Leopard on a Razor Wire

LEOPARD
on a
RazorWire

ecademyPRESS
www.ecademy-press.com

Michael Callender

Leopard on a Razor Wire

First published in 2011 by

Ecademy Press
48 St Vincent Drive, St Albans, Herts, AL1 5SJ
info@ecademy-press.com
www.ecademy-press.com

Printed and bound by Lightning Source in the UK and USA
Designed by Michael Inns
Artwork by Karen Gladwell

Printed on acid-free paper from managed forests. This book is
printed on demand, so no copies will be remaindered or pulped.

ISBN 978-1-907722-65-3

A CIP catalogue record for this book is available from
the British Library.

Contents

Prologue

WHEN WRITING the book which is essentially a narrative of adventure, my incessant concern was that unlike a Sir Ranulph Fiennes, or a Sir Chay Blyth or a Mike Horne, I am an unknown entity. I have experienced this before when I embarked on a venture of motivational speaking. Despite a lively video and a highly professional glossy leaflet spelling out my varied adventures and close escapes in some exotic and remote corners of the world, the exercise was a dismal flop. "You do not put a polar bear hunt on the cover!" a well known celebrity speaker scolded me at the time. Therefore I was in a maelstrom as to how to pay justice to the script of 'Leopard on a razor wire'. Some five years ago I asked a famous buccaneer in the form of Simon Murray CBE to read it which he duly did. He encouraged me to take it further. So did a military titan, General Sir Anthony Farrar Hockley (a prodigious author and an acknowledged historian on the Korean War), who exhorted me to persevere as a writer. After a barrage of rejection slips, I put the script in a drawer, forgot about it, and wrote a book 'Roaming with a rifle, adventures of big game hunting in Africa and other faraway places' which was published successfully as a limited edition by Trophy Room Books in America. In recent retirement, I resurrected the manuscript, updated it, and began to search for an option to having this published.

The process of updating the script came naturally. On to the scene enters a Maxime van Hanswijck de Jonge, himself an author of three books who lives near me in Provence, who suggested that I download a programme from the Internet, Photo Filtre, to enhance the quality of pictures for the book and he provided me invaluable input in teaching me how to use it. And suddenly it struck me! I had this exciting piece on the wild & red blooded Republic of South Africa, but who would be compelled to buy the book? Apart from certain locations where I am known for good reasons or other such as Kingston, Jamaica (the home of Sir Henry Morgan, the infamous pirate - one of England's greatest sons in my estimation) and a very boisterous place in my time; Johannesburg, South Africa's brawling mining town, and corners of the UK where I'd spent my formative years, I was a virtual unknown. This monstrous thought began to assume an incessant irritation, like a persistent tsetse fly or a malaria ridden mosquito, as I scorched along the auto routes of France to Calais to catch the Channel Tunnel to Folkestone, early December, 2010. And then ensued an extraordinary set of circumstances that set my mind alight. I have always had a fertile imagination – a vital requisite for those aspiring to the pen- and the ten days spent in sliding on the ice & snow around the West Country in pursuing game with my rifle and shotgun, and braving London's congestion to visit friends and relations, provided me with some chance encounters that emboldened my inner self.

I was staying with Wendy Durlacher - the widow of my best man, Dick – a very special friend of many years standing. We'd spent a trying afternoon in tracking the whereabouts of the aforementioned Maxime, who was lost somewhere between Marseilles & London, owing to the blizzards that were hammering Britain. He was expected at the Shikar dinner the following evening. Having finally unearthed him at his hotel, I walked from Wendy's house in Victoria road, Kensington to the 'Builder's Arms' – a yuppie haunt – in search of a beer with my writing material in tow. I needed to capture some recent ideas on paper. The inn was busy & I settled down to scribble some notes when a fellow asked if he could use the same table. We got talking & he asked where I was from which I told him & he also resided out of the UK. In walks his mate - a tall, saturnine Al Pacino type with piercing black eyes, a roughed up face and the handshake of a cement mixer. I questioned him on his unusual accent whilst his companion was fetching drinks. "Louisiana" he rasps in a voice to match his handshake. I asked him if he'd been a pugilist to which he responds- "no, but I've been a killer!" "What, big game, or something of that sort," I reply. He leans across in a conspiratorial manner. "I'm part of a brotherhood. Where you from?" I informed him I'd spent forty years in South Africa to which he replies: "Stacks of South Africans in our band of brothers, good men." By this time his mate had returned with drinks in hand. "I'm a Green Beret, we can kill!" By this time our conversation was being relayed to a knot of impressed yuppies in our vicinity. "What do you do?" he barks, glancing at my pad & pen. "I'm completing a book", I reply. "You don't put us in the book or you're dead!" By this time the yuppies were beginning to look nervous. "Tell us about your book" asks his mate. I expound on the chapter I've written on certain warriors I've encountered in the Republic. "There are some extremely potent men down there", I added, elaborating on the Rhodesian SAS men, the Recces, the Parabats and the 32 Battalion. This raises a derisive snort from the Green Beret. He turns to his pal. "Remember how we busted four SAS fellows in that car park not far from here?" This was getting too much and I began to hold doubts to their credibility. These were per-chance, con men! In the meantime we'd exchanged e-mail addresses! My suspicious mind led me to believe that the two men had extracted theirs from the table, leaving mine in their possession, a cardinal error on my part, as I searched for their slips with no success. "I've lost your e-mail details", I said. "Can you write these again"? They looked at me strangely & I seriously began to think I was subject to a set-up– they'd follow me into the street and deprive me of my wallet. "How much is your book?" grunts the Green Beret. "Put me down for two – one for me and one for my friend" who, by this stage, was wearing a grin to the moon. With this he hauls out of his pocket a fistful of dollars. This is now entertainment to be shared by the yuppies around us. "Have a beer", I asked the two sitting across from me. "No, you have one on us. You'd better not bullshit us about that book or we'll come after you!" My short drink had converted itself into three pints of 'old hookey' and a rich conversation few would believe. I eventually shook their hands and made my way into the snow. My sense of jungle survival I'd learnt from many years in a tough city, Johannesburg, led me to wait in the shadows in case of pursuit. But I was under no threat. Later that night I emptied my pockets & found two e-mail addresses. These men were not on the take but were on the level. I'd done them a disservice! It will be a pleasure to see my work in their hands - my first sale!

Then the night of the Shikar dinner which is always a most enjoyable event — 150 hunting/shooting men well out of sight of the Greenies brigade exchanging notes on the 'wild sports' within the hallowed portals of the Cavalry & Guards club, Piccadilly. Interestingly enough Simon Mann was invited to say a few words (refer chapter 8). The evening was, as is customary with Shikar club dinners, a truly entertaining and amusing occasion where I managed to pre-sell a number of my latest book! Andrew Prendergast and Alan Macintosh to take note!

As I lay awake in the early hours of the morning following the Shikar dinner, the thought hit me- take the plunge and contact the men who will help you sell the book with tributes. Ideas were rampaging through my mind by four am by which time I had concocted the essence of this Prologue, a Miscellany including the genealogy of the author and some informative notes on certain illustrious characters that I've had the fortune of meeting during my life, and perhaps an apologies page which was the proud input of my cousin, Peter Geikie – Cobb (referred to later in the chapter). But in the cold light of dawn, the haunting spectre of self doubt resurrected its ugly head. I could run a serious risk of positioning the book as a spoof. This was to be well avoided as there are some highly revered and internationally respected figures contained in the manuscript. I therefore had to strike a careful balance between a Spike Milligan comedy and a serious tome.

More moments of inspiration were to arrive the following day. As I exited the tube at Gloucester Road after a meeting in the West End, the welcoming doors of the Stanhope Arms opposite the station beckoned which led to another extraordinary coincidence. I was in the process of preparing to leave the pub to arrive in impeccable shape for a dinner to be hosted by Wendy Durlacher when two gentlemen enquired as to whether they could take my table as the pub was by this time packed. It turned out that one was a renowned rugby writer from South Africa, Mark Keohane, and his brother who lives in New Zealand, which inevitably led to an impassioned debate on world rugby. Unashamedly, I dropped the name of the Irish rugby idol, Willie John McBride, and the game was on. The brothers would not let me leave without thrusting another foaming glass of 'old hookey' in my hand when they learnt that the company we had pioneered in Johannesburg had sponsored the under 20 Transvaal team in the nineteen eighties.

The next morning I was destined to brave the icy roads to the West Country to join up with an old Downside pal, Jake Francis- Jones, and his charming wife, Diana. As I drove down the motorway, I had more time to reflect on the composition of the book. Further ideas flooded my overloaded imagination and it slowly began to dawn on me that it was feasible to outperform Peter Mayle's book, 'A year in Provence' and, indeed, the recent sensation 'Spud' by John van de Ruit about his schooldays in Michaelhouse, Natal, South Africa, which made it to a film starring John Cleese. Without in any way denigrating the sterling work of the two books, my story centres on *forty years* of life in the 'Wild West' of South Africa! On reaching the picturesque inn in the Wiltshire village of Zeals, I proudly presented myself to the old sea dog, Jake. Some five hours later, not all spent in the country inn I hasten to add, I departed with a volume of colourful snippets on the boys of my generation at school (material for a Downside version of 'Spud'). This brought me to the farm gates of the Geikie – Cobb manor house with my host waiting for me to help me slither on foot down his kilometre long drive, the ice was that severe. I was now in another favourite home where there is a constant hive of activity led by Peter's glamorous wife, MaryAnne, who looks more like Madonna as time progresses, and the antics of two daughters and a son, assisted by a huge dog which is a cross between a Labrador and poodle named Benjamin, and two young puppies. There is unholy chaos and a cacophony of noise raging in the kitchen when I arrive with guns, ammunition, and a safari bag containing clothes, having nearly lost both my legs on the perilous trek down the drive. I should add that young Johnny Geikie - Cobb of eight years of age reminds me of our own grandson in Africa, Buge, in that he is a tough little fellow, an outdoorsman unspoilt by the electronic gadgetry of his age, and fearless. My greeting to MaryAnne at the front door was interrupted by a sharp blow to the back of the neck by an icy snowball hurled by Johnny at the guest. This scenario set the pace for dinner where the three of us stayed up until after midnight reminiscing on the lunatic fringe of the family which inevitably provided me with additional material for the book. Peter's contribution late at night was the suggestion of an apologies page. This seemed a very fine idea until it struck me in the sober light of day that the sheer volume of such an appendage would exceed the book itself!

I had time to further reflect on the structure of the book in between the drives of the pheasant shoot the following day. Another coincidence: a certain dog handler by the name of Jenny greeted me with the immortal words: "I don't believe it, Michael Callender! We used to play with each other when we were small!" Needless to say, this caused huge mirth amongst the guns, the beaters, and the picker-uppers. It emerged that not only did we attend parties in Dorset when we were tiny tots, but she married a Downside friend of mine who eventually found his seat in the House of Lords, The Hon Michael Morris. Jenny then proceeded to wade through another three marriages and here she is, accosting the author! Yet more scintillating trivia for the book! We had a glorious day's shooting on the old Portman estate, where stands the Public School, Bryanston. This is an uncontrived shoot where the guns are practised, ethical, and lovers of the countryside. Needless to say that I was cajoled by my cousin to stop off at an inn after the shoot as he had further ideas for my book. The fun was not to end there as over dinner I was to meet my dearest and only surviving aunt, Julie, mother to Peter and his brother, Ivo. I was raised in WW2 with Julie and another aunt, Sadie, at Pitt House, Semley, near Shaftesbury. Julie is only eight years older than me and fond of describing the author as 'the most horrible little boy' - probably due to when I hid beneath the piano to catch Julie and John Arundell flirting in the drawing room!

The next day found me gliding on the ice towards the Michael de Pelet sixteenth century manor house in Purse Caundle, near Sherborne. This is another of my favourite haunts in the West Country on account of its lively and hospitable hosts, Michael & Charlotte, not to overlook its impressive historical architecture and its magnificent hall decorated by heads of big game – a perfect setting for game trophies. For over twenty years I've had many enjoyable days in this entertaining household. My first book, 'Roaming with a rifle...' provides several paragraphs on this eccentric, renowned field sportsman and big game hunter. My host was in the driveway to greet me, demanding if I'd brought my guns as he had some sport lined up that afternoon. This is in direct contradiction of his remarks, vociferously relayed over the Shikar dinner table, that here was a guest invited to stay for the night who would arrive with guns and ammunition expecting some free shooting! When I suggested, somewhat in jest, to Michael writing a tribute for my new book, he roars "I haven't read your first book! I don't read books" which is vaguely true as according to his brother, Patrick, "he prefers to look at the pictures". After lunch, we proceed into the woods where it was agreed that my host occupy one high stand and I another to shoot a roe deer, but females only. Again, further inspiration for the book as I gazed down at the magnificent countryside of the de Pelet estate. There was wild life in abundance – pheasants, hares, rabbits, squirrels when appears a roe deer creeping along a hedge until it stops behind a gate. I take careful aim with my custom-built .243 rifle which I had brought over from France for this very purpose, breathe out slowly and squeeze the trigger, remembering my reputation as 'One Shot' in Africa and to shoot through the bars of the gate. I watch the deer jolt indicating a true shot and disappear into the woods. My host then joins me as darkness sets in and enquires what I had shot at and where the quarry is. He inspects the gate and exclaims: "This has to get around Dorset - 'One Shot' has shot my gate! You were shooting at a hare -- the bullet hole is low. I didn't say you could shoot hares, did I?" Michael climbs through the fence to look for the roe deer, but to no avail. It was evident that I had shot the gate and not the target as there was no blood spoor. This led to some lively banter as we made our way back to the house. A fortnight later, back home in France, I took a call from Michael to the effect that the roe deer was found in the woods the next morning by the beaters and that I was to be blackballed from the Shikar club for shooting a ram against strict instruction!

At six am the next morning I was to be seen poring over the very impressive book written on big game hunting by a Frenchman, J Vettier and scribbling notes in the kitchen as more ideas were permeating my overstrained brain. "You filching some stories?" demands Charlotte whereupon Michael strides in clad in pyjamas. "You're supposed to be out with Anthony (Michael's game keeper) finding your roe deer" he bellows in his characteristic Gallic style. "I can't, old friend, I have to make my way to Oxfordshire and I daren't be late for the widow of a General where I am due for coffee". I set off in thick fog and unpredictable road surfaces to reach the home of Lady Linda Farrar-Hockley. I arrived on the dot thanks to my Garmin GPS without which I would have doubtless lost my way in the English murk. And then a nostalgic trip down memory lane as Linda and I spoke about her husband, Tony. She told me in halting terms about the tragic end of this Colossus of a man due to Parkinson's disease and this, together with a gentle enquiry from Linda as to whether MaryAnne's body had ever been found in Lake Malawi, brought a mist to my eyes. She is a most remarkable woman who has a fine support team of two fine sons, Dair & Hilary, from the General's first marriage. After two wonderful hours with Linda, I drove back to London with four pheasants in tow, a rifle in the boot, and more ideas for the structure of the book. Dearest Wendy Durlacher-- nothing ever fazes this one -- greeted me on her doorstep whereupon I thrust the .243 and birds into her hands as I rushed off to an appointment in Chelsea.

I returned to France in a jubilant mood. The ten days sojourn in London and the West Country had galvanised me into creating an effective framework for the manuscript. I had been infused with a breath of new life for the book and I had thrust aside the destructive mantle of self doubt, encouraging me to call on my old friends to write tributes: Willie John McBride in Ballymena, Simon Murray whom I managed to unearth in London (he's normally globetrotting), Sir Chay Blyth in Hawich, Scotland, and Colonel Jan Breytenbach in South Africa.

It is not the critic that counts, not the man who points out how the strong man stumbles or where the doer of deeds could have done them better. The credit belongs to the man who is actually in the arena, whose face is marred by dust and sweat and blood, who strives valiantly, who errs and comes up short again and again because there is no effort without error and shortcomings, who knows the great devotion, who spends himself in a worthy cause, who at the best knows in the end the high achievement of triumph and who at worst, if he fails while daring greatly, knows his place shall never be with those timid and cold souls who know neither victory nor defeat.

Theodore Roosevelt (1858 – 1919)
26th U.S.President

Dedication

To Vivienne, Sean, and in memory of MaryAnne

Background

THOMAS PACKENHAM, the author of 'The Boer War', aptly termed the Afrikaner as 'The White Tribe of Africa'. I first encountered members of this tribe in London when I was an account executive at the Lonsdale Hands Organisation working on the Rothmans account. These men representing Anton Rupert's Rembrandt organisation – Rothmans was one of its major products - were big in stature and in spirit. They would have me standing on more than one occasion in the murky drizzle outside their offices in Berk House off Oxford Street in the centre of London saluting Stellenbosch in the Western Cape. With a heavy dose of humour they would remind me in their deep, guttural accents that I should pay homage to Anton Rupert and his entourage in the cradle of Rembrandt, a burgeoning tobacco enterprise that in a short space of time would span the world. Therefore, it was men of the ilk of 'Tienie' Oosthuizen and Derek Robinson, marketing and advertising directors respectively of Carreras-Rothmans, who headed me and my wife in the direction of South Africa. Prior to this, I volunteered to join a task team to promote their cigarette brands in Jamaica, considered then an important business hub in the Caribbean. It was a trite ironic that the 'Black Cat' factory owned jointly by the South Africans and Carreras in the UK was so warmly embraced by the Jamaican government, later to become a vociferous opponent of Apartheid.

Following three rumbustious years in the piratical Jamaican environment, hot on the heels of an exciting military service spent in the deserts of Arabia, I suffered a terrible restlessness. I could not envisage settling down to a humdrum existence in Britain. Its climate was grey and its Labour Government was grey. I was hankering for adventure and I gravitated to a land that promised high skies and untamed frontiers. 'Tienie' Oosthuizen and his merry men had sown the seeds which were nourished by many South Africans I'd encountered in London to explore the controversial Republic. There were inevitably those doomsayers who regarded my quest as wild irresponsibility in taking a wife and a baby to a State that was under threat of a bloodbath.

In 1969 I set forth on a reconnaissance. My first recollection of this domain at the tip of Africa was the impressive sight of the gold mine dumps stippled by the African sun as the aircraft came into land at Jan Smuts airport. Then ensued a hectic six weeks involving a series of job interviews which took one from Johannesburg to Cape Town and it was inevitable that I joined Derek Robinson's former company, Van Zyl and Robinson. South Africa was very different then compared to where the country is today. For forty years, my family and I lived through a pulsating era where we witnessed an extreme shift from the peak of Apartheid to the 'Rainbow Nation' under the ANC regime. My pursuit of adventure was met head on and I felt compelled in later years to write of my experiences in this extraordinary tract of the world.

This book is light on political commentary but I am of the fervent belief that to pass opinion on the emotive issues of Apartheid and the cultural divide that persists between the European and the African blocs – the two dominant pillars of South Africa's peoples - one has to live in this country for a significant period of time to attempt to understand the complex sociology of the Republic. My sojourn in this vibrant land gave me an insight into the Afrikaner ('The White Tribe'), the English speaking, not forgetting the Indian and Coloured sectors, and a glimmering of the workings of the African mind. Since 1750 when the white settlers first clashed with the Xhosas the cultures between White and Black have not fused. Racial disparity is firmly evident and the principle of 'Black empowerment' introduced by the ANC is Apartheid in reverse – a due revenge on the oppressors some will say. The South Africa of today is not exactly what Nelson Mandela envisaged and the fledgling democracy remains at risk with the recent draconian and unconstitutional new secrecy bill which threatens to muzzle the media from exposing corruption and abuse of power. This, coupled with the threat of nationalising the mines - a large chunk of the country's GDP - has led to prominent South Africans of all colours and creeds condemning such measures which would undoubtedly harm South Africa's standing in international circles, thereby imploding the euphoria of the 2010 FIFA World Cup fairy tale which promised a turning point for the country and the defeat of Afro-pessimism. The World Cup provided four thrilling weeks, uniting the country even more effectively than the first democratic elections of 1994 or the 1995 rugby 'Invictus'. Investors began to talk of South Africa being the conduit for the African continent to join the emerging market clique, BRIC.

Nelson Mandela will be remembered as one of the greatest statesmen of the 20th century. His conciliation with 'The White Tribe of Africa' is symptomatic of his pragmatic strength in recognising the inheritance of the ANC of an envied infrastructure that had been forged by the white Nationalist government in its years as a pariah status in the Western world. Under the threat of sanctions such colossi emerged as Sasol - the oil from coal giant; Eskom – the utility behemoth; Iscor – the steel monolith; then the roads, the hospitals, the telecommunications, the legal system, a free press and a developed business economy. The sophistication of such an integrated infrastructure surprised the G8 countries and the ANC. And one must remember that South Africa had developed its own nuclear bomb which is testimony to the extraordinary skills of its scientists and engineers.

The white regime of South Africa was the last to grant independence on the African continent. Its enemies will argue that the freedom fighters had won their battle. The last white government, however, will point to the overwhelming pressure of the Western world forcing their hand. However the prognosis of historians in years to come will present an absorbing interpretation of South Africa. In reality, there is little doubt that if the Afrikaner dominant Nationalist government had granted independence in the late 60s and early 70s when the colonial powers handed over power to their African surrogates at the time of Harold Macmillan's famous address to the Parliament of South Africa in February 1960 –"The wind of change is blowing through the continent" - South Africa's infrastructure would not have developed as it did. The scourge of Communism was rampant in the Cold War period and the Republic could have been reduced to a 'banana state' on the same dismal lines as the current plethora of poverty wracked countries on 'The Dark Continent'.

Many years of living in this country gave one a right to comment on this controversial land. I arrived at the pinnacle of Apartheid and the subsequent metamorphosis of South Africa. The turbulence of the period was perilous with the pendulum vacillating from the Soweto pupils' uprising in 1976, to President P W Botha's 'Rubicon' address to the world in 1988 which plunged the country into a state of emergency, to Nelson Mandela's release from jail in 1990, and to the first full democratic elections in 1994. Throughout this time span the country teetered on the edge of an abyss. During the early nineties many political commentators and analysts predicted a massive confrontation between the militaristic white right wing and the Black Nationalist movement. It was thanks to the enlightened leadership of Nelson Mandela and F W de Klerk, with the support of such men as General Constand Viljoen who tempered the hot heads of the Afrikaner right wing (AWB), that the country escaped a brutal civil war. It's against such a scenario that I was allowed to flourish in a vibrant and stimulating country that provided the opportunity for a host of adventures to be shared with a galaxy of red blooded and inspiring characters.

೮ ✦ ೲ

CHAPTER ONE

The call to adventure

*Every man has his own fantasies, coveted
ambitions, the most private of thoughts. Many
strive to fulfil what they believe is that ultimate
goal. Few of us succeed in being the man he aspires
to so that when he reaches his end, he can whisper
to himself that he has walked the path he
has set himself.*

Hugh Dormer, D.S.O. Irish Guards and S.O.E 1940 - 1944

LONDON IN the 60's was a pulsating place for a young man. "You've never had it so good!" rang out the Conservative Party mantra. Britain was emerging from her shackles of post-war austerity. National Service had, nostalgically for many, reached an end in the aftermath of Korea, Malaya, Suez, Oman, where boys returned as men to their homeland, victorious and battle hardened. The "swinging sixties" evokes memories of Carnaby Street, the cradle of the mini-skirt and the sexual revolution. London was arguably the greatest city in the world in those balmy days before the Arabs invaded the capital to snatch up chunks of prized real estate, coinciding with the opening of the floodgates to the droves of immigrants from Britain's colonies. It was London for the Londoner where the clipped accents of the British public school vied with the colourful rhyming slang of the Cockney. Class barriers sat more comfortably on the shoulder before the Labour Party – the self-styled champion of the working classes - whipped up the resentment that fuelled the intransigence of the unions. The spirit of adventure was incarnated by the need to safeguard Britain's outposts and where there still remained untamed regions to explore. The pride of being British was instilled by the pillars of traditional values – family, school and regiment. These remained standards to be respected and not to be apologised for. Sadly, these heady days were not to last. Harold Wilson and his dreary entourage came to power and the exuberance of the "swinging sixties" was guillotined with the crippling taxation – ninety pence in the pound for the top income brackets – severe foreign exchange controls, and the strangle hold of the unions.

The stifling tube train got to me that wintry day in 1968. The press of malodorous bodies and the incessant hacking coughs, exacerbated by the oncoming of the chilly northern hemisphere winter, was sufficient to break even the sunniest of spirits. I looked around me that morning on the Piccadilly line, uncomfortable in my overcoat, damp from the London drizzle. The expressions of the commuters told the story: a resigned, weary look proclaiming a dreary start to a drab day. I was willing to wager that most of those hapless travellers of the tube had little to look forward to in life –eking out an existence, parallel to that of a rat on a treadmill. The little to look forward to was probably an annual fortnight spent spit-roasting on a crowded beach on the Cote d' Azure or the Costa del Sol, a tight budget permitting. And on that day, I promised that my world would not be fettered by that gruesome tube that tore through the belly of London bearing the commuter hordes to work. I looked long and hard at the sad faces, and I searched for a single smile, a crooked grin. But none to be had. Even the young secretaries and the typists were brow beaten to a grim silence. And it should be remembered that the London of these times remained homogeneous. The Underground was yet to be deluged by the avalanche of immigrants and back-packing tourists. And when the tidal wave of the refugees from the Colonies unleashed itself on the major cities of Britain, induced by the spate of civil wars and the famines in Africa and the poverty of the West Indies, a brave Lord Enoch Powell stood up in the House of Commons and delivered a dire warning in his legendary 'Rivers of Blood' speech of the consequences of unchecked immigration. This predictably created uproar within the ranks of the liberals and the harbingers of the 'politically correct'.

My mind was set as I stood jammed on the escalator lifting me from the bowels of the city to the rain-slicked streets and the leaden skies. I had to get out, back to the sun and the high skies which I had left behind in the deserts of the Middle East, the wilds of East Africa, and the tropics of the West Indies. That evening I strode into the drawing room of our splendid flat in Ennismore Gardens behind the Brompton Oratory in Knightsbridge, and confronted a startled wife - "We must get the hell out! There's more to life than this frightful climate, Harold Wilson, and the drudgery of a nine-to-five job. Are you prepared to emigrate?" It was an onerous proposition for a young wife, three months pregnant. But the idea was sown and it would be two years from that wet November day before we finally packed our bags and headed for the controversial Republic of South Africa.

Harold Wilson and the London Underground apart, I had been destined to pursue an adventurous life. I came from a proud Scots lineage through my father's side and a colourful Norman-Irish ancestry on the maternal line. My sister, Mary, and I were brought up in the early stages of WW2 by Rudi, my paternal grandmother, and from the roof of her magnificent top floor flat in Palace Place Mansions, Kensington Court, adjacent to Kensington Gardens, we would watch the Blitz unleash itself on the docks in the East End. I can recall as a small boy the eerie wailing of the sirens and the probing fingers of the search lights and the ominous drone of the Luftwaffe bombers as they came to destroy the lifeline of London. The Blitz resembled a gigantic firework display and in later years my grandmother would tell me that I would howl with anger at being hustled down with my sister into the basement by our nanny. There is an excellent museum near Waterloo Station that re-enacts London in the Blitz and as one stands in the darkened rooms and listens to the voices played over the audio-visual system, the hairs on the arms begin to tingle and the memories come cascading back. Our generation, the war-babies of Britain, remains a proud lot where we learnt resilience and to endure the privations of a nation at war.

We learnt to read at an early age. There was no T.V. and computers were unheard of. Cell phones and shopping malls were unknown. It was exotic sounding places like Kashmir, Khartoum, and Tonkin that enslaved our imaginations and we'd learn of Clive of India, Cecil Rhodes, Lawrence of Arabia. The Empire conjured up visions of British soldiers fending off murderous Pathans in the Khyber Pass, of Sudanese dervishes being pierced by the bayonets wielded by kilted Scotsmen, of bloodthirsty Zulus being fought hand-to-hand by the Welshmen of the 24th of Foot, of tigers being hunted in the jungles of Assam, of man-eating lions being tracked down by District Commissioners in African outposts. We revered David Livingstone, Robert the Bruce, Richard the Lion Heart, Sir Henry Morgan, and Lord Shackleton. Our icons were men and women who broke barriers such as Sir Chay Blyth and John Ridgway crossing the Atlantic in a rowing boat, or Sir Ranulph Fiennes battling over the ice reaching the South Pole on foot, or Sir Edmund Hillary and his Ghurkha companion, Tensing, reaching the pinnacle of Everest. All very different to today's pop musicians and movie stars. The men that we looked up to, our relations and our peers, were those who fought the Battle of Britain in the skies, who battled the Japanese in the jungles of Burma, who braved the 'U' boats in the icy Atlantic, or the women who nursed the wounded and worked in the factories making munitions. They were men like my grandfather who commanded a battalion in the stench and the gore of the First World War trenches. These were proud people who had never heard of counsellors – they were strong of character but shy of emotional collapse.

Rudi was a little bantam-cock of a woman, indomitable in spirit, always impeccably turned out and magnificently read as they tended to be of that generation. She reportedly was one of the first women to cross the Sudan by camel. She used to tell me bedtime tales of the Bedouins before the peace of the London nights was shattered by the Luftwaffe disgorging their deadly loads on the city. When life became a trite hectic in London from the constant air raids, Mary and I spent the rest of the war in rural Wiltshire with my maternal grandparents. This was the era of Pyt House, the brilliant Queen Anne edifice where my grandparents, Edgar and Nona de Pentheny O'Kelly, lived during the war. Edgar was a formidable figure – tall, erect as a ramrod, and every inch a professional soldier and a hunter of tigers and a wide array of game in his extensive travels. He served in the North Western Frontier of Afghanistan and parts of Africa before the culmination of his career as a Colonel leading 1200 Royal Welsh Fusiliers in the trenches of the First World War. He was heavily decorated, winning the D.S.O. and I read his letters annually describing the horrifying experiences of Gallipoli and the Somme. He was strict and an authoritarian as men were in those days but never a bully and as wary of him as I was at my tender age, I grew up to revere him. It was the Edgars and the Benedictine monks of Downside that gave me the fortitude to deal with the slings and arrows of the world.

A lunatic fringe lurked in my mother's side of the family due to perhaps a large measure of 'Irishness' and a pinch of Catholic inbreeding. In those days the prominent Catholic families tended to inter-marry and hence our connection with the Talbots of Malahide of Ireland and the Arundells of Wardour. Catholics today remain a minority in Britain, although the tradition of marrying within the religion has dissipated over the years. My mother was one of six and two of her younger sisters were raised with me at Pyt House - Julie, only eight years my senior, and Sadie a little older. Sadie looked like Rita Hayworth with her abundant auburn hair and striking looks. An admirer in the form of Hamilton 'Hammie' O'Malley-Keyes would visit Sadie at Pyt House. He was a tall, fair-haired officer in the Irish Guards. Who could forget the free spirited Irishman, a British army light heavy weight boxing champion who could play a reasonable game of backgammon, but that's as far as the intellect went. The swashbuckler was smitten by the charms of the glamorous Sadie following a disastrous six-week marriage to Lady Iris Mountbatten. Hammie was captured by the Germans at Arnhem after landing on a machine gun nest in a glider and was incarcerated in a prisoner of war camp for which he blamed his erratic behaviour as if he hadn't been seriously out of control since childhood and his school days at Downside. After leaving the British army, I stayed with Hammie for a summer in Torremolinos where he and Sadie had settled, well before this charming fishing village was transformed into a mass tourism nightmare. Sadly, at that time Sadie and Hammie were separated, after having reared four children. Hammie - ever an adventurer - ended up marrying a female bull fighter called Betty.

Adventure formed part of our family's heritage. A sepia print of Sir Richard Burton, the nineteenth century adventurer/explorer, hangs in my study. My mother retained a deep interest in Burton and her family albums were littered with press articles and faded photographs of this remarkable character. His wife, Isobel Arundell, is a direct ancestor. Peter de Pentheny O'Kelly was my mother's eldest brother and in the footsteps of many of his forebears he was commissioned into the Irish Guards from Sandhurst, just prior to the outbreak of the Second World War. Peter was an imposing man of 6' 5" in height and blessed with a powerful physique and a thick mane of hair and was a promising athlete, playing for the 1st XV rugby side at Ampleforth, one of the great Catholic schools in Britain. Peter was forced to relinquish his commission after striking a major over a dispute for drinking with an NCO in an Aldershot bar and he promptly enlisted with Lord 'Shimi' Lovat's 4 Commando of 'Green Beret' fame which was regarded as one of the illustrious Special Forces units in the war. He survived numerous front-line engagements in Lovat's lot and after the war he could never settle down, so fiercely ran the fire in his belly. He left Trinity College, Dublin and sailed a small boat to South Africa with the help of two brother Commandos, served as a stipend steward in the Johannesburg Jockey Club, and eventually became a successful farmer in Swaziland, only to meet a tragic end in a car accident. Polo was Peter's passion in addition to his various other pursuits. It is not surprising that Peter, and Tom his younger brother, developed the way they did. Grandfather Edgar had little time for social fripperies, unlike his wife who loved people and parties. My grandfather's method was to bring the boys up under the tutelage of a game keeper, a consequence of which they learnt how to handle guns and horses from a young age. Tom, too young for the war, became a senior racing correspondent for the 'Irish Field', working in Dublin before taking up farming while Peter followed in his father's footsteps and fought the Germans, which he did extremely well. I enjoyed my grandmother's tale of how she treated her sons, both youngsters still in their school shorts, to lunch at the Savoy when they released a ferret in the grill room which created a huge furore with the bemused rodent leaping on to a table and taking refuge in the striking cleavage of a famous actress.

I hold great memories of Peter who taught me to climb trees and he gave me a miniature parachute to use, much to the disapproval of my grandmother. There was one notable occasion when he took me to The Ritz in Piccadilly during my school holidays whilst he was over from South Africa for the Ascot races. Peter, resplendent in top hat and tails, addressed the barman in his soft Irish lilt saying that his life wouldn't be worth living if he didn't serve his nephew with a glass of beer and to hell with my being under-age. He died in a tragic accident whilst I was serving with the Cameronians in Kenya. I telephoned his wife, formally Jeanne Bovet of Johannesburg, and asked whether I could help. Peter was a serious influence in my selecting South Africa as a place in which to live. It was a tragic time for Jeanne and their four boys, and me for losing a favourite uncle. All his sons have done well and it was significant that Hugh, the third, learnt to build rifles after serving six years as an officer in the British army and he sat for a time as the President of the North American Gun Makers Guild.

My paternal grandfather, born in Manor Place, Edinborough, rode horses for Scotland. He was also a recognised marksman and enjoyed initiating youngsters in the art of stalking deer in the Highlands. Sadly, he died while my father was barely ten years of age and I never met this respected sportsman and, alas, the Scots side of the family as my grandmother Rudi decided to leave Scotland to live in London, probably due to the disapproval of her late husband's bigoted Presbyterian brothers for becoming a Catholic. Hostility to Catholicism ruled rife in parts of Scotland in those days and it was ironical that I was to join a famous Scottish Regiment, the Cameronians, who were founded in 1690 by Lord Douglas to fight Catholics. As with my mother's lineage, the spirit of adventure permeated my father's clan, the Callender-Brodies and Callenders. My parents told me the tales of a black sheep of the family, a certain Ronald Brodie, a relative on my father's side. This adventurer ran off at the tender age of sixteen much to his father's fury to enlist with the

French Foreign Legion in 1910 where he served with distinction. I have proof of this as I was presented with his record by a Colonel Hougard when I visited the Foreign Legion's headquarters in Aubagne near Marseilles. Ronald Brodie was a born warrior. After serving in the Foreign Legion, he fought in the First World War, and then survived several actions with the Cameronians, the regiment in which I was destined to serve. When my Commanding Officer, Colonel Charles Mackinnon, interviewed me when I joined the Battalion in Bahrain in 1957, he told me that he'd had the privilege of serving under Major Ronald Brodie and he stated in no uncertain terms that I had a formidable reputation to live up to. The austere-looking colonel obviously thought it unlikely that I would match this inveterate fighter who used to teach the Battalion how to bayonet fight wearing only a shirt in freezing mid-winter weather. I learnt from my father how Ronald Brodie was spirited out of Malta with the help of his brother officers after killing an assailant with his fists while defending an innocent citizen. My mother, fond of this wild Scot, told me how Brodie had the names of battles in which he had fought tattooed on his arms and how he ended his military career with the Horse Guards in his fifties, before finally settling down with his Hungarian wife, an attractive Countess who remained in love with her tough Scot to his death.

Anthony Wellesley-Colley, my father's first cousin, was schooled at Downside as were so many of my relations, and he thirsted for adventure which is not surprising as his mother, my great aunt, had married into a branch of the Wellington family. He was commissioned into Lord 'Shimi' Lovat's 4 Commando - the same regiment that Peter de Pentheny O'Kelly had selected after his fracas in the Irish Guards. Sadly, the young lieutenant died on D-Day. He was hit by a machine gun bullet as he left the landing craft but managed to lead his platoon across the beach before collapsing on the wire defences. The last words to his troop Sergeant who cradled his head as he died were: "Sorry, Sergeant, tell the chaps I couldn't make it". 'Shimi' Lovat makes mention of Anthony Wellesley-Colley in his autobiography 'March Past' when he describes that historic day when only 150 of his 450 Commandos who landed on the beach-head near Ouistreham survived the assault. My father remembered him as an adventurous-minded, cheerful fellow who always wore a smile even when times got tough. In 1994, the 50th anniversary of D-Day, there was a memorial service for Anthony Wellesley-Colley in St Mary's church, Louth, Lincolnshire, and a memorial bench was dedicated to him as the first Allied casualty on D-Day.

It is abundantly clear that my ancestors were soldiers, sailors, hunters and horsemen. I cannot identify one who made fame as a businessman. This is significant, perhaps, as one's own perception of life has been clearly fashioned by my forbears – adventuring, soldiering, hunting remain pursuits to admire and respect, and it is significant that the quest for adventure has been passed down to our children. The option for a conventional way of life has been dismissed for the enticement of wider horizons and independence. Sean, our son, is a charter pilot flying aircraft to some notorious parts of Africa – Angola,Sudan,the DRC, Rwanda to name a few. MaryAnne, his sister, was the co-founder of an adventure company called 'Kayak Africa' that has built an enviable reputation for spear fishing, scuba diving, sea kayaking and remote river exploration. Kayak Africa is based in Cape MacLear, Malawi. MaryAnne survived a number of close calls, including a terrifying hijacking, nearly being bitten in half by a hippopotamus, and a near drowning in an aircraft that spiralled into Lake Malawi from engine failure. Her luck finally ran out, tragically, when she met her end in 2006 through a drowning accident in Lake Malawi, leaving behind her partner, Jurie Schoeman, and two children named respectively Teak and Java.

CHAPTER TWO

A walk on the wild side

One drawback to living many years in this
frontiers land is that one is conditioned to
the adrenalin surge which is an ever constant
companion, rendering other countries
strangely tame.

The Author

SOUTH AFRICA is a magnet for the adventurous minded and the wild
spirited. When asked what it is that drives one to live in this extraordinary
land, the reply is spontaneous: "South Africa is a frontier. It's a wild
place with huge opportunity for the stout hearted. It's not a place for
woessies". South Africans live in a contradiction here in the 'Wild South'
– an apt description for this weird and wonderful country. There are
the extravagant trappings of the First World – the glittering shopping
malls and the five star hotels and the luxurious game camps and the
smart cars and the glitzy restaurants. It's of little surprise that the visitor
raves about the Republic with its wild animals, beautiful beaches and
glorious climate, and little wonder as the pounds and the dollars go a
very far way rendering South Africa as a wondrous holiday destination
for little outlay. One cannot criticize the visitor for being oblivious to
the rank poverty, the horrendous crime and the rampant HIV/AIDS
epidemic. There are some who venture no further than Cape Town and
the perception of South Africa is firmly affixed to this gentle enclave

that is more reminiscent of the Mediterranean than the true Africa north of the Hex River Mountains. One can understand tourists being blinkered when transported from Pretoria to the Cape in five star luxury by Rovos Rail or the Blue Train; by air charter to the Kruger Park in the lush Eastern Transvaal. They will they remain blissfully ignorant of the savage face of Africa – the mindless killings, the appalling squalor of the shanty towns, the rife corruption and the intermittent xenophobic riots that rock the cities . It is welcome that the euphoria remains; tourism is on a gigantic roll. South Africa is high on the international traveller's list and is emerging as an underexploited jewel.

But to live here will always remain a quandary. One only has to turn to the Zimbabwean tragedy on South Africa's very doorstep to understand how dangerously quickly a country can be torn to shreds – just within a decade in the case of Zimbabwe under the rule of that odious megalomaniac, Robert Mugabe. It was nothing short of a miracle that South Africa wasn't plunged into civil war in the early nineties and it took the statesmanship of a Nelson Mandela to steer the country through stormy waters. But it can happen again if the ruling party, the ANC, destroys the dangerously thin remnants of its opposition and South Africa becomes yet another example of the African axiom: *'One man, one vote, once!'* The current acquiescence of Africa's leaders to Mugabe's rotten land grab and his rule of tyrannical brutality illustrates the disregard of the African politician for western democracy. *"Africa for the Africans"* is a mantra that cannot be ignored and the white can well ask if he has a place in this Dark Continent. It is little wonder that the farmers throughout the Republic are restive – close on 1500 have been murdered since independence (1994). It is a fact of life that the brain drain of South Africa's youth and the gifted - and this is not only the preserve of the white but many of the black intelligentsia are following suit - is continuing unabated to the detriment of this country's economy and its professional standards. Scant surprise has been expressed of the Reserve Bank's estimate of R80 – R100 billion Rand having seeped out of the country over the last three decades. So what drives the South African to remain? This is a dangerous rough house of a region where the risks are high and the rewards are no longer fiscal – high taxation, rising cost of living – but environmentally. *It is also relevant to add that for many years the doomsayers have predicted an apocalypse. But the country still survives!*

I have met over the last four decades a legion of adventurers and warriors; carpet - baggers, the men who trade in black Africa; the pilots who fly in guns and out with body bags; the soldiers of fortune who ply their lethal skills in the murkier spots of Africa; and the scores of hunters who brave the risk of gaol in taking rifles into remote places. One drawback to living many years in this frontier is that one is conditioned to the adrenalin surge which is an ever constant companion, rendering other countries strangely tame. The recent experience of standing in an English country inn and listening to the local gentry's quaint conversation about the sighting of a rabbit in a lane caused one's mind to drift to this land of extremes – droughts and floods, snakes and other reptiles & insects, an absence of gentle creatures but where crocodiles and lions abound. Reading the front page of a British tabloid on a London bobby being grievously assaulted by a West Indian youth, led one to reflect that in this country the policemen shot and killed add up to hundreds annually that perish in taking on the roaming bands of AK47 toting hijackers and murderous thugs. There's mayhem unleashed daily on the roads with dilapidated taxis and unlicensed trucks; mayhem in the cities; mayhem everywhere. One begins to question if the tranquillity of places like the Provence in Southern France or Tuscany in Italy is an unnatural dream or if South Africa is seriously out of kilter. The turmoil and the aggression suits not all and a number search for a greater quality of life in other havens. But there are many who cannot live without the adrenalin of a country making history, the entrepreneurial opportunities, the unlimited space, a climate that is unsurpassed and a playground for the adventurer. It is often said that the people make a country. I have had the fortune to travel widely, and to live in other parts of the world, and I've yet to find a more colourful band than right here in this corner of Africa.

✳ ✳ ✳ ✳ ✳

There's a platteland town called Lydenburg in the Eastern Transvaal, a gateway to the Kruger Park and the Lowveld. I was standing in a saloon with the manager of my liquor stores when the swing doors burst asunder in the manner of the Wild West and in strides a huge Afrikaans farmer in the traditional uniform of khaki shirt and shorts and socks rolled over veldskoen. Faan Fourie is a fearsome sight with his ham-like fists and fiery eyes and unkempt mop of hair and unruly beard. He roars in a rich baritone: "Dit is die Nuwe Suid Africa" and the party is on. His eyes swivel around the room and settle on this unnerved rooinek - Afrikaans argot for a Britisher meaning 'red neck' which had its origins in the Boer War. "Who's this manne?" he demands of my manager, Johan Prinsloo. A spate of the taal ensues and he learns that I am a hunter and in my mangled Afrikaans I explain the intricacies of chasing Polar Bear. The big fellow likes this and over the following months a curious friendship forms. I am the first rooinek that is known of who has been offered a farm to shoot on owned by a top ranking member of the extreme right wing, the AWB. Faan Fourie called himself in those days 'Die Leeu van die Oos' (the Lion of the East) and at that time he was the leader of the Eastern Transvaal wing of the controversial AWB. Faan Fourie has an insatiable lust for life. Not one week would pass without some incident whilst he was around.

He wreaked revenge on a traffic officer for having the audacity to paste a fine on his windscreen. Lydenburg turned out to see the unfortunate wretch wriggling furiously with his outstretched arms strapped to two adjoining meters. It wasn't a question of race – the offending officer was white. 'Die Leeu van die Oos' was caught in a speed trap. The officer concerned was unceremoniously bundled into the boot of Faan's vehicle and left there to stifle whilst the wild Afrikaner stopped off at a local inn to drink with his cohorts. A powerful character is Faan and he always seemed to evade prosecution. Possibly his finest stunt was to drive an armoured car through the portals of Johannesburg's World Trade Centre where he interrupted at gun point a working session on South Africa's new constitution being negotiated between Roelf Meyer of the National Party and Cyril Ramaphosa of the ANC. He and his AWB troops held the various political delegations to ransom for a full 24 hours and a picture of the wild-eyed, spade bearded Faan Fourie with rifle lying at hand on the front covers of the national press created a furore.

* * * * *

Before the horrendous demise of Zimbabwe under the rabid Robert Mugabe, six of us were shooting birds in the Lion's Den region under the expert guidance of a character called Steve Seward. The team was an illustrious gathering and included a prominent tobacco rancher, Giles Raynor. He was the same fellow who flew Vivienne and me out of the Zambezi Valley some years ago at the time of a fatal accident when another well known tobacco farmer, Clive Swemmer, was gored to death by a buffalo. We had been hunting in an adjacent camp with Bill Bedford. Bill, now a prominent professional hunter and an ex-SAS soldier, happened to be part of this shoot as was Bob Warren-Codrington, second in command of the Rhodesian SAS Regiment at the height of the war, 1980; Andrew Halstead, a well-known Zimbabwean businessmen, and Michael Deacon and self from South Africa completed the party. I learnt that Steve Seward had shot with Michael de Pelet in Dorset – a small world it is – and he had also fought in the SAS alongside Bob and Bill and predictably the conversation around the camp fire in the evenings was of a lively nature.

Before Mugabe's infamous land grab, Lion's Den was a prized area of Zimbabwe, an extraordinary amalgam of untamed country and vast cultivated fields supporting maize, wheat and cattle. Seward's introductory briefing the evening before the oncoming day's shoot was interesting: "I suggest you all wear long trousers and boots. Shorts and canvas shoes aren't recommended around here – plenty of black mambas around! And by the way, and this applies to those hunters present, don't shoot the oribi, the duiker or the kudu, you'll find them everywhere." We were driving over an escarpment one hot midday when Steve Seward casually mentioned: "that spot we've just passed reminds me of Riley's dinner." We were then fed a story that epitomises the exuberance and the lust for life that seems to permeate this part of the globe. Riley, a local farmer and in those days a bachelor, made an art of sponging off his neighbours just in time for dinner and this practice he applied for some time until it was suggested in blunt terms that he should reciprocate and Riley took his cue and staged a black-tie dinner in the open veldt in the old colonial style of white tablecloth, silver cutlery, and cut glass. The fact that he coerced the farmers' wives into producing a six course meal was Riley's cunning but his heart was in the right place. After dinner the farmers and the women in their finery were enjoying cigars and liqueurs when they spotted a light bobbing around in the bush veldt in the valley below them. Without any hesitation they drove down to investigate to find a farm manager, new to the area, indulging in a spot of night shooting to supplement his larder. The hapless fellow had been caught red-handed and the rugged men of the bush in their tuxedos and black ties gave him a torrid time and sent him packing. But by 3.00 a.m. Riley's liquor had run dry and the only option was to visit the recalcitrant poacher's house for replenishment, this being the nearest homestead to their dining venue in the bush. The wife duly appeared in her night-dress as her husband was in the bath, no doubt cleansing himself from his moonlighting. However, with great grace the chap handed over what he had and readily accepted an invitation to drink until dawn at the dinner site overlooking the valley where he had been caught. Southern Africa breeds stout hearts and generosity of spirit.

* * * * *

Olifantsfontein lies midway between Johannesburg and Pretoria. For years the village remained the domain of the Cullinans, a very wild clan. It was Sir Thomas Cullinan who found the famous diamond that lies on display in the Tower of London and which forms the cornerstone of the Crown Jewels. Douglas Cullinan, his son, used to entertain my grandmother, Nona de Pentheny O'Kelly, on her visits to South Africa to see her son, Peter, and when she learnt of my moving to South Africa, she insisted that I look out for *those very dear Cullinans.* This was hardly an appropriate description! The tribe that I got to know in the late 60's and early 70's were a wild bunch, intensely likeable but very unpredictable.

Mejor was the eldest son of my grandmother's good friend, Douglas, and his reputation had preceded him when I met him at a cocktail party in Johannesburg. At the time he was dressed in a dinner jacket and when I met this urbane character exuding charm I thought that his formidable reputation was somewhat exaggerated. Mejor was a highly talented individual with an excellent brain and blessed with a sporting talent for shooting and big-game fishing. When I first met Mejor, he was recovering from a stomach wound as a result of a dispute with a first cousin as to who was the finer shot. The cousin in question, Tim Cullinan, had fired at Mejor in self defence and despite the bullet entering Mejor's belly, he survived on account of his prodigious strength and was back on his feet in weeks to continue his lifestyle of drinking, fighting and shooting with a little business thrown in between.

Mejor once lent me a polo pony to try out. I don't pretend to be a horseman but I went sailing off into the veldt, thrilling with the momentum of the racing steed until I realised that I didn't know how to arrest the charging animal. I met an ignominious end in a thorn bush, sore but proud. Guns were Mejor's life, not polo ponies. No polo tournament would or could entertain Mejor's wildness. The play would deteriorate into an unbridled Irish brawl. Mejor would fight man or beast. He wasn't particularly big as South Africans go but he possessed the largest hands I have ever seen on a man. His antics could fill a thousand page book and Tom Wolfe, the American writer, would delight perhaps in having this Cullinan as one of his character profiles. There were countless incidents in Mejor's life but there was one in particular that had Johannesburg chortling: Mejor chose to dress up as a fairy godmother for a fancy dress ball but deciding that the soiree was too tame for him, he ventured forth, still decked out in his fairy garb, into Hillbrow, then the Chelsea of Johannesburg, and after a dazzling display of carousing in Hillbrow's night spots he was eventually arrested by the police for disturbing the peace. The granite faced cops – they were mostly white in those days – weren't quite sure how to handle the 'fairy' with bruised lips and a cut cheek bone!

There was the occasion we had been dining with him at his home in Olifantsfontein and at 2.00 a.m. he suddenly sprung to his feet and announced that he was going bird shooting and that I was to come with him. He put his horse groom behind the wheel and we sat in the back of his barouche savouring a fine cognac as we sped off to Standerton, a town in the Transvaal some three hours drive from Olifantsfontein. On the way he counselled me that I must be on my best behaviour as I was participating in a highly prestigious shoot, the host of which was Willy van der Byl, brother of Rhodesia's celebrated Minister of Defence, 'P.K.' van der Byl. Whilst the incorrigible Mejor expounded on the need for propriety I couldn't help but grin, and on reaching the hotel where we were to meet the shooting party, he strode into the dining room calling out "Willy, I have a guest, fresh from Britain, a famous shot!". Willy van der Byl was not particularly amused to receive a gate crasher into his midst. I didn't know at the time but this was the AECI shoot, one of the most jealously guarded events on the bird shooting calendar. The atmosphere became more charged when my eyes settled on a pompous fellow, an inveterate name dropper and poseur that I learnt to take an intense dislike to over recent months, and my threat to banjo this wretch and Mejor's display of colourful language that would have made a barrack room blush, upset the decorum of breakfast that morning. It was a grim looking group of AECI executives that formed the line at the start of the shoot. The Cullinan/Callender team was not entirely to their satisfaction until Mejor knocked down a dozen guinea fowl in a row. Luckily, I had been posted at the end of the line and so went unnoticed. My head was throbbing from the carousing of the night before but I managed to contribute three birds to the morning's drive - a modest percentage of a huge bag. However, over lunch I was able to dispense a little Celtic charm and good humour was restored.

In the late 70's I was the last man to shoot with Mejor Cullinan. The two of us drove to a remote outpost near Vryheid in the Northern Cape, close to the Botswana border. Mejor was on doctor's orders not to drink. Farmers, in general, have iron-clad constitutions and hold scant regard for 'doctor's orders' and the hospitality extended was too great a temptation for Mejor and he leapt into the fray, only to suffer the consequences for the next two days when I ultimately had to leave him to the tender mercies of the cattle-ranchers to drive back to Johannesburg. On his eventual return from the outback, he piled into a party, danced frenetically throughout the night and then lay down and died of a heart attack at the age of 42.

* * * * *

Andrew, a first cousin of Mejor's and a successful fruit farmer, possessed in no small measure the Cullinan wild streak. I was destined to become godfather to one of Andrew's sons, until his second wife the glamorous Janis, put a firm stop to the idea. Andrew matched his cousin's spirited nature and there were several occasions when I would carry Andrew to his doorstep having brokered many a truce in the bars of Johannesburg and Pretoria after rugby tests. Andrew had huge charm and the ladies loved him and his buccaneering style broke a few hearts. He seemed to enjoy my company and we survived many an adventure. He was with me when our son, Sean, was born and I threw an impromptu party at the 'Guild Hall', in those days one of Johannesburg's liveliest venues. This preceded a week of one long and riotous celebration including the memorable occasion when Andrew and the author delivered pigeons to the Top of the Tower, a popular restaurant and night haunt in Braamfontein. It should be explained that Renee and Vic, the co – owners of this hostelry, were the chief customers of 'pigeons unlimited', a venture Andrew & I owned, and in exchange for sackfuls of these birds we dined in majestic style on a regular basis. On this particular evening Andrew and I spotted Mark Edey entertaining a lady friend and we invited them over to join our table. During the cabaret us three men volunteered to shoot balloons as part of the act and up we lurched on to the brilliantly-lit stage when, to the consternation of some 200 diners, we decided to shoot the lights out with an air rifle, believing the balloons to be too easy a target. Then started a fearful fracas and we had to fend off a howling mob baying for our blood, throwing left and rights with merry abandon as we fought our way into the lift. Andrew and I visited Vivienne the next day a little worse for wear, and young Cullinan didn't exactly endear himself to the matron of the nursing home when he climbed into a cot to join a room full of squalling one day olds!

* * * * *

I decided to return home early from Van Zyl & Robinson, an advertising agency where I was employed in those days and referred to in chapter 12, to see my new-born son. I was full of good intentions and felt the model family man until Helgaard Pienaar, a free spirited copy writer, persuaded me to join him for a drink at the men's bar of the Honeydew Motel which was close to our offices. The temptation of an ice-cold beer at the end of a trying day in the chaotic world of advertising was just too much. I was greeted in the dim lit bar by a character called 'Witkop', a scar-faced wild man who would take on any fellow, whatever his size, often for unpremeditated reason. Luckily 'Witkop' had taken a liking to this rooinek. He'd learnt that I had a fair measure of Irish in me which was to his satisfaction. 'Witkop' was in a benevolent mood that night and so were a few other locals in learning of the birth of Sean and before long an unscheduled party was in full sway. Two hours later and with half a dozen beers and bols chasers inside me, I drove home in a company Volkswagen. My head for liquor had always been strong and I was clear of vision and looking forward to seeing the baby. I took a short cut – a one way lane that I knew to be deserted at that time of night – but I hadn't reckoned on a police car lying in ambush which gave immediate chase. Then followed a sort of Le Mans race with the Volkswagen being furiously gunned down a dirt road with the police car in hot pursuit. The latter moved faster than the lurching Volkswagen and I was brought to a Hollywood-style halt with a menacing blond headed brute of a policeman striding towards me with a huge black constable in tow. There was only one thing for me to do and that was to wind up the window to avoid the fumes spilling out over the men of the law. There was a loud expletive. I'd caught the white policeman's hand in the window and his huge fingers presented a tempting target. I'm ashamed to say I set my fangs into these banana-like appendages and I sailed off taking the blaspheming policeman with me. But the black constable had hurled himself onto the windscreen and I'd no choice but to come to a reluctant halt. The door was then pulled open and I was dragged out of the Volkswagen and hurled like an American football into the police van with my head bearing the brunt.

To cut a long saga short, I was handcuffed and taken to the Krugersdorp Police Station where the District Surgeon was summonsed for blood tests. I was a student of karate in those days of the early 70's and extremely fit. I demonstrated my sobriety by completing fifty press ups which annoyed all present as I had been instructed to press my finger tips together with eyes shut, not provide a demonstration of physical jerks, however impressive. Then the fun and games. The blond headed policeman was acting like a pit bull on a chain. He wanted desperately to place his bitten fingers around my neck. The African constable remained a little confused. The District Surgeon had taken the blood sample for testing and I, by now, had recovered my composure and placed my one permitted call to my lawyer. Fortunately, Michael Schneider was at home and I asked him to phone Andrew Cullinan to bail me out. Michael Schneider, a shrewd ring-fighter of a lawyer, questioned me as to whether this was wise! He'd, no doubt, had heard of the wild Cullinans of Olifantsfontein. I explained that Andrew, being a farmer, was likely to have cash on him for his labourers' wages to pay the bail. Michael Schneider, now sadly dead from a heart attack from probably too many clients like myself, agreed to call Andrew against his better judgement and he duly arrived whilst my fingerprints were being taken by the duty sergeant. The blond haired policeman by now had exited in disgust in not being able to lay into the rooinek. In rushes into the police station an excited Andy Cullinan with a wad of notes. He'd been drinking with Mejor in the Cullinan pub in Olifantsfontein and his new wife, the beautiful Janis, had relayed Michael Schneider's message of urgency. Mejor had wanted to join the party to witness Michael Callender's detention in custody but Andrew had exercised an uncharacteristic common sense. Two Cullinans in the Krugersdorp Police Station would have been too vibrant a mixture. Andrew chose his moment carefully, and with a well timed nudge with the heel of his hand, the ink smeared fingers of the prisoner went searing up the sergeant's pristine white shirt. This was too much for the sergeant and he locked us in a cell whilst telephoning for the Captain of the Krugersdorp Police. And then a miracle occurred. Thirty minutes later and on the chime of midnight, this stocky, grey haired police veteran arrived at the station, his uniform thrown hastily over his pyjamas. His gimlet eyes bored into mine through the bars of the cell and then into Andrew Cullinan's. His voice was a bark: "I'm in a mood to detain you gentlemen for the weekend. Explain yourselves. And you", he turned to a subdued Cullinan, "are you part of that bunch from Olifantsfontein? Yes, I thought so". And he turned back to me. He questioned me on my background and as to how I could demean myself in biting an officer of the law. Had I been in the British army, he suddenly asked as he obviously recognised my accent. "Certainly" I said, "in a Scots regiment, the Cameronians". I then detected a subtle softening of voice and expression. "I served with the Transvaal Scottish in the War. I've heard of your lot – explains your terrible behaviour!" said the captain. He released us from the cells and he stared at us for a full minute. Then a slow grin creased his weather beaten face. "Get out of here and go straight home", he growled.

I will not forget that splendid man in a hurry, a tribute to the Afrikaners and an antidote to that blond thug that I'd bitten. The sequel to the saga was that Andrew and I drove in convoy to Johannesburg and celebrated in a nightclub, but not before telephoning the news of my release to our respective wives. Three months later the Court found me guilty of driving in excess of the permitted limit which was generous in those days and the drink and drive stigma was not as severe as today. The legal team of the advocate, Frank Nino, and the lawyer, Micky Schneider, handled the case admirably and the bullet-head blond constable failed to appear in Court and so the charge of 'causing grievous bodily harm' was dropped.

ʔ◆ʕ

CHAPTER THREE

Life on a razor wire

Life is not a rehearsal.
You only get one bite at it. So you had
better make it a big one and live to
the full.

The Author

THE MAN had been on a long training run. He'd been up since the first light of dawn and had jogged the tortuous switch-back which is the old Pretoria – Johannesburg road. He'd run this punishing course for several years in preparation for marathons. He knew every inch of the gruelling hills as this was the final leg of the strenuous 'Iron Man' race, a contest he was well familiar with. It was one of those scorching days in the Transvaal and it was a sweat-stained weary runner that reached his home. He sensed something was very amiss as he strode into the house. His wife looked drawn and troubled, a pale shadow of her usually ebullient personality. In a faltering, subdued voice she described the ghastly tale that had occurred in the small hours of that morning. MaryAnne and Pierre 'Bushy' Bester, both co-founders in their outward bounds adventure business, 'Kayak Africa', had been hijacked and the girl had been close to being raped followed by a bullet to hers and her companion's heads. The story was yet another saga of the relentless crime wave that plagues 'The New South Africa'.

The youngsters, then in their mid 20's, had attended a party near Fourways, a dominant landmark that lies to the north of Johannesburg. Pierre Bester had excused himself early on to sleep in the car and MaryAnne had revelled on. Parties were a luxury in their busy lives where Kayak Africa demanded their full energies to kayaking the Lake of Malawi, abseiling, deep-sea diving, and spear fishing. The young lady climbed into the driving seat at 3.00 a.m. leaving Pierre asleep. She halted at a set of lights when the car doors were yanked open and a gun was held to Pierre's head. Two thugs forced MaryAnne to drive to the cottage they were renting in Farmall, an agricultural area adjoining Chartwell, and demanded money. R30.00 was all the cash the youngsters could muster and the two were forced back into the car with the girl driving with the one African sitting next to her indecently fondling her thighs and the other holding the gun to Pierre's head in the rear. The robbers were angry with their modest spoils and in revenge talked of raping MaryAnne and then shooting the couple. Pierre Bester understood the Zulu dialect and quickly realised that he and MaryAnne were about to die. The young lady was instructed to stop and the thug in front stepped out of the car intent on dragging the girl into the undergrowth when Pierre Bester, realising this was the last chance to save their lives, wrestled with the gun-toting gangster resulting in the pistol discharging a bullet through the roof of the vehicle. Pierre Bester is a powerful man and he managed to throw the thug out of the car, yelling at MaryAnne to start up and drive off. The young lady displayed an amazing calm under this fearsome pressure and without hesitation she pressed the central locking system leaving the thugs hammering on the windows. Pierre Bester had retained the gun in the scuffle and he wanted to chase the criminals across the veldt but common sense prevailed and they drove to the nearest police station to report the hijacking.

Understandably the mother of that girl was in a state of shock. She remains scarred with the memory of that heinous deed. The young couple, resilient and tough survivors as they are, remain seemingly unaffected by their horrendous ordeal. The woman is my wife; the young girl our daughter, MaryAnne.

Johannesburg's newspaper hoardings say it all. The South African citizen is probably a little hardened to the sensational screamers but the foreigner could be excused if he rubs his eyes in disbelief. He could well be in the old Wild West of America.

"Gang rams Woolworths with armoured personnel carrier"

"Fifteen dead in head on taxi collision"

"Bank robbed of R30 million in Johannesburg's central business district"

"Vigilante gang throw thieves to crocodiles"

"Max the Gorilla shot in Johannesburg Zoo by fugitive robber"

"Citizens return fire on muggers in shopping mall"

"Johannesburg – rapist and hi-jacking capital of world"

"Trade union chief stoned to death by strikers"

"Hearse stolen – corpse thrown out"

These lurid headlines are not make-believe but the stark reality of the 'New South Africa'. The country has degenerated into a hi-jackers' paradise and, in a more unpalatable vein, an untrammelled rapist Hades. There are clear reasons why South Africa's law and order has deteriorated so dramatically over the last decade. With the abolishment of the death penalty and the sudden transformation from Apartheid's iron-fist rule to a lenient democratic process, President Mandela's reign sent a signal to the criminal underworld where hardened transgressors of the law could masquerade under a screen of a 'Third Force'. The police force, once feared as an authoritarian arm that stamped mercilessly on any form of crime, has been diluted into a disorientated, unmotivated, and confused body. Poorly paid and of a desperately low morale, large numbers of policemen have been tempted into corrupt ways to bolster their paltry incomes and their perilous life styles. Then there's the ANC's armed wing to consider - the MK (Umkhonto we Sizwe) - which became harshly disillusioned when it returned from exile. In place of an expected heroes' ticker-tape parade through the streets of Pretoria, the freedom fighters were paid out a meagre pittance and unceremoniously bundled into oblivion. Inevitably, many of the MK turned to hijacking, robbery and rape and it didn't stop there. Warriors of the S.A. Defence Force Special Forces – some white, some black – converted to crime. There were no more border wars to fight and redundancy stared them in the face. The ANC's coming to power in 1994 encouraged a tidal wave of illegal immigrants – Nigerians, Zambians, Zimbabweans and Mozambicans mostly – fuelling a sinister trend of drug dealing, arms smuggling, vehicle hijacking and a lengthy chronicle of fraudulent scams that permeates the civil service and the banks and the police force itself. An AK47 could be purchased for a shirt, a forged driving licence for a $10.00 note, or a faked identity document for a crate of whisky. Bribery is swiftly assuming Nigerian levels and the plague is roaring through Government departments and statutory bodies and industry.

* * * * *

Then there are the taxi wars. Black taxis were hailed in their formative years as a miracle for the economy's non-formal sector. But not for long. Taxi gang warfare – Al Capone fashion - erupted on the streets, leaving scores of innocent citizens slain by a hail of bullets in the main thoroughfares of South Africa's cities. The taxi drivers hold contempt for the rules of the road and they are a despised lot for the horrific accidents they cause. There would appear to be no roadworthiness standards and a morass of dilapidated, rusted cars and trucks congest the highways where every day without fail there's a spectacular pile-up on Johannesburg's main arteries. Driving in the city's environs can be likened to a bizarre dodgem car carnival.

On one recent Monday morning I counted two separate accidents on the same stretch of highway, north of Johannesburg, resulting in my having to cancel business meetings. The first was sheer carnage and a grisly sight for fresh eyes at 7 a.m. The six car pile-up was the result of an overturned taxi, the occupants of which were crying in shock amidst corpses strewn across the verge. The second occurred only ten kilometres further down the same motorway where a taxi had inexplicably crashed through the metal barrier dividing the lanes and had taken a BMW head on. More bodies, more deaths, more lost limbs and disfigurements. Shortly after that 'Bloody Monday', I was sitting in a traffic jam and I watched a commuter exchange heated words with a taxi driver. The taxi was typical in its state of dilapidation – bald tyres, rear window devoid of glass, bumper hanging on by wire. The driver jumped out feeling for his gun only to confront an enraged commuter who'd obviously been a victim of being cut-off without warning – a favourite ploy of the taxi drivers. The white fellow calmly threw the howling taxi driver across his bonnet, leant into the vehicle, grabbed the keys and hurled them over a bridge astride a highway. The traffic had remained at a standstill and the early morning commuters of all creeds and colour pressed their horns as a token of respect for the wronged motorist. Incidentally, I counted twenty two shaken passengers emerge out of that taxi– double the legal load.

* * * * *

I was sent an article printed in the British 'Daily Mail'. It was a derogatory, ill-spirited portrayal of South African life: 'whites cowering behind bars living besieged lives from the criminals of South Africa'. Cowering indeed! This impression needs sharp correction. The men and women of this country have been forged over centuries of fighting and turmoil into one of the most resilient and resourceful peoples in the world. Every day they run a gauntlet to reach their places of work but they have learnt to live with mayhem, as indeed have the citizens of Tel Aviv, Bagdad and Kabul. I take note of the young girls driving their way into work, fluffing out their hair, applying lipstick, and chatting on their cell phones. They may have their car-door locking mechanisms in place, their windows wound up, and probably a gas spray canister tucked under their thighs but their spirits remain indomitable as with the young men striding along the business districts, seemingly without a care for caution, but beneath the veneer they remain alert for the threat of a mugging or a gun in the ribs.

We know probably 300 men and women that have suffered the indignity and the trauma of being hijacked and not a few of these have experienced more than one assault. And then on a more sinister note are those that we know that have died at the hands of the criminals. This is no exaggeration, no wayward flight of the imagination. The residents of the notorious hot spots, principally Johannesburg that has earned itself the dubious accolade of the 'crime capital of the world', take their lives in their hands. They face not only the possibility of a gun barrel pressed to their heads as they wait for the electronically controlled gates of their homes to open, but the crossfire of gangsters with police in shopping malls, supermarkets, banks, in the townships and on the highways.

* * * * *

Life is lived on the edge in a violent society and nobody would call Johannesburg a soft city. And the scary reflection is that their denizens have become hardened to death. That is perhaps why they drive too fast, work too hard and drink too much but they all remain inordinately proud of the town. I remember when I met an oil executive at the end of a day's work. He's an interesting man and a fellow hunter. I was looking forward to having a drink with him and to hearing his latest tales of the bush. He asked me how the day had gone to which I replied a cryptic "fine". And then I pondered for a second. "No, not exactly" I added and I told him that three things had occurred that very day. I'd opened the factory at 7.00 am to learn that the watchman had hung himself in the early hours of the morning at his home. 'Welcome' was his name and he had served us well for several years and to deepen the tragedy, his wife was part of our factory line. Then later that morning I was close to having a mobile phone snatched out of my hand. I'd been driving in down-town Johannesburg in an area that resembles Harlem - once proud buildings reduced to squalid, rat infested slum edifices festooned with washing hanging out of broken windows. I should have known better than to take the call from the cell phone. Then the shattering bang and I thought I'd been shot at. The window had been smashed by a spark plug – an old trick – and an arm reached in to seize my cell phone. The light had turned green and despite the cacophony of blaring horns behind me, I was trying my best to clout the robber with my left fist whilst gripping onto the phone with the right. Thankfully my strength prevailed and the miscreant finally backed off, looking at me balefully with drugged yellow eyes. And then a few hours later on the way to meeting the oil executive, I took a call from a Scots friend, Charlie Gough, who told me that he'd just lost a life-long friend, a fellow Glaswegian, who'd died in a hail of bullets from a hijacking that afternoon. Such is a day in the life of Johannesburg!

*   *   *   *   *

In 1987 we were to experience an occurrence where we were fortunate to avoid a possible death. Next to our factory in downtown Johannesburg was the ANC trade union headquarters, Cosatu House. For months on end we would endure a mind numbing chanting of freedom fighter war songs and the noise added to the hideous cacophony of ambulance and police car sirens that would rent the air outside our premises in Bree Street. I arrived one wintry morning to open the factory at 7am. I was confronted by a work force – we employed 70 in those days - wailing and shrieking. It didn't take long to realise the cause of the commotion. Every panel of glass in the building had been shattered and the mess was indescribable. Apparently, we learnt later, a massive bomb of several kgs had been detonated in Cosatu House in the early hours of the morning and I only recently learnt that this deed had been executed by no less a personality than Colonel Eugene de Kock. I happened to read this in his biography '*A long night's damage*'.

This story is a focus on a land of great adventure, of great excitement, of great opportunity. The untimely and unnecessary deaths that crop up in this narrative are simply examples that spring to mind after hours of recollection and everyday conversations. A complete compendium of the horrors of violent deaths that desecrate this proud country would appal the human heart. Economically, South Africa has an infrastructure that is unparalleled on the continent of Africa and, indeed, a host of other nations in the world. The Republic has enormous natural resources and peoples of great potential, many of whom have been lifted from the yolk of suppression and who are improving the quality of their lives. Yet violence continues to blot their outlook and this curse has severely curtailed the investment from overseas that this country is so anxious to attract.

Daily are the occurrences of the shootings, muggings, rapes and hijackings. South Africa is a land afloat with firearms, most of which are illegally obtained. The country is rated in second place behind Colombia in the world for firearm related murder statistics. I was talking to a business acquaintance recently where he told me that only that morning he was caught in a cross-fire between two warring taxi cab gangs. Countless are the stories of Wild West style shoot outs in shopping malls where the law abiding citizen finds himself taking on armed robbers. There was the case of a hectic shoot out in an East Rand mall parking lot where security guards and shoppers chased a gang following a bank heist. One of the robbers was slain in a hail of bullets and he was discovered to be a 33 year old police sergeant. His police identity disc was in his pocket and the gun was discovered to be a police service pistol. In the very basement where we parked our cars in down town Johannesburg – before we vacated the factory premises after the suicide of our watchman and our financial controller being held up at pistol point at the entrance to our factory – a shootout occurred between a bunch of bank robbers and a team of security guards.

* * * * *

The South African has had to learn to cope with the cloud of crime that darkens his life but when he can no longer trust a uniform of the law then the pandemic of violence is rampantly out of control. There's the story of a prominent merchant banker, 'G T' Ferreira, who is fortunate to be alive today. Some years ago, 'GT' was flagged down in a wealthy suburb of Johannesburg by a vehicle with a flashing blue light on its roof. Everything appeared authentic to 'GT' – the flashing lights, the uniforms, the purposeful manner in which the two policemen approached him. And then to his horror he found himself staring down the barrel of a pistol which was discharged at point blank range. He fell to the ground, grievously wounded, whilst the hijackers fled with his vehicle. 'GT' Ferreira spent a week in hospital in critical care. The bullet had traversed his chest through his right upper arm. He keeps the tie as a memento which carries the bullet hole in the centre – a tribute to his quick reflexes and proof of the thugs' determination to kill him.

There was the former police reservist who was deceived one early morning by four armed men dressed in Johannesburg Traffic Department uniforms. 23 year old Byron Niewstad stopped at the roadside, believing he'd been caught speeding in his BMW. A former police reservist and a 95kg boxer, he was a man who could look after himself and police trained at that and he left his vehicle to inspect an authentic speed measuring device only to find a 9mm pistol pressed to his head. The trigger was pulled but the gun misfired due to a faulty primer in the bullet. Then followed a struggle where the valiant Niewstad managed to free himself and the four hijackers raced off with his firearm and watch. No stranger to dangerous situations and having been hijacked and mugged before, Byron Niewstad described the humiliation of pleading for his life. He warned that unless something was done to stop the crime, people would take the law into their own hands and he was quoted as saying "next time, either the hijacker or me will take a bullet. I would rather die than go through this again.........I don't care how fast I'm going, I will never stop for a traffic officer again".

Hardly is it surprising that the alert motorist is loath to stop at night on the command of a flashing light. One is relatively safe with a roadblock, particularly so where soldiers are present, but I experienced a jolt to the nervous system when a police vehicle with lights flashing signalled me to a halt on a deserted road late at night. Two smartly dressed traffic policemen ordered me to stand in front of my vehicle with its full lights on. They asked me to place my hands above my head and frisked my body for a hidden weapon. It was all too quick and too slick for my liking and the thought flashed across my mind that I was to be a hijacking statistic. Fortunately, it was a case of a drink and drive test. In attempting to dial home on a mobile phone I had crossed a white line. I dealt with their aggressive questioning and they could determine that I wasn't intoxicated and they let me go and with relief I climbed back into my vehicle on the realisation that I wasn't to be hijacked.

* * * * *

A recent study by a criminologist highlighted a sinister trend amongst the criminal element. The hijackers, house breakers, muggers and rapists are brazen men living the high life, totally oblivious to death or prison sentences. Known as 'amagents', this breed of criminal is a male aged between 13 and 30. The study involved interviews with forty amagents, some serving prison sentences, and 170 township youths. The purchase of a gun was described as no more complicated than buying beer in a shebeen. The youths interviewed regarded guns as essential 'tools of the trade' and 'symbols of man'. Their attitude to violence was cold blooded, ruthless, and the death of a comrade – at – arms was seen as a cause for celebration of a hero. Life is cheap to these young gangsters. If a comrade is killed, the funeral is an excuse for spinning cars, firing shots into the air and getting massively drunk. To compound this social curse is the ease in which these amagents perpetuate their vile crimes and they are well aware of the inept criminal justice system, the pathetically low conviction rate, and the rampant corruption within the police force.

The citizen in South Africa is confronted with a vast scale of police fraud, bribery, and extortion whose tentacles reach to the very top of the hierarchy and where there is collusion with the Justice Department, the state prosecutors and the court officials in return for bribes from criminal gangs. The Jackie Selebi scandal is a good case in question. The former police commissioner was sentenced at a court in Johannesburg in August 2010 to 15 years imprisonment for corruption and graft. Selebi, a leading light in the ruling ANC party and a former president of Interpol, had been found guilty of accepting bribes from a notorious drug king, Glen Agliotti. Velaphi Ndlovu, a spokesman on police issues for the IFP, a Zulu dominant opposition party to the ANC, made the telling statement "that the sentencing will repair some of the damage inflicted on the SA Police's public image by its former police chief".

* * * * *

Even in the pursuit of one's sport, the threat of being slain by a thug is ubiquitous. Take the pigeon shooting incident near Springs, an hour's drive from Johannesburg. There were several of us gathered on a farm to shoot over a sunflower field where the pigeons were flying in their droves as the newsletter of the S A Wing shooters Association had so correctly predicted. By lunch time we had called it a day, the shooting had been that prolific. I learnt later that week that a gruesome incident had occurred on the very farm where we had been shooting. A sportsman had stayed on that afternoon with his son. The other guns had departed and the two were alone in the sunflower field. Three Africans had approached them, masquerading as labourers of the farmer, offering to collect their birds. This is a customary practice on pigeon shoots and the pair saw nothing unusual in this request. All went well initially until the horrendous moment came when the father was overpowered by the three thugs and killed with his own shotgun. The terrified boy, a youngster in his teens, had bolted off to the farmhouse to summon help by which time the killers had disappeared with the gun and the ammunition. This is the savage side of South Africa, reminding me of another incident related to the pervasive crime that spills over into one's sport. Durban Roodepoort Deep, one of the gold mines on the Reef, operates a shooting range regularly patronised by hunters for rifle practice. It's a popular venue with adequate facilities. I was a regular user on weekday afternoons, testing my ammunition and usually alone without a range officer as I was well known to the staff. I was shattered to hear that a murder had taken place at the range. The hunter, a surgeon, was on his own. Whilst checking his target, a robber had scaled the security fence and shot the sportsman with his own rifle. The criminal escaped unscathed. What is apparent that one is never completely safe in this land, whether driving to work, in one's own homestead, or pursuing one's sport!

CHAPTER FOUR

The brave buffalo

*I have been gored by this awesome animal
and to my dying days I will never forget its
maddened red eyes and its rank smell as I
was swept aside like an irrelevant tsetse fly.*

The Author

I KNOW many big game men who prefer to only hunt buffalo. They reason that this charismatic denizen of the African veldt is by far the most exciting and dangerous animal to hunt and a malevolent fury if things go wrong. Aside from being one of Africa's most impressive trophies the buffalo is possessed with phenomenal strength and bravery. At close quarters a mature bull is an intimidating sight with his heavy muscular shoulders, humped neck and huge gnarled bosses supporting a regal sweep of horn. Little wonder that big game hunters rate this oversized Spanish fighting bull so highly. His toughness is legendary. Once in flight, or in fight, having seen you the buffalo pumps an extraordinary amount of adrenaline which keeps him on his feet long after he should be dead. Even when struck mortally a buffalo continues charging with intent to kill.

A buffalo hunt can be an unnerving experience for the novice. You have to march quickly once on the spoor, trusting that you will catch up to the herd whilst it's still on the move. Once they lie up, and their instinct is to take you into the densest of bush, you'll have great difficulty in identifying a suitable trophy; then there's a further problem with the bulls milling among the cows, when there's a chance of your bullet scorching through the quarry and wounding another animal. Buffalo hunting can be difficult. It's close quarter work and for the first timer it can be a hair-raising ordeal.

The last minute approach to a herd is usually taken on a crawl, leaving the hunter uncertain as to what the pack of dark grey monoliths will do. You creep through the thickets as noiselessly as possible despite sharp stones and thorns, and in your inexperience you probably forget to remove the sling from your rifle that is snagging on stumps, thorn bushes and a host of other obstacles.

Sweat courses into your eyes making it difficult to see the buffalo clearly. All you can make out are swirling tails and twitching ears. The smell is overwhelmingly rank. You wonder why you chose to do this. Then suddenly you are looking a crafty and angry looking *syncerus caffer* in the eye, thinking should there be a solid or soft nosed cartridge in the chamber? Will you kill cleanly or wound? The consequences could be fatal.

It is difficult to describe to the uninitiated this spectre of hugeness, knowing that if you wound it, this member of the Big Five family will become maddened and will want to destroy you. But once you have experienced buffalo hunting, you tend to become dissatisfied with other game with the possible exception of lions. This is, of course, if you have learned to appreciate buffalo. There are some who never return to this sport and I've spoken to certain professional hunters who have said to me that they can sense naked fear in a client when approaching this awesome animal. I'm probably not the first to admit that after 20 or more buffalo hunts the adrenaline still flows abnormally when chasing this formidable animal. I get wound up when stalking these giants of the thickets and I believe this state of the senses is an essential preparation for such a situation. Among big game specialists and seasoned professional hunters, dissension will always remain as to which is the most dangerous of the

Big Five. The African buffalo is often placed at the top of the list. Some place elephant and lion ahead. But whatever their opinion, the buffalo lays squarely in the top three. My own experience of the ferocity of this animal – I was smashed to the ground on my second buffalo hunt – will remain etched in memory to my dying days. I have lost two good friends who were killed simultaneously by a wounded buffalo, and a Rhodesian hunter was gored to death while I was in a neighbouring camp in the Zambezi Valley. Each year I read of others who end their lives on the horns or under the hooves of this massive animal.

Having experienced a charge and a bad battering, I can testify that the buffalo, if wounded, proves to be a remorseless and savage foe. When charging, it keeps its eyes wide open to watch its enemy. It raises its horns when coming at you and finally lowers them just when it's on to you. In my situation, I was able to swivel on my toes in the manner of a matador to avoid the bosses. I crashed to the ground as did the buffalo. I'll never forget the maddened red eyes. Frederick C. Selous, the famous hunter-soldier of the late last century, was one of the many men of Africa who bestowed on the buffalo an evil repute. Not all share his sentiments but most agree that a wounded buffalo can prove to be a nightmare.

How can I forget that buffalo hunt in 1985? I was inching over the rocks, Piers Taylor just ahead of me, crawling towards a buffalo bull with a huge set of horns. My mouth was bone dry. We were in the thick of Charara, a rugged wilderness bordering Kariba Lake in Zimbabwe, a terrain that the Rhodesian Special Forces had used for training in their recent war (1970 – 1980). I would hunt in Charara several times in the following years, but all I knew on this blazing hot afternoon was that I was very apprehensive. I looked at Piers, his long frame stretched over the rocks like a giant python, his binoculars up as he studied the buffalo herd. I glanced back at the imperturbable features of Contella Banda, Piers' chief tracker, and Flex, the strong, silent Batonka tribesman, a poacher that Piers had picked up in the bush some years ago. Contella was grinning and Flex was remaining impassive. These two first class African hunters were to accompany me on many an adventure. Piers motioned me to move forward with a twitch of the fingers, his eyes straining on the buffalo ahead. I was in an awkward firing position. The target was angled in such a way that I was unsure of the precise point where to place the bullet. This was not quite like the rifle range. My rest for my weapon was a rock - a little different to a sandbag! I was uncomfortable, not at all confident, and the result was that I broke the cardinal rule of marksmanship: *don't squeeze the trigger until you are sure of the shot.* To make matters worse my heart was pumping so strongly that I was unable to hold the .375 steady. Everything was wrong, yet I fired at the buffalo. To my dismay the quarry barrelled off into the bush. I had nicked him in the neck.

I fired several shots that afternoon as we chased our prey for over five hours. I had heard of the legendary toughness of the buffalo from my big game contemporaries, and had read stories of the old timers who would fire barrel after barrel at the hardiest wild animal on the African continent. I came to hate buffalo that afternoon. After an hour, we caught up with the wounded bull. It was standing alone in a patch of grass 70 metres from us. I aimed at the point of its shoulder, but the bullet took it too far back and Piers grunted "You've hit him in the stomach, but it'll slow him down". Then followed a further hour of jog-trotting in the oppressive heat of Charara when again we caught a glimpse of the bull in the thick jess. "Fire at him"! bellowed Piers as the buffalo crashed away into the dense thorn bush. "Shoot him again, or we'll lose him!" I took a snap shot from the shoulder and was beginning to despair as we marched swiftly through the thickets, halting only to pick up the thinning blood spoor. By wounding a dangerous animal I had put everyone at risk - Piers, Contella and Flex.

Although the sun was sinking the heat had not abated. Not for a minute did Piers call for a breather except to search for spoor. Then the awful thought struck me that in the approaching dusk we wouldn't find the buffalo. Moreover my strength, despite my conditioning for canoe and road marathons, was beginning to ebb. Contella set a relentless pace. He never faltered on the spoor. And there was Piers Taylor, a man with few peers in the art of tracking. Flex, the reformed poacher, capable of reading spoor like a road map, was up front with Contella. Then came the heart-sinking moment when Piers called a five minute break. "I think we've lost him. The blood spoor's dried up". He turned to me, "Check your rifle. He might be around the corner, and he'll come at us. He's had enough. We've half an hour left before dark. We must catch him – there aren't many left like him these days, probably 44 – 45 inches on the horn is my guess". His words deepened my misery. Not only had I wounded a brave animal, but was at serious risk of losing a very fine specimen with magnificent horns.

The last 30 minutes of that afternoon are welded into my memory. We were trotting along a riverbed when Contella indicated a puff-adder which he had jumped over. We were like a line of marionettes, four men hopping in unison. No time to admire the venomous snake. There was a job to be done. My tongue stuck to the roof of my mouth. I was sensing the light headedness of heat exhaustion and wondered in desperation how on earth I could handle a charge in the fading light. We clambered up a small, rock-strewn kopje, and then down into some of the thickest thorn scrub I have ever experienced - the infamous jess of the Zambezi Valley. Unexpectedly Piers raised his rifle and let off a shot. "There – there!" He was pointing to the fallen buffalo. "Take it from the side but be careful, he might charge". I muttered a prayer to St Hubert as I aimed on the point of the shoulder and squeezed the trigger.

I had fired my seventh bullet that day. Piers strode over to me as the buffalo bellowed his death throes. I looked at Piers and muttered "I don't believe I deserve this buffalo, I truly fouled up." For the rest of my life, I will never forget Piers for that moment. He turned to me with his characteristic piratical grin, gold tooth flashing. "You didn't want to make it too easy, did you? You took us on a marathon on purpose, you bugger!" He stood back and laughed. "You look a sore sight, cap sideways, shirting hanging out, face scratched out of all recognition. I suppose I can put up with you!" The memory of that day will be one of the most vivid as I look back on a lifetime of hunting. I had just taken a remarkable trophy and it was made possible by one of the finest trios in the hunting world.

One year later I was off again to Charara to hunt with Piers Taylor. On the first morning we located a herd of some 200 buffalo standing in a valley. We abandoned the truck and walked in file to inspect them. The adrenaline began to flow as we finally leopard crawled to glass the buffalo. It was 10 a.m., the time of day for animals of the wild to start resting in anticipation of the midday heat and humidity. It was early November, the period just before the first rains of the season were expected, and a time uncomfortably hot for hunting. For an hour we studied the buffalo waiting for a target. But all we could see was a mass of twitching ears and tails. We had to reverse out of the thicket but there was a cow some 80 metres away, facing us in a small clearing in the Mopani scrub. Piers signalled that I should shoot as we had a cow on the license. I took aim on the centre of the chest and fired. The way the buffalo buckled indicated that the bullet had struck home. Clots of blood were proof that the animal had been severely hit. Piers Taylor looked at me with his evil grin. "Callender, if you've fouled up you'll get this up your backside!" he said, pointing to the shooting sticks that Flex was carrying.

We marched for an hour in single file, with Contella leading followed by Piers, self, and Flex bringing up the rear. The cow was taking us in a straight line and the blood spoor was clear and easy to follow. However, my initial elation on a one-shot kill was quickly evaporating and I was thinking the unthinkable - *it's waiting for us.* A cow buffalo is not that much smaller than a bull. In fact the largest horns recorded in Rowland Ward belong to a cow. As with a lioness or a female elephant, a cow buffalo can be as mean and aggressive as a bull. I could sense tension in the team as we threaded our way through the thick jess. The vegetation was so dense that we passed an elephant standing a mere 15 metres away; the huge grey mass was virtually invisible in the thickets.

Contella Banda was carrying Piers'.458 rifle. This was intentional as this highly skilled tracker was being groomed as a professional hunter. After two hours Piers called for a break. "We should be on it any moment". He turned to me. "You ready? The animal may just pounce on you!" Piers had that remarkable calmness and humour in tense moments. He guessed correctly that we were all highly strung that morning.

Thirty minutes later as we were struggling through the jess, Contella raised his rifle without warning and fired a shot. The buffalo had been waiting for us and Contella had caught a glimpse of it a mere 20 metres ahead. Without hesitation, I removed the detachable scope from my .375 and eased a round into the chamber. Piers turned to me and said quietly: "Be prepared, it could come any moment!" We reached a clearing. Contella to my right was studying the ground for the spoor. Piers was behind me when he suddenly yelled, "here it comes! Shoot! Shoot!" The bush erupted and the cow charged directly at me. I raised the .375 and shot directly into the chest - a fatal mistake on a charging buffalo as I was to learn later. As I stood there with rifle raised it looked as if the buffalo had been switched into slow motion – a perception due to my adrenaline rush. In reality the reverse was happening, and the monolith was coming at full speed. As we discovered later the distance between me and the bush from which the buffalo exploded was a mere 10 metres. Despite their bulk these animals can cover this distance in a few seconds. I was now icy calm and, as the maddened beast reached me, I raised myself on tip-toe like a Spanish bullfighter and pirouetted to take the brunt of the charge on the curve of the horn. I was smashed to the ground. I will never forget the blood-red eyes, suffused with savagery, as it crashed to the earth on its front forelegs with the boss missing my forehead by a hairs' breadth. St Hubert was with me that day. If that boss had struck me, my skull would have been smashed to a pulp and I would have died. And I was so fortunate that the crazed animal hadn't wheeled on me and trampled me to a bloodied heap as is often the habit of an angry buffalo. My first reaction was to run my hands over my genitalia as I had taken the full force of the charge in the groin and then I hobbled to my feet and shot at the dying buffalo with Piers next to me firing simultaneously.

The drama in that clearing in Charara had lasted probably for 10 minutes but to me the maelstrom had seemed an eternity. Countless men have experienced a charge in the pursuit of big game hunting and all have a tale to tell. Most of them agree as regards to that extraordinary icy calm which permeates the nervous system. This is due to a secretion of the adrenaline gland that accelerates the heart and stimulates the inner strength. Another important thing I recall about that morning was how my rifle had spun into the air and crashed heavily to the ground. I clearly remember clutching my groin and grabbing the Browning .375 and working the bolt. What a relief that the weapon was in good working order. That is perhaps why I continue to hold great respect for this reliable .375 weapon which has been my constant companion in the bush over the years.

The sequel to the buffalo charge is worth recounting. Piers decided that I had to be taken to the hospital in Kariba to be checked out. Halfway through the journey the truck stalled in a deep mud hole. I had severely stiffened up by this stage and I was in great discomfort and decided that Flex and Contella were capable of digging the vehicle out. Piers had other ideas: "get your backside into gear – we're stuck!" He relented when he saw that I was in pain but I was out of the truck swearing like a trooper, stumbling to the rear of the vehicle. I waded into the mud and shoved ineffectively alongside Piers, Flex and Contella. I was very sore and a little sorry for myself and the final indignity occurred when I slipped and fell face down into the glutinous mud. I was wearing shorts and all Piers could do was to hoot: "Hey, hey, the doctor will believe you've been trampled on – he'll have something to say all right!"

The nurse at Kariba hospital instructed the mud caked apparition to strip and lie on a trolley to wait for the doctor. Her eyes bulged as she took in the huge black shadow running across the base of my stomach. I still marvel to this day how my crown jewels were left intact and how the buffalo's boss hadn't smashed my forehead. The doctor, a cheerful Scot, bustled into the theatre. "Piers, you again! What have we here? Another buffalo accident, eh? I have two a day up here. The stupid buggers walk through the bush and cannot understand why they get stamped on". He ran his hands over me, asked the odd question, and then jabbed his fingers without warning into my spleen. The room swam in front of my eyes and I almost passed out. This was nearly as bad as the pain from the buffalo running over me earlier that day. He turned to Piers. "There's no sign of any haemorrhaging – yet! Give him salad but no solids. If there's any sweating or nausea in the night get him back here immediately". Piers retorted "And that goes for alcohol?" I caught the doctor's eyes that were creased with amusement. "He can have a whisky, but not the bottle. I don't know why you chaps do this for fun. You're mad, all of you." We bade farewell to a splendid man, a true bush doctor that you read about in novels. He just looked at us, shaking his head.

* * * * *

A memorable buffalo hunt took place at Deka, Zimbabwe, adjoining the Wankie Game Reserve. The previous day I had driven up from the Transvaal to join Piers Taylor at his Matetsi camp. It was a very tiring journey after little sleep as I had been in a canoe race in the Crocodile River in the Eastern Transvaal, a race in which I had the dubious honour of finishing last. I had been caught in a whirlpool and had struggled to keep the boat upright and in so doing I had lost my paddle, a cardinal error in canoeing. A well meaning fellow competitor had collected the paddle as it sailed past him, leaving me to steer my canoe for about seven kilometres with my bare hands. It was a hot, humid day, and I had narrowly missed stepping on a snake. So my mood was bleak as I crossed the finishing line a good three hours after the field had gone home. However, two fellow canoeists, Tony 'Moggy' Lightfoot and Andrew Gutchi were waiting for me, bless them, and they restored my spirits with several cans of beer. These cheerful, lively men pestered me to party the night through at the Montrose Hotel but reluctantly I declined. I had to drive 350 kilometres back to Johannesburg, collect Vivienne and my gear, and then immediately on to Matetsi near Victoria Falls to hunt buffalo – a further 13 hours behind the wheel. The renowned British sailor, Sir Chay Blyth, an ex-paratrooper who first hit fame by rowing across the Atlantic in 1966 with Captain John Ridgway, also of the Parachute Regiment, had been a trifle bemused when I said farewell to him at Jan Smuts airport, two days prior. He asked me what I was getting up to that weekend and I told him I was racing a river in a canoe and then immediately on to hunt buffalo, one thousand kilometres north. "You're mad", he said, "You are bonkers!" He could well have been right.

From Matetsi camp we motored 50 kilometres south to Piers' Deka concession. Piers had allotted me a buffalo remaining on his license and granted me the compliment of hunting on my own with his trackers, Contella and Flex. Contella was close to being appointed one of the first black professional hunters in Zimbabwe and he was to back me up that day. The morning was memorable in more ways than one. The area lacked the beauty of the Zambezi Valley or Charara, but had its own distinctive appeal with huge basalt boulders, broken by patches of savannah which was interspersed with Mopani woodland. Contella stopped the truck in a pretty glade of palm trees and pools of water. He wanted to check out a bull elephant that regularly fed in the area. As we slowly trekked through the sun-dappled clearing, Flex motioned us to halt. Lying on a prominent rocky outcrop was a proud male lion approximately 100 metres from where we were standing. The impressive looking cat lay there observing us without a care in the world. We left it in peace and shortly after caught up with the elephant with its back to us, totally oblivious to our presence. Unlike buffalo, I cannot claim extensive experience of elephant. Under the care of Contella and Flex, I inched forward to within 10 paces of the giant. "Fifty pound tusks" whispered Contella as we watched it feeding. The elephant suddenly wheeled. The breeze had shifted direction. "Slowly, slowly" whispered Contella as we walked backwards. My heart began to thud when the elephant started to flap its ears, creating a noise like sailcloth in a stiff wind in its readiness for a mock charge.

Within an hour we were on to buffalo tracks and by this time the rising wind added an extra dimension to the hunt. "We're looking good – 200 plus or minus in this herd" murmured Contella. I looked back at the imperturbable Flex. This immensely strong, granite-hewn African nodded. Not a talkative man, Flex, but very useful in a tight corner as I recalled from that buffalo charge in Charara, three seasons past. We spooked the buffalo five times that morning, and the sun had reached its zenith. It was hot, certainly into the upper thirties and my shirt was sodden with sweat. We had run with the herd, and crawled on our bellies, and my hands and arms were scratched by the cruel 'wag 'n bietjie' thorns and I was beginning to feel a serious thirst but Contella kept us moving forward. His bush sense was magnificent as usual and we never lost sight of the quarry. We arrived at a clearing. Contella asked me to give him a leg up a tree. He remained up there for about 20 minutes, then glanced down and gave the victory sign. Contella then missed his footing, fell out of the tree, and sprawled on the ground temporarily winded. Flex thought this a huge joke, whereas I was concerned that Contella had not only broken a bone but had spooked the prey. Mercifully he clambered up, unhurt.

"There's a bull this side of the herd" he whispered. "Not great horns but take him". We were shooting for provisions, not trophies, so the size of horn was not a factor. The bull obliged by stepping out of the thicket at a distance of about 50 metres and presented me with a reasonable shot. It was partially obscured by the tall grass so I had to estimate the line between its shoulder and chest. Once I could see its head clearly, it was easier to decide where to place the shot. I clamped the rifle against the tree to steady my aim and squeezed off. The shot felt good and I looked at Contella who gave me the thumbs up. I glanced at Flex. He was happy. There would be meat at the camp that night. We walked slowly up to where the bull had been standing. We heard the death bellow and there it lay. The 280-grain solid had done its job.

Piers was waiting for us back at camp. "Let's see what you've done!" He grinned. "How many shots, Contella – the usual six or eight, eh?" Contella and Flex, one of the greatest hunting teams that man could be blessed with, roared at this. "One bullet, eh?" responded Piers. "At last you're getting the hang of this. About time. About time".

* * * * *

The Zambezi Valley conjures up a kaleidoscope of images for the dedicated hunting man. Since arriving in South Africa in 1969, I had listened to the stories about the valley – the beauty, the ruggedness, the abundance of game, the heat and the river. The valley is nothing short of a Mecca for big game enthusiasts and in this stretch of pristine wilderness where the mighty Zambezi flows, I have experienced a host of thrilling adventures. The opportunity for hunting out of 'E' camp came in June 1988 at short notice. Louis Serrurier's fellow hunter was forced to cancel one week prior to the safari and there was one man Louis knew who could be relied on to drop everything at a moment's notice when the opportunity to chase buffalo was involved. I took the call on a Sunday morning and without hesitation agreed to join Louis and his wife Diana with Vivienne in tow. It was through this particular adventure that I came to meet Bill Bedford, then a keen and experienced hunting enthusiast who today rates as one of the most successful hunting operators in Zimbabwe.

I well remember that hunt. I was carrying a .500 Webley Express 'Army and Navy' double-barrelled rifle – a mongrel of a gun. The stock didn't fit, the 30-inch barrels were top heavy and it was inevitable that the weapon was to prove a bane. We were on to a herd filing through a clearing in the thickets and a buffalo hesitated for a second, presenting a side shot. I reacted promptly and let loose with the right barrel. I could hear the distinctive thump of the bullet striking home as the buffalo cantered off. Bill Bedford and his tracker, Bandit, and I waited for twenty minutes, allowing the animal to stiffen up and for the adrenaline to wear off. We picked up the chase and I spotted it standing 80 metres away in an open patch, looking fairly sick, and I raised the .500 Express to my shoulder and squeezed off. *A misfire!* Just a click as the firing pin struck the primer on the Kynoch bullet. With an oath, I re-chambered a fresh round and signalled to Bill and Bandit that the buffalo had run off in a straight line ahead of us but that it had been effectively hit from my initial shot.

Minutes later Bill climbed a large anthill to inspect the ground ahead. The cover was reasonably open in this section of the valley and I saw him raise his rifle and fire at the buffalo which was lying prone in a weakened state. There are certain hunters who resent their quarry being shot by a back-up and I certainly have never asked a colleague to fire simultaneously in dangerous situations or otherwise, and I admit that at the time I was annoyed at Bill's action. However, in a situation such as a wounded buffalo, it can make sense for the man closest to it to dispatch it. It saves the animal from suffering and one must remember that a wounded buffalo is a very dangerous and unpredictable beast.

I sat alone that night after the others retired. As I stared into the embers of the fire with a whisky in hand, I pondered on the misfire experienced earlier that morning and what might have happened had the buffalo decided to charge. That evening I promised myself two things: firstly, I would dispose of the .500 Webley Express. If a hunter has not got total confidence in his weapon, he must discard it. And secondly, I would never use old ammunition again. Furthermore I vowed to reload my own cartridges, a practice that I adopted from then on. Immersed in thought, I heard lions roaring in the distance and as I gazed at the slow swirling waters of the Zambezi River, I reflected how savage and yet how beautiful the bush could be. The misfire that morning also caused me to reflect on another experience with a cow buffalo twelve months earlier. Piers Taylor had arranged for me to shoot a buffalo needed for lion bait for an American client. This had been booked for early in November, 1987 in Pier's Charara camp. My father had died the week before this hunt and I had requested my sister in London to defer the funeral until the following Saturday. "Why?" she had asked. "What's wrong with Wednesday as originally planned?" "A matter of business", I replied. "Business my foot", she had snorted. "You're hunting, aren't you, dear brother." Yes, she was correct, I had replied, but our father would grant his blessings from the heavens and he would condone delaying the funeral for a few days was my stated belief. He remained to his death a deeply interested party to his son's hunting exploits and enjoyed hearing stories of the African bush when I used to visit him in Dorset.

Piers' camp was close to the Wafa-Wafa military base used in the Rhodesian war by the Special Forces. I slept little that night, it was so unbearably hot. At 5 a.m. we set off to hunt a buffalo. Even at that early hour, the temperature was scorching. This was early November, well past the end of the normal hunting season. At 10 a.m. we came across the spoor of a sizeable herd. I had the Webley .500 Express and was determined to show Piers how I could use a double. I had reasonable success with the weapon on the range, although the barrels were too top-heavy for my liking, but the Webley 'Army and Navy' was my first double and I was eager to use it.

This was my third buffalo hunt. I was beginning to feel an old hand at the game. Following the charge in Charara, I was confident that nothing could go wrong. After an hour on the tracks we reached a herd standing in Mopani bush. We took our time on the approach. The wind was behaving sensibly, not that there was much of it, but the heat was oppressive and the rocks were hot to the touch. It was very unpleasant and the temperature must have been well over 40 centigrade. Mercifully, I was well conditioned to heat. At the time I was training for the 'Iron Man' race. I broke the rifle and slipped in two cigar-sized Kynoch solids. Using a rock as a rest I aimed at the buffalo which was standing away from us at an angle, dictating a raking shot from a distance of approximately 50 metres. As I squeezed off, the animal decided to shift position at this crucial moment.

I groaned as the buffalo cantered off with the herd. I had hoped I had missed it completely and I dreaded the wrath of Piers. "Let's trust we've a miss on our hands, otherwise we've got one hell of a job if you've scratched that buffalo and it's got back into the herd!" muttered Piers darkly. And for all to see there was a droplet of blood. Piers was grim looking. "You've creased it on the flank. It's probably not feeling any pain but we've got to find it. Hell, I need that bait by the end of today or we are in trouble!" One thing about Piers Taylor is that he leaves you in no doubt what he thinks if you've messed up. He tells you to your face that you have screwed up in the choicest of language. Piers Taylor is a hard taskmaster. That's why he is one of the best in the business. Zimbabwe produces great hunters, particularly where dangerous game is concerned, and he ranks right up there. Berated and shamed, I felt as big as a field mouse that desperate morning. The American client was arriving that evening and it looked as if there would be no bait for his lion hunt.

Two hours later we had to call a halt in the searing heat. All of us, including Flex, the strong man, were suffering symptoms of dehydration. We had marched, jogged and raced with the herd in that inferno in Charara. Piers had instructed Flex and Contella on one occasion to beat the buffalo herd towards us as we crouched behind an anthill, searching desperately for a bloodied buffalo in the pack. This was my first experience of buffalo being driven directly at us and it was very, very unnerving. "Stay still," Piers instructed. "They'll part around the anthill. They won't trample you, although you deserve it!" he added without pity. Piers ill mood hadn't abated; in fact it had grown worse as the heat of the day soared into the mid 40s centigrade. We were to learn later in Kariba when collecting Gene Bishop, the American client, that we had been hunting in a temperature of 45 centigrade! As we clung to that anthill with the buffalo galloping past, Piers let out a low whistle. "There it is – just a scratch on the left flank." As we walked back to the truck - stumbled would be a more apt description - Piers summarised the position. "Your bullet creased the flank. If that buffalo hadn't moved, you would probably have hit it well and brought it down. However, unfortunately, we have to report a wound and I haven't another animal on license, not even an impala, so we are a bit stuffed for bait. I'll have a quiet word with the game department. Perhaps they will relent. Otherwise we're in trouble".

I felt very subdued that night as we dined with Gene Bishop and his lady friend, Sheri. The conversation was desultory and I had no appetite for food or alcohol which was obvious symptoms of dehydration. I couldn't help notice with a certain black humour that Piers had skirted the problem of the lion bait over dinner. He, too, was feeling the effects of the extreme heat and like me, spurned beer and whisky for soda water. Fortunately, Gene and Sheri kept up the conversation that evening. *God knows how they're going to cope with the heat*, I thought in my despondent mood as we drove back to camp.

We left Sheri in camp the following morning. I was feeling stronger after some sleep, fitful as it was. All I could do was to fantasize about shooting the scratched buffalo with one shot by 9 a.m. It was not to be. Piers, the trackers, and I slogged it out on foot for four uncomfortable, hot hours before finally catching up to the herd. The buffalo were lying down. Not even the sentry bulls were standing guard as is their custom, the heat was that oppressive. We lay for an hour watching the herd. Gene Bishop had remained back at the truck with Flex for company, which was probably sensible. Charara was a cauldron. Even the rocks were too hot to touch, the sun was that searing. "Let's go, we are wasting our time," Piers finally spoke.

As the four of us walked back to the truck, Piers told me that he had come clean with the game department who'd mercifully regarded the superficial wound as a miss. "Gene has only three days to get his lion and already we're behind schedule", said Piers. "We'll have to try for a buffalo early tomorrow morning. No animal will budge in this heat. I'll take the shot, Mike. No offence meant but I've got too much at stake". On the way back to camp Contella spotted a group of buffalo climbing out of a small ravine below us. Piers asked Gene whether he could borrow his .375. I then witnessed one of the finest shots in my hunting career. Using the fork of a sapling, an unstable rest, Piers crouched into a firing stance and lined up on a cow that was reaching the crest of the ravine. The range was 200 metres at least. My heart was in my mouth as I knew what this meant to the success of the American's lion hunt. Piers fired and the buffalo buckled and tumbled slowly backwards into the ravine. It was a spectacular shot and an awesome sight as the huge animal cart-wheeled through the air. Later Piers told me that he had aimed 12 inches above the spine. A truly magnificent shot which had saved the day.

Then the fun and games began. Flex, Contella and I were given the task of retrieving the buffalo from the bottom of the ravine. I'm strong for my size, but I suffered that next hour as the three of us manhandled the huge carcass piece by piece out of the gully. First we had to gut the animal, then hack it into quarters, and finally drag the massive slabs of meat out of the ravine. Contella and I heaved the buffalo with a rope over our shoulders with Flex, the big Batonka, shoving from behind to make the job easier. Four times we repeated the exercise of hauling the buffalo pieces out of the steep ravine over a distance of 100 metres. It wasn't fun, particularly watching Piers and Gene devour a bag of oranges. But then Piers had saved the situation and Gene was the client and I deserved my fate for creating a near crisis.

By the time we loaded up, it was past midday and I was due to fly to Harare to catch a connection to London. We had left it late and I was close to missing the plane out of Kariba. In the excitement, all of us had lost track of the time and I was facing a shocking predicament of missing the funeral. Piers drove the truck at breakneck speed. Back at camp, I hastily bundled my belongings together, wished Gene and Sheri luck with the lion, said farewell to Contella, Flex and the camp staff, and hurtled off with Piers to Kariba. We made it in the nick of time. The aircraft was actually taxiing to the end of the runway, preparing for take-off and Piers had to use every ounce of his influence to halt the plane. I and a porter raced across the tarmac and I must have been a weird sight reeking of sweat and buffalo and covered in dirt and blood stains as I entered the cabin. There were some very astonished tourists aboard – a German tour group as it transpired - and a very pretty and sympathetic air hostess. She was used to hunters and soldiers so she told me whilst the group from Germany continued to gape at the dust-streaked character swilling cold beer at a furious rate.

I managed to scrounge a bath in the staff quarters of Harare Airport and despite the ingrained grime of the tub it was the finest that I could recall for many a moon. I made the funeral and delivered the eulogy in the Norman church in Marnhull, Dorset. I stood by the grave, said farewell to my father, looked up at the leaden sky on the wintry November day and thought that only 24 hours ago I was in the heat of the Charara with Piers Taylor, his hunting team and the American who had come to look for lion. I resolved in the graveyard to heed Taylor's words: "Stick to buffalo. Persevere. You've had a tough initiation." And twenty years on I would remember those words.

* * * * *

From then on, buffalo hunting came right. The .375 FN Browning became an extension of my right arm. I pay tribute to this weapon, the very gun that cart-wheeled into the air in Charara. I've taken game ranging from the largest monoliths down to the tiniest animals with this reliable and accurate weapon. The .375 has downed polar bear, lion, buffalo, hippo and leopard as well as the tiny steenbok and duiker. I must have fired over 2,000 rounds in practice on the range in preparation for numerous sorties to the bushveld, mountains and deserts. I've also learned to use a double barrel with good effect. The ignominious .500 Webley was sold and replaced with a magnificent .475 Jeffrey No. 2 double, a well-balanced weapon that fitted me and proving highly accurate.

Each buffalo hunt carried its own indelible set of memories. I have kept five heads out of my forays, including my first that measured 45 ¾ inches and which ranks well in Rowland Ward. Then there were the horns of the cow that was close to taking my life in Charara in 1986 and a fine dagga boy shot with Bob Warren-Codrington in Chirisa in 1997. The horns of this particular buffalo are average in width but the huge scarred bosses are commensurate with an old loner bull. The body of this bull was immense, the largest I've ever taken. I was pleased to shoot this grand master nearing the end of its life.

Also in my collection is a Red Dwarf forest buffalo taken in the Congo, and a North-Western species collected in the Central African Republic. The Red Dwarf variety is the smallest of the buffalo family where four species occur in Africa: the Cape buffalo, the Nile, the North-Western and the Red Dwarf. The latter is an unpredictable creature whose habitat stretches across the central band of the African continent. It is primarily found in the rain forests of Cameroon, Congo and DCR (Democratic Republic of the Congo - formerly Zaire). Although half the size of its Cape counterpart, the Red Dwarf is more aggressive and is known to charge without provocation. As its name suggests, the animal is red in colour, with horns akin to the Asian water buffalo which curl backwards – very different to the other African species – to give this forest animal greater freedom of movement in dense vegetation. It may appear less intimidating than the Cape variety but they account for the deaths of several unwary Africans each year in the jungle. In fact, in remote regions such as the Congo, this is the species that has escaped the ravages of untrammelled poaching. The Africans leave them alone; such is their reputation for ferocity.

Then there was that unforgettable hunting escapade in Charara – again my beloved Charara - when Johan Bellingham and myself, accompanied by our wives, joined up with two Zimbabwean hunters. For reasons of security on account of Zimbabwe's present political chaos, the two hunters will be code named as "A" and "B". The full story of this particular hunt and how Johan and I landed in an African jail is covered in chapter 7. 'A' and I were looking for a bull buffalo along the shores of Kariba Lake in the Charara reserve. Two hours after sunrise we picked up a reasonable herd of about fifty animals. However, the problem was that they were grouped in a large clearing, and the nearest target I could fire at stood approximately 200 metres away. So 'A' came up with the brave idea of laying an ambush and he duly instructed his trackers to beat the herd towards us. We took up position behind an anthill that, mercifully, was wide enough to afford some protection if the herd decided to stampede. The plan worked brilliantly. The buffalo milled around, eventually becoming restless and snorting nervously when they picked up the trackers' scent. Then the herd began to gallop towards us (a reminder of the scratched buffalo adventure in Charara). For those hunters who have yet to experience stampeding buffalo, the sight is awesome. On came this blackish-grey tidal wave. I held my .375 ready. At this stage 'A' and I were conversing openly. Whispers weren't needed as the noise was deafening. The herd parted several metres before the anthill, for no reason, and the buffalo broke into a walk. Perhaps the trackers had used their senses and had backed off, allowing the animals to calm down. In the lead of the right column was a presentable bull. It was young but the bosses were fully formed and the horns would measure in the high 30s. On came the bull as 'A' and I remained crouched behind the anthill. I began to wish that I had brought the .475 Jeffrey double with me as the huge beast was virtually on top of us, a mere 15 metres away. It was still unaware of our presence. I fired at what seemed point blank range at the bull that was now abreast of us. The shot was placed on the point of the shoulder. I was totally oblivious of the herd streaming past us on the other side of the anthill and I watched with sheer amazement as the bull galloped off – a perfect illustration of how incredibly tough these animals are. It had taken a 286 grain solid bullet in the centre of the heart and yet had sufficient adrenaline to run a further 50 metres! On this occasion we didn't need to wait around to allow for the animal to stiffen. We ran in the direction of the bull and found it standing, head turned looking at us. We knew it was mortally hit, yet the strength and resolve of this animal was phenomenal. I shot it again from 30 metres and it sank to the ground letting out the characteristic death bellow. Yet another example of the buffalo's legendary courage and awesome strength.

* * * * *

The North Western buffalo deserves mentioning. This is a valued addition to my trophy collection. Being a buffalo enthusiast I had collected the grand slam of this species in Africa. The North Western buffalo, three-quarters of the size of its Cape counterpart, has a similar configuration of horns and the same coloration and physique. It was the fourteenth day into the hunt in the Central African Republic with Andre Roux, and I had already collected some excellent specimens including the Lord Derby Giant Eland and Giant Forest Hog, both highly prized trophies which are indigenous to the Central African region. We left camp at 6 a.m. and two hours later we were on to the spoor of a sizeable herd that promised some bulls. I was confident that clear, sunny morning in the C.A.R. I had taken all my trophies with off-shoulder shots with the .375 FN Browning and my eye was well in. Men who had hunted in CAR drummed into me the importance of mastering the off-shoulder shot for such animals as the Giant Eland. This species, they insisted, often dictated snap shots. To digress for a second: many hunters make the cardinal mistake of practicing with shots taken from a bench rest. Seldom does it occur to them that the big game hunter should become accustomed to firing off shoulder. A charging buffalo or elephant will not allow the hunter the luxury of a rock or a branch as a rest. The same rule applies when hunting such animals as Giant Eland or Bongo. They are there one moment and gone the next. Before leaving for the C.A.R, I had practised constantly with the

.375 and .475 double-barrelled Jeffrey. I accustomed myself to standing shots, and sitting shots ranging from close range up to 100 metres. I designed a practical target device and called it *'Callender's Clanger'* - a six-inch steel plate suspended between metal stakes. I used it to compare the effects of my reloads, and noted with interest that a solid .375 bullet penetrated the steel neatly whereas the 500-grain cartridge for the .475 rifle created a sizeable bulge but little penetration. The beauty of this self-invented target was the resounding 'clang' that would follow the strike of the bullet, thereby eliminating time spent on inspecting the target. I thoroughly recommend this technique to hunters of big game.

Back to the buffalo. An hour later we caught up to the herd. The gentle breeze remained in our favour and we were able to follow the slow moving pack quite comfortably for another hour or so. Martin, the senior tracker, signalled a halt and we crouched behind a tree to view a bull that had meandered off to the side of the herd. I wasted little time in raising the rifle to my shoulder to fire. The bull was angled with its head facing away, and I took a bead on its left flank, intending the bullet to rake through the engine room and settle under its right shoulder. That is precisely what happened. It was a fine shot, worthy of a dependable rifle and a remarkable bullet. The buffalo ran for 10 metres and then sank to its haunches and died.

* * * * *

It all started at a pheasant shoot in England, and in the pub after the day's sport, my host, Simon Albertini, asked about big game hunting. I gave him a brief expose on the sport and expanded upon the thrills of buffalo hunting. Albertini, much to the consternation of the villagers in the pub, bellowed: "That's it, Cobby- (my first cousin, Peter Geikie-Cobb, was in the party) - we must hunt buffalo!" A year later, the two Brits came to Zimbabwe to hunt with Bob Warren – Codrington as the guide in Bill Bedford's Dande concession. Simon Albertini wrote shortly after his return to London: "What a memorable week, with so much excitement and laughter in the company of first class people. I'm not sure life gets any better!" Apart from the constant humour, the buffalo hunt was crammed with thrills. The Dande area where we were hunting had taken 900mm of rainfall and the bush was exceptionally thick. Riverbeds that were normally dried up at this time of year were running full and the Angwa River was flowing beyond belief. I'd never seen such vegetation in Southern Africa and the grasses were almost ten feet tall in places. Bob Warren-Codrington took me aside at the start of the first day. "This is going to be hairy and we'll be lucky to even catch sight of buffalo. Explain to your pals that we've never seen the bush as thick as this". The Dande concession is a vast tract of ground and the water was that abundant that we would battle to find the game. We had three buffalo to shoot in seven days.

But fortune was with us the following morning and one hour after leaving camp we came across the spoor of a herd of fifty buffalo or so. Half an hour later we sighted them from a small ridge from where Bob was able to take Peter through the drills. The plan was to ambush the herd and we cut a direct line through the foothills and within thirty minutes were on to them. Unfortunately the vegetation was so thick that a shot was out of the question. There were reasonable bulls in the herd, but the buffalo were milling around in impossibly thick grass. I could sense Bob's concern that we might have to ditch the herd due to the dense vegetation and at that very moment they caught our scent and crashed off. We gave chase and then the fun and games ensued. Never before in my buffalo hunting career had I found myself in a situation where we were literally plumb in the middle of the herd, in a similar vein to a bird shooter amongst a flock of guinea fowl in a mielie field. *CRASH!!* A group of buffalo charged off to our left. Bob and I instinctively raised our rifles to the shoulder. The two men fresh from Britain were looking at each other in alarm. *CRASH!!* Another bunch burst out to our right. We could not see the galloping buffalo as the grass was over our head. *CRASH!!* A further group careered away to our front. And, finally, there was yet another eruption when the balance of the herd stampeded behind us.

All this pandemonium had taken place a few metres from us. The Britishers' eyes were a sight to behold – olives on cocktail sticks! Vivienne was also with us. She is experienced with buffalo at close quarters so she had some idea of what to expect. Bob looked at me, shaking his head. He'd never experienced anything like this, nor had I – further testimony to the unpredictability of buffalo hunting. The Britishers asked, after the excitement had died down, whether we'd been in danger. Bob Warren-Codrington answered: "generally, buffalo will want to escape. However, if they can't see you they could charge. Anything is possible in this thick bush. I've never seen it like this, so all of us better have our wits about us!" The herd had dispersed in all directions and we decided to follow the tracks of one of the splinter groups that had run off ahead. An hour later, we caught up to twelve buffalo, two of which were bulls. One sported a reasonable spread of horns but the bosses hadn't knitted together and therefore it was too young to shoot. The other was more mature and a representative bull with a horn measurement of approximately 38 inches. We were above the herd on a small rise and after glassing the buffalo, Bob decided to take Peter Giekie-Cobb and Makusa, the tracker, to prepare for a shot. Fifteen minutes later a rifle shot rang out. I looked at my watch, an old hunting habit, and it showed 10.30a.m. - three hours after disembarking from the truck - and the temperature by now was well above 30 centigrade. Peter had taken a frontal shot on the bull that had been standing straight on, and by all account the bullet had been well placed. We then waited for the death bellow, but in vain. I glanced at Bob. He looked at me and I knew what he was thinking - we were in for a tense follow up in this very thick cover. After half an hour to allow the buffalo to stiffen up, we walked up to where it had been standing. Just a thin trace of blood was evident. I was prepared with my .475 double; Peter had my .375 and Bob Warren-Codrington was armed with his .450 double. The game was on. We left Simon and Vivienne with one of the trackers and moved forward. Bob asked me to cover the right flank, he would look after the left and Peter would take care of the rear. Makusa suddenly pointed to a bush 20 metres ahead and there laid the bull, facing us, seemingly dead. Bob fired a shot for insurance, unnecessary as it transpired, and there was Peter's trophy, brilliantly taken through the top centre of the chest. A fine shot with no fuss, no hesitation, and no panic. In photographing

Peter with his trophy, I couldn't help but think that here was a softly spoken, gentle mannered fellow, without any pretence or bravado, who'd completed the job with the minimum of fuss. The British at war! I was proud of my cousin. Bob had done a first rate job in guiding Peter and full marks to him. Makusa, the tracker, excelled in tracking the buffalo. Simon had kept his nerve. He had never ventured into Africa before, had never experienced the bush, let alone a herd of buffalo stampeding in elephant grass at very close quarters. And Vivienne, she's a natural in a tight corner – never flinching, always stoical and calm.

Simon Albertini's buffalo hunt two days later also proved to be a heart-stopping adventure. I was in camp that morning, writing notes while waiting for Bill Bedford who was on his way to join us from Harare, when I heard a shot in the distance. Then an hour went by. Then two further shots. I thought, "Uh! Uh! What's going on out there? Anything can happen in this thick stuff". Shortly afterwards, Bill roared into camp in his Land Cruiser. "Just seen Bob and the two Brits. They're cock-a-hoop. Albert's shot a good bull." I was thrilled. After Peter's effort he had quite an act to follow and he had succeeded.

Bill Bedford, Vivienne and I went straight out into the bush after a light lunch. Bill took us to the very spot where Johan Bellingan and Alistair Travers had met their tragic deaths (covered in chapter 7). It was a poignant moment standing there in the riverbed. We held a minute's silence in respect for the fallen hunters. Bill then explained precisely how the accident occurred and I appreciated hearing at firsthand how the ghastly incident actually happened.

That night over dinner we heard the full story of Simon Albertini's buffalo. It has been an amazing hunt, possibly even more eventful than Peter Geikie-Cobb's. He had taken a shoulder shot and the buffalo had fallen, giving the impression that it would die in minutes, but it had risen to its feet and cantered off with the herd. Simon had justifiably believed that he had scored a bull's eye. After three years in the British army, Simon was experienced with rifles and he'd frequently stalked red deer in Scotland. Fortunately, there was ample blood spoor for Makusa, Bob and Simon to follow. Visibility was down to a minimum, so tall was the elephant grass, and after 800 metres involving an hour of tense, mind-blowing tracking through dense cover, Makusa pointed to the bull which had turned to wait for the hunters. Mercifully, the buffalo wheeled, then ran up an incline whereupon Simon raised the .375 and fired off a snap shot. The bullet took the buffalo in the spine and it collapsed on the spot.

I went out with Bill Bedford the following morning to hunt buffalo. I was shooting a non-trophy buffalo for the tribal community's annual feast day celebrations and Bill had granted me this privilege. Luck was with us as we encountered fresh spoor immediately outside the camp and we were on to a herd within half an hour. Cephas the tracker took us in an adjacent line to the buffalo that was slowly meandering though the thick vegetation. After two kilometres we closed in to intercept the herd. We climbed up a small hillock to lay an ambush. Then, taking us by surprise, out strolled three bulls that were totally oblivious to our presence. I couldn't believe my luck – a clear shot in this thick terrain. I lined up the .375 on the shoulder of the bull in the middle of the trio, and without hesitation squeezed the trigger. The buffalo lurched on the impact of the .286 grain solid and toppled to the ground only twenty paces from where it had stood. This was one of those rare buffalo hunts where everything had slid into place without complication: an early sighting in the cool of the morning, an easy track, the herd oblivious to our presence, a clear target and an accurately placed shot. Bill ribbed me as we walked back to the truck. "I can't understand it – no incidents, a hunt without drama!"

That afternoon, another buffalo adventure took place. This was one of the scariest buffalo hunts that I have ever countenanced in the wilds of Africa. The Tribal Trust in the Dande region had called up Bill about a herd wrecking their cotton fields and had requested help from his hunting operation, Ingwe Safaris. As we drove to the village, Bill warned me that this could be a goose chase. He told me, however, some years before, he and Bob Warren-Codrington had been hauled out of bed early on a New Year's morning by the same Tribal Trust to deal with two dagga bulls found standing in the middle of the village. After recovering from serious hangovers, Bill and Bob went to investigate later in the day and found the bulls still grazing in the centre of the village and dispatched them without ceremony. When we reached the village, we met the two 'guides'. One reeked of beer and the other was a somewhat surly fellow with an arrogant manner. These two led us into a patch of riverine where the buffalo had been sighted. It was a bizarre situation: a beer-reeking guide and his disagreeable mate leading a column, including Bill, myself, Bill's three trackers and Vivienne through deep riverine looking for buffalo.

The early stages of the foray proved uneventful. We marched along a riverbed without any sign of buffalo. Bill turned to me rolling his eyes as if to say that this was a pure waste of time. We then entered some of the thickest vegetation I have ever experienced, including the infamous jess of the Zambezi Valley. We came across fresh signs of buffalo spoor at which stage Bill moved Cephas ahead of the column and relegated the inebriated guide and his surly companion to the rear of the line. I had my .475 at hand and could foresee some hairy moments ahead. Cephas suddenly halted and pointed and there was a buffalo standing five metres away. We couldn't make out the head or tail, the vegetation was so dense. It crashed off creating a fearsome din in the riverine thicket. The humidity was oppressive and my shirt clung to my back. On we crept, our senses fully tuned for the slightest signal of buffalo. Then followed a stampede and it struck us that we were surrounded by a herd in this stretch of dense vegetation. The buffalo continued to mill around us for a full hour. At one stage we passed a narrow gap in the vegetation and saw what looked like a lone buffalo bull waiting in ambush. Bill and I were on our hands and knees peering into the darkness of the riverine and to contemplate taking a shot would have been perilous. The dense bush could easily deflect a bullet and we had no clear sighting of the animal. We thought that we were imagining things and crept on leaving the gap behind us. We were then blocked by an impenetrable wall of riverine and we crawled backwards, only to discover that the buffalo we'd seen was virtually on top of us. It had walked through the gap to watch us. It couldn't see us but could certainly smell us. It was probably only three metres away when it wheeled and stampeded in the opposite direction. I looked at Bill; he looked at me. We rolled our eyeballs. We were taking a grave risk of buffalo charging a line of eight people and a hideous accident could occur at any moment. Dusk was falling when we finally emerged out of that patch of riverine, and all of us breathed with relief. We were very shaken, except the beer-drinking African who had probably remained totally oblivious to any danger. On the return to camp, Bill and I debated why a herd of buffalo would confine themselves to that patch of dark and dank vegetation when they had the vast Dande concession to roam at will. We could only put it down to the fact that lions visited the village from time to time, looking for livestock, and that this small herd felt secure in the thick riverine.

* * * * *

Buffalo have proved to be more fascinating than any other species I have had the privilege of hunting. I've tracked them until my throat is burning with thirst and I have crawled unseen to within 10 metres from them. I've watched them wallowing at watering holes, milling in tall grass, browsing in Mopani woodland, lurking in thick jess. I've encountered them in rain forests and in savannah glades. No wild animal has captured my imagination quite as forcefully as the buffalo. Maybe it is because I have experienced some very tense moments – and I have countenanced extreme danger several times in my life– with these wild bovines. Maybe it has something to do with the terrain that these massive creatures inhabit. Buffalo are true survivors and they will select the densest, thickest, most hostile country in which to lie up. They are powerful, brave and proud. If the buffalo wants you, he'll come for you with one intention which is to kill you. This explains my deepest respect for this awesome monolith of the wild which, even in death, evokes an overwhelming aura.

CHAPTER FIVE

Chartwell - A rural retreat

With some trepidation we glanced around the
stretch of veldt and thought that this piece of ground,
bare save for one tree and a loose wire fence around
the perimeter, would require many years of taming.

The Author

IN 1969, I stood with my wife, Vivienne, in a field looking over a valley, free of power lines and buildings, and in the distance we could see a line of blue hills and we decided that this was to be our home. The ground was bought for a bargain as it was unfashionable in those distant days to live so far out of Johannesburg. But we had a hunch about this charming, rustic area – its remoteness and its glorious sense of space appealed to us. We could not foresee that three decades later we'd be within walking distance from a sophisticated shopping centre replete with restaurants, a theatre, and a supermarket that can match the finest in Europe. We could not envisage that on our doorstep would be created the Dainfern Golf Estate which was rated recently in the top ten of most valuable property developments in South Africa. After years of bumbling along as a rural backwater, we were the focus of property developers and speculators where our properties were beginning to soar in value. We were one of the few areas left that make up a greenbelt, and this rarity dictates value.

The origins of Chartwell are interesting. George Albu, a mining magnate at the turn of the century, purchased the farm Chartwell for its mineral rights. This piece of real estate measuring approximately 2500 acres lies 30 kilometres north west of Johannesburg. After Albu's death, the Chartwell farm was split up into agricultural holdings where tax benefits could be gained from farming livestock. When we first came to live in the area, developed properties were few and far between and the ground remained relatively unchartered. Buck roamed the vales and the Jukskei River remained unpolluted, leaving the water open to canoeists. This was horse-riding country, free of fences, and children could bicycle without danger down the dirt roads. Doors were left open at night and armed break-ins were unheard of. Law and order prevailed in those halcyon days. We employed a gardener that was a bad lot and he ran off with certain of our valuables and cash whereupon I called the local police station and they sent an imposing looking black sergeant. He and I tracked down the culprit who was hiding under an iron bed in a disused shack close by. He put up a fight but we managed to handcuff him and justice was met. If one attempted this deed today, one would find oneself in the dock.

Chartwell was a charming country retreat lying well beyond the tentacles of urban sprawl. I would ask the owners of the dispersed properties in the vicinity if they minded if I shot the pigeons that swarmed across the veldt. Most obliged happily, including a friendly soul who would bring me cans of cold lager as I stood beneath the pines to hide from the pigeons. There was one dissident, a belligerent fellow called Voget who lived opposite the entrance to our drive. His delight was to call the police to have me arrested for disturbance of the peace. The idiot would fabricate stories about shotgun pellets landing on his head and then he'd watch through binoculars from his stoep as the police would duly arrive at my home. Eventually he gave up trying to deprive me of my sport when he could see the constabulary enjoying a glass of brandewyn and trying their luck on shooting clays.

One of the charms of the area was the thrilling sounds of the lions that roared at night from the game park across the valley. On one occasion when we were down at the coast with the children, a few of the cats escaped. We heard the news on the radio and this gave cause for an impromptu lion chase and the hunters and farmers of Chartwell were out in their droves with their rifles. It was touch and go before there was a casualty and fortunately the Wild Life Department caught up with the lions, one of which had romped through a Greek corner café making off with a dozen lamb chops in his jaws (or so the story goes!).

Chartwell was an idyllic place for the first ten years of our life in South Africa. Rich and poor lived harmoniously together, aside from the unfortunate Voget who sold his property – probably in a fit of pique that the police never arrested me – to a friend of mine I used to work with called Rick McCarthy. There was a friendly fellow called Gerrie Breedt who was so poor that he couldn't afford flooring. I used to take him some Guinness which he enjoyed; there was an old man called Kruger who had a charming courtesy and a cantankerous character called Dick Wilson who was a city engineer and who wasn't afraid of using his knuckles to settle an argument. We had an Irish family called Ian and Vi Findlay as neighbours. Ian had been a policeman in Nairobi and he had remembered only too well the wild antics of my regiment, the Cameronians when they served for a short period in Kenya in the late fifties. Ian was a nature's gentleman and we saw eye to eye on many matters unlike his contrary wife, Vi, who constantly waged war with me until a peace treaty was eventually drawn. She meant well and she was certainly a character, totally unafraid to say what she thought. They had two daughters, Deidre who now lives in Dublin, and Alison whom we watched burgeon from a gangly twelve year old into an attractive lady who married a wildlife doctor, Hamish Currie. They live in Cape Town and we remain good friends.

There were drawbacks living out in the sticks. We'd come back in the early hours of the morning to find a veldt fire raging on a neighbouring property. The fire brigade was too far away to call out and in any case veldt fires were not their domain; the responsibility lay on the shoulders of the property owner. The serious droughts in the early eighties increased the threat of these vicious conflagrations that could place homes and gardens in serious jeopardy. For three years in a row we must have turned out on six occasions each winter in the middle of the freezing night to help neighbours. Amenities in those days were a long distance away. Restaurants, cinemas, and supermarkets took half an hour in the car. The nearest shops were at Fourways – a notable landmark as the description implies – which was a hitching post consisting of a vegetable shop run by 'dirty' George whose favourite trick was to pinch ladies' posteriors - hence his nickname - whilst winking at their male consorts; a hardware store; a pharmacy; a café owned by a Greek known as Eric; and a petrol station. Chartwell was linked to Fourways by a single lane road which had just been tarred six months before our arrival in the area. For three years one virtually had the road to one's self and I remember well gunning my ancient Mercedes as fast as it could go and it would be a feat to reach 100mph without the vehicle blowing up.

On the subject of helping out neighbours, we were having dinner with friends of ours in the area, Harry Hall and his wife, Patricia. Harry, an old Etonian, had fought as a British paratrooper in the war and was a colourful individual as was Patricia - a glamorous, charming lady. Harry took a call from Eric the café owner whilst we were on the desert course and he hurried back into the dining room urging me to get my gun ready to help out Eric who had an armed robbery in his café. We rushed from the dinner table, grabbed our weapons, and hurtled down the road to Fourways. We stopped the car some distance from the café and stealthily made our way through the grass to save Eric when Harry in his slightly inebriated state stumbled into a ditch and cursed aloud as his pistol fell into the mud. We reached Eric to find a drunken African sprawled across his counter, comatose and out to the world. Neighbours helped each other in those early days of Chartwell. I went to the aid of Ian Findlay when he telephoned me to help him out with a snake which had slithered into his borehole pump house. I duly dispatched a large rinkals (spitting cobra) with birdshot. Ian Findlay was highly impressed with my accuracy but I put him right some days later whilst drinking his whisky that the gun I was using was a shotgun and not a rifle!

And then came the dark clouds of crime. The first serious assault in the area left the women of Chartwell in a state of jangled nerves. A cottage was broken into in the dead of night and the young married couple were badly beaten up and threatened with rape whilst the home was ransacked. Hot on the heels of this incident was the ghastly assault on a crippled woman who had her face run over by a scalding iron. Nick Leonsins, then Chairman of our Chartwell Owners and Tenants Association, was shot at in the entrance to his property which lies at the corner of our road. The bullet missed his brain by millimetres. "It's a strange feeling to be so close to death" he later told the press. Police found powder burns on Leonsins' shoulders indicating the shot had been fired from a mere distance of three feet. A paramedic on the scene was overheard to comment: "The angels were with him". Nick Leonsins, then the chief executive of a large publishing group in Johannesburg, gave a press interview in his office. "Criminals do what they want and get away with it. If they want a war, they'll get a war. I am not prepared to lose South Africa. The country is barbaric and anarchic", Leonsins told the throng of newspapermen. I have known Nick for many years and I worked with him closely on the Chartwell Block Watch system. Crime began to escalate in the early nineties and this was the signal to start building walls, erect electrified fencing and to lock our doors at night. Rotweillers and Dobermans replaced smaller house pets. The Block Watch system was initiated and the locals took turns to patrol the neighbourhood complete with a vehicle flashing light system and a loaded firearm on the front seat.

This was the era before the hijackers ran riot and we learnt to carry guns to work. Bandits did not enjoy the easy access to guns as they do today and the police in the 70's and 80's remained a potent force. We had a factory in the bowels of Johannesburg and every so often the alarm would be triggered off and always at the most inconvenient hours. I would set off with the Doberman for company – a big fearless hound named 'Bullet' - and a loaded rifle. On one occasion when I was out of town on a hunting trip, the factory alarm sounded off and Vivienne solicited the help of a neighbour, the aforementioned Rick McCarthy who kindly agreed to escort her to the factory at midnight. He had his handgun ready – a wicked looking weapon with a long barrel - and the two accompanied by 'Bullet' drove the several kilometres to the factory in downtown Johannesburg. Rick McCarthy took his part seriously jumping from pillar to pillar in the factory, holding his cannon with two hands, praying for something to shoot at. We were in his home celebrating New Year's Eve a few years ago when we heard gun shots in the distance. This galvanised McCarthy, much to the despair of his charming wife, Jane, into having me fetch a firearm from my house up the road and I duly returned with a rifle perched on the pillion of our son Sean's motorbike and off we set with Rick McCarthy leading the way in his 4 x 4 twin cab truck looking to blow away a criminal in the neighbourhood. It was Marion, Rick's daughter – a literary agent living in Sydney– who reminded me recently of the story as she'd been at the same party and she'd watched the vigilantes lurching down Spencer Road festooned in dinner jackets with long barrels pointing into the sky.

Chartwell is fortunate to have a lion tamer, a charismatic lady called Vicky Brooker. I had met Vicky shortly after we arrived in South Africa, her parents being friends of the Beith family. She is an amazing character who wrestles with full grown lions, unarmed and without guards at hand, and who can summon a diverse collection of zebras, wildebeest, and other antelope to her side by a mere whistle through her teeth. She has a way with wild animals and film crews regularly solicit her skills. Vicky was recently summoned from a dinner party to attend to her zebra which had kicked a hole in her fence and was clattering around Chartwell causing mayhem with her neighbours' gardens & dogs. However the story does not end there. The hole in the fence attracted the attention of two unsavoury characters that were intent on a robbery. To their horror, they were confronted by two yellow baleful eyes belonging to a large lion tethered to a tree! The driveway was apparently littered by a string of cigarettes left behind by the thieves who had gapped it through the hole in desperate flight. Vicky came to our neighbour's aid, at our suggestion, in relocating a wild warthog which he kept as a pet on his property adjoining ours. He was reluctant to let it go, despite the animal nearly ripping his own Rottweiler to death. But clearly something had to be done as the creature insisted on breaking through our fence to climb into our dog kennel. Initially I found the experience to be novel and he was an endearing creature who liked to stare at my Giant Forest Hog trophy hanging on the stoep. He obviously thought he had met a cousin! However, he became a handful in tearing up the French drain & then decimating the staff's mealie patch. Action was needed and we called in Vicky with the reluctant agreement of the neighbour and the friendly warthog was transported to a more suitable environment.

Then the squatters arrived. With trepidation we watched a cluster of six shacks spread like a forest fire on a farm owned by a fellow called Klaff who lives today in America. Misguidedly he'd given permission to an African family to occupy a corner of his twenty acre property on a temporary basis whilst they looked for a permanent residence. This was the signal for hundreds of illegal squatters to pour onto Klaff's property and the Chartwell Residents Association had to move like lightning to spur the municipality into action. In those days before the 'New South Africa', municipalities worked and reason prevailed. The Chartwell residents assisted the police in manning a check point to control the influx of squatters and for a while the preventative measures succeeded. The ANC then came to power in 1994 and the Sevenfontein squatter camp began to swell where the original cluster of six shacks had swollen to 7000 despite a Supreme Court ruling in favour of the landlord, Klaff – now an absentee in the USA as aforementioned – deeming the squatters illegal.

The spate of crime then developed into a torrent and the owners and residents of Chartwell saw the writing on the wall. Action was needed or the values of their properties would dissipate. Thanks to the tireless efforts of a handful of Chartwellians running the land owners' association, certain cooperative owners contributed a significant sum to protect the area. This resulted in a thirteen kilometre electrified fence circumventing Chartwell North and a single access entry point to the area with a sentry manned boom. At the time of the squatter invasion I was talking to a senior executive of Johnic Properties, the developers of Dainfern, and I asked him what he thought of my investing in a piece of ground behind our property. He was adamant in his reply that I shouldn't waste my money as the future for Chartwell remained bleak. He went on to state that in his belief the local municipality had no sympathy for white landowners and that the Sevenfontein squatter camp was not only here to stay but that it would swell to alarming degrees. I thought that this was an odd response from a property executive whose task was to promote Dainfern, a development well ahead of its time where a third of an acre would sell for a vast amount of money on account of its sophisticated golf course development, and an efficient security system. Ironically, Dainfern was adjacent to the squatter development – a truly Third World situation of rich and poor living cheek by jowl! I decided to ignore his advice and take the opposite direction by purchasing the property with Grahame Wilson, who lives in the same road and whom I make mention of in chapter 8. The Supreme Court ruling has been upheld and the squatters are on their way and Klaff – the absentee landlord – has sold his ground to a large property developer who will create a second Dainfern. The property values of Chartwell have increased tenfold over the last five years.

However, it would have been foolhardy to remain complacent over the ever present threat of crime; it remained a blight over Chartwell, as with most cities & their conurbations in the Republic. A typical example and one that occurred once a month on average was the sounding off of the alarm on our property. Inevitably, the timing was impeccable – between the hours of midnight and dawn when one's spirits are at their lowest ebb. Mumbling obscenities with one's sleep pattern so rudely interrupted, the running shoes would be tugged on, and one would stumble out into the grounds clutching a sawn off shotgun in search of a robber hiding in the undergrowth. At one's peril would one ignore the alarm as this would signal to any hidden house breaker that here was a soft target. On one occasion, I overlooked a broken window in the sitting room – there *had* been an entry into the house on that very night! It was evident that the intruders had been scared off with the sound of the alarm & the imminent arrival of the security team. We discovered human faeces in a garden bed – a sure sign of housebreakers. These were possibly the same criminals who had broken into a neighbour's house that same night where the wife – her husband was away- had sensed an intruder in the house, called the security team, and hid in a locked bathroom. She never recovered from the shock and placed the property on the market shortly after.

The interesting point to note on Chartwell is that despite its turbulent history and its perceived remoteness, most of the owners have stayed put and there's a reason for this. Despite the Jukskei river being polluted with the canoeists moving further afield; and the buck disappearing either from poaching by the squatters or by the encroaching development in the area; and signs of witchcraft making its way into Chartwell (two fields along from our property was the scene of a form of satanic ritual which was reported to our security team and they found candles burning with strange objects placed around them), the open spaces remain intact, the bird life is prolific (120 different species we've counted on our property), the sunsets are pure magic, the stars shine brightly in the less polluted air, and Chartwell's lightning storms are a wonder to behold - Chartwell & adjoining areas feature some of the most vivid lightning storms in the world, attracting international special interest groups. Each morning we would awaken to the sounds of guinea fowl that bred on our stretch of the veldt. White faced whistlers and Egyptian geese began to flock into the neighbouring property where a pond has been specially created for them. We would find francolin nests in our field and behind us a wildlife enthusiast introduced springbok and blesbok, now counting for some thirty heads.

We have experienced vast changes in Chartwell. No longer can the fields be walked over with a shotgun in hand and the snakes are scarcer but the wailing of the police cars are a distant sound as are the ambulances and the sporadic gunfire that have become a way of life in Johannesburg's suburbs. And still today can be heard the roars of the lions at night, perhaps not quite to the same clarity as in the old days when the region was less built up, but the wonderful sound remains.

CHAPTER SIX

The Grand National of marathons

The soul of the Comrades, that special confrontation between an exhausted body and mind, and an ailing but unbeaten will.

Dr Tim Noakes – Sports Trust Medical Consultant

I WAS driving my family back from a holiday on the north coast of Natal when I joined a throng of spectators standing on a bridge watching a thinly spread procession of runners enter Durban and I then remembered that this was the special day when a handful of long-distance athletes brave the Comrades Marathon. This was back in 1972 when only an intrepid few – in contrast to the big fields of today - chanced their luck on the tortuous 90km route linking Pietermaritzburg to Durban. In 1921 thirty four runners decided to pay tribute to the fallen in the Great War and from this humble beginning there grew into what has become one of the great foot races in the world. It was an engine driver on the SA Railways, Vic Clapham, a survivor of the First World War, who sought permission from the League of Comrades of the Great War (later to be changed to the South African Legion) to use their mantle under which a race was to be staged between the two cities. The Ex-soldiers' Association and the Athletic Commission remained cynical of Vic Clapham's dream to remember the fallen – the race would be far too long and strenuous to survive for any period of time. The competitors in the early Comrades Marathons were mainly ex-infantrymen and it was the veterans of the Second World War that resuscitated the waning fortunes of the race. The Collegians Club of Pietermaritzburg are to be acknowledged for nurturing the Comrades, building it into the Grand National of road races where unusual stamina and fortitude are the requirements for this most gruelling of marathons. The entries began to balloon from the 70's under the capable auspices of the Collegian Harriers and where inveterate men like Mick Winn and Bullet Alexander formed the Comrades Marathon Association.

In line with the jogging explosion during the last thirty years, there has been a proliferation of marathons and ultra marathons the world over. In South Africa, the Comrades Marathon has emerged as one of the most coveted of goals for the long distance runner. The average field for the first ten years after World War Two remained at some 50 athletes only. By 1970 the ranks had increased to 400 and in current times the field has swollen to 15 000 runners reaching a peak in 2000 where 20 000 runners celebrated the Millennium.

It was in a gym owned by an odd-ball called Keith Gordon that led me to the start line of the 1978 Comrades Marathon. I had never really taken serious cognisance of this great race, although the valour of the men, and the few women who dared this feat, had impressed me since that occasion when returning from a holiday in Natal. I remarked one evening after a work-out to Keith Gordon that I was becoming increasingly irritated with a fellow member of the gym who couldn't talk on any other subject than his competing in the Comrades Marathon. "Have a go" prompted Keith "and I'll second you". Keith Gordon interested me. He was Jewish but ate copious amount of red meat, had never seen the inside of a synagogue, was colourfully profane, he had a Scots name, and married to an attractive gentile lady called Marlene. He was eccentric, unusual, maverick and a gifted athlete. He represented South Africa in the Maccabi games at wrestling and his knowledge of the human physiology was exceptional. He became a gifted sports physiotherapist resulting in his appointment as the All Blacks' rugby physio on their 1970 tour. In the early 80's it was

Keith Gordon who took me under his wing after a serious parachuting accident where I'd split my fifth vertebrae and he had me running the roads within four weeks of that mishap, despite my doctor warning me off any serious exercise for six months!

Keith Gordon propelled me into training for the race only four months before the event. Normally a novice to the Comrades will allow for a full year of steady initiation, a gradual introduction to one of the severest physical challenges a man can confront. But not Keith. "We'll show him!" he says. "Start running tomorrow". This advice was bordering on the foolhardy but Keith is built like that and the timing was right. Vinuchi (Pty) Limited, a corporate neckwear enterprise which I'd started with the help of Vivienne, was in its infancy and it was not doing very well. It was a bleak period of our lives and I needed a healthy distraction to those grim days and thus I started running with a long-standing friend of mine, Tony Beith. I was relatively fit and reasonably strong at the ripe age of 40 before I found myself training with Tony's ensemble, a fine bunch of men who accepted me into their Comrades school. Their advice was, however, disturbingly conservative. Give this year a miss, they'd say, and aim for the 1979 Comrades. However, this well-intentioned collection of long distance runners with several Comrades beneath their belts, had underestimated my iron resolve to beat the fellow from the gym and to earn some desperately needed income at that.

And so commenced the unenviable spartan routine of the Comrades runner: the awakening at a wintry dawn to don the running shoes and run the mandatory 15 – 20kms in the dark. Over the weekends, we would build up to distances of 30kms to 40kms, acclimatising to the midday heat. The body began to melt and the face assumed a skeletal profile of sunken eyes and drawn cheeks. There were, however, hidden bonanzas such as the need of copious draughts of beer forming a vital part of the carbo-hydrate diet. The Comrades runner can eat anything in sight and those inclined to foods of a sweet nature have a veritable field day. In those months preceding the big day I noticed a variety of intriguing symptoms. My trousers were in danger of falling off my hips and I'm a lean man; I could drink with impunity and never suffer hangovers; deep slumber came my way despite my childhood inheritance from WW2 of being a light sleeper; my woes at business became less of a nightmare as stress began to fade. And then the wonderful revelation that my days as a cross-country champion in my youth were standing me in great stead and that I could earn some useful money at this game. I began to slur my speech at parties appearing to be inebriated with a cigar of a dubious pedigree– as this was all I could afford – hanging out of my mouth, boasting about my racing the Comrades. The Comrades runner remained a rare breed in those days of the late 70's and I was considered a freak in the salons of society that I irregularly frequented and so the wagers were struck. I would carefully jot down the bets in a black note book out of sight. These ranged from small amounts of money to larger sums- depending upon the race times that I had to meet- to boxes of Cuban cigars, to cases of rare wines. I couldn't afford to lose as I hadn't drawn a salary for six months, so stringent was our business in those early days of its existence. I trained hard with Beith, Bigham, Hunter-Blair, Holmes and others with Keith Gordon constantly probing me about my progress. Clive -the Comrades fanatic in the gym – looked on with a complacent smirk on his face. "He'll see his arse!" I overheard him on more than one occasion in the showers. But then there was a splendid chap called Casper Greef, a Comrades silver medallist many times over. He used to observe me quietly as I pounded the boxing bag in Gordon's gym and I would go to him to eke out valuable crumbs of advice.

As the days grew nearer to the great race, my nerves began to stretch. I had no doubt that I could complete the 90kms but the question was how quickly I could cross the line. To break even on the book including the cigars and the wine and the whisky, I had to come in on 8 ½ hours which was daunting enough where my training colleagues were predicting that I'd be lucky to break 9 hours on my first Comrades. But my major target was 8 hours 15 minutes where I had wagered the big money – the equivalent of a month's salary. As the days ticked closer, the more neurotic I became of any slight tingle prefacing a head cold, or the merest twinge in a muscle foreboding a strained tendon. I held nightmares of contracting flu the day before the race or pulling a muscle in a training run. It didn't help to be called *looking ill* by acquaintances that hadn't seen me for a few months and *ill* one did look: sunken eyes, a skinny frame, a shrunken backside. The bets came rolling in, so preposterous were my antics of reeling around in a drunken gait with evil smelling cheroots drooping out of my mouth. But the charade obviously worked as I well remember the sniggers of disbelief at the dinner table.

Came the great day. We withdrew the children from school for the occasion and we drove down the day before to friends, Michael and Anne Benson, prominent pig farmers and polo players in the Karkloof district in the Natal Midlands. I was a constant source of amusement to Michael and his family as my method of hyping myself for the race was to wander around his farm muttering *"Go!"* with right fist punching the air. I didn't get much sleep that night at the Benson home. I was more concerned about waking in time and I dozed in fitful snatches as my mind played ducks and drakes in the early hours of the morning. My thoughts kept reverting to the gruelling hours spent on the hills surrounding Johannesburg and I must have notched up close on to 2000kms, learning how to handle the fierce inclines and the steep descents that the Comrades course is infamous for. My days of cross-country running at school and in the army had stood me in good stead for the hot tarred roads linking Johannesburg to Pretoria. Out there on those long winding paths, the marathon man learns the loneliness and the pain of the long distance runner. Invariably I'd run alone in the races, as was one's choice, where my mind would meander in a strange pattern. I'd ponder on a business problem or I'd fantasise to forget the discomfort of the salty perspiration in eyes and mouth, aching joints, and tired limbs. I would dread the injuries which each long distance runner is prone to: the tendonitis, the pulled hamstring, the strained Achilles heel, the torn cartilage, not to forget the minor irritancies which can turn to a living hell after 30kms into a marathon – the bleeding nipples, the burst blister, the torn toe nail.

The start of the Comrades is an unforgettable experience for the first timer. Up to 1979, runners' seconds were still allowed on the route and the field was confined in those days to a mere 2000 runners, a fragment compared to the 20 000 that lined up for the Millennium just over twenty years on. I stood there in the chilly dawn amidst an apprehensive throng of runners, mostly men then, with Tony Beith and Reginald Hunter-Blair - an ex Sandhurst cross country champion – standing in silence beside me. We were nervous as we didn't know what to expect. Sure, we'd driven over the route and we'd seen the monster hills and the tortuous descents but we'd never set actual foot on this notorious switchback linking Pietermaritzburg to Durban. I took stock of the picture around me and most of the runners were standing muted, alone in their thoughts. They were lean, athletic, determined looking. A few appeared overweight or seemingly ill-prepared for the occasion but in those days of the Comrades, the average athlete was a well trained, seasoned long distance runner.

We stood there patiently waiting for the famous cock crow, the traditional sound emitted by a veteran of the race, Max Trimborn. He was a former deep sea diver repairing war-damaged ships and completing eight comrades, achieving fourth place in one event. I began to stamp my feet waiting impatiently for the pistol to be fired. I'd done my homework and the hours of pounding the roads were behind me. I'd taped the nipples, put Vaseline on the feet and the pits of my arms and groin, and was now set on the serious business of running the 90kms to Durban. The gun went and the field set off under the glare of the arc lights and the television cameras. So great is the charisma of the Comrades that still today television covers the event continuously from the start at 6.00 a.m. to the cut off at 5.00 p.m. The crowds are to be believed. The entire population of Pietermaritzburg had turned out to cheer on the runners and it would be an abnormal man if he didn't experience a lump in his throat as he made his way down the centre of the city.

I ran the race that day in 8 hours, 8 minutes - 580th out of 3094 runners including seventeen women, disposing of the theory that novices, unless highly talented, would be lucky to break the 8 hours, 30 minutes barrier. It was a grand day with Johnny Sach serving me as a splendid second. Keith Gordon had delegated John to second me as there was a needier runner in his gym asking for his help. He was at my side virtually the whole way with bucket and sponge in hand. The drinking tables in those days were few and far between and a vital job of the second was to keep his charge well stocked with fluid. I vividly remember every milestone of that course: the infamous Polly Shorts, the cruel hill that destroys the athlete on the up run from Durban; the Harrison Flats before the monster Inchanga mountain leading into the halfway point at Drummond, where the crowds amass to will the runners on; the soul-breaking Botha's Hill; the landmarks of Hillcrest and Gillits; the leg jarring Fields Hill leading into Pinetown; the cresting of Berea; and the final run down into Durban. The pain, the heat of the midday, the ominous signs of de-hydration were forgotten. It was to do with the fact that I was beyond the reach of the telephone, leaving the bank manager and pressing creditors well behind me that made the Comrades such an unforgettable day in the Natal sun. It was to do with the sweat-streaked, agony filled faces of one's fellow runners in the last twenty kilometres of the never-ending, twisting road; it was to do with the thousands upon thousands who lined the road exhorting you on; it was to do with the sight of my battered old Mercedes carrying Vivienne, MaryAnne and Sean – the children aged nine and five years respectively – and the ever present, indomitable Johnny Sack carrying the bucket and sponges.

In the field of that 1978 race, there was an ex-Springbok rugby player, Wilf Rosenburg that I knew, and he went through the halfway mark exactly in the same time as I: three hours, 55 minutes, and ultimately finishing in nine hours 25 minutes. He wrote an article for the press. His words sum up the agony and the ecstasy of the Comrades: *"the Comrades isn't a race. It's murder. There's nothing harder in the world. But at the halfway mark, I was starting to think it was easy. I had covered the first 45 kilometres in three hours 55 minutes and was even contemplating a silver medal for a finish under seven and half hours. I was feeling strong, and remembering a conversation I had a month ago with Don Walton, another Springbok rugby player to compete in the Comrades. 'You've got to be strong at halfway,' he said, 'because the rest is murder. If you're not strong halfway, you might as well get in the car and go home.' Then out of the blue disaster struck. I broke down. The tendons at the back of my left leg ripped. My muscle went into spasms. The pain was excruciating and*

I started swallowing pain killers. But they didn't work. I felt like I was running on hot coals. I was so concerned about aggravating my injuries that I stopped drinking my water which added to my distress. Every step was torture for me now. Behind every hill was another hill, but bigger. You don't believe those hills. Inchanga just keeps going on up into the sky like a staircase to hell.........There were runners much worse off than I was. Guys limping, guys crawling, ambulances going up and down the line. Many staggering along with sightless eyes...........twenty kilometres from the end of this race, a man comes face to face with himself. Never in my rugby career did I push myself to these boundaries of exhaustion. What I got to show for it is a bronze medal and an inner sense of achievement".

Keith Oxlee, another famous Springbok rugby player, described the sensation of crossing the line comparable with receiving his first green and gold blazer: "It is a truly great moment". Perhaps the other ultra marathon in South Africa that can compare with the charisma of this truly great foot race is the Two Oceans which is staged over 56 km around the Cape Peninsular.

Four years later, the call of the Comrades enticed me back to this famous race. I had a strong incentive. Alan Tucker, a good friend of mine and a noted sportsman in his own right as a yachtsman and oarsman, challenged me to run for a silver medal beating the 7 hours thirty minute cut off. There's a saying amongst Comrades athletes that you are *running, not jogging* if you beat the eight hour fifteen mark; that you are *running seriously* if you make the silver medal cut off. Since the inception of the race, there are only some five hundred runners that can achieve the silver medal, despite the swelling ranks of the field in recent years. To achieve a silver, the pace you have to maintain is five minutes a kilometre which is seriously daunting when the immense distance and the punishing terrain is taken into account. My bets with Alan ranged from seven hours to eight hours. If I managed to beat the seven hour mark, I would be in for significant money and in the exalted ranks of the top two hundred runners. The seven and half hour barrier remained lucrative. But a performance exceeding eight hours would dig a deep hole in my pocket to Alan Tucker's benefit. I started to train in earnest in December and I called in the services of Reginald Hunter-Blair and Tony Beith and an ex New Zealand national sprinter, Tony Watson. Reg had notched up a sub-seven hours in the previous year and he was the man with the experience to teach one to break this testing barrier. I learnt to run hills at a faster rate than before – thanks to the speed training set by Tony Watson - and I began to understand the skills of varying one's pace and the breaking of the seven hour barrier began to assume a possibility.

Three weeks before the race, Alan Tucker took me aside and asked if I could structure a betting scale for him. "I'm not sure I'm with you -are you telling me that you're proposing to race the Comrades?" I spluttered with disbelief. He replied in the affirmative. "But there are only three weeks to go and, besides, you haven't qualified." "I'll be there" replied Alan with a calm confidence that unnerved me and we struck the bets. I gave him the big lure at nine hours believing that he might just attempt this barrier and by doing so blow up and withdraw to my financial benefit. But I knew how determined this individual could be and his winning the Cape to Rio yacht race under his captaincy bore testimony to Alan's grit and competitive spirit. But to take on the Comrades where his longest distance to date had been twelve kilometres was lunacy. Athletic, the man might be, but to countenance the Comrades with three weeks to go was the act of a madman.

Since 1978, my first race, the Comrades field had grown at an unprecedented rate and the field had swollen to double the size. 5500 runners lined up in the cold dawn waiting for the cock to crow. I stood in the drizzling rain with Reg Hunter-Blair and Tony Beith, musing on the spectre of Alan Tucker struggling up that staircase of hell, Inchanga hill. I was in a more hyped up state than that four years previously as I had a serious task on my hands and that was to earn a silver medal, if not the glory of beating the seven hour barrier. At the crack of the gun I shook hands with Tony Beith and Reg Hunter-Blair wishing them great runs, and off I sped past the cheering crowds in the breaking dawn. It was drizzling and I was running in two vests with my forearms covered in black marker ink giving me my time splits. I was feeling strong and I was confident that the silver medal was mine together with a fair slice of

Alan Tucker's disposable cash. I ran alone. I prefer it this way as one is unencumbered and there hasn't been one major road race that I've run with somebody, let alone in a 'bus' as many runners choose to in the ultra distance races. I reached the Chicken Huts some twelve kilometres out of Pietermaritzburg to find a struggling Hunter-Blair. I ran with him for two or three kilometres but he was plagued with stomach cramps. I felt disappointed for him as he is a talented long distance athlete and he'd set his heart on six hours forty-five minutes. Five kilometres further I came across the familiar tall figures of Lewis Gerber, John Feek, and John Sawers running together. They are seasoned veterans of the Comrades with Feek and Sawers holding silver medals. I'm going to enjoy this, I murmured, as I surged past them with a raging ego. "I'll be waiting for you at the finish" I taunted them. "Slow down, you're running far too fast", they urged me. "I'll wait for you at the finish" I shouted as I raced on. I strode the route with a mission and I reached the halfway point on exactly three and half hours, making the possibility of a seven hour finish a distinct reality. And then the wheels came off. I began to develop pains in my legs that I'd never experienced before and the words of a strong Comrades veteran, Chris Griffiths, came back to me. "If you want silver, you must learn to pace yourself. Ninety kilometres is over two marathons back to back and you must reach Drummond, the halfway mark, strong and with plenty to spare. If you don't, then the game is over. You may as well walk the rest". Another seasoned silver medallist, Bob Tucker – Alan Tucker's elder brother - would put it another way: "You jog to the start which is the half-way at Drummond, and then you run to the finish".

Up Botha's hill, just past Drummond, I was reduced to a walk. As I stumbled down the fiercely steep Fields Hill, my mind began to descend into a fog. I couldn't focus on my time splits. I was running on depleted reserves. I 'hit the wall' in Pinetown and I wanted to crawl under a tree and lie down. I was truly spent and I was close to giving up the race until it was Reg Hunter-Blair who caught up with me as I was limping into Gillits. He had gained a second wind and was running to his true form. "Keep going – don't give up. The Cameronians never give up!" and those words from an officer of the Gordon Highlanders did the trick. I willed my legs to function and I managed a painful stagger at which stage John Feek came surging past me. "I warned you, Mike. I told you!" were his words. I reached the crest of Berea and I remember muttering through gritted teeth to a fellow runner on how far to go. He urged me to keep it up and I was still in time for a silver.

But I didn't make the coveted silver medal that day. I was close to it but the magic prize was slipping out of my grasp. It was the longest Comrades run ever staged – 91.4kms owing to a detour around a road works at Pinetown. Under the normal distance, I might have come in on the silver mark. The last three kilometres were hellish. I was dehydrated, cold from the rain that had accompanied us for most of the way, and hurting desperately in my legs. I made the finish to find Reg Hunter-Blair waiting to consol me. Both of us had had disappointing days. He'd made the silver mark but he'd set his sights on the sub seven hours barrier, a prize that is attainable only by the elitist of the Comrades runners. In my case, I crossed the line on seven hours, 38 minutes - eight minutes behind the silver medal cut off and I'd achieved 669th place out of 5500, ranking in the first 12% of the field. Eight minutes is a life time in this race but it's a sobering thought as Bruce Fordyce, the king of the Comrades, reminded me at a recent lunch that those extra two kilometres at Pinetown equated to probably twelve minutes at the pace which I was reduced to over the last ten kilometres. It is always easy, however, to say *if only...* I'd missed the silver medal cut-off, the prerogative of the top 500 long distance runners in South Africa.

But there was more drama to unfold. We were in the stands, spirits restored due to several beers, when I saw a sight which left me rubbing my eyes in disbelief. There was Alan Tucker wobbling in on nine hours, fifteen minutes! I'd given him ten hours at the best, remembering he'd never run distances in his life, not even a 21 kilometre race. Here he was, defying all odds, conquering one of the most gruelling road races in the world in a time which most seasoned Comrades runners give their eye teeth for! I hobbled painfully down the stands to the finish line and embraced him. All Alan could do was to open and shut his mouth like a goldfish – nothing was coming out! His hair was standing on end and he was out for the count. I helped him to the grass and stood over him, shaking my head. It didn't take him long to recover his composure. "Hard luck" he croaked when he heard that I'd missed the silver.

Three weeks later Alan and I stood on ceremony at the Wanderers club with several others who'd been privy to the series of wagers that Alan and I had struck. All present witnessed the solemn occasion of two grown men, legs restored to their original strong self, handing each other identical cheques to the sum of R3500.00. It transpired during that evening of serious carousing that Alan Tucker had camped on the course over the three weeks before the start and had spent the days running up and down the monster hills of Inchanga, Botha's, Fields, Cowies, and Polly Shorts. The furthest distance he'd put in was 20 kilometres. The man best suited to racing oceans or rowing in regattas had conquered a 91.4 kilometre switch- back course from Pietermaritzburg to Durban with the scantest of training! Alan Tucker went on to compete in two more Comrades, finishing one within the silver medal cut-off which says something for this gifted athlete.

The Comrades was to see me once again in 1985 to take part in a field that had grown to 9000 runners. I had put in little training for the event, relying on my fitness built up for the 'Iron Man' and I had invested in one long training run alone of fifty kilometres. I entered the Comrades for nostalgia and curiosity: nostalgia knowing that this would be probably my last Comrades race, and curiosity to see how well I'd fare with such little time spent in specific preparation. Three months earlier I'd scored a reasonable triumph in the 'Iron Man', a gruelling twenty-two kilometre canoe leg, one hundred and ten kilometres of cycling in the hills surrounding Hartebeespoort Dam, and the tortuous marathon of forty-two kilometres over a fiercely undulating course of the old Pretoria – Johannesburg road in the searing midday sun of a Highveld summer. It's worth mentioning here that Bruce Fordyce – he still today is regarded as the 'King of the Comrades' on account of his extraordinary feat of winning the race nine times consecutively (1981 – 1990) - was manning the last water table in the 'Iron Man' before the excruciating hill known as Summit Road leading into the stadium at the Jewish Guild. It was his words to me that galvanised my wracked body and leaden legs into a final desperate surge up that devilish hill leading to the finish. "Mike, get a grip! There's a woman ahead of you. How can you allow yourself to be beaten by a woman!" I looked up that hill that resembled Everest and it was a very hot afternoon edging 35 centigrade and I saw the form of Liz Mulder, the leading woman and an athlete that I knew. Using my last vestiges of energy I caught up with Liz and her husband Pieter and the three of us were captured on television breasting the tape in line. Bruce Fordyce remains a highly respected figure in the world of sport and he's a humble man despite his immense achievements in long distance running. He'd set a record for the USA fifty miler championship, Chicago 1984; three times winner and record holder of the London to Brighton fifty miler; he held for some time the record for the world 100 kilometre championship; and today he's the CEO of the Sports Trust and winner in 1997 of the State President's Gold Award for Sport.

I knew I was in good physical shape for the 1985 Comrades, but as the hours ticked towards the start, I began to hold serious misgivings as to whether my legs would last the distance. The canoeing disciplines required for the 'Iron Man' had strengthened my upper body, and the cycling regimen had developed some serious thigh muscles. But the time invested on the road itself had been pared to the barest minimum – sufficient for a standard marathon that is part of the 'Iron Man' - but any Comrades competitor knows that there are no short cuts for this race, particularly as this year was the 'up run' from Durban to Pietmaritzburg (the race is alternated every year). The first thing I noticed as I made my way to the start at the Durban City Hall was the swelling numbers of the field. I'd left it late in my complacency that morning and I had a job to force my way into the seething press of bodies thirty minutes before the cock-crow. As is my usual style in races I stood alone in the dawn, taking in the thousands of spectators against the sound of ' The Chariots Of fire' over the loud speaker system, the smell of wintergreen and the hum of nervous talk amongst the runners.

I ran reasonably well that day and the fitness stored from the 'Iron Man' worked for me. The highlight of the race was running with Jackie

Mekler (Five times winner of the Comrades in 1958/60/63/64/68 only surpassed in number of wins by Bruce Fordyce, Hardy Ballington, Arthur Newton, and Wally Hayward) up the notorious Polly Shorts hill – a mind-numbing, punishing obstacle that tortures the runner a cruel ten kilometres from the finish. I'd met Jackie many times before this day and he's a great athlete and an excellent man and his presence was of great comfort as I ran with him for at least twenty kilometres. He exhorted me on as I staggered up Polly Shorts and I had to keep running for my own pride as on account of Jackie Mekler's standing in the annals of the great race, the television crews were filming him and this included me and the others in his entourage as he led us up the steep staircase of Polly Shorts before the descent into Pietermaritzburg. Due to the presence of Jackie Mekler, I featured on television according to the many calls I received over the subsequent week after the event. There was the one occasion when we did walk – Jackie Mekler had relented – but only for a minute or two before he cajoled us into a stumbling run up the last two kilometre stretch of that horrible hill and that's when the cameras had a field day, much to the interest of those watching the race on television who knew me. I came in on a respectable eight hours twenty-four minutes which I was well satisfied with. I beat my old rival John Feek whom I passed at the top of Polly Shorts where the welcoming sight of Pietermaritzburg unfolds for the weary runner. I had a quick word with John Sawers two hundred metres on, an Irishman who usually teamed up with John Feek for the canoe marathons and for the Comrades, and I was proud that I had passed these silver medal veterans – sweet revenge for the 1982 race!

I stood in the stands amongst a crowd of 20 000 jammed in the Jan Smuts Stadium in Pietermaritzburg watching the runners come in. On the previous occasions I'd been pleased to leave the race soon after finishing but I decided today to digest the true drama that unfolds in the final hour of the Comrades Marathon. I watched the agony contorted figures limping in, some bent double, others cramping horribly. There were the walking wounded with torn cartilages, sprained tendons and bleeding blisters. These were the men and women who'd made the Comrades their pinnacle of achievement. I saw in that last hour tides of runners surging into the stadium oblivious to the cheering of the crowds, lost in their own torment of pain and exhaustion.

It is easy to become complacent with one's own achievements and to be diffident about the back trackers that struggle to make the eleven hour cut off which in recent times has been extended to twelve hours. It's only when one actually witnesses the heroic endeavours of those that have spent an extra three hours on that punishing route that the real appreciation of the meaning of Vic Clapham's Comrades comes to full light. I witnessed in that darkening afternoon sights that stirred the soul: runners that were collapsing outside the stadium where compatriots stopped and risked their medals to carry the fallen to the finish line. I saw a woman crawling across the line, her anxious mate exhorting her to the finish where she made the cut off by thirty seconds to spare; and then the sadness of watching the stricken faces as they stumbled towards the line, only to hear the gun go off signalling the end of the race, depriving them of their coveted medal. In 1984 I had competed in the New York marathon and I had seen many runners pulling out, complaining vociferously of blisters and other minor ailments and I thought back as I was striding through the boroughs of Queens, the Bronx, and Manhattan, of the men and women that had completed the Comrades with ripped tendons, torn ankles, not to forget the blind runners with their guides. South Africa seems to breed them tough - a legacy of its turbulent history. In the dying minutes of the 1985 Comrades marathon, I watched with a lump in my throat the batches of runners tottering around the stadium, many limping with shoes in hand, their feet a bloody mess. The St John's ambulance men were busy and the medical tent was crammed with men and women struck with exhaustion, dehydration and cramp.

Since the dismantling of Apartheid, the elitist ultra marathoners from all over the world have been drawn to Natal to contest this famous race built on the backs of the soldiers who gave their lives on the battlefield. We have seen a band of top runners from Russia, Poland and Romania come in to compete alongside the best of Britain and the USA. No longer is the rare privilege of breasting the tape as the winner after ninety kilometres of arduous slog the sole prerogative of South Africans. Men of the ilk of Attila Kovacs (Hungry); Alberto Salazar (USA); Jaroslaw Janicki, Dimitri Grishine and Vladimir Kotov, all of the USSR, have won in recent years. Bruce Fordyce remains the holder of the fastest time and South Africa still fields the majority of gold medallists thanks largely to the performance of our black athletes where running is a natural strength.

The words of the great Springbok cricket fast bowler, Peter Pollock (Springbok selector and uncle of Shaun Pollock, the recent captain of the South African cricket side), perhaps sums up the spirit of the Comrades Marathon: *"There just had to be something that makes a man want to challenge his own sinew, muscle-fibre, guts and determination and pit himself against one of nature's most gruelling tests".*

Today there are runners from around the world who are listening to the call of this extraordinary foot race. Bristol Clayton of Connecticut, USA, said in *1984 "It's the toughest; the course is one huge heartbreak .....I heard it was a mountainous race and that was no over exaggeration!"* He'd learnt about the Comrades from the South African athletes in the London to Brighton race and he was impressed with the quality of these runners. There's Dick Goodman of the USA, aged 65, taking three medals. *"It is the most scenic, colourful, and spectacular road race in the world".* In the early stages of its history, those men who attempted the Comrades constituted a handful of pioneers who ran the course in remembrance of the fallen dead whom they'd fought with. From these humble beginnings, the Comrades marathon has developed into arguably South Africa's single greatest sporting event – from 34 runners in 1921 to close on 20 0000 in 2000. There are numerous ultra distance marathons in SA and overseas but the Comrades stands alone because of its unique origins and its high standing in the annals of the great foot races in the world.

℘ ✦ ℭ℞

CHAPTER SEVEN

Death and close encounters in the wild

A life without adventure is likely to be unsatisfying, but a life in which adventure is allowed to take whatever form it will is sure to be short.

Bertrand Russell

I WOULD like to pay tribute to a great friend and hunting companion, Johan Bellingan. I had known him since 1980 when he was a partner in Rand Merchant Bank started by Johan Rupert, son of Anton Rupert of Rembrandt tobacco fame. Johan then started on his own and formed Prima Bank. He was born in the Orange Free State and at the height of his career served as Chairman of the Board of Trustees of the University of the Orange Free State.

Bellingan had an aggressiveness to his nature and a toughness that belied a big heart and over the years we became staunch friends. Our approach to life and the principle of work hard, play hard was a philosophy we held in common. We would meet regularly at the Johannesburg Country Club where in the change rooms he and I would confront the 'bunny-huggers' who'd insist on expressing their displeasure at our hunting antics. The two of us, well out numbered, would handle their antipathy without compromise and Johan, well within earshot of the greenies, would bellow across the showers as to where I was hunting over the forthcoming weekend. The tall, solidly built Afrikaner was a foil to this Brit/South African and he had a healthy respect for the British, despite his traditional Boer upbringing. Inevitably, there would be a clash of personalities and I cite the occasion when we were dining at his home in Sandton, Johannesburg at the time of the Falkland War. Some fourteen guests were present when he coolly stated as we were about to commence dinner that the British soldiers were a poor match for the Argentineans. I exploded. The cream of the British army had been dispatched to the Falklands: The SAS, the Paras, the Scots Guards, and the Marines. No finer troops in the world. Bellingan had meant this as a joke but I'd swallowed the bait and I was livid. The dinner party was reduced to a shambles, or certainly the first two courses were ruined, as I unleashed both barrels at the big Afrikaner who sat glowering at the top end of the table and there were some extremely nervous ladies present. Fortunately, the dark clouds evaporated by the desert course and good humour restored, largely through the influence of some fine brandy, but not without a harsh scolding from our respective wives.

There was the occasion in the Kalahari when Bellingan and I were hunting on Gert Koekemor's property, a vast game ranch measuring thousands of hectares near Gobabis, midway between Windhoek and the Botswana border. We were hunting kudu and eland with the help of Koekemor's Bushmen trackers. Gert Koekemor possessed one of the happiest, contented dispositions known to man. Only once did I see Gert phased and that was when Bellingan and Callender were arguing heatedly one early morning over a trite issue – the age and weight of a kudu that I'd shot the previous evening. Bellingan's bellicose nature was at the fore that morning and my own fuse was burning brightly. Gert's face had lost its usual amenable expression with the sight of the two men squaring up besides the weighing scale and he had to intervene to restore order. After that potentially explosive fracas, the hunt settled down peacefully and I shot a kudu bull with an off – shoulder shot from 150 metres; my eye was in from ten days of buffalo hunting in the Zambezi valley from where I'd just come. Bellingan had driven up on the sound of the shot with several

Bushmen clucking excitedly in their dialect. The big Dutchman looked down at me from the hunting truck: "You know what they're saying, Meneer? They're saying that you are one of us the way you shot that kudu. They were making you out as something from outer space with that naked head of yours, until this shot!"

A year after that unpleasant experience in the Kariba Police gaol (as described in chapter 10), Johan Bellingan was gored to death by a buffalo. It was a tragic, sad ending of a great friendship. Johan Bellingan had spoken to me the day before he flew up to Harare with Denise, his wife, and Ernst his son. He'd arranged a buffalo hunt with Alastair Travers, co-partner with Bill Bedford in their recently formed hunting operation, Ingwe Safaris. I wished him well and we agreed to speak to each other as I was hunting at the same time in the Eastern Cape. Then the appalling tragedy. I was fast asleep when the constant ringing of a telephone called me out of bed at midnight. I had hunted that day near Middelburg and had taken a record Vaal Reebok. With me was a young local farmer, Kurt Donian, and we were staying in a farmhouse between Middelburg and Steynsburg. I took the call and it was a distraught Vivienne telling me that Johan and Alastair had both died earlier that day from a buffalo goring. Bob Warren-Codrington had phoned from Harare having heard the news from Bill Bedford. I had difficulty in getting back to sleep, haunted by the nightmare of a buffalo taking out two experienced hunters – one, perhaps, but two fine men losing their life on the horns and hooves of a buffalo bull was hard to bear.

Seven years later Bill Bedford led me and Vivienne to the exact spot where the ghastly accident had occurred on Bill's Dande hunting concession on the escarpment of the Zambezi. I'd been briefed in detail by Bill Bedford and Bob Warren-Codrington just after the killings but Bill replayed the sad saga that hot afternoon as we walked over the ground where the two hunters had lost their lives. The buffalo had been shot high on the shoulder with a .375 solid by Johan Bellingan early in the morning. Throughout the day he and Alastair Travers and the trackers had followed up without success. That night they'd heard hyenas and they'd believed this to be an omen that the buffalo had died. At sunrise, the search continued and shortly after this, the buffalo broke from thick cover in a riverbed and stopped momentarily on the opposite embankment approximately 80 metres from the hunters. Alastair Travers fired using a solid from his .458 and hitting it but the buffalo ran on. The two hunters sprinted across the riverbed and scrambled up the bank catching a brief glimpse of the bull. It had taken off into open country looking for cover and in doing so it retraced its steps to find shelter in the thick vegetation near the riverbed. Bill Bedford was able to explain all this in fine detail as he and the Ingwe Safari trackers had scrutinised the tracks of the two hunters and the buffalo in order to recreate the detail on the accident.

This ghastly tragedy was a freak accident. The direct turnabout of the buffalo on its footsteps had led the animal into an unpremeditated head-on collision with the two hunters. Alastair was half way up the opposite riverbank in front of Johan, when he took the charge head-on. Alastair was hurled backwards into the donga and the buffalo then turned on Johan, ripping him open with its horns and then proceeding to trample him into a bloody mess. The major horror of this accident was that Johan's wife Denise, and their son, Ernst, were at the top of the donga with the trackers. It was unlikely that they saw the hideous goring but they, as Bedford put it, would have heard the screams as Johan died on the buffalo's horns. Johan was killed virtually instantly but Alastair Travers had lain in the riverbed, stomach torn open and intestines bulging out, whilst the trackers ran back to the camp for help. Alastair died on the rescue aircraft on the way to Harare.

Hundreds of hunters over the years have met their end with buffalo. Having been close to death myself from this awesome monolith, I can well understand why many game hunters rank the buffalo as the most dangerous of the Big Five.

* * * * *

Andrew Fraser was a sportsman, adventurer and traveller. The youngest son of the 15th Lord Lovat of wartime fame, he was educated at the famous

Catholic College, Ampleforth and Magdalene College, Oxford. His adventurous spirit and quest for dangerous sports included bobsleighing for the British team, pig sticking on horseback in Pakistan, exploring the Venezuelan jungle, riding a horse over the Andes, and spending six months in war-torn Angola to research a documentary on Jonas Savimbi. Andrew Fraser was an avid big game hunter and a member of the exclusive Shikar Club which I have the honour of belonging to. This splendid man epitomised the best of British values: valour, honour, loyalty. He was charged by a wounded buffalo whilst on a sixteen day safari near Mount Kilimanjaro, Tanzania in 1994. Andrew Fraser had shot and wounded the buffalo which then took cover in thick bush from where it made its charge, tossing Fraser and causing severe injuries from which he died.

* * * * *

We were in 'E' camp in the Zambezi Valley in June 1988 with Bill Bedford and the Serrurriers when we picked up some horrifying news on the bush radio. A friend of Bedford's, Clive Swemmer, had been gored to death by a buffalo earlier that afternoon. He and a friend had been hunting from 'G' camp to the east of us and Bill had shared a beer with him at Makuti only the evening before. All we could gather was that Swemmer had wounded the buffalo in the notorious jess which the Zambezi Valley is renowned for. Jess is a frightening vegetation in which to hunt because of its heavily tangled thickets interspersed with razor sharp thorns. Apparently Swemmer had fired a second shot that failed to kill the animal. He had become snared in the thorns and was then gored to death. It was a very sober camp that evening. Bill Bedford knew Clive Swemmer well; he was a prominent tobacco farmer, much admired and well liked in Zimbabwe's farming and hunting community. Vivienne and I had to return to Johannesburg a day earlier leaving behind the rest of the party as I was due to join Johan Bellingan in Namibia the following week. That's how I first met Giles Raynor who flew us out of the Zambezi Valley on a brilliant clear day. We were rewarded with a wonderful farewell to the valley as over the escarpment streamed a huge herd of buffalo, some three hundred strong in our estimation. Giles Raynor flew us at low level to view this magnificent sight. The Swemmer tragedy was well known to Giles as they were close friends and fellow farmers.

*   *   *   *   *

Something about the aura of a lion is blood curdling. Many hunters claim that this powerfully muscled killing machine is the most dangerous animal in the world, excepting the tiger perhaps. The lion is a hunter, one of the finest in the animal kingdom. It is carnivorous, fast as lightening, fearless and extremely powerful. I haven't experienced a lion charge as of yet but I have spoken with men who have and I have read accounts of past and present hunters who survived the hair-raising occurrence of a lion coming full tilt at that them. They will all agree that the apparition of a huge yellow ball of roaring fury hurtling at you with speed is one of the most terrifying experiences imaginable.

Bill Bedford, a constant hunting companion over many years, came close to death when he wounded a lioness in the Zambezi Valley. He decided to follow up with a shotgun. In his wisdom he'd selected birdshot believing this to be the solution for a highly dangerous wild animal lying up wounded in dense bush. With him was Bob Warren-Codrington and Bandit, Bedford's faithful Matabele tracker, following the blood spoor into the treacherous jess. The lioness then barrelled out of the undergrowth without warning, despite Bandit and Bob Warren-Codrington tossing stones into the undergrowth – an old hunters' trick to elicit a warning growl from a wounded cat. The roaring lioness sprang at Bedford who was in the lead and knocked him to the ground and commenced tearing at his forearm which Bill had flung up to protect his face. Bob Warren-Codrington and Bandit were powerless to shoot at the risk of wounding Bedford who was being flung from side-to-side like a rag doll. Eventually the brave Bandit saw his chance and placed his rifle against the lionesses' head and pulled the trigger, killing the lioness. We received the news shortly after Bedford's release from hospital. "Never again will I go after lions with bird shot" he vowed. "It was a mad thing to do."

* * * * *

Bob Warren – Codrington was not to remain unscathed. I received an e-mail from him last year: "I joined your club when I was knocked down by a buffalo cow. An unfortunate incident where we walked, by chance, on to an old cow, unwounded but grumpy and alone. She charged through thick bush and I only had one shot at about 4 metres. I was knocked flying but avoided any serious injury, possibly due to the effect from my shot and the fact that the animal's horn hit my binos on my chest. One cylinder of the binos was crushed! At the time I had two clients from USA with me (father & son) who finished the animal off before she could have another go at us. The first shot struck the base of the neck which forced her to stumble before she hit me. My injuries were superficial and I was back in the field three weeks later. Quite an experience and very fortunate to get off so lightly".

* * * * *

There's the story of Ian Henderson, a scion of a famous Rhodesian family. His father won a V.C. in the Matabele uprising at the turn of the century. The family game ranch, 'Doddieburn,' is renowned throughout the land. Ian built for himself a formidable reputation as a professional hunter in the 50's and 60's. I met Ian Henderson in Johannesburg in the company of Piers Taylor who purchased the Matetsi concession from Ian. Ian Henderson was knocked down by a charging lion in Botswana after he'd fired off a snap shot when the cat had sprung at him out of a bush without warning. His client couldn't get a clean shot into the lion which then turned on him and sank his fangs into his chest, crushing his ribs in the process. The lion returned to Ian Henderson, biting him several times on the arms and the groin, leaving him drenched in blood. Both took shelter under a tree and dispatched the trackers to raise help from camp. By the time the truck had returned four hours had elapsed but the nightmare was not yet over. Ian Henderson was driving the truck with a savagely torn arm and both hunters were now in severe pain and suffering seriously from loss of blood. To add to their woes, a bull elephant erupted out of the bush and charged the truck leaving Ian Henderson to order his gun bearers to fire into the air to frighten off the elephant but their day wasn't over when they finally reached camp in the small hours of the morning. Bandaging their wounds the best they could, they then had to continue driving for eighty miles along a dirt road to the Victoria Falls hospital.

I always enjoyed meeting up with Ian Henderson and hearing his stories on hunting. His brush with death is marked by a distinct limp but this remarkably humble man – one of the famous big game hunters of his era – will tell you with a wry smile that his confrontation with that lion was all in the days work.

* * * * *

Short of being charged, I have certainly found myself in some hairy situations with lions. I was hunting with Bill Bedford in Charara on that occasion when Johan Bellingan and I had had that unpleasant experience with Mugabe's CIO as described in chapter 10. At dawn one morning, Bedford, myself, the National Parks Board game scout and Vivienne (who persuaded us to let her come against our better judgement) set off for the blind which we had rigged up the previous day. We parked the truck about one kilometre from the hide and we walked along a dry riverbed and crept into place at first light. The silence was broken with a distinct rustling of the leaves around the hide. We could sense the presence of lions. Bill slowly eased himself up the bole of the tree which formed the mainstay of the blind in which we were crouched. I kept watch on the bait hanging seventy metres away. Then to my consternation, a young male lion padded across the front of the blind and I could have stretched out my arm and prodded him in his rib cage, he was that close. I glanced at Bill and he was looking grim. He signalled down to me that we were surrounded by 11 lionesses and their cubs.

For ten minutes or so, we remained motionless. We could hear the lionesses stalking around the hide. Then the young lion referred to earlier walked into the rear of the blind where Vivienne and the game scout were crouched. It stood for what seemed a life time and then it turned and left. Vivienne was an asset that morning. She hadn't panicked remaining calm. At this stage I had lost interest in the bait and kept my eyes on Bill who remained motionless except for his head which he swivelled slowly from side to side in order to keep track of the lionesses. He was now as anxious as we all were and we sensed the danger surrounding us.

Suddenly Bill roared at the lionesses and that was my cue to leap to my feet with the .375 at my shoulder. I aimed at a lioness 6 foot away, her tail switching and ears pinned to her head. She was in a crouch, ready to leap into the blind, and this was no mock charge. Behind her in line lay another six lionesses with cubs. Bill Bedford urged me not to kill as I aimed at the lioness, intending to shoot at her feet when she came. Eventually she slunk off with the other lionesses. We stayed put for thirty minutes, not daring to move until we thought we were out of danger. We headed for the riverbed with Bill in front and me at the rear. The pride, however, weren't to leave us alone. They followed us on the bank until we finally reached the truck. Bill and I and the game scout – we agreed with Vivienne that she best remain behind – returned to the blind an hour before dusk. The lionesses were there waiting for us and minutes after our arrival they started to stroll backwards and forwards close to the hide, looking at us in a sinister manner. We decided to cut our losses and leave. We were inviting danger and there was no sign of a big male. We had already been in a tight spot that morning and why invite a replay.

The next day, after a buffalo hunt in the morning, we decided to look for lion in a different area. The plan was that Bill Bedford would take the truck and drag a chunk of buffalo meat while I walked along a riverbed with the game scout and a tracker. We agreed to meet at a point some six or seven kilometres distant, thereby allowing two hours to meet up before nightfall. If I saw a good lion I was to shoot it and I liked the idea. The only problem was that the 7 kilometres turned out to be half the distance again and darkness was setting in when I realised that my hapless tracker was still dragging a chunk of buffalo meat to draw lions into the area. I ordered the tracker to cut the bait, and just in time as the lions started roaring on both sides of the river bed. I cursed Bill Bedford under my breath. First the doomed blind and now this. The three of us quickened the pace and all we wanted were the lights of the truck in the distance. Another 30 minutes passed during which we came close to colliding into a solitary bull elephant. Then the lions began to roar again. They were now uncomfortably close and it was becoming dangerous. Lions at night fear nothing and this is when they are at their most lethal. I worked the bolt of the .375 in readiness for an attack.

We finally saw the lights of the truck far down the riverbed but the lions were all around us and their roaring was blood curdling. I reckoned at any time there would be a swift charge from any direction. We broke into a jog trot which was a risky thing to do as a running form is a magnet to a hunting lion. On reaching the vehicle, I was angry with Bill Bedford who was probably the most contrite I'd ever seen him. He was worried as I was and had considered taking the truck down the riverbed to meet us. It was wise that he didn't as the truck could have stuck in the sand, increasing the potential danger for us all.

On the following day, I shot a lion without the assistance of bait. Bill Bedford first spotted a male lion and three lionesses at the base of a tree some 500 metres distant. Between us was a stretch of broken ground and the wind was in our favour. The male was young but it was a reasonable trophy and we deserved the prize after the close encounters over the past two days. The four of us, Bandit and the game scout included, moved stealthily using the dead ground as cover until we reached a large bush from where we could study the lions. The male had remained put but the lionesses were restless and were pacing back and forth and it seemed we had little hope of approaching closer to the quarry for lack of cover.

We'd reduced the distance to an estimated 150 metres and I could have taken a shot at that range but the grass was too thick threatening bullet deflection. Bill and I then crawled to a small bush 70 metres ahead of us. It was a slow, painstaking and agonising process with thorns embedding themselves into our skin and razor sharp stones drawing blood from our elbows and knees. It was very hard going as all of the four cats were now on their feet and looking in our direction. On and on we crawled and I had difficulty in dragging the gun in such a way that it made no noise. I also had to ensure that the muzzle remained free of dirt as this could foul up a shot. We continued this painful stalk until we reached the sparse bush. It took us 30 minutes to cover a mere 70 metres.

The lion was now on its feet and the cats were looking directly at us and Bill was whispering if I was ready to take a shot. My hands were shaking from that long and difficult crawl and also from a liberal dose of old-fashioned nerves. But what I had done was to find a slim branch to steady the .375 as I wanted an accurate bead on the lion - and so did Bill Bedford as he admitted afterwards. He was as anxious as I was for a one-shot kill. Having been savaged to within an inch of his life by a lioness the previous year, he didn't relish a repeat performance. I waited for the lion to stand broadside and the moment it did I fired. The lion buckled on the impact of the bullet and collapsed to the ground, whirling in circles as if it was trying to bite its tail. Then it charged off with tail rigid in the air, the tell-tale sign of a heart shot. The three lionesses were now looking straight at us and we had to remain on our bellies beneath that sliver of bush for what seemed an eternity.

Finally, the lionesses took their eyes off us, and we watched them slouch off into the distance. We gave them 10 minutes and then walked up to find the lion stretched out some 30 metres from where he had been shot. I was pleased. The lion had been hunted properly, shot cleanly and had died without pain, and it was most satisfying that we had got it stalking on foot and with the challenges of the approach.

* * * * *

I was hunting lions in Ngamiland with David Lincoln, a young hunting professional on a concession 90 kilometres north-east of Maun, Botswana. We spent six long, hot days scouring the vast concession in the Kalahari scrub searching for the lions that only the week before had broken into the Tribal Trust lands bordering the concession and had taken a number of cattle. It was tedious, monotonous work involving endless hours of perching on a truck looking for tracks or breaks in the fence. We eventually came across fresh spoor but the lions were lying up in the Tribal Trust land beyond the boundary of our concession. We camped on the spot, hoping for the lions to cross our concession line. It was desperately frustrating for us as we heard them roaring at night and it was tempting to move in and take them at dawn but if we were caught we'd be in jail and we'd lose our guns and David Lincoln his professional licence.

To alleviate the hours of tedium on that hunt, Lincoln and I would talk of the many stories of lion in Botswana. We spoke about the Chobe safari area to the north of us which was notorious for lion – incurred deaths. We recalled the grisly tale some years ago of a 15 year old American tourist who was dragged out of her tent in the dead of night and devoured in front of her terror stricken companions in the flickering light of the camp fire. It was a ghoulish scene as the unfortunate victim could not even scream as she was wearing braces on her teeth.

David Lincoln told me of a case that very year of some serious veldt fires which had depleted the Makgadikgadi and Nxai pans of the grazing and the small game resulting in hungry lions ambushing the local inhabitants on game tracks, outside their kraals, and even at bus stops. Several deaths had been incurred amongst the terrified natives in the area. He told me of a cook from one of the hunting camps in the Okavango Delta who had made the mistake of wandering into the bush after dark and meeting his end on the claws of a lion. A week following the incident, an African at Kasane near the Zimbabwe border was weaving his way to his hut after drinking in a shebeen and was mauled to death by a large male lion. The body was found a day later, half eaten by vultures. And then shortly after that, a safari camp guard in the Chobe game reserve was savaged to within an inch of his life.

The Chobe safari area is notorious for lions wandering into camps at night. I personally had some experience of this when I was running in the early eighties along a dirt road in the grounds of the Chobe game lodge with an American. The pace was progressing smoothly until I noticed the fresh spoor of a large male lion. The American wasn't quite as unsettled as I was on the presence of lions as he was naïve as to the ways of the animal kingdom and he must have thought that I was a wimp when I told him that it was time to turn back. Once ensconced in the safety of the Chobe game lodge, I explained to the New Yorker over breakfast that the area was highly dangerous as far as lions were concerned. I told him of a recent incident outside the very gates of the Chobe game lodge where an African had been dragged off his bicycle by a lion which proceeded to maul him to death.

*   *   *   *   *

In this modern age of computers and jets and where the world is shrinking to a village, it's difficult to comprehend that nature still exists in its raw state in a developed country that is South Africa. There was a veritable uproar in the Eastern Transvaal, a mere five hours drive from Johannesburg, where an angry group of villagers confronted the Kruger National Park authorities for confiscating their stockpile of lion biltong. The lions were escaping through the Kruger Park fences, complained the villagers. Their spokesman put his case: "we are forced to kill these beasts before they maul us to death and kill our stock. This is a village not a game reserve, and we therefore can't live with dangerous animals like lions roaring around here and threatening our lives!" The officials of the Parks Board replied that it was unacceptable for the villagers to accumulate mounds of fresh lion meat, piles of biltong, heaps of lion skins, an assortment of traps and a cache of unlicensed hunting rifles!

*   *   *   *   *

More deaths in the African bush have been caused by the hippopotamus than any other animal or reptile in Africa, with the crocodile coming a close second. Our daughter, MaryAnne, was canoeing with Pierre Bester, her co-founder of their adventure company 'Kayak Africa'. They were 50 metres from the shore line at Cape MacLear, Malawi. The pair was surprised at the terrific din the hundreds of Africans were creating on the shore line but they were unaware that there was a female hippopotamus cruising behind the canoe with jaws agape. Pierre Bester then sensed danger and turned his head just as the hippo's incisors literally scraped his back. Both were hurled into the water and they swam for dear life to the shore to watch helplessly as the hippo demolished their valuable klepper kayak. I saw the damage at first hand when Pierre bought the relic down to Johannesburg and he told me that he would have been ripped to pieces if the hippo had taken its bite one inch forward.

* * * * *

I was hunting buffalo in the Zambezi valley with Bill Bedford when we came to a large pan some 5 kilometres inland. The water was covered with a dense carpet of coarse lily and there seemed to be no life until we noticed the spoor of a lone hippo. We had hippo on the licence and I had never hunted this tusked beast of the river. We returned that afternoon to find the hippopotamus basking in the centre of the pan, its head above water but the rest of its body immersed in the stagnant pool. For one long hour we lay motionless on the bank looking at this baleful creature staring back at us. It was a hot afternoon and Bill Bedford began to doze off, leaving me to ponder where to shoot the animal. I remembered his comment earlier that morning that one was best advised to take a shoulder shot on a hippopotamus as it required extreme accuracy to kill it with a headshot. I also recalled that the target area was just below the eye which measured a mere inch. This was a challenge to any hunter as the dire consequences of a badly placed shot weren't worth contemplating.

Whilst lying on the bank of the pan I looked at the 2000 kilogram monster with its razor sharp incisors capable of biting a crocodile in half. I reflected on this mammal's ability to fight ferociously for days and I have seen two hippo bulls ripping at each other in the Chobe River. The terrible, bloody wounds that these creatures are capable of inflicting on each other are not a pleasant sight, even for the blood-hardened hunter. I mused on their extraordinary capacity for travelling considerable distances across land and the terrifying threat they impose on itinerant Africans in the bush.

I poked Bedford in his ribs to wake him. His casual attitude was irritating me and all I could think of was that scary mouth agape as the hippo came at us from the water. 50 metres would appear to be a safe distance but a thrashing behemoth barrelling out of the pan at full speed creates a shocking vision. I wanted to shoot the hippo but kept delaying the moment of truth as it kept on submerging and it wasn't staying still. Dusk was now on us and I decided to shoot the hippo when it next rose out of the water. I settled the cross hairs an inch below its left eye and fired. Then followed an immense swirl and silence. A hippo sinks when it's dead and this is due to the build-up of gases in its system and only after seven hours or so will the carcass float to the surface. Bill Bedford was relieved and I was drained as it had been a severe test of concentration that afternoon. There hung a lot at stake at the finale with that shot and my trusted .375 hadn't let me down.

Just after dawn the next morning, we approached the pan and there was the hippo floating on the surface. We had an interesting task ahead of us as it was lying in the centre of the pan. I looked at Bill Bedford. He looked at the trackers. Bill Bedford looked back at me. "You shot it, Mike, you'd better retrieve it". "There could be a crocodile in there!" I muttered. "Don't worry; we'll have guns trained on you. You can't come to harm!" he replied cheerfully. The trackers were grinning as they thought this was a big joke. But all I could think of was landing the hippo and I wasn't that worried about crocodiles as I thought that we were too far inland – a very foolish assumption. I stripped down to my underpants and jumped in with rope in hand. As I slowly waded through the slime on the bed of the pan, it struck me that I was, in fact, being extremely foolhardy. The murky water could easily harbour a croc and there would be little that Bill and his crew on the banks could do to help in the event of an attack. I cursed the ooze and the weed and began to wonder what the hell I was doing in this evil-smelling pan. After a very unpleasant journey through potentially treacherous water, I finally reached the hippo and tied a rope to one of its feet. Bill then started the winch and the massive mammal was finally brought to land. The bullet had entered the brain, striking the precise spot at which I had aimed. This had to be one of my finest shots.

My second experience on hippo was decidedly more hazardous. On this occasion, we were hunting with Athol Vrylink in the Luangwa Valley in Zambia. Ian and Jeanette Fraser-Jones had joined us in this particular hunt and our primary purpose was to shoot lion and leopard. We had drawn straws for the hippo license and Ian won the honours. We set off before dawn on the morning designated and shortly after leaving the truck we spotted a hippo emerging out of the riverine and walking toward us to reach the water. The three of us crouched behind a clump of grass ready to ambush the mammal. As it turned broadside, Ian dispatched a shot and the hippo raced off in the direction of the riverine. I fired at it with my .475 Jeffery but this didn't stop the monolith. I was struck at the time by the awesome speed of this huge creature. Now the game was on. Blood spoor led to the thick riverine. We waited 20 tense minutes for it to lose its adrenaline.

Vrylink remained remarkably calm as he was used to close quarter work and a wounded hippo in riverine was routine to him. He was a good man to have in a fight. My nerves were stretched and the waiting seemed an eternity. I did my best to appear nonchalant whilst checking my equipment. I glanced over at Ian Fraser-Jones who looked as if he'd seen happier days and I managed a grin as I patted my double-barrel. This was the medicine for a charge in dense bush. Then came the moment of truth when Vrylink said in a quiet tone, "Let's go. Watch out. It may come at us at any moment. Keep your wits about you".

We had just entered the dark riverine when Vrylink suddenly raised his rifle and fired. The hippo had been standing a mere 50 paces from us while we were preparing for the follow-up. It must have heard us and was waiting in ambush. I fired a shot immediately after Athol and the hippo sank to the ground. I believe that Athol's shot had done the trick. We approached with caution and Ian Fraser-Jones applied the coup de grace. We had a lot to thank the Gods for that morning as there could have been a very nasty accident in that riverine.

* * * * *

I've hunted along the Zambezi River several times and I've seen the mass of hippo and crocodiles which serve as a constant threat to the fishermen and the canoe safaris. I wasn't in the valley on that occasion when a group of German tourists were tripping the river and the guide, Philip Longden (23) of Harare, was bitten through the foot by a hippo which had attacked their canoe. The five tourists survived unscathed but their guide had to be airlifted to Harare with a gangrenous foot which had to be amputated. Only the very next day, five kilometres downstream from the aforementioned accident, four men were fishing off a motorboat which was attacked by a hippo. The boat overturned and sank and the fishermen found themselves stranded on a sandbank. One of the fishermen, Alistair Gellatly (40), swam across the Zambezi to summon help. He was seized by a crocodile but survived the attack by ramming a fist down the croc's throat. Badly injured and suffering from shock, Gellatly crawled into the reeds and collapsed as dusk fell. Meanwhile the others remained marooned unarmed on the sandbank when, by a stroke of fortune, a paddle floated by – believed to be the aforementioned Philip Longden's –and they had a weapon to fend off the crocodiles during the night. In the meantime, the semi-conscience Gellatly lay as potential bait for the lions and hyenas which infested the area and to make matters worse his blood was creating a strong scent for these predators. That wasn't his only problem. He thought he was going to die when a bull buffalo walked menacingly towards him. Lone buffalo bulls tend to be aggressive and are known to attack humans without provocation but, instead of goring Gellatly, it remained close by as if standing guard against the lions and hyenas. At dawn Gellatly was able to stagger several kilometres along the river before being sighted by African fishermen. He was eventually flown to hospital and shared a ward with the other survivor of a river attack the previous day, the same Philip Longden.

* * * * *

There was a story of extreme heroism that occurred near Mana Pools in the Zambezi River. A Johannesburg businessman, Hugh Lloyd (45), lost an arm whilst saving his teenage son, Jeremy during a canoeing safari. A crocodile seized the boy who was floating on a life jacket and his father and a 19 year old Briton, Alex Shaw, tackled the crocodile which tore an arm off Lloyd. The guide was quick to apply a tourniquet to staunch the bleeding which saved Lloyd's life. Alex Shaw survived with a crushed arm and Jeremy escaped with bites on his left arm and buttocks

* * * * *

We have a son, Sean who is a charter pilot flying in the hot spots of Africa ferrying supplies of all description. He spent three years as a bush aviator based in Maun flying tourists into the neighbouring Okavango swamps. The Okavango Delta is one of the last unspoilt retreats in Africa, and famous for its crystal clear swamps and flood plains. These are teeming with hippo and crocodile which frequently threaten the mokoros – hollowed out tree-trunks - which the local Africans use for fishing. Certain South Africans that I know abjectly refuse to set foot in such craft and I do believe them to be somewhat faint hearted but then Sean and other pilots who have flown this region will tell you of the regular capsizing and near misses with death. To illustrate such, an Australian tourist on honeymoon died from a crocodile attack and shortly afterwards a Swiss visitor was fortunate to escape with his life after a hippo upturned his mokoro in the same stretch of the swamps.

* * * * *

Crocodile attacks never fail to give me a chill down the spine, particularly when I reflect on the time I stood waist deep in the Kasane rapids in Botswana angling for tiger fish. I was foolhardy then, some twenty years ago, when I allowed myself to be tempted to stand in the crocodile infested waters, the lure for tiger fish was that strong. I was with Sean and it was only at the end of the day's fishing when we were returning along the banks that I saw the spoor and I turned to our guide - a young man called Hartley - who confirmed that these belonged to a large crocodile. I was furious with myself at risking not only my life but that of my son's that afternoon in the Chobe River. And talking of this very river, I recall Ian Green's bravado of training for the Iron Man race in a canoe in these waters infested by hippo and crocodile. He couldn't understood my refusal to join him in this madcap venture and he duly transported his canoe up to the Chobe game lodge which he had just renovated and which he later purchased from the Sun Hotels group. A week later he was there to greet us at the Kasane airstrip with his partner, Jonathan Gibson. I thought he looked a little crestfallen as I shook his hand and he had to admit that my reservations on canoeing down the Chobe River were well justified. He told me of his hair raising ordeal. He was paddling furiously down the river when in front of him rose this huge hippo with jaws open and it was a miracle that he remained alive to tell the tale.

৪৩ ✦ ৫৪

CHAPTER EIGHT

The warriors

The many enjoyable encounters between us reflected
a brotherhood of warriors. Your appreciation for
those who were willing to risk their lives for their
noble beliefs has been well expressed in this book.

Brigadier General Zvika Kantor (ret'd),
Israeli Defence Force

THE HISTORY of South Africa has been a litany of skirmishes and strife since inception. In 1510 the Portuguese noble, Francisco d'Almeida lands in Table Bay and fights the Khoikhoi – nomadic sheep and cattle herders who had moved south from Botswana. D'Almeida and fifty of his men are killed. The first permanent settlement of Europeans is led by Jan van Riebeeck in 1652 where the Dutch East India Company bases itself in Cape Town and where follows constant clashes with the Khoikhoi. Thirty years later the first French Huguenots arrive in the Cape shortly followed by German mercenaries which led to the founding of the Afrikaner people. Two hundred years later, the white settlers clash with the Xhosas and the constant warring between the two groups over the next decade culminates in the killing of the Xhosa king, Hintsa. Shortly after saw the killing of sixteen thousand Xhosa by the British colonial forces that included a number of British settlers who'd landed in the Eastern Cape in 1820. Then came the Great Trek of the rebel Afrikaners migrating from the Cape into the interior to flee from British rule, skirmishing along the route with Black tribes. Shortly after follows the proclamation of the Boer Republic of the Orange Free State and the subsequent clash with the Basothos. Then ensues the British conflict with the Zulus, commemorated by the crushing defeat of the British at Isandlwana and the famous stand of the Welsh 24th of Foot at Rorke's Drift where 11 Victoria Crosses were awarded. A few years later the Boer War is fought with 50,000 obdurate Afrikaners, assisted by a handful of Irish and European mercenaries, taking on the might of the British army in a savagely fought contest at the turn of the century where the technique of guerrilla warfare was initiated on a grand scale. Thus it can be seen that the story of South Africa has been a succession of fighting – Boer & British settlers on the Eastern Cape frontier warring with the Xhosas (the largest tribe in South Africa); British fighting the Zulus for supremacy in Natal; Boers fighting the British in the Boer War; and Boer & Brit fighting as allies in the two World Wars. Then not to forget the mercenary armies of 'Mad' Major Mike Hoare's 5 Commando that involved fighting in the Belgian Congo (now the DRC) in the nineteen sixties, liberating Stanleyville from the 'The Simbas', saving hundreds of European hostages, and restoring order to the Congo; and Eeben Barlow's Executive Outcomes (EO), the potent mercenary force made up of men drawn from the SADF Special Forces conducting successful actions in Angola and Sierra Leone. This impressive military litany perhaps goes some way in explaining the pugnacity of the Republic standing on its own against the world in the Apartheid era.

This chapter is dedicated to the warriors of recent times. I start with a character called 'The Phantom Major' and he's a neighbour of mine and I'm a fortunate to have him as a friend. The story unfolds like this. A close friend, Ian Green whom I have referred to in previous chapters, rang me in a buzz of excitement. "Fellow's just left my office. Wants us to invest in a big game hunting venture – Mozambique –virgin territory - we can make some money and free hunting.........he's given me the figures. I've told him he has to meet you. Expect his call." Ian Green was bursting with enthusiasm – as was normal – and whoever the supposed professional hunter was, he certainly inspired Ian. Ian Green was a born entrepreneur.

His various enterprises covered platinum and chrome mining, hotels, and a liquor business which I was to subsequently purchase.

I then met the man behind the hunting venture and he certainly cut a plausible figure. But when he told me that he'd been an ex-armourer in the Rhodesian SAS at the height of the bush war, a warning bell intuitively began to jangle. Fortunately I had contacts which could verify his claim. His business plan was well formulated but he was looking for a contribution of up to 90% of the capital required in an industry which is notoriously mercurial and thus it was imperative that his credentials could bear up to close scrutiny. So I rang a hunting friend, Billy Bedford who'd served in the SAS. Bedford's response was immediate. He'd never heard of him but he'd talk to a friend of his, Bob Warren-Codrington, a major in the SAS. This he did and I had Bob on to me in a trice. "We've no knowledge of X. I suggest you ring Grahame Wilson, our Commanding Officer". The jungle drums were throbbing. I phoned Grahame Wilson, and in his customary polite manner he told me that no such person existed. I thanked him, not realising where he was calling from. Grahame Wilson and his men of the SAS had brought an abrupt end to the big game hunting venture in Mozambique.

A few weeks later Bob Warren-Codrington, who'd served as second in command to Grahame Wilson, came to stay with us in Chartwell. I was cleaning my rifles at the time when he joined me in my gun room before dinner and I learnt that he'd just been having a drink with his former C O. I asked Bob where this Grahame Wilson lived and I was cheerfully told that he happened to be my neighbour! I had read of this extraordinary fighting man, the most highly decorated member of the Rhodesian Security Forces. An excellent work, 'The Elite – Rhodesia's Special Air Service', happens to lie in my book collection and contained therein are profiles of certain SAS men. The one entry that remains devoid of a photograph is 'The Phantom Major' who declined to be pictured. I called Jack Crutchley – another SAS officer of a previous generation - whom I knew was close friends with a certain Lt-Colonel Brian Robinson, generally known as Rhodesia's Mr SAS for honing the regiment into one of the most professional units in Southern Africa. He could confirm that the 'Phantom Major' was Grahame Wilson whom, as it transpired, was selected by Brian Robinson when Grahame applied to join the SAS.

In fact, I was to spend an entertaining evening with Jack, his wife Ros, one of his sons, Andrew, and the aforementioned Brian Robinson who obviously held great respect for Grahame. I could readily understand Brian Robinson's formidable reputation listening to him. I first met the SAS legend with Jack Crutchley in the Durban Club. He's a short, lean man with a strong face and with eyes like a scanner. You sense he's assessing you and you realise you're in the company of an inveterate warrior. I was curious to meet Grahame Wilson whose many daring deeds, mostly enacted solo, earned him the Grand Cross of Valour, the Silver Cross, and the Bronze Cross, making him the most highly decorated soldier in the Rhodesian Security Forces. Only one other member of the Rhodesian Security Forces was to receive the G.C.V. - South African born Captain 'Schulie' Chris Schollenberg of the SAS and later the Selous Scouts.

What immediately strikes you when meeting Grahame for the first time is his expression and the softness of his voice. This is no Rambo as of the celluloid world. Here is a quiet, courteous, well rounded man with a charming wife, Carrie, and two fine children. But it doesn't take an observant man long to realise that Major Wilson is a man of profound depth and shrewdness of brain and once you have earned his confidence and his empathy, you are fortunate to have a loyal friend. I experienced a tragedy of losing a canoeing partner in a river race and he was one of the first to call and suggest we meet. He was one of the few – apart from the canoeing fraternity – I could speak to intimately of this terrible loss of a friend of thirty years standing. He's known death and it should be remembered that certain of his valorous deeds were executed in a klepper canoe in the Zambezi River.

* * * * *

Jack Crutchley can be an overpowering figure, and he won't mind my describing him thus, as many not of his ilk are wary of him, but then strong men are often envied. One has to admire this product of Michaelhouse School who gained the distinction of being awarded the Sword of Honour at Sandhurst, a rare achievement for a colonial boy and he's rightly proud of his military career, including a term in Aden with the Rhodesian SAS. When he was serving with the SAS, he and a C/Sgt Bob Bouch were in charge of the initial selection for C Squadron, a demanding time for all who made it. The location was the rugged Matopos Hills, south of Bulawayo in the then Rhodesia. Bob Bouch was to lose his life, tragically, in the early stages of the Rhodesian war. We met under interesting circumstances in the offices of Barlows (then one of the larger South African conglomerates) where I am quietly writing up an order with a charming lady in the public relations office. In bursts a tornado in the form of one Jack Crutchley. He looks at me menacingly and barks as to who I am. I reply and at the mention of Vinuchi, the company that Vivienne and I pioneered, I could see his face darken with mistrust. Jack is a true WASP and the mention of an Italian sounding clothing company was to be regarded with deep suspicion. "See he sharpens his pencil!" Jack orders the PRO and storms out in the same style as he's blown in. "Who on earth is that?" I asked. "Jack Crutchley" the lady laughed. "You'll get to know him. I'm sure of that. You've got a lot in common" replied the perceptive female. She was right. A fortnight later I was bounding down the steps of the WITS University change rooms in running shorts and little else. I was putting in some heat training for the forthcoming Iron Man race and climbing the steps was the same Jack. "Where do I know you from?" he growls and I remind him of the occasion in the Barlow offices. "I have sharpened my pencil" I hastened to add. "Okay, okay, cut the crap", he grunts impatiently, "and what are you training for, can I ask?" "The Iron Man", I reply. This was to Jack's liking and from that day a friendship was kindled. Jack Crutchley went on to head several companies for Barlows and his final accomplishment was to hold the chair at Romatex, a very sizeable textile operation within the Barlow empire.

Still today he pulls my leg mercilessly about my hunting. "I hunt with a bow" he constantly reminds me. "Any old fool can bring down the big five with a heavy calibre rifle!" I have yet to learn what Jack has shot with his bow but his energy remains undiminished despite his age. He is two years older than me and if he's not canoeing the Inanda dam in the Valley of a Thousand hills, he's thundering over the horizon on his motorcycle. Recently Jack had the gall of lecturing me on my lifestyle and that I should retire gracefully from such challenges as cycling up the Mont Ventoux in Provence but I remind him that I have sufficient energy left in the legs to do such things. "Ah", he says, "but I hunt with a bow!"

* * * * *

Many of South Africa's modern combatants have had difficulty in adjusting to peace time. Lanseria Airport is a stone's throw from our home in Chartwell and it was a regular sight to see fit, bronzed young men stride purposefully through the concourse carrying a grip. One recognised the men of Executive Outcomes (E.O.), the highly potent mercenary force made up primarily of ex-Recces and Parabats. I had the chance of meeting an enigmatic adventurer, Simon Mann, over a dinner in Cape Town with Hamish Currie (refer Miscellany). A product of Eton, he served as an officer in the Scots Guards before graduating into the SAS. A chance meeting between Mann and a certain Tony Buckingham in London – the latter operating his company, Branch Heritage owning oil fields in Africa – led to a partnership where Simon Mann's role was to liaise with E.O. Founded in 1989 by Eeben Barlow who had served in Colonel J Breytenbach's legendary 32 Battalion, E O could be considered as the forerunner of the modern private military company. This feared, uncompromising unit of approximately four hundred strong - mostly ex Special Forces soldiers from the Reconnaissance Regiment, the Parachute Regiment and 32 Battalion - built such a formidable reputation during the 1990's that certain regimes in Africa hired this band of men to protect them from rebel uprisings. Angola and Sierra Leone are notable examples. The first significant contract for E.O. was the successful recapture of

Buckingham's oil site in Soyo, Angola. Simon Mann led an abortive coup in 2004 destined to overthrow President Obiang of Equatorial Guinea – a corrupt despot in the mould of Mugabe - and was recently pardoned whilst serving a thirty four year sentence in the notorious Black Beach prison in Malabo, Equatorial Guinea. A sad sequel for this man of arms and what got into him in his latter days, God only knows.

* * * * *

Legionnaire 131,318. Simon Murray. I first heard of this extraordinary character at a dinner hosted by Mary & Gordon Richdale in Johannesburg. Gordon, then Chairman of Hill Samuel, proceeded to tell me of this colourful buccaneer who had written a book on his adventures in France's famous mercenary force, the French Foreign Legion. I was no stranger to this legendary warrior band, having listened spellbound to tales from my parents on a relation, a Ronald Brodie, who'd run away from home at the age of fifteen to enlist with the Foreign Legion in Sidi Bel Abbes, the HQ in Algeria. As a boy, I had read voraciously the PC Wren books and had made my mind up in following the footsteps of Ronald Brodie into this band of hard men – but the Cameronians had first call!

As Irish luck had it, Simon Murray was a member of the Shikar Club and he had received a flyer from a mail shot I had despatched to my fellow members on the book I'd written: 'Roaming with a rifle...' Thereupon, he had delivered by one of the cars he owned – a London cab of all things - a special leather bound edition he usually reserves for his VIP clients for his investment fund (Johan Rupert & Henry Kissinger amongst them), containing a personal message beautifully inscribed in copper plate, to Philip & Mary de Laszlo's home near the Thames. My sister was intrigued with the cab – I told her that this was Simon's method of breaking every traffic law in inner London - typical of this pirate that puts Sir Henry Morgan in the shade. I could carry on in reams. For more refer to the Miscellany.

* * * * *

Talking of the SADF Special Forces, there's one figure that stands tall, a certain Peter Barry, commonly referred to as 'P.G'. Our friendship was spawned on the banks of Emmarentia Dam, Johannesburg, when I observed with interest this huge figure squeezing himself into a racing canoe. He made an ungainly sight wobbling precariously around the dam and I was curious to learn more about this unusual looking fellow. I introduced myself and it emerged that 'P.G'. had spent four years with 2 Reconnaissance Battalion. The term 'Recce' draws respect in this country as this highly elite band can be placed on a par with the SAS and this has been verified by conversations I've had with members of the latter. 'P.G'. had served most of his service fighting in Angola. "I've shot a buffalo" he once remarked to me proudly. "What with?" I asked, knowing well the answer. 'P.G' shuffled his feet a little awkwardly. "With an R4 rifle" he had to admit. "But we had to eat, Michael". I remain with this vision of Barry crawling up to the unwary beast of the wild, unleashing a torrent of bullets on the excuse that he and his men were short of dinner! Despite his considerable height and bulk, he's a nimble man and he was a Transvaal champion in the eight hundred metres event. He completed the 'Iron Man' through which he became a gifted cyclist and he recently finished the renowned Cape Town Argus race measuring 100 kilometres in three and half hours. 'P.G' fits firmly in the adventurer bracket. The soft life is not for him and he is one of that daring breed that forsakes a comfortable lifestyle for trading in dark Africa. Three weeks out of four he vanishes from Johannesburg and he's to be found in such murky spots as Luanda, Angola, and Maputo, Mozambique, trading cigarettes, liquor, and pharmaceuticals.

* * * * *

Through such men, one encounters other men of action such as Sej Dunning. 'P.G'. called me up a few years ago when I was preparing for a hunt in the Pamir Mountains in Tajikistan bordering Afghanistan. Sej

Dunning was then engaged in flying supplies to Kabul and other parts, and 'P.G.' had reckoned that Sej could provide me with invaluable advice on equipment and medicines needed for the Pamirs. Like 'P.G.' Barry and many South Africans, Sej is a big man in the full sense of the word. The conversation was riveting that evening in a Sandton bar and the topics veered from the Pamirs to the Angolan war where my two drinking partners had first met. "I was always bailing out ruffians like this fellow", laughs Sej and I was to learn later that this was exactly what Sej did. For twenty years he'd served with the SA Air Force, specialising in helicopters, and he quickly became a legend amongst South Africa's Special Forces. He was fearless in action, flying his helicopter in the face of fire, rescuing the Recces and the Parabats from perilous positions in Angola. Sej today heads a contracting business involving some seventy aircraft including twenty helicopters operating out of Kabul, Afghanistan; Sej Dunning is an exciting man involved in an exciting business — an adventurer in the true mould.

I had occasion to fly to a guinea fowl shoot on the Botswana border with two majors. Piloting the aircraft was Major Sej Dunning and sitting next to him in the co-pilot's seat was a fellow warrior and a friend of old, Major Grahame Wilson. My day was made as I watched these two men of arms setting about the guinea fowl with determination and between the drives I had the opportunity of murmuring to Sej: "not quite like knocking off the Cubans!", "or Mugabe's mob!", I remarked in turn to Grahame.

* * * * *

David Christie is a tall, heavily built, impressive looking man. He was the Adjutant of the Cameronians on that sad occasion in 1968 when the regiment was disbanded to Scotland's grief. As coincidence had it, he inherited my platoon in Kenya in 1959. He married a South African girl called Anne and after a period of running his property company in Cape

Town, David Christie received a vocation to the church and became a padre for the South African Police (SAP) and the Wits Rifles regiment. We used to meet at the Wits Rifles Officers annual dinner. The Wits Rifles were affiliated to the Cameronians as were other regiments from various parts of the world, including the 7th Ghurkhas. David and his bride were posted by the church to the grimy industrial environs of Vanderbyl Park, a culture shock after the gentle Cape. I asked David with his SAP connections if he'd take me to some of the more notorious hot spots in the townships and he duly obliged. Our tour covered the ill famed Sharpeville and a number of the front-line stations of the East Rand including Katlehong that had experienced some of the fiercest hostel fighting in the nineties. As we drove down the mean streets of Katlehong under a dark, grey sky, my imagination ran rife with visions of ululating Zulu warriors streaming out of the hostels to rush the barricades manned by their foe, the ANC followers. I could picture burning buildings and the debris of battle littering the streets. My ears rang with the sound of gun fire crackling from the casspirs in which crouched the policemen – black and white – from the Internal Stability Units and it was appropriate that it was in Katlehong where David Christie and I had a very close brush with death. Shortly after leaving the SAP station, in stormed a black policeman who shot and killed the captain with whom we had been conversing with a mere ten minutes ago, before turning the gun on himself. David Christie believed that the policeman was in a state of deep depression as were so many at that time.

* * * * *

Talking about soldiers/adventurers, there's one extraordinary man that has enriched my life with his sheer spunk and courage. He personifies the expression 'guts'. David Barr is an ex-US Marine who fought in the Vietnam War as a crew chief of a Huey Helicopter Gunship. After his stint in Vietnam where he racked up 57 air medals, he went on to serve in the Israeli Parachute Brigade in 1975 -1977 and had the distinction of being awarded honour man for his battalion. He moved on to join the RLI and within two months was a troop sergeant fighting in the Rhodesian bush war. He then volunteered for the SADF and completed the selection course for the Pathfinders in 44 Parachute Brigade and fought the Cubans in Angola with 32 Battalion, known as 'The Buffalo Soldiers'. Serving as Colonel Jan Breytenbach's gunner – 'Gunnie' as the legendary Colonel would refer to Dave Barr - a landmine blew up Colonel Breytenbach's vehicle, ejecting him clear and leaving Dave Barr pinned under the blazing truck. Colonel Breytenbach returned to the truck risking his life and pulled Dave Barr clear. The Colonel then called for medivac and High Command said *no,* let the soldier *expire*! A helicopter pilot, however, heard the heated exchange over his radio & told High Command *to go to hell* and evacuated Dave Barr. After nine months in hospital and four amputation operations to his legs and serious burns on many parts of his body, Barr straps on his prosthetic legs and 9mm pistol around his waist and returns to train paratroopers in machine guns and providing encouragement to the paraplegic and quadriplegic victims of the South African bush wars. I experienced this exemplary practice of Dave's when he phoned Jurie Schoeman, our son in law, giving him some well needed cheer when Jurie had his leg amputated (refer chapter 19). As Jurie later described it to me ," he gave me some excellent advice on how to deal with the matter and I assumed he was calling from Johannesburg and not California" – that is the man Dave Barr is.

I first encountered this character in the early 80's. Monty Brett, who commanded 2 Para Battalion and who was to lead his troops under the command of Colonel Jan Breytenbach in the 1978 Cassinga raid, phoned me and suggested that I meet David Barr as he had an idea in mind. I arrived early for the appointment and was talking to Monty Brett and Charlie Gough when I heard a clumping of two metal legs and in walked this extraordinary warrior who had fought for four separate armies. His firm hand shake and his candid eyes struck me immediately and there started a friendship that continues today. With the help of men like Charlie Gough and Mike McWilliams of the Parabats we raised a significant amount of money for Barr to tour South Africa on a Harley-

Davidson motor bicycle, a machine that is his consuming passion. Barr visited hospitals and nursing homes to give fellow war victims hope and inspiration and this he did in spectacular style by jumping out of aircraft assisting fellow paratroopers with lost limbs to fly the skies. On one occasion he lost one of his artificial legs on a descent and a Free-State farmer was watching incredulously as he saw a limb whirling out of the sky to land in one of his meilie fields! David Barr doesn't know the meaning of giving up and in 1990 he embarked on a solo journey around the world astride his beloved Harley-Davidson. It took him three and half years to cover eighty five thousand miles spanning six continents and he has written two books on his adventures and in so doing making the Guinness Book of Records. He had the grace to mention my sister and brother-in-law, Mary and Philip de Laszlo, who had invited him on several occasions to their home in London. We keep in regular touch and David Barr visits us whenever he sets his tin legs in South Africa.

* * * * *

Monty Brett! I first encountered this ebullient character at the Beith's cottage on the Natal South coast after I had completed my first Comrades marathon in 1978. Monty Brett was seconding Tony Beith. Monty was at that time commanding 2 Para Battalion when the country was at war with the Cubans in Angola. In his inimitable style he persuaded me to be interviewed as a potential officer for his Battalion. He needed men who had military experience, he told me, and he knew of my career in the Middle East with the Cameronians. I duly reported to Military Headquarters in Pretoria punctually at 6.00 pm, only to be told that I was last in line to be interviewed and on my reckoning I could be waiting for anything up to six hours if the assembly of potential officers – all eager young men in their late teens and early twenties - was any yard stick. I enquired politely if I could obtain a drink in the Officers mess only to be firmly told that interviewees were not allowed to drink. This was sufficient for me to take off for the nearest hostelry to catch up on some reading. I settled down quietly with a beer at hand and opened Denys Reitz's famous account of the Boer War – "Commando". The sight of the aspirant officers bedecked in their candidate officers' insignia – the white flash on the epaulettes – took me back to my own days as an officer cadet at Eaton Hall.

Before joining the British army I became a meat porter at London's famous Smithfield meat market. I was serving my apprenticeship in a meat importing firm known as Sheed Thompson and Company which was owned by the Thompson – a friend of my mother's. It was a successful company and I obviously made my mark as Mr Thompson offered me a retainer whilst I served in the military. I declined his offer, however, as I could not envisage spending seven years working in the market at night and sleeping by day. For a young fellow straight out of school, Smithfield presented a fair challenge and ill suited for the squeamish as depicted by the fights with meat hooks which were not uncommon if terrains were pirated. The hours were long and breakfast would take the form of a pint of beer and a meat pie consumed hurriedly in the pubs that stayed open for the Smithfield market. One of my contemporaries was Terry Spinks, the British lightweight boxing champion at the time, and I was privileged to know him. He was a cult figure and he enjoyed my style of coming to work in dinner jacket trousers as on certain occasions I'd dash from a debutante ball to the market. I appeared an oddity to the porters and something of a toff with a British public school accent but I mixed well with these ruffians and Smithfield was a suitable grounding for the barrack room that was to come.

The barrack room! Winchester Barracks was a relic of the Victorian era. Cold, bleak and forbidding was the home for the Rifle Brigade and the 60th Rifles – the Green Jackets as these elite regiments were known. It was my mother's connections that gained me entry into this illustrious lot and it would appear that the Green Jackets, the Irish Guards, the Scottish regiments and the Cavalry were favoured by my relations. There were four of us potential officers housed with 36 odd riflemen in our platoon and at first an uneasy atmosphere hung over the barrack room with the PO's (potential officers) being looked on somewhat resentfully by the hybrid mix of the platoon – Liverpudlians, Cockneys, Irishmen, all thrown together to be prepared for duty in the trouble spots of the British Empire. A clash was inevitable and being possibly the most spirited of the four, I was the PO singled out for retribution. I entered the barrack room one evening to find my boots brimming with urine with a sea of hostile faces leering at me from their bunks. The other PO's appeared to have taken flight and were nowhere to be seen. But there was one kind fellow who whispered advice "watch out for the boot". It didn't take long to recognise the perpetrator of the crime. Matthews was his name, an ugly looking Liverpudlian with a demonic scowl made even more evil with his buck teeth. I looked at him and the sneer on his brutish face told the story. "What's the boy born with the silver spoon going to do about his boots" he whined in his nasal accent. "I'll deal with you, Matthews" I responded but I was not as confident as the tone of my voice. I thanked the boxing instructors of Worth and Downside that day. The bout lasted twenty minutes before the barrack room squad pulled Matthews off me. He was slowly choking me to death but not before I had jabbed his left eye into a bloodied pulp. Justice had been done and Matthews spent three days in hospital. He'd won the fight but I'd gained the high ground and never did I have an ounce of trouble from that day and the barrack room settled down.

However, I was punished for my deed and I was on Adjutant's orders the following morning. The Adjutant was something of an effete man and he hadn't exactly covered himself in glory in Malaya as I was to learn later. In addition to being confined to barracks for a week, I was admonished with the words "potential officers aren't supposed to demean themselves by fighting". He went on to say that there would be no place for me in the Green Jackets as an officer if I succeeded in passing the War Office Selection Board (WOSB), a feat that remained very doubtful in his view. I considered this verdict to be desperately unfair and I spoke to my platoon sergeant - Brown was his name - as I would have thought that a defence of honour was to be expected of potential officers. This excellent man agreed in expression but out of a professional loyalty to his officers, he couldn't exactly state his mind. He did this later when I returned from the WOSB

Examination Board where I'd passed the five day trials for acceptance to the Officer Cadet Infantry School, Eaton Hall. With me at WOSB was an officer candidate from the Green Jackets, the Honourable Julian Byng, who was to become a lifelong friend.

Close to the city of Chester lies Eaton Hall, the Westminster family home. It was an ugly edifice and as rumour had it the Duke at the time didn't protest too loudly when the War Office expropriated the ancestral home for use as the Officer Cadet School for Infantry Regiments. Eaton Hall consisted of an incongruous collection of buildings including the main palace, an impressive forecourt, a collection of Nissan huts and the famous clock tower from which, sad to say, a few young men in the history of Eaton Hall jumped to their death when the pressures of Eaton Hall became unbearable.

The cadets were drawn from all corners of Britain. There were the men from the Brigade of Guards; The Royal Marines; Scotsmen from the Black Watch, the Highland Light Infantry, the Cameronians; Welshmen from the Royal Welsh Fusiliers; Irishmen from the Inniskillings. Eaton Hall was effectively ruled by the Guards. In my time, the Commanding Officer was Colonel Basil Eugster DSO OBE MC Irish Guards. He was a friend of my mother's by coincidence and his two sons had been at Downside with me. The Regimental Sergeant Major was D.T. Lynch DCM Irish Guards, irreverently dubbed by the cadets as 'Noddy'. Colonel Eugster was a tall man but RSM Lynch was a giant in comparison – 6"4' high and girth to match. Our generation in the British army coincided with some very celebrated RSM's. The three most noted were RSM Britten who eventually became a stage and television personality; RSM Lord of Sandhurst fame; and RSM Lynch. The latter's huge stature and his awesome voice reduced us cadets to trembling jellies. It was rumoured that Lynch had driven an unfortunate Irish Guardsman with the flat of a spade into the Libyan Desert until all that remained of the poor devil was his head jutting out of the sand! Then the Sergeant Majors. The names! CSM Blood of A company and CSM Leach of C Company. Blood was seconded from the Coldstream guards and Leach from the Scots Guards. Lynch, Leach and Blood were the bane of us cadets, and there were other illustrious men of the ilk of C.S.M. Owen, and Sergeant Pickles. These were the backbone of the British army, an active and proud army in that era, and these men were at the height of their profession – formidable, strong, indomitable soldiers who'd seen action. The Commanding Officer and the Adjutant at Eaton Hall were traditionally drawn from the Brigade of Guards. The other officers were picked from the various regiments of the British army and they were good as a posting to Eaton Hall meant a guaranteed rung for promotion.

Eaton Hall was an adventure, and the secret of handling the four months of arduous training and to avoid the temptation of jumping off the clock tower, was to work hard and play hard. On more than one occasion I ran close to being RTU'd (returned to unit), a disgrace which was not worth countenancing. I and a fellow cadet called John Lodge of the Military Police were caught poaching the Duke of Westminster's pheasants. He would pilot his Vespa scooter around the hedge rows and I'd perch on the pillion cradling a .303 rifle. The purist bird shots will shudder at the spectre of shooting game birds with a rifle but shotguns weren't part of our armoury, unlike rifles, mortars, light machine guns, hand grenades and bayonets. Our method of poaching was rudimentary. Lodge would revv his Vespa at the appropriate moment and I'd discharge the .303 at a pheasant startled out of the hedgerow with the noise. We'd limit our bag to four pheasants and then carry these triumphantly into our Nissan hut and roast the birds on the paraffin stoves. All went well for the first half of the course at Eaton Hall. Lodge and I were the intake's heroes bringing back such exotic food which we'd wash down with beer or whisky, whichever was available, and then the inevitable. I should state at this stage that to make time for shooting Westminster's game, I had discovered from a fellow cadet - an explosives expert called 'Thunderflash' Emery - a short cut to the tedious spit and polish procedure designed to produce a gleaming boot. 'Thunderflash' Emery's closely guarded secret was a swift but skilful application of Luton's hat dye which he taught me providing he had his share of pheasant. Our poaching activities were progressing without hitch until the day when a game keeper nearly arrested us. We hadn't heard the low growling of the land rover behind us with the noisy revving of the

Vespa. I was busy lining up my shot on a plump cock pheasant scuttling across the field when Lodge sensed we had company. We turned to see this red-faced countryman stumbling towards us, shrieking unprintable obscenities when Lodge had the foresight to accelerate down the hedgerows with the land rover in hot pursuit. A grand prix ensued over ditches, across ploughed fields and, through streams before losing the enraged keeper and we escaped with Vespa and rifle intact but without our pheasants. It didn't take long for the resultant witch hunt to focus on the Lodge/Callender duo and we were in front of the Adjutant. Fortunately the Adjutant had a sense of humour and we gleaned he was more attuned to equestrian sports than shooting but we were threatened with the ignominy of being RTU'd and we were made to vow that the Duke's pheasants would never again be threatened. The story made the Sergeants' mess and CSM Blood capitalised on this by storming up to me on the parade ground, shrieking "march in time you 'orrible little pheasant plucker!".

Came that dark day when it rained. We were standing to attention on parade waiting for the fearsome Blood to inspect us before the morning drill session. The CSM came marching onto the parade ground, ramrod erect in his freshly pressed uniform with the white sash resplendent down his scarlet tunic, pace stick tucked under left armpit, and boots gleaming – not from Luton's hat dye of course! Until up to this fateful morning, there'd been an 'Indian summer' and Eaton Hall had enjoyed exceptional weather but it was raining steadily today and 'Thunderflash' Emery hadn't fully explained the sensitivity of Luton's hat dye to wet conditions!

The CSM was in a particularly evil mood that morning. I was in my usual place in the middle of the front rank. Before he reached me, CSM Blood had three officer cadets doubling around the parade ground for petty offences such as a 'gungy' (dirty) belt buckle or a 'spider' (a speck of dust) in the rifle barrel. Officer Cadet Callender stood proudly in all his glory, confident that his battle dress was in perfect order, belt gleaming, everything shining in the right places. Something, however, was desperately wrong with the CSM. His head kept bobbing in a strange way. Up went the cheese- cutter cap, gimlet eyes boring into mine, and then down to the tarmac. Five or six times this happened. I lost count, I was so unnerved by the strange movement of the CSM's head. Sergeant Pickles' face behind Blood was a picture – a mixture of rank disbelief and pure astonishment. Blood finally spoke. It was a ghastly sound. A mixture of a snarl and a croak. "Mr Callender, Sir, (the NCO's at Eaton Hall had to address the cadet officers by the title of Sir – but few ever meant it) bend your 'ead down very slowly and tell me what you seeee!!! Take your time Mr Callender, Sir, and tell me what this smelly black 'orrible puddle is all about!" Blood's menacing note had risen to a piercing shriek. I peered down and I saw this murky pool coagulating at my feet and this was a truly obscene sight. My boots were beginning to look like a skinned pheasant, a light pink and devoid of colour. The Luton's hat dye was staining the forecourt of Westminster's ancestral home! CSM Blood's hard eyes, devoid of expression, lasered through mine. And then Blood emitted a weird howl that could be heard a mile away. "Take this nasty man away. Get 'im out of my sight. This 'orrible man has painted his boots. Criminal offence. Take 'im away! Get 'im out!!!!" I was doubled off the parade ground by Sergeant Pickles of the Coldstream Guards and into the guard house.

I was to learn later that CSM Blood had nearly collapsed from a stroke when he reached 'Thunderflash' in the second row. Two puddles of Luton's hat dye desecrating Westminster's gracious forecourt! We were sentenced to two weeks of "jankers" – the term given to punishment duty such as peeling potatoes, swabbing out the toilets and other distasteful chores including three special inspections during the day in full kit – and ceaseless merriment raged in the Sergeants' mess at CSM Blood's expense.

Each day there was an incident at Eaton Hall – that august establishment for nurturing the flower of British youth for officerdom. I remember vividly the terrible journey to battle camp, lying on the floor of the three ton truck believing that I was dying. I'd spent the previous night in Chester carousing with Jock Ormond of the Black Watch, a gentleman of a wild disposition, and 'RTU' Sally, a noted siren of Chester, drinking shots of Scotch whisky and devouring platefuls of oysters that Sally had insisted on ordering and which we could ill afford. Oysters are demons with whisky and play havoc with the innards, I was to learn too late. Ormond had his head out of the rear flap of the truck, retching ceaselessly on the way to the bogs and hills of Transfynnyth where we were to practice battle for two weeks. I remained on the floor groaning on a field stretcher with my fellow cadets of the ilk of Lodge of the Military Police, Nick Stobbs of the Royal Marines, the Honourable Julian Byng of the Green Jackets, Tony Gould of the Ghurkhas and the evil Emery (Regt unknown) peering down at me, chorusing "Ormond and Callender have a dose of RTU Sally" in a burlesque of the Benedictine chant.

Battle camp will be remembered by every officer cadet that passed through the portals of Eaton Hall. Two weeks of very uncomfortable self-survival. The more skilled of us with the LMG (light machine gun) took out the farmers' sheep with unerring accuracy. Those of a rural upbringing became experts in blasting the trout out of the streams with hand grenades, a ruse that Captain Oddy of the Parachute regiment, one of our instructors, had perfected as rumour had it. These antics were encouraged in a strange sort of way – a form of initiative expected of an officer no doubt - and the farmers were not unhappy at having their livestock decimated on a systematic basis over a fifteen year span (Eaton hall operated from the end of the Second World War to 1960 when National Service was terminated by the Labour government) as they were compensated handsomely by the War Office. But all of us at Eaton Hall would never forget Transfynnyth in Wales for its incessant rain, the freezing weather, the mud of the trenches that we had to sleep in. And on top of this the torment meted out by the 'enemy' to whom the task of capturing the Eaton Hall cadets was delegated to the hardest of the British army. God help you if you were caught by the Kings Liverpool's or the Parachute Regiment or the notorious Highland Light Infantry as such soldiers held a mean disposition towards officer cadets.

And then the glorious finale. The day of the Passing out Parade - the graduation of the officer cadet. How we thrived on that clear, brisk winter's morning in marching in Guards style with the band playing, with the Adjutant in his finery astride his horse and the impressive Colonel Eugster taking the salute with the selected dignitaries present. And then those inimitable NCOs from the Guards – they were all there: RSM Lynch, CSM

Blood, CSM Leach, CSM Owen, Sergeant Pickles and others with pace sticks, red sashes on the splendid uniforms, gleaming boots (unassisted by Luton's hat dye) and those awesome cheese-cutter hats. We marched off the Duke of Westminster's forecourt with pride and in perfect time and even the NCOs had to admit at the party in the Sergeants' mess later that day that 'we had put up a good show'.

It was late, close to midnight, when I found myself facing Brigadier Du Plessis, the OC of 44 Para Brigade. The scenario was set where the Brigadier sat at the head of a long table flanked by the Commandants, Monty Brett and Lewis Gerber of 2 Para and 3 Para Battalions respectively, followed by a sprinkling of majors and captains. I faced the Brigadier from the other end of the table. It was somewhat of a bizarre interview with Louis Gerber trying to keep a straight face as my Afrikaans left a lot to be desired and Brigadier Du Plessis' command of the English language was somewhat slight. The interview was a hopeless non-event as the Brigadier wasn't overzealous to see a 40 year old Britisher leapfrog over a batch of keen, aspiring young men being interviewed as potential officers and in those days *uitlanders* were still regarded with more than a little suspicion by the die-hard Afrikaner. Monty Brett believed the interview had been a roaring success, but Monty would remain cheerful if Pretoria was in flames. I met up with Louis Gerber, who was to became a full colonel as OC of 44 Parachute Bde, sometime after the famous interview and he still laughs to this day at the Brigadier's bewildered expression as to what on earth was this rooinek doing, thinking he could pole-vault into the 2 Para Battalion with a commission circumventing basic training. The outcome may have been very different if Colonel Jannie Breytenbach had conducted the interview! Well, my conscience was at rest. I had volunteered to fight for King and country.

I keep in close contact with the irrepressible Monty Brett who now resides with his attractive wife, Kim, on their 60 acre holding in Nottingham Road, Natal. Monty sits on the Nottingham Road landowner's association and inevitably he's in charge of security for the area. He is to be seen on most days striding down the high street of

Nottingham Road distributing largesse with his wicked .457 hand gun discreetly tucked away in his shirt band.

It was through Monty Brett that I had the welcome opportunity in 2008 to sit next to Colonel Jannie Breytenbach and his wife at a dinner given in honour of him. We had met before at a 'Vinuchi Sporting Occasion' in 1991 which I make mention of later in the chapter. It was an honour for me to spend an evening with arguably the most illustrious warrior that served in the SADF since WW2. Having met several of his soldiers in my travels it is not difficult to understand his awesome reputation as a front line leader. Contemptuous of military politics and constantly in conflict with the High Command in Pretoria, Jannie Breytenbach was a bush fighter supreme. He left the SADF as an officer in the Tanks in 1955 to join the British Royal Navy, a fact few know of, gaining a commission in the Fleet Air Arm in which he served as a navigator and a pilot and took part in the Suez landings in 1956. He returned to the SADF in 1961 with an English wife in tow where he founded 1 Recce (the SADF's equivalent of the SAS), the famous 32 Battalion a.k.a. 'The Buffalo Soldiers', the legendary fighting unit in Angola, and 44 Parachute Brigade wherein he led the successful parachute jump into Cassinga – one of the major airborne assaults since WW2. After 37 years service, Jannie Breytenbach retired in 1987 and has written a number of books including his latest 'Eagle Strike' covering Cassinga. The Breytenbach family is multi faceted. Jannie's brother, Breyton Breytenbach, is the celebrated author and poet who lives in Paris and, contrary to what is read in the press, they speak to each other, although very different in political stance. "We're brothers after all and blood is thicker than water" Jannie will tell you.

History has a strange habit of changing fortune. Colonel Jannie Breytenbach and his 32 Battalion successfully vanquished the Cubans and their surrogates, the MPLA, in Angola. Recently as two years ago, the Colonel was visited at his home in Sedgefield, Western Cape, by a high ranking dignitary from the MPLA, informing him that the Angolan government would be honoured if Colonel Breytenbach accepted a gift of some 250,000 square hectares in the south west corner of Angola where the Cunene River meets with the Atlantic Ocean. In a nutshell, Dos Santos and his MPLA regime detest the Cubans for being heavily slighted as soldiers when the Cubans pulled out of the Angolan conflict. The MPLA had finally cottoned on to Breytenbach's pseudonym *Carpenter* which he had used in his various missives on the war and realising this was the very same warrior who'd decimated Castro's Cubans, and ironically their very own, decided to grant this eminent soldier a significant chunk of their country in the belief that this would be protected from the rapacious mining giants. The Angolan government had done assiduous research on the Colonel, unearthing amongst many other attributes that he remains a devoted conservationist of Africa's game. A worthy reward for a man who has devoted his life to defending the Republic's borders.

* * * * *

On the topic of paratroopers, Charlie Gough, a British army soccer captain and Sir Chay Blyth, the famous British sailor, were close friends in the British Parachute regiment. The CO of their battalion, Colonel Anthony Farrar-Hockley, was to become a famous general and confidant of Maggie Thatcher. These three men I got to know through the circumstances of the *'Vinuchi Sporting Occasion'* referred to in chapter 12. In 1966 two British paratroopers, Captain John Ridgway and Sergeant Chay Blyth, rowed across the Atlantic for 92 days covering 3000 miles in a tiny boat measuring only 20 foot long and five foot wide. This feat was made more remarkable in that these two soldiers had no experience of the sea. In those dreary days of Harold Wilson's Labour government and when the proud Empire was shrinking and the economy was faltering, Britain needed a dose of strong medicine such as this daring adventure, straight out of the pages of 'Boy's Own', and the intrepid paratroopers were lauded as heroes around the British Isles. I had always wanted to meet Chay Blyth, and the 'Vinuchi Sporting Occasion' presented me with the opportunity to pluck up courage and call this great adventurer. I eventually obtained his number through the Royal Thames Yacht Club, and the brusque response in a Scots accent wasn't too encouraging. I explained what our event was all about and who the preceding guest speakers had been, hoping that this blatant name-dropping would impress him. However, it appeared not by the sound of his cryptic reply - "I'll think about it!" "Can you call me back this morning" I replied, trying to appear as confident as I could with this seemingly obdurate man. "I'll think about it!" remained his laconic response. He did phone me back and he asked me to make contact with a certain Charlie Gough. The next day, I met a craggy faced Glaswegian standing at the bar of the New Club in Loveday Street, Johannesburg. Charlie Gough, his reputation as a British Army soccer captain (1962) preceding him, had been contracted to captain a leading Johannesburg Club, Highlands Park(1965 – 1973), and had remained in South Africa forging a successful career with Waltons becoming a main board director, before starting his own business. The preliminaries over, we immersed ourselves in the days of the British Army in Jordan. The Cameronians, in which I was serving at the time, and the Parachute Regiment had shared a line of defence in 1958 in the desert surrounding Amman, in preparation for battle with the enemies of King Hussein. And, incidentally, the Brigade Major happened to be Farrar – Hockley whom mention is made of in this chapter.

A strong factor in my favour with Charlie Gough was my Scots background and my service with the Cameronians. This was to his approval and an uncle of his had served in the Cameronians in the 2nd World War and this was a regiment that was essentially Glaswegian in rank and spirit. "So you were one of those 'poison dwarfs'?", Charlie asked me with a wry smile. The Regiment had earned this sobriquet from the Germans when the bulk of the battalion had marched behind the swirl of the bag-pipes to fight the barge men of Minden in 1960. 'The Battle of Minden' in West Germany created a furore in the House of Commons and the Cameronians sorely needed a leader of the ilk of Colonel 'Mad Mitch' of the Argyll & Sutherland Highlanders to save the regiment. The Cameronians were thrown to the mercy of the pusillanimous Labour government of the time which precipitated its disbandment in 1968. Chay had obviously briefed his soul mate of the Parachute Regiment to vet me and I had won my spurs. Chay Blyth, ultimately knighted for his services to yachting, is a short, barrel-chested Scot from Hawich – the border wars country over centuries passed. One can understand why this extraordinary man became the first to sail single handed around the world nonstop against the prevailing winds and tides. His strength of character saved him when he nearly perished when his tri-maran 'Beefeater 2' capsized off Cape Horn in 1984 and Chay spent 19 hours in freezing water before rescue. The man is an adventurer, through and through, and his book, 'A fighting chance' with a message inscribed to me – "next time I go you come with me!"- stands proudly in my library. Chay initiated the B.T. Global Challenge, a global race for amateur sailors, and he created a trans-Atlantic rowing race which remains an endurance feat of note. Sir Chay Blyth has helped hundreds of people, including the disabled, to test the strength of the seas and provide them with an adventure of their lifetime.

* * * * *

The path laid down by those two tough Jocks, Chay Blyth and Charlie Gough, led me to one of Britain's most revered soldiers, General Sir Anthony Farrar-Hockley GBE. KCB. DSO & Bar. MC. They would describe him as 'the soldiers' soldier' and speak of his skill in handling officers and men of the Parachute Regiment, of his impatience with ineptitude and inefficiency, and of the optimum standards he set in war and peace. Anthony Farrar-Hockley had enlisted under-age at the outbreak of the Second World War in the Gloucesters, from where he was commissioned in 1942 into the fledgling Parachute Regiment. He fought in North Africa, Greece, Italy and France and after the war he rejoined the Gloucesters, fighting in the Korean War. He was then Adjutant of the Gloucesters who put up their heroic stand at the Battle of the Imjin. Anthony Farrar-Hockley rejoined the Parachute regiment to command the 3rd Battalion and subsequently became Commandant of the Parachute Brigade, following which he was promoted to Major

General as Officer Commanding land forces in Northern Ireland and then on to command the Fourth Division in Germany. He has written a number of military history books and today stands as the official historian of the Korean War to the universities and schools. He became a close confidant to the British Prime Minister, Margaret Thatcher, as an advisor on military matters.

It was a great honour when the General agreed to address the '*Vinuchi Sporting Occasion*' at the Ellis Park rugby stadium, a venue especially chosen so that selected free-fall parachutists of the SA Parachute Regiment could stage a jump – a fitting tribute to one of the founders of the British Parachute regiment. The stadium lay silent and you could hear a pin drop as the famous warrior told the heart - wrenching story of how 650 Gloucesters defended a key position on the Imjin River in South Korea against ten thousand Chinese. For two days, the isolated Gloucesters fought heroically against the Chinese hordes until their ammunition ran out. The heroism of the Gloucesters – akin to the valour shown in the Charge of the Light Brigade in Crimea, or the 24th of Foot at Rorkes Drift in Zululand - earned them the sobriquet 'The Glorious Gloucesters' that stands intact today. 622 men out of the original band of 650 defending that hill in Korea, isolated from their British and American allies, were killed, injured or captured. The climax to the General's address was the account of his incarceration in a bamboo coffin, six feet by three feet, as punishment for daring to escape six times, and his immortal words towards the end of his speech: "if only one of those guards had just shown a morsel of kindness I might have broken".

The General told me he'd enjoyed his day, a valued compliment from this hero. In turn, we hadn't had to work very hard at Vinuchi to draw the cream of the South African Special Forces, including the aforementioned legendary Colonel Jannie Breytenbach, and some high ranking officers of the 44 Para Brigade including my old friend, Colonel Lewis Gerber, such was the lure of General Farrar Hockley. It is pertinent to add that the seating plan for the head table included some kindred spirits including Colonel Ian Mackenzie, Colonel Jannie Breytenbach, Colonel Lewis

Gerber, and the two illustrious Majors – Jack Crutchley & the 'Phantom Major', Grahame Wilson, all of whom are mentioned in this chapter. And not to forget my inveterate friend, Charlie Gough, who had suggested that I invite his former CO as a guest speaker to the 'Vinuchi Sporting Occasion'. For most years after this magnificent happening Vivienne and I would meet Sir Anthony and his charming wife, Linda at their home near Pangbourne until his sad death in 2006, and he would always ask with a charismatic smile "And tell me, Michael, about those wild officers in the Cameronians?"

* * * * *

Another soldier that served in the 2nd World War who enriched my life was Colonel Ian Mackenzie DSO and Bar. Within five years he rose from the rank of Second Lieutenant to Lieutenant- Colonel, ultimately commanding the 6th Battalion, the Royal Scots Fusiliers, at the age of 30. He experienced continuous action from being posted to France in 1940, from the retreat of the British Expeditionary Force from France, up to the fierce battle at the Gheel bridgehead when the British forces were attempting to smash their way through to link up with the 1st Airborne Division at Arnhem where he received his DSO from Field Marshall Montgomery in person; then with his Battalion leading the British forces across the Rhine, earning in the process a Bar to his DSO. Returning to South Africa, he became Chairman of the Standard Bank Investment Corporation from 1973 – 1985, and pursued a host of activities, including masterminding African Finance Consolidated, a family business often referred to as AFC; collecting Africana – books and art; running his game farms in Sabie Sand and Deka, Zhimbabwe, and his trout fishing lodge 'Santa' in the Eastern Transvaal; big game hunting and shooting throughout Southern Africa and other exotic destinations. In addition to his full life, he received a Doctorate of Law from Rhodes University and was Chancellor of the same university from 1977 to 1990. The Colonel was a fully rounded man and not to forget his family role. His charming wife, Anne, whom he met and married in Scotland, and his two sons and two daughters continued to perpetuate the family dynasty. However, tragedy was to strike the Mackenzie clan not long after the Colonel's death where his son, John, and his grandson through Jane, his second daughter, were to die in a plane crash at Rand airport.

I used to be invited on certain occasions to the Chairman's private lunches where I would be placed on his right in position of honour amongst South Africa's captains of industry. During lunch the Colonel would mutter under his breath: "Michael, buffalo hunting is much more interesting than this business talk and, by the way, I'll have to teach you not to get knocked down next time!" The Colonel was alluding to an accident I'd experienced in Zimbabwe where I'd been gored and close to losing my life as covered in chapter 4. His funeral was a fitting end to his illustrious life. There was not a dry eye as the pipers of the Transvaal Scottish of which Ian Mackenzie was the Honorary Colonel played a lament down the crowded aisles of St George's church, close to his home, Stone House.

* * * * *

I include in this collection of warriors a very special person that entered into our life. I have always harboured an admiration for a tiny country surrounded by hostile Arab states that will never rest until this biblical land is driven into oblivion. Well before I arrived in South Africa, I would read avidly of Israel's battles from the War of Independence (1948 – 1949) through to the Yom Kippur war of 1973. Mere mention of Israel's leaders, David Ben Gurion and Golda Meir, Moshe Dayan and Ariel Sharon, was sufficient to get the blood racing in adventurous hearts. I suppose that my military experience in the Middle East had a direct bearing on my interest in this turbulent part of the world and it was paradoxical that I was to live in a country which was supported in her times of need by a handful of nations and Israel was one.

I met Brigadier General Zvi Kantor, the Israeli military attaché, in his office in Pretoria some years ago. I needed material on Israel for a script I was working on and I telephoned for an interview with the General. He needed some persuading, and he found my request somewhat irregular as he put it. To gain access into the heavily guarded military attaché's office is a complicated process, particularly so for a first time. Once in, the ordeal is by no means over. You are facing a tall, stern looking Israeli tank officer who has fought in the Yom Kippur and Lebanon wars. He listens politely as you stumble through your synopsis. After an hour or so you say to yourself – that's it, the Israeli is not impressed and you shuffle your papers together preparing to shake hands and thank the General for his time. And then a smile, like the sun breaking through a wintry day. "When do we see you next, and send a manuscript through".

Regularly for the two years of his duty we saw Zvi and Michal, his attractive blonde wife, and we would meet for dinner at each others' homes. Being reasonably well versed in Israel's military history, I could talk to Zvi for hours on end and it was truly enthralling to hear at first hand of such illustrious warriors as Ariel Sharon, Colonel Danny Matt, the legendary paratrooper, now a General as Zvi recently informed me, and others who fought gallantly for the brave country. Zvi would tell me that he was fond of Ariel Sharon and he'd served under him in many a tank battle. We were privileged to celebrate the 50th anniversary of Israel at the Embassy. One evening, the Kantors brought the Russian military attaché (Naval) and his wife to our home for dinner. It was a hilarious experience as Commander Alexei Moissev from Moscow loved hunting and drinking. We'd been warned that Moissev would have us up till dawn. The Kantors weren't far wrong as Moissev would find any excuse to propose a toast and he was in his element standing at the head of the dining table on the stoep raising his glass to the various game trophies adorning the walls. We had a return match at his home and my head was near to bursting following numerous toasts of vodka to Israel's rapprochement with Russia and his friendship with Brigadier General Kantor; to the Marco Polo sheep trophy that I'd hunted in Tajikistan; to the noble sport of hunting; to the Mil-8 helicopter that had borne me to the Pamir Mountains. The last gave cause to Zvi to claim triumphantly "We used to shoot your Mil – 8s out of the skies!" "How could you shoot such beautiful things" riposted Alexei, by now in full flight and he even toasted Vivienne's fur coat that she was wearing for dinner. "The mink is a symbol of the might of Russia!" roared Alexei Moissev. The Russians didn't believe in central heating and the Moissev house in Pretoria was close to freezing and hence the women wearing their fur coats. By this stage Zvi, Michal and Vivienne were reeling as they are frugal drinkers and they had to endure this rampant Russian until two in the morning.

It was a sad day when Zvi was recalled to Tel Aviv. However, we keep in touch and only recently we had a glorious reunion in the Luberon Valley, Provence, with Svi, Michal, and two friends of theirs from Israel where we celebrated in regal style. So from the first uncomfortable meeting there blossomed one of those solid friendships that enrich a life. We'll have to go to Tel Aviv soon which will promise to be a rewarding experience.

*   *   *   *   *

It was a momentous occasion when a Cameronian and a Gordon Highlander were to meet after a gap of fifteen years in the military museum of Dundee, Northern Natal. It was akin in a modest way to the historic encounter between Livingstone and Stanley as both of us officers of Scottish regiments had had a fairly adventurous life by any standards. I had first met Rob Gerrard outside the Balalaika kroeg in Sandown - an appropriate venue perhaps – where he had just completed a seven year stint in the British armed forces, first serving with the Gordon Highlanders (1959 - 1963) which his father, Colonel BJD Gerrard DSO & Bar had commanded in WW2, and then seconded to the Sarawak Rangers (1963 – 1966) in Malaysia. Our conversation veered towards our experiences in exotic places such as Borneo, Malaysia, Thailand, Jordan and the Arabian Peninsula. A friendship blossomed from that chance encounter for some 25 years where, amongst many riotous escapades, I had served as his best man at one of the most uproarious weddings ever known to man putting Hugh Grant's comedy '4 weddings and a funeral' into the shade; to a nerve-racking Le Mans style race from Johannesburg to Durban in the midst of night; to sinking a pairs scull at a prestigious regatta at the Roodeplaat Dam; and many, many more carousings which beggar belief. Rob's business life was as vibrant as his military career where he ran the WK Croxton trading agency taking him to China on a regular basis before a messy irritancy with another company led him to return to his favourite Natal, his birthplace. Rob then continued to flourish in a new career which suited his multi faceted nature which commenced with working with David Rattray of the Anglo – Zulu wars fame before he struck out on his own, becoming a recognised authority on the Zulu and Boer Wars. He is the author of five books on these subjects, is a Fellow of the Royal Geographical Society (1998), and a Member of The International Guild of Battlefield Guides (2010).

A certain Colonel Michael Goldschmidt who had commanded The Royal Leicester Regiment a.k.a. 'The Tigers' inflamed the resolve for the author to resume contact with Rob Gerrard. I happened to be standing on a peg next to the colonel on a shoot hosted by the renowned Michael de Pelet and whiling away the time prior to the arrival of the birds, I mentioned Rob Gerrard knowing the Colonel had been to Ampleforth. The reaction was spontaneous – "holy mackerel – where do you know him from!" The pheasants started streaming in and we continued the discussion later that evening in Michael de Pelet's Grand Hall beneath the crocodile & buffalo trophies which Rob Gerrard would have fully approved of. It turned out that Michael Goldschmidt was three years his junior at Ampleforth. He described Rob: "He was a killer as a flank forward and a very fine athlete. Please give him my very best regards. He might also be interested to receive his father's citation for his DSO. I have a book on the DSO medal".

I called Rob from Malawi when I returned to Africa shortly after the aforementioned shoot in Dorset. Thus it led to the celebrated reunion which was witnessed by Braam Cronje, the Dundee farmer. We had a lot to catch up on in 'The Miners Arms', including the story of how Rob had survived an ambush in Zululand where he shot one of the culprits and the other criminal was caught shortly after and both are in gaol. Natal will feature on my Africa itinerary for many years to come and this will include Rob Gerrard and his modus operandi at Isandlwana.

* * * * *

It is a fitting conclusion to this chapter on the fighting men to hold a bosberaad on the battlefields of South Africa with a staunch friend who is a Boer in every sense – by birth, in size and appearance, and in strength of mind and body. Later that day after meeting Rob Gerrard, we found ourselves and our wives taking sundowners sitting besides the picturesque lake on Cronje's farm conversing in quiet tones whilst appreciating the kudu and the waterbuck making their way down the hillside to drink. The conversation drifted to the many battles and skirmishes fought in Natal, many of which were close to Braam's farm in the Dundee district. Braam Cronje is a multi faceted fellow and in addition to his prowess as a farmer and sportsman, he is well versed in the history of his country. The conversation between the Boer and the Brit was riveting and furious in pace as the sun set over the brilliant landscape of Northern Natal. My view expressed to the small gathering was that fighting was in the blood of South Africa's diverse people, whether they are Zulus, Boers, or the English speaking. This explains Shaka, the Zulu warrior chieftain; 'Sailor' Malan, the Battle of Britain ace; General Jan Smuts, the titan who was revered by Winston Churchill; and the warriors of recent times – General Constand Viljoen and Colonel Jannie Breytenbach. I referred to Braam's namesake and distant relative, General Piet Cronje, the scourge of the 51st Highland Division at Magersfontein and I quoted a description of the General from Conan Doyle's work 'The Great Boer War': *"a hard, swarthy man, quiet of manner, but fierce of soul, with a reputation among a nation of resolute men for unsurpassed resolution".*

Braam responded, describing the emotive account of the Battle of Blood River on December 16th, 1838, where his great, great grandfather and 470 Voortrekkers led by Andries Pretorius formed a lager on the Ncome River in Zululand, beating off 10,000 of Dingaan's Zulus. After two hours of furious fighting over 3000 dead were piled against the wagons with the Boers suffering only three wounded. The corpses were dumped in the river and the water ran red and hence the name 'Blood River' which is commemorated annually by *The Day of the Covenant*.Some years later a similar heroic feat was enacted by the 24th of Foot, where less than a hundred Welshmen repelled 4000 Zulu impis with Martini Henry .450's, drawn bayonets and rifle butts at Rorke's Drift, not far from Cronje's other farms near Dundee and Helpkemaar. The discussion then alluded to the heroism and gallantry of both sides in the Boer War displayed at Magersfontein, Spion Kop, Colenso, Modder River, and Paardeberg to name only a few of a long litany of fiercely fought battles throughout the vast country of South Africa. We discussed the Generals - Lord Roberts VC, 'Bobs' as he was affectionately called by his British troops - a leader revered for not only his military prowess but his concern for the welfare of his soldiers. This was a seasoned campaigner of India in the Wellington mould, and a hardened warrior in the 2nd Afghanistan War 1878 - 1880, and he is acclaimed to have earned the affection of regimental officers and soldiers on a deeper scale than any leader of the British Army at the time. Then the courageous Sir Redvers Buller VC but of questionable military intelligence; of 'Fighting Mac', General Hector Macdonald who was sent for to replace General Wauchope killed at Magersfontein. A grizzled Scot who had worked his way through the ranks as a private to reach the pinnacle as a general, he could speak to his highlanders in their own rough vernacular to lift their spirit from their drubbing at Magersfontein. And the Irishman, General Fitzroy Hart, the leader of the 'Faugh a Ballagh' boys – the Inniskilling Fusiliers, the Dublin Fusiliers, the Connaught Rangers, all forming Hart's famous Irish Brigade. Hart was the quintessential fighting man's General, impervious to danger and not short of hauling a laggard through the ranks by his ears to express his dislike of shirkers!

This led to Braam interrupting: "Michael, it sounds as if the British army consisted only of Scots & Irish – such as you & Gerrard!" We were well into our whisky by this stage of the evening and I roared with this appreciation of the Celt from my Boer companion. I countered his injudicious comment with a sober riposte: "As Celts, Rob & I would be tempted to agree with you but it should be remembered that virtually every regiment in the British army fought in the Boer War, and those stoical men from the counties of England, not to forget the Guards regiments and the Rifle Brigade, stood firm against the withering fire of your hard - bitten guerilla fighters! These dependable, solid troops might not possess the brilliance and daring of the passionate and explosive Celtic men in their trews and kilts, but they formed the bulk of the British army. And we should not forget the auxiliary forces such as Major Mike Rimington's 'Tigers'. These were regarded as the most effective scouts for the British – some 200 colonial horsemen who wore leopard skin bands around their slouch hats to distinguish them from the Boers as they spoke the taal and Zulu and they looked like the enemy.

And then Braam painted a picture of his leaders: "We've covered Piet Cronje at length but then there were other great Boer generals, the steely, experienced veldt leaders as Louis Botha and Piet Joubert who led our men in Natal; Koos De la Rey, a solemn and austere man with hawk eyes; Christiaan De Wet who led the *'Bitter – Einders'*; and there were characters such as Danie Theron, the famed scout. They led the fellows who blew up trains, could gallop at the speed of wind whilst firing their Mausers with unerring accuracy - they gave the world the meaning of *Guerilla*".

I concluded before we sojourned to the homestead for dinner. "When we were studying modern history at school, we were given the Boer War to read up and discuss. All of us in the classroom would debate on how a bunch of frontiersmen could hold up the might of the British Empire. This at a time when the British were at the peak of their empire and their soldiers were battle seasoned and hardened by constant campaigning in Africa. The Boer War in contrast to the atavistic savagery of the Zulu Wars was a chivalrous conflict. As the military historian Ian Knight described it: *"The British did not generally hate or fear the Boers in the same way as they hated or feared many of their black enemies.....whilst the troops seldom had any qualms in destroying Zulu or Maori homes, for example, or blowing up Pathan villages. Many soldiers felt deeply uncomfortable about the policy of forcibly removing Boer civilians to concentration camps and burning their farms. This mutual respect manifested itself in a number of ways, including the care afforded by each side for the other's wounded".* Unlike the Zulu conflict, atrocities were few and far between. For example, compare the defeat of the 51st Highland Division at Magersfontein, where chivalry was extended by the Boers to allow the Scots to attend to their wounded, to the carnage at Isandlwana where 1300 dead Welshmen were slashed open from sternum to groin; some had been scalped, some mutilated, their genitals cut off and stuffed into their mouths; where two small drummer boys were discovered hung up by their chins on butchers hooks. To us schoolboys, the Boer War was an adventure on the wide open spaces of the veldt. We conjured up visions of slouch hatted wild looking men racing across the countryside on horseback, firing at the 'Khakis', and disappearing to lay another ambush amongst the rocks and dongas of the veldt. It's when you have spent forty years here that you get an inkling what this war was all about. Both sides were replete with hard, tough men but both essentially white and Christian. On the British side there were men from the Australian outback – 'Breaker' Morant for good example; the Rhodesian irregulars, seasoned bush fighters who had fought the Matabele; the New Zealander contingent; and soldiers from the Indian army."

Braam concluded: "Facing them were the men who were descended from the Huguenots, supported by a band of rebels fighting against the mighty British Empire including a collection of French, Dutch and Irish mercenaries. The Boer forces had townsmen - english speaking businessmen and men of the professions - but the hard core were the sunburnt, tangle haired, bearded men of the veldt, the hunters and farmers who were accustomed to living a hard life with a rifle and bible in hand. These were the men who were cheered on by the world to give the British a come- uppance for their empirical arrogance".

৪৩ ♦ ৫৪

CHAPTER NINE

The Duzi Rats

To the lost man, to the pioneer penetrating a new
country, to the naturalist who wishes to see the wild
land at its wildest, the advice is always the same –
follow a river. The river is the original forest highway.
It is nature's own Wilderness Road.

Edwin Way Teale

SOUTH AFRICA produces immensely talented endurance athletes – something to do with the pressing call of the great outdoors, the constant drive to conquer challenges, the eternal quest for adventure. There is a river called The Umsindusi in Natal – commonly referred to as 'the Duzi' - that snakes its way from Pietermaritzburg through the 'Valley of a Thousand Hills' to Durban. The Duzi is not the largest river in South Africa by any means. It's not the most savage river compared to the Umkomaas or the Tugela, but it hosts perhaps the most charismatic of all the river races in the Republic.

A lot of sports have been sanitised by marketing and over-exposure, but the Duzi stands for a genuine test of skill, endurance, strength and extreme fitness. There is something simple, rugged and old fashioned about this ultra distance race. There are many dangers: one can get trapped by rocks and get sucked under; hitting one's head on a rock and toppling unconscious into the water; a limb can be broken while portaging the boat over rocks and dongas; a head can be cracked open on a low-lying bridge; there's the chance of getting stoned by hostile locals; of suffering from sunburn and dehydration from the extreme heat; or catching unmentionable diseases from the bacteria in the water. Anyone of athletic ability can aspire to run a road marathon; few are equipped to finish the Duzi. Well before I entertained the notion of tackling this awesome race, I recall the televised interviews with the competitors – both the front runners and the back markers. I was struck by not only their will to complete the race as well as they could but their capacity for life. These hardy men, and not to forget the handful of gutsy women, were doing it because the Duzi was a challenge – a tough, tiring and painful challenge but nevertheless fun at the same time. The likes of Graham Pope-Ellis, Danny Biggs, Tim Cornish, Mark Perrow, Martin Dreyer and others worthy of mention as leaders of the Duzi were infinitely more flesh and blood than certain of the sleekly packaged sporting icons that we are exposed to today. The 12O km canoe marathon staged over three days is Africa's answer to the Grand National steeplechase or the Oxford and Cambridge boat race.

There's a spate of reasons why the 'Duzi rats' – the accolade given to the river men who've completed more than five races – return year after year to brave the stifling heat and humidity, the gruelling portages over steep, bush-strewn hillsides, the challenging rapids – some of these daunting – and the ever present risks of incurring the infamous 'duzi guts'. In the days when the 'Valley of a Thousand Hills' was abundant in game and reptiles, canoes were rudimentary affairs constructed out of canvas and wood. It took an adventurer and renowned naturalist, Dr Ian Player (brother of the famous golfer, Gary), to persuade a handful of like-minded men to the race the Duzi. The inaugural event of 1952 took the intrepid group four days and nights to complete the 120 kilometre stretch through untamed country and unchartered waters. Since those early days the mystique of the Duzi canoe marathon has steadily gained notoriety and the mere mention of the Duzi pricks the ears of canoe marathoners and adventurers. The race now shares a similar status with the Comrades, a sister Natalian event, but unlike the Comrades which rates up to 20 000 runners, the Duzi is restricted to a mere 1500 to 2000 canoeists. The explanation to this is the mixture of risk that confronts the athlete. Not many perish in the river – perhaps one in every second event – but there is the perennial hazard of the gut wrenching water-borne disease caused through contamination by the hordes of locals that reside in the valley. There's the threat of heat stroke and dehydration where temperatures can reach up to the mid 40's centigrade. In addition to the challenges of the extremities of climate, the rapids of the river, the habitual hazards of the 'Duzi guts' and the awesome hills up which the river men have to carry their boats – 'Burma Road' is a prime example – there are other hazards such as the black mamba, Africa's deadliest snake, that struck Colin Van Heerden in the 2002 event. This canoeist was within an inch of dying according to the Umhlanga hospital and the tremendous spirit of the Duzi was at the fore when fifteen boats stopped to help the stricken Van Heerden with Natal Canoe club mate, Greg Eayrs, standing shocked by the horrible incident. The Duzi paddler lay in a coma for 36 hours, and it was a miracle that the athlete survived, thanks to a helicopter hovering on hand to airlift him to hospital.

Snakes aside, the Duzi River is vulnerable to the robbers that roam the valley and a week before the 2001 event, an armed ambush sparked new safety fears for the race. A party was picnicking at a spot just belong the Inanda Dam when four armed men walked out of the bush saying they'd come to swim when seconds later the group was surrounded, stripped of their clothes, and robbed of their 4 x 4 vehicle. "We're lucky not to have been shot or raped. We'll never in our lives go into that area again, but we are really worried about the Duzi canoeists" stated the spokesman for the group. Three days later a young contender for the Duzi, 20 year old Hank McGregor, was robbed by panga-wielding thieves whilst he was training near the 'Island' rapids. During the Duzi race several years ago two lonely paddlers at the rear of the field were robbed of their watches. This led to the organisers warning canoeists training for the race on the dangers of the Molweni valley that stretches below the Inanda Dam. The organisers are quick to state that the Duzi is no exception to South Africa's rampant crime problem. This explains the presence of 150 policemen on foot plus a further 200 on motorbikes and platoons of soldiers, in addition to the divers, and the helicopters to protect the canoeists in their drive to conquer the Duzi.

The purist canoeist tends to avoid the Duzi. He'll call it a freak race or as one lady Springbok paddler described it: 'The Grand National of the Canoeing Calendar'. Akin to the Grand National run at Aintree - this majestic horse race that enthrals millions of television viewers that have never sat on a horse - the Duzi has a majesty of its own, a vast following on television where sportsmen and armchair onlookers alike are glued to the live coverage of this spectacle, in spite of the unlikelihood of their ever taking to paddling a canoe. I could write volumes on this red-blooded adventure. I would not be the first but I will endeavour to provide the reader with a graphic account of what this extraordinary obstacle course is all about.

*   *   *   *   *

In 1991, I partnered in a double boat with Tony 'Moggy' Lightfoot. We were of the same age and of the same fitness level and we'd proved our compatibility in the mighty Fish River two day event and the strenuous Vaal marathon -120 kilometres in two days- and we entered the Duzi with confidence and high spirits. We had a cracking start and sailed down the Umsinduzi passing boat after boat and a lot of them youngsters. We had a spectacular pile-up at Mission to the entertainment of the crowds massing the bank at this relatively manageable raid where we finally managed to disengage ourselves from the jumble of boats that had piled up on the rocks and continued down the river.

But then disaster struck. Moggy, the veteran man of the river which he indisputably is, can be prone to break all reason and act in a very curious way when logic and common sense are discarded. Thus when I bellowed at the compulsory 'Finger-Neck' portage: "Stop! Stop! We have to get the hell out! This is going to be a f...up!" Moggie was undeterred by the sight of hundreds of canoeists streaming over a hill which was the portage.

They'd got out in time with respect to the rules of the race. And all he could shout was "Paddle, man, paddle!" We turned the corner and we knew from the furious roar of the infamous Finger-Neck rapid that this was a serious boat breaker and, indeed, there sat one disconsolate Duzi racer, his boat in a heap of shredded fibreglass, waving his arms furiously. "Get out! You'll smash up!" We were too late. We were committed to an ignominious end. "Hold on" shrieks Moggy and then the canoe catapulted into a morass of foaming water and evil-looking rocks and we were in half, literally. The force of the water jammed Moggy in between two rocks, trapping his foot whilst he valiantly clung on to his half of the boat. I'd been swept down river and I honestly thought that my end had come. The river was raging at this point and I surfaced at least a kilometre downstream to find the other half of the canoe barrelling towards me. I managed to leap on to it and haul it to the bank with a great degree of difficulty as the river was deep at this point. And what was serious was that I'd swallowed copious amounts of the contaminated river and I was a sure candidate for the dreaded 'Duzi guts'. I struggled back to find my partner gripping onto his half of the boat, unable to free his foot. I heaved the submerged craft or what was left of it, off the rocks and prized my partner's foot free. Luckily no bones were fractured.

I looked long and hard at Moggy with a dark scowl on my face and at least he had the grace to appear crestfallen. "Sorry, Mike" the gravel voice rumbled. "We got it slightly wrong!" "*We got it wrong. You got it wrong!*" I barked. I looked at him again for a long time and then broke out into a peel of laughter. "Those youngsters we passed", I was now hysterical with mirth, "They are going to have a field day!" And a field day they certainly had. As we trudged up the dirt track to the water point at the top of the Finger Neck portage, each carrying a piece of the canoe, there were taunts of "Here come the young raging bucks!" The youngsters we'd overtaken earlier on were returning our medicine.

Tony Beith, our second, was there to greet us at the finish of the first day. We were one of the last in, our boat spliced together with a branch. Beith was taken aback at the sight of his two charges and the smashed up canoe. We all believed the boat was irreparable and we pleaded with the officials to bend the rules. But, predictably, they remained intractable. There's a strict regulation that boats cannot be replaced in the Duzi and this applies to river racing in general. We were in for a merry nightmare. It began to drizzle and we had to join the two pieces with rivets, then apply resin and catalyst, and force dry the resin with a blow-torch. It was a major piece of reconstruction requiring hours of interminable labour in the light rain and we were seriously tired after a gruelling day. Tony Beith was a power house in maintaining our spirits and his contribution to mending the smashed canoe was invaluable. It wasn't until eleven at night that we wound our way out of the valley in search of food. We were tired and we were cold and we needed solid sustenance for the day ahead.

We completed the next day without major incident although the canoe was wickedly heavy with the extra burden of 16 steel rivets and many overcoats of resin. But that night brought the dark devil of the 'Duzi guts'. I was on my hands and knees vomiting and I crouched on the loo seat for most of the night with a dose of heavy diarrhoea. I was sharing a room with the stalwart Tony Beith in the bleak, cheerless hotel we were billeted in and he remarked as he was taping my shoulders at five in the morning that I was looking a very sick man. "Keep it from Moggy", I urged him. "We'll finish the race first".

I looked around me at the start and I could see bodies lying prone – all victims of the contaminated water - and I was to learn later from the press reports that 90% of the field had contracted severe gastro-enteritis and raging fever, some of whom were admitted to hospital. Dr Ian Walton, the Pietermaritzburg medical officer, had stated: "Without today's sophisticated medicine and hospital facilities, many competitors of the Duzi canoe marathon might have died!" Walton explained the problem further: "There had been a period of drought before the start of the Duzi, but when it rained just before the race, because of a build up of contamination on the banks, all the faeces was washed into the Duzi".

Just after the string of rapids preceding the last flat stretch to the finish line at the Blue Lagoon, the 'Duzi guts' began to overwhelm me. I'd kept my weakening state away from Moggy but he could sense my parlous condition being the experienced canoeist he is. I was in a state of fever and cramping badly and I paddled the last 16 kms in a daze. I was in a bad way and to compound my misery, I was expected to speak to the Duzi committee on the handling of the Ian Green trophy which twelve of us, including Tony Beith and Moggy Lightfoot, had contributed in respect of his death in the race the previous year owing to a heart attack. I ran a temperature of 103° that afternoon and I deemed myself lucky that I had managed to finish.

* * * * *

Then there's the tale of Tony Beith and his son, Gareth. The two powerfully built men had decided to challenge the Duzi as a father and son team. They'd done the training and completed the qualifiers before Gareth took off for Scotland for the Christmas break. One week before the start, Gareth – a young fellow of a somewhat wild disposition – returned with glowing reports of the Scottish lasses and the Edinburgh bars. The young man was a trifle out of condition and on the very first portage known as Campbell's was heard to remark to his father: "What the hell is that!" pointing to the line of canoes snaking up the formidable hill through the cane fields. "That's Campbell's portage, and we're only at the start of it, young man, all thirteen kilometres of it!" replied Beith senior. Back in the river, Gareth managed to topple out on a flat stretch. "He just fell out, can you believe it? He was in behind me one moment, and out the next!" Tony Beith told me at the finish of the first day.

Then the fun started in earnest the second day. I was paddling with Lionel Benham – also a grandmaster (competitors over 60) and a highly experienced river man - when we heard a shout from the banks at the Confluence Rapid. The Beith pair had taken a tumble and repairs were needed to the rudder system. Later in the race we saw David and Chris Beith, Tony's sons who were seconding their father and their step brother. I asked them how the Beith boat was faring to learn that the duo were just behind us before the final stretch to the finish. Moggy Lightfoot was seconding Lionel Benham and me and we waited in vain for the Beith combination at the finish line.

As dusk was beginning to fall, I asked the marshalling team if there was any news of the Beiths but the response was negative. Understandably David and Christopher Beith were beginning to agitate so we decided to back-track and attempt to find them in the remote areas of the Duzi valley. At that moment an army truck careered around the corners crammed with soldiers clutching R1 rifles and a canoe sticking out at right angles. We called the truck to a halt and there was the hilarious sight of three grinning big white men, one canoe and thirty black soldiers. We had to hear the story and we got a blow by blow account – yet another in the litany of dramas in the history of the Duzi. They'd mended the boat at the Confluence where we last saw them and off they set only to have the rudder system fail in a turbulent stretch of the water. The force of the river took them into the fork of a submerged tree and there they sat suspended whilst canoes rushed past either side of them. Tony Beith had had the Duzi up to his teeth by this stage, what with his son toppling out of the boat for no reason and then being side-swiped by a pair of novices at the Confluence Rapid and now this! With some difficulty in the raging waters, the pair salvaged what they could out of the canoe which remained jammed in the tree.

And then out of the blue emerged a paddler nursing his smashed canoe down the river. His boat was tied together by branches. He was a big powerful man, as many are in the race, and he was a prop forward in the Roodepoort Rugby team, a club notorious for robust play. They shook hands and down they went – three men in a tub – hanging on for dear life to the rugby player's broken canoe. It was miracle that they survived the rapids – some of them fairly fierce at this remote stretch of the Duzi – without the aid of paddle or rudder until they could venture no further. The boat had breathed its last sigh. So the next problem was posed – how to get out of the jungle. The three canoeists had found themselves deserted in a wild, remote section of the river. They clambered their way through the dense bush in bare feet and Tony Beith stated that he saw at least three snakes with Garth claiming that he nearly stepped on a python! They laboured on until ultimately they hit a track and to their amazement there, in the midst of the jungle, was an extraordinary apparition - a taxi bouncing their way. The genial African driver told them that they were fortunate not to be attacked by a gang of robbers that was known to prowl this particular part of the valley and he agreed to give them a lift to a general dealer store from where they had to make their way back to the finish. As further luck had it, an army truck was standing at the store and the sergeant in charge agreed to give a lift to the three canoeists plus their boat.

They were lucky those men not to have been stranded on the banks of the river for the night. The valley isn't a safe place at the best of times. "It was an adventure", Tony Beith told us weeks later. "Here we were, clinging on for dear life to this rudderless canoe as we bounced through rapid after rapid only to come to a grinding halt in the middle of the densest bush you can imagine. We were nearly bitten to death by hordes of mosquitoes and a swarm of wild bees, and the snakes! I swore I saw a black mamba and we were ripped to pieces by the thorns and our feet were in a mess as we'd lost our shoes in the river. We'd nothing to eat, nothing to drink and we were beginning to hallucinate. But that huge Afrikaner rugby prop was magnificent. He kept us laughing and the black taxi driver! He was a fat, jolly fellow and all we had to give him was an empty water bottle and a racing cap. Then those soldiers. They loved the drama and we kept them amused with our story. But thank God we got out of there without our throats slit!"

* * * * *

There are so many incidents around this famous race that are too numerous to recount within the brief framework of this story. On one Duzi , I remember hopping over a deep ditch with Tony Beith at the start of the infamous Ngumeni portage – a mean climb of three kilometres and peering down at an imploring white face looking up from the depths of the hole. "Help me – please someone help me!" We were too committed to stop but we did alert a marshal not far from the unfortunate paddler.

There was the occasion of the 1998 race, where three canoeists bringing up the rear on the first day were attacked by a gang of thieves. In a manner reminiscent of the famous Rorke's Drift battle in the Zulu war, the three stalwarts fended off the thugs using their paddles as bayonets. Finally they were able to jump into their boats and paddle off with their assailants running along the banks hurling rocks at the unfortunate canoeists.

It's a well known adage of the Duzi that you must know your partner well. There was the case of a wild spirited character called Noel Attwood-Smith who decided to tackle the Duzi in a double in the sixties when anyone could enter the race, without qualifying points and without any canoeing experience, and where there were no cut off times. He'd never canoed in his life and despite his prowess as a rugby flanker – he played for Natal in the celebrated company of Tommy Bedford and Keith Oxlee – he was ill equipped for an event of this ilk. The pair capsized at the Ernie Pierce weir 800 metres from the start and they fell out at every rapid en route until they struggled in at the finish at 9.00 p.m. well after dark. Noel wanted to pack it in but his partner had other ideas. For the two remaining days, the pair limped down the Duzi, battered and bruised, and the only method in which Noel's partner succeeded in persuading his mate to continue was to lay a trail of smarties along the portages. They finally made it to the Blue Lagoon. It had taken them 27 hours!

* * * * *

The Duzi is renowned for the fights between the competitors and over the three days it's not uncommon to see grown men squaring up to each other. The pain, the pressure and the temperature can lead to heated tempers and shortened fuses. Talking of such fights, Lionel Benham and I nearly came to blows during the second day of the race in 2000. It was a scorcher of a day and Lionel was beginning to needle me about my tardiness in securing my splash cover to the cockpit on the put-ins. We had grounded the canoe in readiness for a portage when I saw no sign of my partner. I then heard a loud splashing noise and there was the fellow basking in the shallows like some elephant cooling off. This was too much and we started slagging each other, Lionel for being slow on the portages because he was running unfit, and me for being useless with my splash cover. The row reached the ears of several passing canoeists, most of whom were many years younger as us grandmasters are a rarity in the Duzi, and in turn the ranks of the onlookers on the bridge ahead were regaled by the same canoeists that there was a serious rumpus going on between two old 'toppies'. Moggy Lightfoot happened to be there and he told us later of the hilarious reports reaching the bridge.

I recall one race when at the start of the second day – the Duzi Bridge – this big Afrikaner chasing a horde of picanins who'd been helping themselves to his Mars bars that he had painstakingly taped to his cockpit. The large, muscular canoeist was to be seen haring after the pack of six urchins into the distance, bellowing like a wounded buffalo bull. He would be late for his batch start, I conjectured at the time.

* * * * *

The Duzi canoe marathon, a uniquely South African event like the Comrades, sadly sees the back of many first timers. The event is hard, admittedly, and hazardous. Hazardous in terms of life loss: the Ian Green saga, for example, where the young, fit man of age 40 died of a heart attack at the foot of the Guinea Fowl portage; hazardous to limb – many an entrant fractures an ankle or breaks a bone; and hazardous for other reasons such as the canoeist who was bitten by a black mamba. The odd drowning does occur and hospitalisation is necessitated through heat stroke, exhaustion, and gastro-enteritis as aforementioned. The rapids are daunting, particularly on the last day around Burma Road, but then there are the 'Duzi Rats' who live for one race and one race only and that's the Duzi.

I will always remember the 2002 race with nostalgia. It may be my last; I am not sure at this stage. As strong and as fit as one fortunately is for a man approaching his mid sixties, the event is so strenuous that sense is beginning to raise its head, but who knows. If 2002 was to be my last Duzi, it certainly was one of the most memorable. It was Bruce Fordyce, the Comrades marathon king, who gave Moggy Lightfoot and me the idea two months before the race. We were putting some endurance training in at Emmerentia Dam, the home of the Dabulamanzi canoe club, where Moggy Lightfoot, Tony Beith, myself and a handful of other grandmasters have been members since the days when the club was a small but elitist body and when the canoeing sport was fledgling. Today the Dabulamanzi is the largest of its kind in South Africa with five hundred odd members. Bruce, always of a quick wit and sense of humour to match, jokingly suggested that us two would be probably the only grandmaster pair and the oldest in age in the race and we should apply for the celebrity batch to which he and his partner, Gary Boast were invited. To give the man his due it was his idea but it was Moggy who must take the credit of badgering John Oliver, a leading light in the Duzi committee, to allow us into the celebrity batch. The honour has huge advantages. One starts third out of thirty batches in the cool of the day – if you can call 30 degrees centigrade at 6.00 a.m. cool – and the benefit of being part of a colourful collection of famous names: men like Gary Teichman and Henry Honiball, the legendary Springbok rugby players, and a host of other sporting luminaries such as Brett Taylor, an ex welterweight boxing champion of South Africa, and a score of others.

At 6.20 a.m., we entered the water at Campbell's Drift, and already at this early hour the temperature was well into the 30's centigrade and sweat was beginning to pour off us. We were in for a blistering day. Down we roared over the Ernie Pierce weir, the first obstacle and a mere 800 metres from the start. Already the race was claiming victims and by a narrow squeak we avoided crashing into a submerged boat, its crew desperately trying to save it from the hordes of canoeists bearing down on them from the chute of the Ernie Pierce weir. We portaged around the Commercial Road weir hot on the heels of Bruce Fordyce and Gary Boast, a short lived experience sadly, and then churned through Taxi Rapid and Low Level Bridge. There was no stopping the two grandmasters but then came the sun and the heat. The 8 km Campbell's Portage through the cane fields was a true test of grit, strength and stamina and already at this early stage of the race the strain was beginning to show on the faces of the river men.

The drama of the Duzi on that first day began to unfold at the notorious Guinea Fowl portage, over half way into the first leg of 40kms. I saw strapping young men sitting on the ground, wearing the '1000 yard stare' given to front-line soldiers. There were canoeists on hands and knees, or lying spread eagled from the ravaging heat as by 11.00 a.m. that morning, four hours into the race, the temperature had reached the 44 centigrade mark (102 degrees Fahrenheit!). We had taken a swim on that first day, just after the 'Hole in the Wall' rapid, leaving Moggy Lightfoot without a hat and with the loss of a shoe. The tough veteran raised in the Rhodesian bush had to hobble up the steep Guinea Fowl portage with one shoe. Whilst climbing up this cruel hill, my mind went back to 1990 where Ian Green, a close friend of mine, tragically died from a heart attack at this very spot. I made a mental note to talk to the organisers to nail a plaque to the tree where he'd collapsed.

Then followed the really arduous and unpleasant stage of this particular portage – the steep descent into 'Devil's Cauldron' where the canoeists have to heave and haul their boats through dense bush and rock-strewn dongas. The journey through 'Devil's Cauldron' – so aptly named – commands brute strength and those competitors who hadn't paced themselves suffer the consequences. We arrived at the finish line in one piece to find scores of exhausted, dehydrated canoeists in various stages of disrepair. There was Jomo King, the President of Transvaal rugby- a member of the SA Rugby Football union board and a Duzi veteran- lying sprawled on the ground, out for the count. The sun had wreaked a savage toll and we learnt that several competitors had to be casevaced out of the valley by helicopter.

The start of day two brought cooler weather and we could thank the Gods for this. We had borne-up well from the previous day, despite some severe cramping experienced by Moggy Lightfoot and an injury to my left hand which threatened to be a hairline fracture. This had been incurred through a collision into the rock face of the Tegwaan Rapid the previous day. We were doing nicely up to the first half of the 50 km leg of the second day. We had shot the tricky Confluence Rapids well and had taken the Marianny Foley rapid into our stride when disaster struck at Big Bend – a long surging rapid which takes many an unwary canoeist by surprise. A submerged rock tossed us into the water and the two grandmasters found themselves entwined with each other with myself on top and Lightfoot underneath, bouncing off a chain of nasty-looking rocks. What was unnerving was the sight of the boat that was careering down the fast flowing river in the direction of Durban. Mercifully we disentangled ourselves and I managed to catch up with the boat just in the nick of time before our craft wrapped in half. It took a herculean effort to empty the canoe and then we saw to our concern a lady canoeist being swept up in the swift current of the rapid. Lightfoot was already peeling off his splash cover to swim out to the panic stricken woman but then the spirit of the Duzi came to the fore. We yelled at two powerfully built canoeists surging down Big Bend in a double to save the terrified lady and they struck out for the rock where she was clinging onto for dear life and managed to taxi her down to calmer waters. This is what the Duzi is all about – the camaraderie, the spirit, the bigness of heart, all of which were exemplified by those two gallant river men.

Us chastened grandmasters gritted our teeth after our Big Bend swim to complete the final sixteen kilometres to the finish of the second day. This involves a mind numbing slog across the massive Inanda Dam where usually the wind reduces the athletes to gibbering wrecks but we enjoyed a sudden stroke of fortune: two lively youngsters gave us a welcome slipstream accompanied by the leading women's' Masters pair, both seasoned veterans of 50 years apiece, one of whom was the daughter of the legendary Ernie Pierce, a pioneer of the Duzi. We then caught up to an amazing sight: a grizzled looking veteran with a close-cropped cannon ball of a head on top of which perched a school boy cap – an incongruous sight but he was going for all his worth – with a slip of a girl, his daughter perhaps, who could not have been more than eighteen years old, paddling furiously with face turned to one side and eyes clamped shut. She was battling with exhaustion but the sheer determination on her face will never be forgotten. I muttered to Moggy: "You think we are taking strain but take a look at this!" So there we were, four canoes romping across the Inanda Dam in record time due to the slip-streaming opportunity that had sprung our way. Talking about the women of the Duzi, they deserve special mention for their grit and courage. Forming approximately 10% of the field, they stand proudly and not all are fearsome looking amazons. Some are slight in physique, other are into their mature years – the 50 year old master pairing for example.

We were pleased with our result for day two and we finished strongly, a good omen for the final leg. Day three dawned with the sun streaming, promising to be a hot day but fortunately tempered by a breeze. I spent a few minutes talking to an official in the information tent where I learnt that there had been a higher than usual casualty rate through broken boats and severe dehydration. I was to learn of one canoeist having his ear half ripped off in a rapid but had soldiered on after receiving stitches. I heard of another who had battled on to finish despite serious wounds to his head following a tumble in a rapid, and of a high number of serious heat exhaustion cases. Fortunately no deaths.

As I stood with Moggy Lightfoot at the start, I absorbed the vibrancy of this race. There were some six helicopters revving up before undertaking their vigil along the river; there were the squads of mounted police and the police off-road motorbike riders, all dressed in striking yellow shirts. Then the military that were there to patrol the river to discourage evil-intentioned marauders, remembering the backmarkers' experience of assaults in previous years. And there were the multitude of 4 x 4 trucks manned by the seconds of the canoeists. The noise, the hum, the dust, the television crews all created an electric atmosphere and I thought of the organisation that goes into staging this race which is mind-boggling. The men and women behind the scenes deserve medals and so do the sponsors that make the event possible for the 1100 odd crews that battle the river.

Before entering the water at 6.30 a.m., I cast my eyes around the brilliant scene taking in the throngs of canoeists with boats on shoulders and not a few of them wearing the signs of extreme exhaustion against the back drop of the announcer summoning the competitors into their respective pounds. Added to this was the rough bonhomie of the rugby players, and the constant chirping of Bruce Fordyce and other sporting notables that made up the celebrity batch.

Now for the third and final day and the race is by no means over. Awaiting us are some of the biggest rapids of the river. We could play for safe, and portage 'Burma Road'. In all of Moggy Lightfoot's six Duzis and my five, not one of us have opted for this monstrous climb that peaks at a 45 degree incline – an obstacle that leaves the cursing canoeists heaving their 18kg boats over rocks and bushes, slipping on the uneven, muddy track. In the old days only a few chose to canoe around Burma Road on account of the risk of the big rapids taking the competitor out of the race. Today it's the reverse. Burma Road may prove a safer route but friendships have been broken for life by this inhuman trek through dense bush. Graham Pope-Ellis, the undisputed king of the Duzi, was to talk of Tim Cornish – an ex-British canoeing champion – in the context of Burma Road. Pope-Ellis, winner of twenty odd Duzis, had partnered Tim Cornish on four occasions to win the doubles race. In 1981 a weakened Cornish, just out of his sick bed with tick bite fever, had kept going for three days in the unrelenting heat. Cornish vomited incessantly up the killing Burma Road portage but pushed on grimly. Graham Pope-Ellis said after that race that Cornish had more guts than any competitor he'd met in 20 years of top-level sport. Tim Cornish three years later was to take the crown in South Africa's first ever 'Iron Man' race.

We took two severe swims before reaching the last stretch – the 12 kilometre stretch of flat water that leads to the finishing post. Behind us lay the long, surging rapid known as Little John which we had portaged around; the Graveyard which we had negotiated successfully; and the notorious Island Rapid which can gobble boats. We had shot the last rapid under the pipeline well and we were home and dry. We were also in good physical shape apart from my injured hand and we paddled the final furlongs under a bright sky but cooled fortunately with a breeze. We turned the last corner and in the distance could be heard the loud speakers and the crowds lining the bank and we were home. Out of the 1120 boats that started the Duzi in January, 2002, 980 completed. The two grandmasters reached 916th place. Of the casualties, one will be written into the records: the canoeist that was bitten by a black mamba and for thirty hours battled with his life. It is not difficult to realise why each year hundreds of canoeists return to 'the Valley of a Thousand Hills' to challenge the famous Duzi. They will risk the ravages of Duzi guts, severe bruising, broken limbs, extreme exhaustion and even their lives, but the Duzi canoeist is a resilient breed: hardy, an optimist by nature, and, above all an adventurer.

CHAPTER TEN

The agony of Zimbabwe

*No one who has been at a British public school or
served in the British Army can feel entirely out of
place in a third world prison.*

**John Simpson quoting Roger Cooper in his book
"A mad world, my masters."**

ZIMBABWE'S HISTORY has been wracked by turbulence since 1965 when the white minority government of Rhodesia, as it was called then, declared UDI. And then ensued a long and merciless civil war with Rhodesia being forced to capitulate in 1980 from international pressure and the withdrawal of support from its powerful neighbour, South Africa. Robert Mugabe inveigled himself into the presidency and over the next two decades systematically destroyed a once proud nation that was the breadbasket for Southern Africa. In March, 2008, the tyrannical rule promised to come to an end and Mugabe's Zimbabwe African National Union- Patriotic Front (ZANU-PF) lost a general election to Morgan Tsvangirai's Movement for Democratic Change (MDC). Mugabe predictably rejected the results of the election. *Zimbabwe is mine* he was fond of reiterating. He unleashed his security forces on his own people, massacring hundreds, arresting thousands and displacing tens of thousands. Using violence as a lever, Mugabe forced the opposition to retain him as president and remains today in control of the police, the

CHAPTER TEN

military, and the Ministry of finance. His network of patronage remains intact. Tsvangirai, in contrast, has remained powerless as farm invasions continue, and his own members suffering abuse at the hands of the security police.

Zimbabwe's spiral to its current state of outright lawlessness commenced with Mugabe's reign of terror that was unleashed on Matabeleland a mere three years after Mugabe came to power in 1980. The spate of mass murders adding up to over 22000 dead, involving wholesale torturing, raping, and ubiquitous burning of villages by the infamous Korean trained Fifth Brigade, effectively decimated Joshua Nkomo's ZAPU, reducing Zimbabwe to a one party state. *'Breaking the silence'* - a detailed dossier on the atrocities in Matabeleland- was compiled by the Catholic Commission for Justice and Peace (CCJ) and the Legal Resources Foundation. This report describes in detail the horror camp, Bhalagwe, where women were seized as 'wives' by the soldiers, others raped with sticks up their vaginas, men with their testicles bound with rubber strips. Digging graves was a daily chore and the Fifth Brigade, assisted by Mugabe's goons the CIO (Central Intelligence Organisation), played sadistic torture games with the inmates. At the time the Matabele genocide was played down by the West. It was unfashionable to take to task a newly elected leader of a former white colonial power, allowing the government in Harare to dismiss the accusations as figments of sanctimonious missionaries' imaginations. Since then the atrocities of Mugabe's Fifth Brigade have been unearthed and the current reign of terror is a repeat of the 80's where the same intimidatory tactics are being used against the opposition party, the MDC, and their supporters including the white farmers. Mugabe's land grab was triggered off by his defeat in the 1999 National Referendum when he proposed to alter the Constitution to provide him with life presidency. The man's dark side returned to the fore and he set about usurping the 4000 farms owned by the 'white racists' for daring to assist the opposition party.

Tomes have been written about this evil and odious dictator, of his manipulation of the 1980 UK pledge at Lancaster House to finance the purchase of white owned farms, where after a decade of Britain granting the equivalent of US$44 million, farms were looted and then abandoned; the personal ownership of a web of companies including diamond concessions in the Democratic Republic of Congo (DRC); of his condoning the CIO and his ragtag mob - 'the war vets' - raping the mothers, wives and daughters of his political opponents. Zimbabwe, once the agricultural showpiece of Southern and Central Africa, is on the verge of famine. According to the UN, six million Zimbabweans –half of the population- face imminent starvation. Mugabe blames his destruction of a once proud country on the British colonialists, propagating the notion that he is the victim of a concerted racist conspiracy. His bizarre fantasy cuts little ice in Zimbabwe itself where he was clearly outvoted in the elections of April 2002 and 2008 but where he manipulated the vote and stole the elections. Strangely, his twisted deeds avoid censure in neighbouring countries and incongruously from the regional superpower, South Africa, which has sat in silence whilst Mugabe has unleashed his gory campaign of murder, extortion, expropriation and rape.

Zimbabwe is a nation in transition, as Tsvangirai insists, but how is it that 'Mad Bob' remains on the throne? I had the opportunity of questioning the fragile alliance of Tsvangirai and Mugabe with Fergus Blackie whom I'd known at Downside. Fergus had served as a High Court judge and he had been victimised in revenge for sentencing Patrick Chinamasa, the Minister of Justice, to three months in prison for two counts of contempt of court. Fergus had been thrown into gaol for seven days. The country's judiciary had collapsed, Fergus told me, and the high courts were filled with Mugabe's henchmen following the quitting of Anthony Gubbay, the former Chief Justice, as a result of death threats issued by the 'war vets'. Fergus was of the opinion that Tsvangirai's strategy to strengthen his support base in Parliament was to show little grudge against the dictator, despite the attempt on his life in 1997 where Mugabe's thugs tried to hurl him out of a tenth floor window in Harare, being beaten to within an inch of death prior to the 2008 elections, and losing his wife of 30 years marriage in a car smash which smacked of foul play. However, Fergus continued, the vision of Tsvangirai's shaking hands and appearing cordial with the dictator confounds his supporters, and indeed the international community, leaving the question *just who is in charge?* Any belief that Mugabe has relinquished power can be shattered with the screening of British TV's Discovery programme screened on 3/8/09 that disgusted the viewer with the continued brutality in Zimbabwe by Mugabe's police and military. The land invasions continue unabated and what is particularly loathsome is the recent funding of Mugabe's war chest from an appropriated platinum mine to the tune of $100m facilitated by the unprincipled financier, Billy Rautenbach, an infamous toady of Mugabe and his clique.

This sad country continues to be mesmerised by the corruption and paranoia of its ageing bully, a liberation 'hero' who grasped the leadership of Zimbabwe but who , in an only too familiar refrain, came to personify the tragedy and broken promises of so many states on the African continent. Mugabe joins the grotesque parade of horror figures – Africa's 'Big Men': Uganda's Idi Amin, Liberia's Charles Taylor, Ethiopia's Mengistu, CAR's Jean – Bedel Bokassa, Zaire's Mobutu, Equatorial Guinea's Obiang, Gabon's Omar Bongo and many more.

I can clearly recall when the land grab started in April 2000. I was in Provence, France, at the time and I remember talking to an American who'd lived in Zimbabwe for two years. He wanted to know – as did a number of internationals living in the region – what was going to happen and would the expropriation of farms spread over into South Africa. "Unlikely", I answered, "Unless Thabo Mbeki, our leader, refrains from taking a strong stand." How wrong I was proven. Mbeki persisted in his policy of 'quiet diplomacy' for the entirety of his political tenure until he was dismissed in disgrace by the ANC in 2008. His Foreign Minister, Mrs Nkosazana Dlamini-Zuma, attacked the South African press for lashing Mugabe. She lambasted the media for presenting a negative picture and failing to paint a balanced picture of events both in Zimbabwe and South Africa. But, more tragically, it was the UK's Labour party that had been brainwashed by Mugabe's vitriolic rhetoric on Britain's colonial past. The British government had shown timidity and inertia on the mindless destruction of a country, once a proud member of the Empire. And in face of growing antipathy from the world, Mugabe had the gall to present his face at the Earth Summit in Johannesburg, August, 2002. Using the Summit as a platform to hurl insults at Tony Blair (who was present in the room at the time) instead of explaining why he had catapulted his own country into collapse, the wretch gave Sam Nujoma, the President of Namibia at the time, encouragement to follow suit at the Summit and harangue the luckless Blair. "Here in Southern Africa we have one problem and it was created by the British". Nujoma, another leader who seized rule at the end of a gun, emulated Mugabe's rant: "First you enslaved us. On top of that you colonised us. You took all our wealth and you built up your country and you made Africa poorer". Thabo Mbeki, the architect of NEPAD- the New Partnership & Development campaign for soliciting the support of the West & G8 countries to foster economic development in Africa - must have shuddered with Nujoma's threat: "I just want to make it categorically clear that if the EU does not lift *sanctions against Zimbabwe*, the whole of the African Union will also impose economic *sanctions against Europe*. Either there is peace or war, and we don't want a war. Change your attitudes. If you won't change, we are going to get you".

I first visited the country in 1973 when it was known as Rhodesia. The country was at war and there was a patriotic fervour that permeated Salisbury (now renamed Harare). I could remember the bars and restaurants crammed with soldiers on leave and the mood was optimistic. The war was confined to the rural areas and the Rhodesian army supported by the South Africans were holding Mugabe's ZAPU and Nkomo's ZANU at bay. There was no talk of defeat in those days. I returned in 1984 to hunt buffalo. The war was over. As with South Africa, world pressure had been brought to bear on this once proud country. The mood was mixed. There was a strong school of thought that Mugabe would respect the constitution laid down at the Lancaster House talks in 1980 and would withhold from tampering with land ownership and that his bellicose rhetoric was to appease his war veterans. The well managed farms remained the bastion of the economy. Most of the men that I knew in Zimbabwe were hunters and farmers. Prior to the land grab they remained confident of their future. They were sons of Africa and had no volition to move. "Better the devil you know" they would often say and, indeed, in the early years of the newly independent Zimbabwe, the country boasted one of the best schooling systems in Africa; tourism was healthy; and the Department of Wildlife and National Parks continued to be a fine exemplar in the African continent for protecting its abundance of game.

I am one of the few South Africans who has seen the inside of a Zimbabwean jail. It all started when Johan Bellingan, a close hunting friend, asked me whether it was safe to hunt north of the South African border. He'd heard from reliable sources many a disquieting tale of hunters' misfortunes when they ventured into Black Africa. Corrupt officialdom, interminable road blocks and the threat of civil wars are the constant perils that face trophy hunters. I reassured Johan as after all, I reasoned, I had survived six forays into Zimbabwe. I told him that the men we would be hunting with exemplified the highest standards and ethics set by the Rhodesians with their traditions of hunting big game passed down over four generations of settlers. I told him that the area we were destined for contained some majestic terrain and held an abundance of game equal to what any serious hunter could ever wish for. I lauded the wilderness called Charara where we were destined to hunt for its abundance of flora and fauna to be found in the open savannah and Mopani woodlands that teemed with lion, leopard, elephant, buffalo and a wide variety of smaller game. Johan was convinced and in September, 1990, the two of us plus our wives took off from Lanseria in Johan's Beech Baron. Our spirits were high during the three-hour flight to Kariba, a small town on the shores of the lake. Kariba evoked vivid memories of previous hunting safaris including that unforgettable buffalo accident where I nearly saw my last moments on earth. I was well acquainted with Kariba's bars, the airport, and the infirmary of course. Kariba was named after the flooding of the Zambezi valley in the early 1960's where several labourers perished during the construction of the massive dam wall. John Gordon-Davies' best seller, 'Hold My Hand I'm Dying', was inspired by this watershed in Rhodesia's history.

We landed at the airport unassisted by air control that was not functioning that day, or perhaps it never existed! We then had to wait for two hours for Customs and Immigration to arrive from Kariba, some twenty-five kilometres distant. Despite the torrid heat, which was well into the high thirties, and the absence of any adequate catering facility, time slipped by as we were briefed on the safari by the two Zimbabwean hunters who will be referred to as 'A' and 'B' for security reasons. I had hunted with 'A' for several years and 'B' was his partner in their newly formed safari company. The immigration officials finally arrived and then disaster struck! I had no visa. I'd brought my South African passport, leaving my British passport behind that obviates the need for a visa. I asked the young African official to refer to his superior in Kariba, which he did, but he returned saying I would have to fly back to South Africa immediately. It was a desperate situation as the hunt was in jeopardy and some quick thinking was required. I told the rest of the party to have lunch in Kariba while I sorted out this dilemma with the British Consulate in Harare. Following five hours of frantic phone calling from a dilapidated booth to Harare and Johannesburg, I eventually managed to persuade the local immigration chief over the phone - we hadn't met face-to-face at this stage – to contact the British Consul who had been a gem. He had gone out of his way on a Saturday afternoon to instruct my son at home to phone him back with my British passport details. It had been a very close call and I would have had an extremely irate Bellingan and two impatient Zimbabwe hunters to contend with if I hadn't solved this problem.

On the day we were arrested we were relaxing in a motor launch, believing that we'd earned a rest after eight days of hard hunting in the grilling heat averaging 35 centigrade. Johan had shot two good buffalo bulls and I'd taken a lion, a buffalo and an excellent waterbuck. We were having a fine time, downing cold beer and discharging bonhomie as we fished for tiger and bream. And then our festive mood suddenly turned to a dark disquiet. A shout from the shore from Bandit, the head tracker, drew our attention to a lorry bristling with armed officials from the National Parks and Wildlife Department. 'A' and 'B' were then summoned to Kariba, leaving us to speculate what was afoot. We began to seriously worry when darkness set in and our Zimbabwean friends hadn't returned. Nine hours later they drove into camp, their grim expressions telling the story and three hours after this we were in front of the local warden of the Parks Board and we were told there were discrepancies with our permits, and that we were hunting in an area reserved for local hunters, and that our hunt was terminated forthwith.

Worse was to follow. Johan and I were to be detained in the Kariba jail. 'A' and 'B' were exonerated from this unpleasant ordeal on the technicality they were hunting legally as Zimbabwean citizens in a National Parks area closed to international hunters which includes South Africans. An African jail is never a pleasant experience. We were stripped of our belts and socks and there was a glimmer of dark humour as 'A' and 'B' and Vivienne and Denise Bellingan were allowed to bring us something to eat in the jail. They had to see the funny side at the picture of the big Afrikaner and the rooinek standing helpless behind bars. But it was a grim situation, exacerbated by the sight of our fine trophies lying in a heap outside the cell including the lion and the buffaloes. Johan and I opted to sleep on the cement floor outside the filthy cell with its overflowing latrine and lice ridden blankets but peace was short lived. At midnight a drunken constable prodded us with his AK47 forcing us back into the cell. One positive aspect was that we were alone, giving us time to assess our predicament, and one major worry was the prospect of the aircraft and the guns – and we had some valuable weapons with us - being impounded which was a distinct possibility.

Sleep didn't come easily on that hard, lice infested floor and I cogitated on Roger Cooper's inimitable statement prefacing this chapter. I had a lot to be grateful for in my upbringing to facilitate this unpleasant ordeal. An upbringing in the environment of war-torn Britain, a Benedictine schooling, and the British army as it was then, tuned one well for the vicissitudes of life that can sometimes be cruel and adverse. The men of my generation were conditioned to meet hardship and the standards set in those days would instil a resilience to misfortune and privation.

At the age of six I was dispatched to Worth Preparatory School, the main feeder establishment for Downside. That first day of school was unnerving for a small boy. We sat in silence in the train ride from Victoria Station to Crawley, Sussex – our caps skew on our heads and socks hanging around ankles. We remained in a forlorn state on the bus before disembarking at the striking quadrangle of Worth School. But we began to cheer up as we sensed adventure, trudging our way up the hill to the junior school run by Dom Jerome - a kindly figure who manifested a fatherly affection for us small school boys. Worth served as an excellent prelude to the big school, Downside. The Benedictine monks had us boxing at the age of seven and we struck out at each other like demented midgets with pillow-cases on our mitts. By the age of ten I was the champion of my weight and the pillow cases had shrunk to the semblance of a sixteen ounce boxing glove. We were to thank the monks of Worth for indoctrinating us in a sport that Downside remained supreme until boxing was banned in schools by a pusillanimous Labour government. That Downside could be acclaimed as one of the greatest boxing schools of its era was affirmed with the very last public schools tournament held in the country in the nineteen seventies between Downside & Winchester. As with most Catholic schools in Britain and the Commonwealth, Downside placed heavy value on the manly sports of boxing and rugby. Boxing was compulsory for every boy in the school in the Lent term and hence to become a school boxer as champion of your weight earned a supreme distinction. I was destined for the boxing house Caverel that had won the inter house cup for fifteen years in a row, having gained distinction in the sport at Worth School, but the furthest I could reach in the heavily contested welterweight division were the semi-finals. Such gifted boxers of the ilk of The Hon Jamie Drummond (Captain of Boxing) and De Domenico - blocked my aspiration to becoming a school boxer.

The four schools annual tournament between Downside, Clifton, Cheltenham and Malvern was an eagerly awaited gladiatorial fixture. It was of little wonder that Downside was a successful boxing school. The Benedictines and the Jesuits espoused the maxim 'boxing and beating is good for the soul'. Transgressing the rules led to the choice of one round with the boxing coach or a whipping at the hands of the headmaster, Father Wilfred Passmore, known to the boys as 'Pod'. This legendary leader of Downside could certainly wield a cane but being short sighted was capable of collecting his victim around the neck or the thighs. I had a problem with Pod. My father and he had met at Downside as pupils. Both entered the legal profession together and both remained friends for life. I was therefore expected to be an exemplar but, sadly, in the eyes of Pod I was a sub standard reflection of the father. I was a natural target for Pod's ruthless 'cleansing' programme for those Downside boys who dared to question his authoritarian stamp on the proud school. Passmore was a clever monk, not only in the intellectual sense, and he could have fitted in as one of those wily monsignors in the inner sanctum of the Vatican. He influenced a four hundred and fifty band of Roman Catholic scholars, the majority of which commanded stout hearts and strong bodies. That the bulk of this medley of high spirited youths endured Father Passmore's Machiavellian rule was evidence of his strength of character. This awesome figure, the grand vizier of Downside, lauded the scholars but silently thanked the athletes, the latter bolstering the then enviable reputation of the school.

I enjoyed Pod in a strange sort of way. I certainly respected this uncompromising monk of imposing stature and jutting chin, and the reason I enjoyed Father Passmore was that his intransigence and his benevolent brutality – let's describe it as that – forged a spirit that flamed internally and emitted a message to the outside world that a product of this great school of that generation would be difficult to subjugate. Despite the constant battle of wills between Father Wilfred Passmore and myself, there was no malice and I was to receive a most heart-warming telegram from this titan on the birth of our daughter which read: "My Dear Michael, all my congratulations and good wishes on the birth of your daughter. May she be blessed always and give you and your wife much happiness. It is a long time since I saw you. Do not forget that you are always most welcome here and please remember me without fail to your father .With all good wishes, Your old friend, Wilfred Passmore".

Another great monk of that era – Father Aelred Watkin, the housemaster of Caverel, played a strong role in my life at Downside. I could eulogise at length on this charismatic man of the cloth who once wrote of me in a school report: "Michael Callender, sadly at his tender age, already manifests a premature rebelliousness. He has a diverse character but, if properly nurtured, will flower in a productive manner". Father Aelred married Vivienne and myself and I will never forget this scion of a noble family - one of the greatest intellects of the Catholic clergy of his time and a future headmaster of Downside.

Father Aelred called me into his study one cold winter's day and said "I will have to cane you. For a fourteen year old, you have the audacity of masquerading as a wine connoisseur. I found in your locker a ghastly, nasty smelling plonk. For this I am giving you four lashes, following which I'll deliver a sermon on wine!" I revered Father Aelred. He understood loners and students of rebellious character because he found them interesting, as they were out of the stereo-typed mould, he told me on one of my visits to the school. It was a sad occasion when I last saw Aelred in the Downside Abbey. He was looking frail and close to death. I took him back those years past and my heart warmed at his enigmatic smile. "You were a difficult boy and rather different. I trust you've settled down. Go well and God be with you". I learnt so many valuable approaches to life from that marvellous monk who merited a full page obituary in the London Daily Telegraph.

I left Downside with a sore backside. Pod had wreaked his final revenge on the very morning I left the school. Twelve lashes on my naked buttocks was my farewell present on account of a grand finale. Six of us high spirited boys had organised a thrash in a barn lent to us by a friendly farmer and the celebration was in full swing with a full flow of liquor and a string of local lasses to help us along when at 4.00 am the door burst open and the menacing figure of Father Ceolfrid O'Hara framed the entrance. Who split on us we would never know but Father Passmore was there to greet us in his study. David 'Archer' Hardy collected sixteen lashes and I was next with a count of twelve, followed by Ted Maynard who was accorded the same lashing. Hardy has died since and so has Ted Maynard. It might have been Pod's handy work, who knows! When I recount this tale, most look at me cynically as if to say he has to be exaggerating. However, Jake

Francis-Jones (refer Miscellany) in his home in Wiltshire recently testified to me that Robin Watson was dragged off the bus as it was leaving the quadrangle in 1955, the year before I left, on his very last morning at the school for having got his leg over one of the 'hags (serving wenches in the dining hall) and despite vigorous denial received the identical punishment as I from Pod.

"Boxing and beating is good for the soul!" The wheels of the train hammered out the refrain as we returned to London after my painful farewell to Downside. I've returned several times since. I enjoyed my days at the school. In fact, I was there recently with my wife and I made a point of revisiting the infamous landmark of Pod's study. I stood in the narrow dark corridor, now derelict, where the school villains lined up for their weekly punishment and I remarked triumphantly to Jake Francis-Jones: "there – Jake, the blood stains!" Vivienne and Diana, Jake's wife, peered fretfully at the worn carpet. They were hardly amused as their appreciation of corporal punishment didn't exactly match Jake's and mine. On one visit, I recall talking to the Headmaster of the time - Dom Phillip Jebb – on the possibility of our son, Sean, spending a year at Downside to gain an A Level . "The school has changed, Michael, since our time. It's not quite the tough place it used to be". "A good thing, Dom Philip?" I asked. "Not really, no" was Dom Philip's pensive reply. It was an apt answer in my book.

Johan and I were released from jail at 9.00 a.m. the next day. We were charged with illegal hunting in an area reserved for local residents and fined Z$100 (US$40.00 at the time). The charge was bizarre as we had National Parks managers accompany us during all stages of the hunt. We were told we were free to leave and we rejoined 'A' and 'B' and the wives who'd spent the night in the hunting camp. We decided to leave Charara and fly onto Vic Falls as our hunt was over, our trophies confiscated, and we weren't going to hang around Kariba to lick our wounds. There was a bitter taste in our mouths as we made our way to the airport and Johan had refuelled prior to our incarceration– by the grace of God as it turned out later – and we packed our luggage and guns and reported to the control tower to log our flight. Then the nightmare started. We were told by the airport officials that the CIO required us for further interrogation and we were to remain at the airport. We then knew beyond any doubt that we were to be singled out as targets for harassment. The CIO is Zimbabwe's secret police, mostly comprised of former guerrilla fighters in the Rhodesian war. These are little better than thugs, feared by Zimbabweans and distrusted by the police force at that time.

We had to kick our heels for at least an hour before the CIO arrived. This ragged looking band demanded that Johan and I escort them to the aircraft where they proceeded to strip the plane, including the women's toiletry bags. It took every ounce of composure to check our tempers on the tarmac at the sight of a lewdly grinning CIO operative shaking a tampax beneath our noses. Our self control was further tested as the CIO pranced around our luggage strewn across the tarmac. To add to our discomfort the temperature had reached the 40 centigrade mark. The game had just begun – we were being callously toyed with – and we all knew it. We were then instructed to take our weapons into an office and the charade started all over again. They scoured our documents, shouting and threatening in a vile and obscene manner. Johan's papers were in order but they had fun and games with the absence of entry stamps in my weapons permit. They made hay of this and it then dawned on me that before leaving the police station earlier that morning, I had shown a CIO operative this very same permit, asking for an official stamp to avoid any potential complication at the point of departure; I'd explained that owing to the mix up of the visa, the official had failed to stamp my weapons permit on the day of entry. He had waved me on, stating this was not needed. He was obviously in on the plot.

All six of us, including 'A' and 'B', were then escorted back to the police station. After two hours of sitting on our backsides, I volunteered to determine under precisely what pretext we were being detained. I found myself wandering into the CIO section that was separated from the main police precinct by a grill door. There was one young CIO operative present and he was a mere twenty years of age or so. He waved me to a chair and glared at me with malevolence. In then pounded five other CIO ruffians and they began harassing me. A state of confusion reigned in the CIO office and after ten minutes I had enough of this chronic line of interrogation. "Silence, please!" I roared above the din. "One question at a time!" To my surprise the motley gang obeyed and then followed a two hour ordeal. The accusations ranged from gun running to illegal foreign exchange dealings to poaching. Every crude tactic was used – jostling, threatening postures, crowding, and the tired old trick "You've been betrayed by your friends". I was asked whether I'd been in the military, this due perhaps to the expression in my eyes. It must be remembered that the CIO were drawn mainly from former terrorist cadres, although some of them in the room were far too young to have been involved in the war. I was resigned to spending another night in the cells when 'B' was ushered in. He gave me an imperceptible wink but he looked drawn. Apparently the party had been worried stiff at the length of my absence. 'B's interrogation session lasted an hour, 'A's half an hour, and Johan Bellingan's a paltry ten minutes. What the CIO had neglected to do was to separate us, thereby allowing us plenty of time to co-ordinate our story, although a complicated story was not required. The only infringement of the law was that 'A' and 'B' had allocated their allotted trophies from the annual Hunters' Association lottery to Johan and I but the underlying problem was that Kariba's Immigration chief had been severely miffed by being overruled by the British Consol in Harare who had issued the temporary visa. The chief's domain had been transgressed – and petty bureaucrats don't particularly like their suzerainty threatened!

To our immense relief, and particularly for the wives who were at this stage understandably fretful, we were told by the police that we were free for the night but to report back at 7.00 am the following morning. We were suitably thirsty and proceeded to the Breezes Hotel only to find a further charade in play. It was a like Peter Sellers farce to watch the CIO hide behind pillars and crouch behind sofas making themselves to be an absurd sight. There was one comic moment when 'A' made a telephone call from the reception desk to enquire about the whereabouts of his 3 ton truck (this had broken down on the way to the camp site the previous evening when Johan and I were languishing in jail). Engrossed on the telephone, 'A' hadn't noticed a CIO operative creeping up to eavesdrop on his conversation and this in full view of a party of astonished American tourists. By this stage the hotel was crawling with CIO lurking in every nook and cranny and we decided to curtail our conversation in the bedrooms in the likelihood that these had been bugged.

Unfortunately, our harassment was by no means over. We reported at the Police headquarters on the dot at 7.00 am where we were ignored for an hour. Our patience was now running dangerously thin and we demanded an answer from the CIO who shrugged us off with the infuriating statement "Wait until we are ready". 'B' called us together and by this time the women were close to despair. "We'll have to call a lawyer from Harare, otherwise we'll be detained indefinitely". This 'B' did and within half an hour we were handed over to the Kariba Police. Obviously the telephone lines had crackled at a furious pace and the CIO's hands had been forced. It was also clearly evident that there was no love lost between the CIO and the police -then a relatively well disciplined force compared with the rabble of today - and the surliness and aggression of the CIO were replaced by the pleasant dispositions of the police, but we were informed that we had to stand trial in the Karoi Magistrates Court the following morning. I left the women with Johan in the Breezes Hotel and drove back with 'A' and 'B' to the hunting camp where I had a chance to say farewell to the trackers and skinners. It was an emotional parting as Bandit and Adom, both trackers I knew from previous hunts, had been deeply concerned over our internment and, like most Africans in Zimbabwe, they hated the CIO.

The case was tried the next morning in Court and Johan Bellingan and I were fined Z$800.00 each for hunting with incorrect permits. We were free to go but the nightmare continued. We were accosted by the chief immigration officer at the airport. I looked curiously at him as this was the fellow who had originally thwarted my entry into Zimbabwe despite the intervention of the British Consul. He had the largest nostrils I've ever seen on a man, monstrous rolls of fat around his neck, and foul breath to boot. He was the ugliest immigration official I've had the displeasure of encountering in all my years of travel. He informed us with relish that there were further formalities to complete and we were to return to Kariba. I glanced at Johan Bellingan and he was white with anger. 'A' and 'B' were looking desperate and Vivienne and Denise were close to tears. At the immigration office we were ordered to complete new forms, stating that we were guilty of a criminal offence. We were then taken to the police headquarters to be fingerprinted and we had to sign a Prohibited Immigrant document. This was an iniquitous and unfair act as far as the women were concerned.

The ordeal continued. At the airport we were told that we had fifteen minutes to clear guns, ammunition and complete currency and departure forms. The immigration officer adjusted his watch so we would lose five precious minutes and Johan noticed this and urged us to move as swiftly as possible. We rushed through the formalities and we had to race for our lives to the aircraft and hurl the guns and luggage into the cabin. Johan had no time for any pre-flight checking procedures and within seconds we were airborne. During the return flight to Johannesburg, the four of us reconstructed the chain of events that had occurred during the preceding 48 hours. Despite our clearance by National Parks and Wildlife, the police and the Magistrates Court, the CIO had obviously schemed to hold us for an indefinite period. Although Nelson Mandela had been released from prison the year before, there remained a paranoiac dislike for South Africa from certain countries north of the border. Probably jealously. We were extremely lucky not to have faced the same circumstances twelve months earlier. There are many grim stories of detentions and imprisonment of innocent South African tourists at the hands of the sinister CIO. We were fortunate in having 'A' and 'B' in place to arrange appropriate legal representation and their good standing with National Parks and Wildlife had helped. Without their support, the CIO and the immigration chief of Kariba could have triumphed at our cost and misery.

Later we were to learn that if we had not taken to the air by 6.00 pm, we would have been detained for contravening the Prohibited Immigration act and could have been incarcerated in jail for an indefinite period. We had escaped by a matter of seconds and woe betide us if Johan had not refuelled the aircraft when he did and also for noticing the chief immigration officer adjusting his watch. For seven years I avoided Zimbabwe but not on account of the Prohibited Immigration charge. That was revoked within one year following the intercession of certain influential citizens in Harare. It was the sheer anger of having a hunt disrupted in such a vile manner. The following year I took off to the Arctic to hunt polar bear. I wanted the pristine white wilderness to purge the memories of that dirty, ugly experience at the hands of the CIO and the foul immigration chief of Kariba. I sincerely hope that one day they will be eaten by the lions of Charara!

Above: Author in pensive mood at the Ouagou forest camp, Central African Republic, after a search for Bongo. (Refer chapter 16)

Below: A 'dagga boy' Buffalo in the thickets of Chirisa, Zhimbabwe.
Note the .475 double Jeffrey rifle

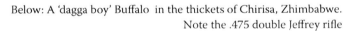

Above: Braam Cronje, a prominent farmer in Northern Natal. I first met Braam when he was shoot captain on the Wales international shoot in the Orange Free State.
(Refer chapters 8 & 14)

Right: Harry Manners, one of the last of the 'Old Timers'. A legendary elephant hunter of Mozambique with his famous tusks, *the second largest recorded.*
(Refer chapter 16)

Above: Retrieving the hippo from
an inland pan covered in dense
weed in the Zambezi Valley.
(Refer chapter 7).

Above: Angling for Tiger
fish in the crocodile & hippo
infested Chobe River near
Kasane, Botswana. L/r:
Author, Tom Mackie, Steve
Finnemore and local guide.

Right: Author & Sean as a
boy shooting guinea fowl &
francolin with dogs
in Standerton district,
Transvaal.

Above: The Lord Derby Giant Eland, one of the most exotic and sought after big game trophies to be found in the central belt of Africa. (Refer chapter 16).

Right: The founders of Kayak Africa – MaryAnne Callender & Pierre Bester. From humble origins, Kayak Africa has grown into a leading outwards bound enterprise in Southern Africa offering kayaking, deep sea diving and extreme adventure trips. (Refer chapter 19).

Below: The old team at work on the Breede River marathon .(Refer 17).

Above: The hunting group in Charara, adjoining Zambezi Valley. From l/r: Bill Bedford, Vivienne, trackers, Johan Bellingan,and Alastair Travers. Johan Bellingan & Alastair Travers were to lose their lives from a buffalo attack in a later hunt in Dande, Zhimbabwe.

Below: Author & 'ghillie' in Lake Chilwa, Malawi which sports some of the finest duck shooting in Africa. (Refer chapter 14).

Above: The Vinuchi Sporting Occasion. From l/r: Vivienne in foreground, Author, Gert Potgieter (ex World record holder of the 400 metres hurdles) and the legendary Irish rugby icon,Willie John McBride, captain of the 1974 British Lions team that overwhelmed the Springboks .(Refer chapter 12).

Below: The trackers with Author after a buffalo hunt in the Central African Republic. The buffalo featured is the North West species, slightly smaller than the Cape Buffalo which is the largest of the four species in Africa (refer chapter 16).

Above: The Molopo river guinea fowl shoot. Shown l/r: Dennis da Silva, David Seward, Christo Mackeurtan(co shoot captain), Andrew Allen(co shoot captain), Neil Hobson, Author. (Refer chapter 14).

Below: The Vinuchi team competing in the First National Bank road relay race – the largest corporate race in the world at that time. L/r front row: John Feek, Michael Tindall, Author, Ian Green, Tony Beith. L/r backrow: John Sawers, 'P G' Barry, Rob Gerrard. All are mentioned in chapters 6/8/9/13/17.

Above: Tony Beith and Author in the Visgat rapid in the Vaal River canoe marathon.

Below: Searching for the elusive Forest Sitatunga on the banks of the Mambili River, a tributary of the Congo. Few white men have travelled this river. (Refer

Above: Running in the Two Oceans ultramarathon – a scenic 56 km course staged in the Cape Peninsular and rated one of the great foot races in S Africa.

Below: Vivienne in a French Congo rain forest – her ability to speak French kept the trackers alert! (Refer chapter 16).

Above: The Giant Forest Hog, shown here in a remote area of the Central African Republic, is a nocturnal creature and rarely seen. (Refer chapter 16).

Below: Vinuchi Sporting Occasion (refer chapter 12). From l/r: Penny McBride, Author, Alan Jordaan, Willie John McBride, Jannie Breedt (Springbok no 8).

Above: Author's buffalo on back of Piers Taylor's truck in Charara, Zhimbabwe. This particular specimen well into Rowland Ward with a 45 ¾ inch horn measurement. (refer chapter 4)

Below: The buffalo as featured in the adjoining pic with Piers Taylor. (refer chapter 4)

Right:
Sean competing in Iron Man.
(Refer chapter 13).

Below:
MaryAnne & her partner Jurie
Schoeman of Kayak Africa.
(Refer chapter 19).

Above: Shooting quail in lion infested country in Matetsi, Zhimbabwe. L/r: Author, Piers Taylor, Adom, Flex, Jonathan Taylor. (Refer chapter 14).

Below: Eric Stockenstroom, tracker, and self with the Red Dwarf Buffalo taken in the Congo River basin in the French Congo. (Refer chapter 16).

Above: Mayhem at the Mission rapid, Duzi canoe marathon. Author wearing white cap shown in foreground. (Refer chapter 9).

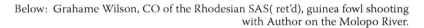

Below: Grahame Wilson, CO of the Rhodesian SAS(ret'd), guinea fowl shooting with Author on the Molopo River.

Left:
The marathon leg
of the Author's first
attempt at the Iron Man.
Note the considerable
distance between each
competitor. Johny Sack,
an excellent second and
athlete, shown in pic.
(Refer chapter 13).

Below:
Moggy Lightfoot &
Author, the oldest men
in the race, prior to the
start of the Duzi – fit,
fresh, and ready to go!
(Refer chapter 9).

Right:
Bruised and a little battered
at finish of Duzi!
(Refer chapter 9).

Below:
Shooting white faced whistler
ducks on Lake Chilwa,
Malawi. L/r: Author, Tony
North, Ted Siebenman with
locals holding ducks.
(Refer chapter 14).

Above:
One of the last pictures
of MaryAnne before her
tragic accident on Lake
Malawi. (Refer chapter 19).

Left:
Sean shooting Ernie Pearce
weir just after start of Duzi
canoe marathon.

CHAPTER ELEVEN

South Africa at war

War is an ugly thing, but not the ugliest of things. The decayed and degraded state of moral and patriotic feeling which thinks that nothing is worth war is much worse. The person who has nothing for which he is willing to fight, nothing which is more important than his own personal safety, is a miserable creature and has no chance of being free unless made and kept so by the exertions of better men than himself.

John Stuart Mill – English economist and philosopher (1806 – 1873)

IN THE 70's and 80's, South Africa was in the thick of war. At war with the UN who was screaming at the Republic for its Apartheid policies. At war with the revolutionaries who were torching the townships. At war in the process of keeping the tribal factions at bay. At war in the defence of her borders with her back to the sea and her front to hostile Africa. In the closing years of the twentieth century, South Africa was fighting for its survival, a pawn in a game where the two Super-Powers, America and Russia, were jostling for supremacy. Well may have the course of history been altered if the SA Defence Force had not turned back at the urgings of America's Pentagon and C.I.A. and had marched on a mere 100 kilometres further and seized Luanda in Angola. The promises of compensation were never promulgated and it was not long after the columns of Africa's most powerful army had retreated behind its lines that the U.S.A's liberal bloc championed international sanctions against this country.

South Africa was a vibrant panorama in those turbulent days - army trucks brimful of soldiers in camouflage fatigues trundling down the highways, fighter jets screaming across the Highveld's azure sky on their way to far flung airfields, Dakotas rumbling overhead, their cavernous bellies transporting paratroopers and the paraphernalia of combat – artillery pieces, hospital supplies, and ammunition. A textiles executive from Italy was driving with me to the SA Bureau of Standards in Pretoria and he was stupefied at the military convoys and the war planes overheard. Alike so many visitors to this country, he was ignorant of South Africa's war footing, so clouded was the country's image with the Apartheid issue. I explained to the gentle mannered Italian from Como that the men in uniform and the aircrews above us were on their way to the battlefields that stretched across a wide swathe of Africa to the west. The border wars were a way of life for the young men of the Republic, whether National Servicemen or Permanent Force. This was a proud time for the South African and vivid in my memory are the words of a veteran naval officer of the Second World War. He was lost in the Johannesburg Country Club and I was showing him around the grounds when he turned to me and said "You're British, aren't you?" "Why?" I answered. The visitor replied: "The young men that I've met here and in Cape Town are as we used to be. It's a fearful shame that we no longer have National Service. Did you serve?" I told the venerable old boy that I had done my time in the Middle East.

I was very proud that our company Vinuchi designed and manufactured a wide array of ties and cravats for the various units of the S A Defence Force. Through this, I met an interesting array of military personnel ranging from generals, colonels and majors to the fighter pilots and the air transport men to naval officers. Thanks to my service in the British Army, my face fitted and business was a pleasure with these men of arms, Afrikaans and English speaking. I was a constant visitor to the various messes of the artillery, tank corps and the regiments of the Transvaal Scottish, South African Irish, the Wits Rifles and a number of others including, naturally, the Paratroopers. I was invited to sit in a Mirage simulator and those fighter pilots I met were as the adventure books depicted: focused, fit men above the average cut. Military product formed a special niche in our production line and our reputation extended to the GHQ Pretoria. It was therefore inevitable that I found my way to the forward positions which was arranged for me by the kind courtesy of General Neil Webster. I happened to know his son, Norman, and I ran with him regularly in preparation for the Comrades.

Invitations for visits to the border were highly coveted and I was privileged to find myself winging my way in 1982 in a Hercules transport to Oshakati, South West Africa in the company of some fairly distinguished men. Sitting in a bucket-seat in the transport, I glanced around in the gloom of the fuselage and I could pick out various heads of industry and I thought how could I explain to this illustrious group that only the night before I had rolled a Mercedes Benz three times, that I'd celebrated my survival from this brush with death into the early hours of the morning, and that my head was thudding and that I was feeling very fragile, due not a little perhaps to a bout of delayed shock. At the rear of the aircraft I studied a knot of young men wearing crew cuts and looking very fit and sunburnt and I made my way down the noisy transport to find out more. They were courteous but short on words. I found out later that I'd been talking to the Recces, the elite of SA's covert forces.

We touched ground at Oshakati and we made our way to our billets. The military base was awesome – huge, bristling with heavy artillery pieces, and abuzz with soldiers, helicopter pilots and the usual back-up personnel. The man in charge was the legendary 'Witkop' Badenhorst. He was a Brigadier, later to become a General of whom fighting men would speak of with great respect. Dinner in the Officers Mess was eventful and the Brigadier was in roaring form by midnight and I plucked up the nerve to walk across and talk to him. I wanted to meet this inspirational soldier at close quarters. I asked him if he could arrange an early morning call to arouse me for my run around the perimeter of the camp. "For what time?" the impressive figure barked. "5.00 a.m." I responded, "And Gert Potgieter will be with me". This famous athlete had held the 400 metres hurdles world record for fourteen years and was sharing my tent. "Will he just – then we must see to it that you'll be ready for your run". Gert was standing with me and he was not going to comply. "The rooinek's running on his own, Brigadier". It was already 2.00 a.m. at this stage and Gert proceeded to regale 'Witkop' Badenhorst with the story of my rolling a Mercedes the previous evening. The Brigadier then turned to me and asked if I'd served in the military and this gave me the cue to embellish upon the fighting reputation of the Cameronians which I believed he enjoyed. I walked back to the tent with Gert Potgieter, pleading with him as I would have given my front teeth to run with this great Olympian athlete but he wouldn't be dislodged and we continued to converse in hushed tones in the tent whilst our other two room-mates, Chris Ball and Piet Badenhorst, both to become banking titans, snored softly into the remaining hours of darkness.

I couldn't sleep that night. I was thinking of the Scottish regiment that I had served with in the late fifties. I slipped out of the tent and walked to the perimeter of this huge military camp and stared out into the flat and featureless terrain of northern South West Africa that lay silent in the brilliant moonlight. I glanced up at the chiselled features of the lonely face which was peering out from his elevated observation post, telephone at hand and R1 rifle cradled in his arms. The sentry gave me a cheery wave from his crow's nest and a flood of nostalgia swept over me in the chill of the pre-dawn.

"The Cameronians are going through a rough period. The regiment is short of good NCO's. You'll have your time cut out, Mr Callender" were foreboding words of the liaison officer for Scottish regiments at Eaton Hall. These words I didn't find particularly ominous after the rough ambiance of the Smithfield meat market and Winchester barracks. Fortunately, there was a big, raw-boned Jock in the intake ahead of me, a Glaswegian called Bill Melville whose Douglas tartan trews and Glengarry cap presented a recruiter's dream for the Cameronians. I had read various accounts of this famous regiment I was destined for and one in particular stood out as it was written by the noted author, John Masters of 'Bugle and Tiger' fame. As a professional soldier, John Masters had met the regiment during the Second World War where a battalion of the Cameronians had fought the Japanese in Orde Wingate's Chindits in Burma. In Master's words:

"They recruited most of their men from the streets of Glasgow and had the reputation of being one of the toughest regiments in the British army. They waged street fights with secreted bayonets and broken bottles. They carried razor blades in the peaks of their caps with which to wipe the grin off opposing faces by a careless back hand swipe from the cap; and potatoes in their pockets in which razor blades were stuck. No one but their own officers could handle them........"

I decided to confer with Bill Melville. "You'll survive" was the cryptic answer given in the harsh Glaswegian rasp. " However, that officer who spoke to you is right. The regiment's short of sergeants and it won't be easy for you to begin with. There's a nest of hard men in there and quite a few have spent time in Barlinnie (the infamous Glasgow jail). Work the jocks hard as they are devils if they've time on their hands". Sound advice from a staunch man who I was to catch up with in the regiment in Arabia and in later life in South Africa where sadly he was to die of cancer in Durban.

My first impression of the Cameronians – one of the eight famous Scottish regiments of the British army – was gained at the deserted regimental depot in Winston Barracks, Lanark where I spent a scant twenty-four hours before flying out to join the battalion in Bahrain. The regiment was then deployed in Sharjah, Bahrain, the Trucial Oman and Kenya, with the principal task of protecting the Trucial Oman states and defending the oil installations in those parts of the Middle East. The evening meal was a subdued affair with little conversation between the officer in command of the depot, Captain Dudley Lucas, whom I got to know later as a good man, and a second lieutenant who will remain nameless. The latter had returned prematurely from Bahrain and he was in a nervous state of note. He'd taken me aside before dinner and he'd muttered under his breath, out of earshot of Captain Lucas, "I warn you, they're savages out there, and the officers! Beware of 'Black' Campbell and Nick Carter. They're mad, all of them!" I discounted the words of the second lieutenant. He was ill, I decided, and I'd summed the poor devil up as a case of shell-shock and something of a nerd. But the warning bells from the Scottish officer at Eaton Hall jangled in my head as I looked at the troubled features of the lieutenant.

The first thing I noticed when I touched down on the stroke of midnight at Muharraq Airport, Bahrain, was the stultifying heat. I felt that I'd walked into a Turkish bath. At this time of year Bahrain's average temperature in the shade would reach 50 centigrade. In fact, just before I arrived in the Persian Gulf, a second lieutenant R G Boyd had died of heat exposure near the Buraimi Oasis in the Trucial Oman. Bahrain Island in the Persian Gulf measures 45 miles in length and 10 miles across at its widest point and consisted of two primitive towns, Muharraq and Manama which were linked by a causeway; an oil installation called Awali; and a jebel (mountain) in the centre of the island. D company to which I was assigned was deployed at Muharraq where we shared the officers' mess with the Royal Air Force. Bahrain's terrain was similar to most parts of the Persian Gulf – sand desert with the sprinkling of odd oases of date palms and tiny mud-built villages. Bahrain in those times had remained unchanged for centuries and a far cry from the metropolis of today. Air conditioning and fresh food supplies were rare commodities and entertainment was limited to an open air cinema.

The battalion kept fit through forced route marches and simulated battle assaults on the jebel. There was a regular relay race between the Cameronians and the RAF which the Jocks won hands down. Six of us were selected to represent the regiment under the tutelage of Lieutenant John Irvine, a Sandhurst cross country champion and John would work us hard. Each runner completed two miles and we'd train in the broiling midday sun with our leader exhorting us to run flat out with the help of a megaphone from the rear of a military jeep. One may well ask what is two miles but believe me in that debilitating heat reaching 50 centigrade and running on oil-based roads, the athlete would be close to collapse at the end of his stretch. Downside school had trained me well as our Colonel was a firm believer in his junior officers climbing into the boxing ring and cross country running and his stern figure was invariably present at the Bahrain relay races and at the ringside for the boxing tournaments in Kenya. There was one very painful occasion when I'd been on a 24 hour route march across the island and on reaching my billet in a state close to exhaustion, I decided to slake my thirst in the Officers Mess. It was midday on a Saturday morning and I felt I deserved some beer. I fell into disreputable company. There was Flight Lieutenant Paget Bellin, a big blond haired South African, and two other lively RAF officers – all very competent aviators – sending it at the bar and I was invited to join the party. Two hours of fairly hectic arm-raising elapsed and in walks my company commander, Captain Donald Sinclair. "Callender", he says "go easy on the gin. You're running for the battalion in an hour's time!" "Oh no!" I replied. "No, no, no. The race is next weekend". "It's today, Callender and you'd better get going or the Colonel will have your neck!" This was all to the mirth of Paget Bellin and his cronies and they had known, the miscreants, that we were racing the RAF that very afternoon. I'd downed at least six beers and as many large gins to recover from the route march and in those days we had to survive on one pint of water to last the twenty-four hours gruelling slog across the burning sands and here was I expected to belt along a two mile leg under the baleful scrutiny of Colonel Charles Mackinnon. The first mile was a red blur. The heat was oppressive and the road was melting and I found myself on hands and knees retching when the shadow of Colonel Mackinnon loomed over me. "Get to your feet and run, man. You're a disgrace to the regiment!" From the rear of the field I finished in sixth place and the battalion's honour was restored. We handed out a merciless beating to the RAF that day and I had my revenge on Paget Bellin and his crew.

Paget Bellin! I first met this indomitable South African on the second night of my joining the battalion. On first encounter, Paget can cut a domineering, aggressive figure – but once the barrier had been broached, here was a fun loving buccaneer and an excellent pilot. But that first encounter is worth telling. "Pongo, what's your name?" He barked down the bar in the Officers Mess which the Cameronian officers of D company were sharing with the RAF. I looked around me, pretending that this aggression was being targeted at someone else. "No, you, you lily white ponce of a Cameronian officer!" This was beginning to get to me. "Yapi (a derogatory British military term for South Africans) - wash out your mouth and stop behaving like a pig!" I retorted. This was too much for the big South African and he took a swing at me, and again thanks to the tuition from Sergeant-Major Wallace and the Benedictine Monks, I ducked with reflexes in good order and his fist jammed in the wooden panelling of the wall of the officers mess. I took careful aim with my right foot and caught him in that section of the anatomy where the buttocks adjoin the scrotum. With a howl of rage and a modicum of pain, he wrestled to disengage his fist. The giant South African glowered down at the middleweight Cameronian. "Well, I'll be f......d!" he roared. "Have a drink, you cheeky pongo!" Then blossomed a ripe friendship. One day I invited him to join me in a 24 hours route march including an ascent over the Jebel. Paget had always denigrated the foot soldier as cannon fodder and added to which he was irritated, as were the other RAF officers, of the jocks continuously beating up the less warlike airmen on the Muharraq air base. "Poofter stuff, marching!" he'd snort derisively. "Come with me, then" I responded. On the day he insisted on striding ahead of my platoon, his big feet pounding the rock-strewn sand. But then the wheels came off and his stride inexorably lessened until was he was reduced to a limping shuffle. The man was in agony, much to the glee of the jocks, but I had to admire his staunchness. I helped the groaning Bellin to the Officers Mess after I'd dismissed the platoon and I eased him onto a stool and bought him several beers. "Listen, pongo," Paget managed to croak after he'd downed two beers in as many minutes, "I'm returning the compliment. Next saturday I'm taking you up in my fighter plane. You had your day today and mine is coming!"

I duly reported the following week at 07.00 am on a blazing hot morning where the humidity was already soaking my shirt to the skin and up strides Paget looking distinctly the worse for wear. "Right, hop in". I clambered into the cockpit excited at the prospect of being taken on a pleasant joy-ride around the shores of the Persian Gulf. I glanced across at Paget. He was looking awful for a fit strong man. His hands were shaking, and his eyes were blood-red. "Haven't been to sleep. Downed my last scotch an hour ago. Those officers of yours are dangerous company". Paget had been invited over to the B Company mess by the wild Captain Nick Carter. "You mean to tell me you're going to fly when you're still pissed. You're mad. Stark-steering bonkers. I'm getting out!" "Stay put, pongo. You caused me horrible blisters on your bloody march across the sand and now it's my turn!" With that, we streaked down the runway and screamed to the heavens in a vertical position. For the next half hour I didn't know what had hit me. Paget Bellin had the bit between the teeth. He would barrel roll without warning, he would dive bomb the Arab dhows in the sea, he would skim a mere five metres above the ground and I thought I was about to meet my maker. And then I began to get the hang of things. I can now understand how Paget flew single-handedly a Spitfire from England to South Africa after he'd left the RAF. He was a very gifted pilot and he was in his full element behind the throttle that hot morning. For two hours we cavorted over the Persian Gulf and just before we grounded, Bellin targeted a fishing boat. "We'll give him one hell of a fright!" he shouted above the roar of the engines and he aimed the fighter plane at the vessel. We were screaming across the sea at full bore at about the height of the vessel's mast and as we flashed by, five sets of flashing teeth and arms and legs appeared to fill the cockpit. I looked down to see the Arabs flailing around in the sea. "There are sharks in there, Paget!" I yelled over the din of the engines". "Good riddance!" was his reply. "Stinking wogs!" Paget Bellin was certainly not of the 'politically correct' mould.

Twenty years later I bumped into the South African quite by chance in Johannesburg. I had always wondered what had happened to that big, swaggering pirate and there we stood in the street looking at each other. "It's the pongo!" he cried, laughing. I replied "You're the yapi who got his fist stuck in the panelling at the Muharraq mess!" We had an impromptu party that night that took us into the dawn. As I write Paget is somewhere causing mayhem in Natal. He'll like this anecdote, except the memory of his route march across the Arabian sands with the Cameronian jocks.

After Bahrain came a brief sojourn in Kenya. This East African colony was a jewel, a vibrant country with the European settler in jubilant mood after the Mau Mau uprising. Kenya was prospering. Its agricultural production was at an all time peak. Its tourism and big game hunting industry was booming and its wild life infrastructure was under efficient control. Kenya in those days of 1958 was a very pleasant station for a soldier. I can recall the pristine cleanliness of Nairobi's streets and its hotels, the

Norfolk and the Stanley in particular, and the legendary Muthaiga Club were superbly run establishments where the ice cold beers and chilled gin and tonics would be served by impeccably attired staff in starched whites and red fezzes. I can remember the hunting trucks rumbling down the streets and this was the Kenya that Robert Ruark immortalised in his best seller 'Something of Value' and for a young subaltern in the British army, Kenya opened many doors. There were the farmers who allowed me to shoot Thomson gazelle for the pot in return for a bottle of whisky from the Officers Mess at Muthaiga camp. There was the generous hospitality extended by the settlers in their homes and this was the era of the white hunter and his client. There were the polo tournaments, the boxing matches against the Kings African Rifles, the company exercises in the bushveldt and the forests of the great Kenya outback. The women were sporting pearl-handled revolvers in their handbags and there was the rough camaraderie of the ranch owners. Kenya was a great experience and there was no doubt this was where the seeds were sown for my call to Africa in later years. After the harshness of the deserts, and remembering that many of the Cameronians had been serving in Muscat, the Trucial Oman, and Bahrain for well on two years without a break and with limited recreational opportunities, the Kenya posting was a Shangri La. To this extent I can speak of the intransigence of the Cameronian soldier in Kenya from raw experience. For the two weeks that I served sentence for leaving a live rifle bullet on my dresser in my tent, my task as extra orderly officer was to scour the seedier bars and brothels for the wayward jock looking for cheap thrills. The military police were on hand to assist in this unenviable job and their prowess in using boots, fists, and truncheons were often needed as it should be remembered that the Glaswegians of this generation were notorious for their mercurial behaviour. The spirit of the Gorbals and Barlinnie, giving rise to that famous book 'No Mean City' written about pre-war Glasgow, was very much evident in the battalion when I joined it. Those were the days when Members of Parliament were not expected to be called upon for help. The army NCO exercised his right in 'banjoing' a recalcitrant soldier behind the latrines and the troops knew where they stood.

I was into the second week of my sentence of duty orderly officer, surviving on three hours sleep a night after patrolling Nairobi to keep peace and order and undertaking battalion duties during the day. One evening, in my jaded state, I dropped into the Equator club for a quick whisky and sitting at the bar my mind flitted back to HMS Duneira, the troop ship that had transported the bulk of the battalion from the Persian Gulf via Bombay to Mombassa, Kenya. There was a reason for me to ruminate on that famous British navy warship that for thirty years had ferried men at arms to trouble spots of the British Empire. One particular night I was serving as duty officer. I found myself in the middle of the ship where from both sides I heard this extraordinary cacophony of noise. To the left were the officers in full flight. They were celebrating the escape from the tedium of the deserts and the constant dangers therein. To the right of the ship the naval ratings and the jocks were locked in a stupendous brawl on the lower decks. The jocks had found fault with their sleeping arrangements and the turbulent Glaswegians had taken a deep dislike to the unfortunate sailors. It was true pandemonium and I had little hesitation in summoning the full complement of military police that waded into the fracas with their truncheons.

I was immersed in thought of that night aboard the Duneira when my reflections were shattered by an unholy disturbance in the Equator club. This was an establishment owned and run by a character called Ron Partridge for the well-heeled local fraternity and the tourists and the hunters with money to spend. In lurched a rifleman from my own platoon, as chance had it, a saturnine jock, one of the battalion's hard men, by the name of McCluskey. He was drunk, very drunk. He looked a menacing figure as he thrust his way into the centre of the dance floor – knife in one hand and a bottle of whisky in the other. "Get him out of here" Partridge whispered feverishly into my ear. "I'll do that, Mr Partridge. The deal is membership and an evening of my choice on the house". "Just get that horrible soldier out of here" urged a panic-stricken Partridge. "I have a deal?" I muttered under my breath, my eyes fixed on the bellicose Jock. It should be explained that Ron Partridge was an effeminate man, and many took him to be more than that and Partridge had a vendetta against the junior officers of the Cameronians. He considered them to be of an inferior caste to mankind and not worthy of membership of his precious club. But men of the ilk of John Irvine, Nick Daglish, Nesbit and others shared my view and we walked with impunity into the Equator club when we felt like it. Now was the occasion to avenge Mr Partridge's lack of respect for the Cameronians' finest. "Deal" whimpered Partridge. "But get him out of here!" By now Partridge's shocked clientele was mesmerised by the demonic Scot and this is where I chose my moment to stride across the dance floor and I grabbed McCluskey by the arm and steered him to a dark corner of the nightclub. "McCluskey, pull yourself together!" I hissed". The granite faced Jock peered at me malevolently, knife gripped in one hand. "I've my lost my ma – I've lost my ma" he kept repeating and the hard man had tears in his eyes, probably for the first and last time in his life. I then took a decision, an unconventional decision at that, but probably one of the finest in my career in my humble opinion. "My driver will take you back to camp. I won't report this but don't give me any more trouble or to the driver or to the guard duty. You hear me, McCluskey, and not a word of this to anyone". From that day I never had one ounce of trouble from Rifleman McCluskey. I was to learn that after I left the battalion he was sent to Shepton Malet, the military prison in Somerset for serious offenders, for assault and battery.

The famous day arrived for the cocktail party that our Colonel had decided to throw for the locals. It was a gesture of 'gain the hearts and the minds of the civilians'. The occasion was destined for disaster from the outset when one considered the nature of the officers we had in those days – men better equipped for battle than social niceties. Sandy Lindsay, the battalion's signals officer and normally a sensible man, allowed the event to go to his head. With encouragement from the wilder officers such as Nick Carter and 'Black' Alan Campbell, Sandy decided to use a thistle – a suitable emblem of Scotland – as a rifle pull-through down a selected matron's cleavage. The ear-splitting shriek silenced the hubbub of the cocktail party and Sandy's social graces were brought to an abrupt halt by Major Reg Parkes, the President of the Officers Mess.

There was the occasion of my being called upon with the assistance of a sergeant to act as a guide for an Irish Guards' platoon into the bush. The Kenyan highlands were teeming with game and some of it highly dangerous as the black rhino which were plentiful in that era. Thus, myself and the sergeant found ourselves in the middle of a file of Irish Guards who were fresh out of Caterham, the Brigade of Guards Depot near Aldershot, England. Our job was to act as observers to test a new survival ration, in addition to assisting as guides in the terrain we knew well. I found the lieutenant a pompous idiot. The Irish guardsmen, however, deserved some pity as their white skins and large feet encased in standard issue heavy marching boots suffered not a little degree of discomfort. In those days sunburn and blisters were considered self-inflicted wounds, a chargeable offence. The sergeant and I observed with scepticism the behaviour of the lieutenant who insisted that his platoon march through the bush in parade-ground formation. The noise of course was deafening. Then came a confrontation with a very angry rhinoceros. My sergeant suggested in his choicest Glaswegian vernacular that I take charge of the situation. He had accompanied me on more than one crocodile shoot (crocodiles were considered vermin) and the occasional gazelle hunt. I took the subaltern aside, suggesting that the troops remain motionless so as to allow the rhino to move on. Not a bit of it. The officer replied in no uncertain terms that I was a mere observer and that he was in control. Shaking my head, I collected the sergeant and the two of us took sanctuary on a small kopje to view the fun. On marched the stoical Irish Guards stomping through the vegetation, with their leader swinging his arms as if on guard duty at Buckingham Palace. His bravado evaporated minutes later when the rhinoceros grew bored with this charade and decided to charge the line at full speed. "Hold your positions!" yelled the silly lieutenant. "Steady now!" His men knew better and they scattered in all directions – up trees, down ant holes, anywhere to escape this fierce behemoth bearing down at great velocity. "Stupid wee bairstard!" was all the sergeant beside me could mutter as chaos unfolded beneath us. The rest of the day, the two Cameronians firmly ensconced themselves in close proximity to the Irish

Guards officer in the event of another mishap in the bush. He didn't like it one little bit but there was nothing he could do about it.

It was a sad day when the regiment was recalled to the deserts. The citizens of Nairobi heaved a sigh of relief but the officers and men had hardly settled down in their newly found paradise before they found themselves being hustled back to reinstate law and order in the sands of Arabia. The Cameronians were part of 24 Independent Infantry Brigade and their duty was to act as trouble shooters in the turbulent Middle East which was in foment. There was trouble brewing in the Lebanon, Kuwait and in Jordan following General Kassem's overthrow of King Faisal in Iraq. We found ourselves in Aden amidst the flies and the discomfort of the army camp at Khormaksar. This camp was in a state of deterioration with tattered tents and inadequate ablution facilities and we spent a highly unpleasant two weeks amidst sand storms, over crowdedness, and a lack of laundry facilities. Mercifully the resident regiment, the Yorks and Lancs, were up-country on operations which alleviated the congestion somewhat but we weren't a happy battalion by any stretch of the imagination.

Rumours were now rampant. We knew we were destined for an exciting assignation but the cloak of secrecy was well maintained, right up to the point when we embarked on HMS Bulwark, one of the veteran warships in the British navy. Only when we were about to set sail were we told over the tannoy that we were heading for Jordan. This was riveting stuff for a young subaltern, perhaps not so novel for the older officers who'd seen action in Malaya and those who'd served in the War. As history would reveal, it was touch and go that the Cameronians and the Parachute regiment sent to protect King Hussein of Jordan were not propelled into a full blooded battle. We disembarked at the Port of Aquaba and were flown by Valetta's and Dakotas to Amman. Then followed a period of my military life which will never be erased from memory. We were billeted in tents on top of slit trenches which were dug by the soldiers amidst a constant stream of the most colourful language open to imagination. There were a handful of miners that chipped through the hard stony ground but the average jock was better suited to fighting and he found the task alien to his nature.

We now knew from our briefings that King Hussein of Jordan had called upon the British government for assistance on account of the revolt in neighbouring Iraq; and assassination by his own army was a distinct possibility. We and the men of the Parachute regiment remained on the barren hillsides surrounding the Amman airfield for three months with little to do except to stand ready waiting for an enemy attack. To alleviate the boredom we kept fit through endless patrolling of the surrounding countryside, drink in the evenings with one's fellow officers, and sleep fitfully in the torrid heat. But it was a rewarding experience for many reasons. The friendships – I came to know well three excellent men over those three months: Major Hugh Mackay, CO of D Company, his deputy, Captain Jim Orr, and Sergeant Major Henderson. It was Hugh Mackay, previously Adjutant of the regiment, who after I'd just joined the battalion in Bahrain, found reason to call me "one of the worst behaved officers that I've ever had the dubious pleasure of setting eyes on". I cannot be precise about the reason for his invective as I was frequently in hot water for a host of spirited adventures, inspired in the main by the incorrigible Captain Nick Carter. In the confines of a hot tent that served as our company officers' mess, you got to know men well. Hugh Mackay was an excellent professional soldier and was so was Jim Orr who returned to the Parachute regiment after the Cameronians were disbanded in 1968, rising to the rank of Lieutenant Colonel. And then Sergeant Major Henderson, a massively built Scot with a splendid thatch of hair that spread over his body and a deep voice that could rumble menacingly. I was quite touched when Hugh Mackay shook my hand on my demobilisation and asked me whether I shouldn't sign on with the words that I'd marginally improved since my early days with the regiment!

I can recall those days in Amman and I remember the patrols in the searing heat, the constant thirst and the swarms of flies. I remember the well-disciplined paratroopers with whom we shared the task of protecting King Hussein. On one occasion I took my platoon to Bethlehem where the Cameronians were well remembered from the days in 1936 when the battalion was stationed there. My impressions of Bethlehem and Jerusalem were of awe. Up to the late 50's those biblical towns had remained virtually unchanged since the days of the Crusades. I still recall the stark beauty of the valleys vegetated by Cyprus trees, the scrubby hills, the experience of swimming in the Dead Sea. I can also recall the paucity of good things to eat and the squalor of the filthy sleeping bag and the longing for sheets and hot water. I can remember the sight of the early snows on the hills at the time we withdrew from Amman in October 1958 when the defence of the airfield was handed over to the Parachute regiment. On that particular day, the regimental Pipes and Drums played the beating of the retreat in honour of King Hussein and Pipe-Major Matheson and Bugle Major Allan were presented to the monarch.

We flew to Aqaba where we exercised in the mountains bordering Saudi Arabia and guarded ammunition dumps scattered throughout the desert. It was after one of these duties that I can well remember to my dying days the occasion of the Pope's death. I was trudging through the sand, leading my platoon after a 48 hour vigil protecting an ammunition dump, when to my surprise I heard a tremendous racket emanating out of the Officers Mess with flag flying at full mast. This was odd, I thought, as it was only 08h00 in the morning. I put it down to an addition to the Royal Family or other such eminent occasion. After standing down the platoon, I entered the mess to be greeted by a throng of officers bellowing with gusto "Drinks on the left-footer. The Pope's died!" There was no malice, no suggestion of religious bigotry but just a red blooded prank on the one Catholic officer of the regiment at that time. I should explain that the Cameronians were originally formed from a strict Presbyterian sect known as the Covenanters whose function in the days of the seventeenth century was to fight Catholics. A steadfast tradition of the Cameronians was that a Catholic could serve as an officer but never command the regiment. Every Sunday, the RSM issues the order "Roman Catholics, fall out". I dreaded the first church parade in Bahrain. I had imagined that there would be a meagre patter of feet marking a small element of Catholics exiting the parade ground. But to my relief, I heard a crash of boots and it appeared that a full third of the regiment responded to the RSM's call.

Life as an officer in the Cameronians was never dull and there were constant challenges for a young man. From that morning I faced my platoon for

*the first time in Bahrain – and to a young subaltern fresh out of Officer
Cadet school they looked a fearsome lot with their hard expressions and
sunburnt, lean bodies – to the day I flew out of Nairobi (the battalion
returned to Kenya from Aqaba), the First Battalion Cameronians (Scottish
Rifles) served as a rough university that equipped a man to survive the
jungles of life. As unpredictable and as uncompromising these Scottish
soldiers were, they had huge hearts and one learnt to hold affection for
the Glaswegian jock. It had to be remembered that this regiment had
won a long roll of battle honours fighting in all corners of the earth since
its inception in 1689 under the first Colonel of the Regiment, the Earl of
Angus, son of the Marquis of Douglas. The Cameronians were essentially
a fighting regiment as exemplified by the words of John Masters and which
is to be expected from them with their history of Clan wars and fighting
the English. In battle the regiment earned itself an awesome reputation,
alongside its sister regiments from Scotland, making it one of the most
feared of fighting units in HMS armed forces. One will never forget those
officers and men and for an adventurer the battalion was a fertile seeding
ground. I made many solid friends in that regiment which took us from
Bahrain to Aden, to Kenya and to Jordan. I have kept in contact with men
like Jim Orr and Hugh Mackay, Brian Leishman, Dudley Heathcote, and
the reverend David Christie and who could ever forget the irrepressible
captains, Nick Carter and 'Black' Alan Campbell. I always enjoyed it
when I was in the revered company of Sir General Anthony Farrar-Hockley
who served as the Brigade-Major in Jordan when I was there. "Remind
me, Michael, of those wild officers in your regiment" he'd say with a wry
smile. "Nick Carter and Alan Campbell, amongst others," I'd reply. "That's
them. They were very wild "said the General.*

The crash of artillery at 5am had the four of us sitting bolt upright in
our camp beds. Piet Badenhorst looked at his watch cursing what the
hell was the rumpus all about. Chris Ball suggested that we were under
attack. Gert Potgieter gave me a very knowing look as I reached for
my running shoes but the eminent bankers remained in the dark as to
the reason behind the barrage of the big guns renting the air. I ran the
perimeter that morning with the sun coming up in the desert. I ran past

lines and lines of ratels (two man tanks), eland armoured cars, hippos and buffels (mine protective personnel carriers), huge artillery pieces bedded down, and the ever-alert sentries in the crows nests scouring the featureless terrain of northern South West Africa. We were, after all, in an operational camp, one of the most important to the High Command in Pretoria. I appreciated that early morning call, the most original that I have ever experienced. The guns of Oshakati put the standard alarm clock to shame.

* * * * *

The second border visit was another adventure. On this occasion I was clear headed to digest the briefing that we received at the military headquarters in Voortrekkerhoogte. The world was tightening its noose on the Republic and our Foreign Minister, Mr Pik Botha would vociferously defend the country's right to stand against the Russian and Cuban backed enemies on its borders. The presentation was lucidly executed and made fascinating reading and we clambered aboard the Hercules with patriotic fervour. We were going to meet the men on the front.

We landed at Katima Mulilo, the 701 Battalion base situated on the northern shores of the Zambezi in the Caprivi Strip. This was a strategic defence position where the borders of Botswana, Zimbabwe and Namibia converge. We were magnificently hosted by the SA Defence Force and were witness to an impressive mock battle staged by the 701 Battalion, a white officered unit, unusual to the extent that this particular battalion was the only officially English-speaking force within the SADF, all others being bilingual in English and Afrikaans. The Katima Mulilo border post was essentially a monitoring function for local activity, recording river traffic and refugee movements as a result of the devastation and strife in neighbouring war-torn Angola.

We boarded a Dakota to fly to a neighbouring camp called Omega in West Caprivi to visit the Bushmen Battalion and I was seated next to the public affairs director of the United Tobacco Corporation. I observed shortly after takeoff that the aircrew was unusually active and I glanced out of the window to see the wing on fire! The crew remained remarkably cool but the man from UTC was in a state of panic and I couldn't blame him. I had marked up some close calls to death in my time and I was somewhat used to situations of danger but the poor fellow at my side was in need of support. He implored me to talk to him and I obliged. I suggested that an order for our needy company would be welcome and this was to be granted if we survived. By this stage the wing was blazing furiously. It was a rare occasion to watch an aircraft wing in full flame whilst in flight and not a few aboard that morning thought that their end was nigh.

We landed at what appeared to be at full speed in Katima Mulilo. The air crew, cool and professional to the last, had contrived to extinguish the blaze and we climbed out of the Dakota a sober lot, somewhat shaken and happy to be alive. For two days we were grounded and for those 48 hours we were looked after in regal fashion. We were fortunate to be stranded in this scenic spot on the shores of the Zambezi River and two infantry officers were seconded to the four of us who opted for tiger fishing as opposed to whiling away the time sitting in the sun and drinking in the Officers Mess. We had a wonderful experience of cruising up and down the river, trying our hand at Africa's finest fresh water sporting fish, the tiger, so called for its vivid markings and its razor sharp teeth.

I never received the order from UTC. The fellow resigned shortly after my return to Johannesburg. Katima Mulilo will always be in my mind and not long after that incident I was destined to revisit the area in a further quest for tiger fish.

CHAPTER TWELVE

Tie breaker

WHEN COMPILING the book, I was reluctant at first to include the story of Vinuchi Pty Ltd, the company that Vivienne and I created. Narratives focussing on business tend to be pedestrian, particularly in juxtaposition with the adventurous tales in this manuscript. As I suggested earlier in the book, I was not a natural businessman; however, I had to generate money to support a family and fulfil an adventurous life style through sheer energy, sometimes misdirected, to compensate for a lack of natural business acumen. I can well understand how business leaders and money oligarchs are created. They are indoctrinated with a materialistic ethos from the cradle, often at the expense of the finer values of life. Brash Johannesburg, where I spent my prime years, flaunted the magnetism of the shekel and I surprised myself in surviving such a climate of raw consumerism.

I had to work from an early age as most of the family fortunes had been erratically managed and there was no safety net to fall on. My father set the pace He was the senior partner in London's leading Catholic legal firm that went by the Dickensian name of Arnold, Fooks and Chadwick. He was highly acclaimed for his work by certain luminaries as Cardinal Basil Hume and august bodies such as the Vatican but his reverence for money didn't exactly match that for matters of the church. My mother had a better understanding, curiously enough, of monetary affairs where she displayed certain cunning on her investments on the stock exchange and pursuing a hobby of antique dealing. However her business dealings were conducted in a mercurial manner – her parents hadn't trained her from the cradle!

I had a driving motivation to work for myself. This was a natural leaning of a loner spirit who from the start of his working career suffered a degree of volatility in his career path. After leaving school with a self belief in his writing skills, bolstered with A levels in History and English Literature, I aspired to becoming a journalist after completing my military service. I was dissuaded by my despairing father: "You will die of drink and penury as a newspaperman!" I countered with a suggestion that I join his legal firm. This was received by a gentle but firm rebuff as it was clearly obvious to my father that I was better suited for rat catching than a career in law!

After experiencing an exciting military service in the Middle East, I had to knuckle down to a job of my own making. In the London of the "swinging sixties" a significant number of my contemporaries, most of whom had served in the forces, had gravitated into advertising. It was a profession that was not overtly fussy who it took in. Strangely enough in those days, several top advertising men were of military stock and a commission into the armed forces served as a university degree. Colonel Varley, of Colman, Prentis and Varley was of such an ilk and I commenced my career in his agency followed by a stint in the Lonsdale Hands group. I then gravitated into marketing beverages for Cantrell & Cochrane(C & C), a company of Irish origin that was owned in part by Schweppes and two brewers, Courage's and Watneys.

On arrival in South Africa, I had planned to perpetuate my career in marketing. However I needed a job in a hurry with a wife and a one year old daughter to support and it was expedient to accept an offer from a leading advertising agency in Johannesburg. My sojourn in the adverting industry was best expressed by a copywriter wag that accorded me the accolade of 'the director in charge of outgoing accounts'. The more enjoyable recollections of the advertising world of Johannesburg best come to mind with serving such kindred spirits in the client ranks that I held an empathy with: John Frankel of Tiger Oats; Bruce Dennison and Paul Deppe of Cerebos foods; Ernie Malherbe of Kinekor; Peter Gallo and Tony Niemeyer of Gallo Music; Vladimir Steyn of Satour; Danie Hough, Frank Oosthuizen, and Len Petser of Total Oil, and David da Pinna of Cape Hotels. I also retain warm memories of my agency colleagues such as Marius Jansonnius, Wernher Heyns, Stan Joubert, Helgaard Pienaar and Brian Searle Tripp of Van Zyl & Robinson and David McKinstrey, Philip Cadman, Joh Groenewald, not to forget Rick McCarthy and his creative team at De Villiers & Schonfeld.

There were some hilarious incidents which helped to offset the extreme pressures and stress, often self induced by the agency wheel spin. Bristol Myers sent out their top brass from America to lock into some serious strategic planning with the agency's client service team. This summit was being staged in the boardroom on the eight floor of the prestigious 252 Jeppe Street office block – de V & S occupied four floors – whilst a black comedy was unfolding on the floor below. I had just returned to the office after a tedious meeting with Kinekor, an account I had been charged with by my peers to mastermind, a misguided decision as I was not remotely suited to the glitz and bling of the movie world. My dark mood was given a lift when I encountered a boisterous spectacle: there was Bob Brown, a Svengali like figure with flowing black hair and beard to match, and Alan Mitchell, a big bear of a man, feigning an assault on an infamous siren who took delight in sensually teasing those unfortunate denizens of the creative department of the seventh floor. The seductress was lashed to a chair by a curtain cord and the two bright sparks – one a copywriter and the other a senior visualiser – were giving the pretence of unzipping their trousers. Before the reader gets the false impression of a blue movie unfolding, these two stalwarts of the creative department possessed stable dispositions and both had experienced a bad day as indeed I had. I was invited to join in the charade by which stage the receptionist of the seventh floor, quite a passable brunette underneath the layers of mascara and fake tan, had panicked and was squealing her head off. I well remember the sea of faces peering down the spiral staircase linking the eighth and seventh floors, including those of Grahame de Villiers and David McKinstrey, the 'big men' of the agency, who had some explaining to do to the astonished Americans. Alan Mitchell and I beat a hasty retreat, leaving 'Dirty Bob' – as was his nickname in the agency – to face the music.

The aforementioned Alan Mitchell was an enigmatic character and a highly gifted copywriter whom I took a strong liking to and we used to meet with Rick McCarthy, the creative director of de V & S, at a midway point between the office and our respective homes. There was a bar in the Colony shopping centre, Hyde Park, where the three of us used to reminisce on the idiosyncrasies that abounded in our place of work. Another we enjoyed raising in addition to the romp previously described– our chairman in his wisdom decided to have his top echelon trained in the art of public speaking and he called in the services of Robin Alexander, a well known media personality of his time. To give Grahame de Villiers his due, he had the knack of attracting arguably the finest talent in the advertising industry to work for him - executives and creative men alike. All of us, with rare exception, were articulate people and following a series of these training sessions, which were undoubtedly a chronic waste of time for both Robin Alexander and his class, we were tasked to prepare our individual presentations. Philip Cadman decided to hurl a chair out of the eighth floor onto the street below to illustrate a point he was making about racing cars; Theo Meintjies lulled us to sleep with an earnest peroration on combustion engines. And then it came to my turn. Alan Mitchell had reminded me that morning on the presentation which I had forgotten about. "Alan, I have a brainwave. I'll talk about gorillas. I'll hire a skin and you wear it". I had to bribe Alan with a case of Guinness before he acquiesced to my scheme. Whilst the combustion engine story was boring us to tears, there was an extraordinary din emanating from the corridor. Apparently a very grumpy Mitchell, heavily perspiring in the gorilla suit, had been assaulted by the despatch department manager, Johnny Prince, a delightful fellow whom we all liked. Johnny Prince had never seen a gorilla and it was too much for him to encounter this savage looking apparition smoking a cigarette. According to Alan Mitchell, Johnny Prince was creeping up on him with an empty beer bottle in hand, eager to smash the enemy over the head when he received the fright of his life with the gorilla growling at him: "Beat it my man, I work here!"

Unaware of all this, I kept tugging on the string attached to Alan Mitchell believing he had deserted his post when , at long last, the conference door was hurled open and in lumbered an extremely angry and hot Mitchell. The audience howled the roof down – this was one up on Cadman's performance – and well needed relief from the combustion engine. "Two cases of Guinness you owe me or no deal" Alan hissed from underneath the gorilla skin. But he met his side of the bargain, prancing ungainly around the room making grunting noises and beating his chest and he began to enjoy himself until he overplayed the part, deciding to seize the research director, a visibly nervous female at this stage, under his arm, racing for the exit. By this stage of the evening, our leader, Grahame, was visibly annoyed as his senior men of the agency had not taken to the public speaking exercise quite in the mode as intended!

Another incident which had us chortling into our beer was the Guy Faulkes fireworks party. The agency had won a large account and it was decided to throw a celebration on this auspicious occasion. The revelry was in full swing with an impressive fireworks display cascading over Jeppe Street. A particular highlight of the festivities was a rocket that zoomed across the street through an open window of an office block. The fizzing missile had found its way into a mens' washroom and was ricocheting off the walls, causing the incumbent with his trousers at half mast to holler his head off. A gallery of Gallo Music executives was observing all this from their offices nearby and they were in a position to see a police car come cruising around the corner to investigate the disturbance and they warned us of the raid. They did us a service as we prepared ourselves for the visit from the law. Hume Schonfeld saved the day by greeting the police squad with glasses of brandywyn in the eighth floor reception. Hume's personality could be magnetic and by the time the police came down to the fourth floor to check at first hand the cause of the disturbance, another party was to begin with a tamer display of fireworks than previously staged.

One bleak Friday night I had a most unpleasant meeting with the MD of the agency. He had decided in his wisdom that 'the director in charge of outgoing accounts' was incompatible with the agency. This particular individual will remain nameless but he created irreparable damage to the company by firing several excellent men shortly after I led the charge out of the firm. I announced to my apprehensive wife that I had parted with the world of advertising and that the manufacture of neckwear was to form the nucleus of my new career. Vivienne had made a tie from silk cuttings supplied to her by a friend, Nuschka Roux, who worked in the fashion world. Vivienne has many talents but her ability with her hands is uncanny. She has a mechanical mind and I've watched her dismantle an industrial sewing machine and reassemble it at breakneck speed. I had found the bedrock on which to build a business -- the greatest silk tie company in South Africa was the objective. My one problem was that the clothing trade was an unknown entity. I had been trained in consumer goods marketing -- drink, cigarettes, and beverages - but not in such fastidious products as ties.

On reflection, it was short of a miracle that we drove Vinuchi to where it stands today. Initially we were an aspiring Gucci with dreams of creating a silk tie empire in South Africa - a marketplace more suited to the male world of mining and heavy industry. A born optimist, I took scant heed of the well intentioned advice I received from the clothing fraternity. In their opinion, the market for silk ties in southern Africa was extremely limited and we'd be wiser to consider polyester as the more suitable fabric to manufacture in; and, as the doomsayers' prognosis went, how could we expect to survive against the all pervasive Wistyn family of Cravateur, Wilfie Pimsteen of Skipper Ties, Norkie Abrahams of Regent and the other fourteen manufacturers in the neckwear business hovering like vultures to pick up the pieces! There was one Afrikaans speaking producer, a Mr Human of President Ties, who turned out to be a staunch ally. He had an intuition that our fledgling company could take on the might of the Jewish dominant neckwear manufacturing community. He helped us with servicing our machines and he told me: "You'll get the mining business and the military, your face fits". His prediction was accurate.

The story needs fast forwarding as otherwise the narrative would be bogged down in tedious detail. We will skim over the Woolworths visit to our first 'factory' -- a one roomed office in Rissik Street facing the SARS; the frantic rounds of several banking halls on Friday mornings in downtown Johannesburg drawing out the paltry limit on the credit card to pay the wages of our factory staff; of the discounting of our customers' cheques in bustling End Street in downtown Johannesburg -- this being conducted on the bonnet of my battered hunting truck serving as a delivery van - with our landlord, Izzy Stanger, a splendid Jewish fellow of the old school; of the sharing of Stanger's dank fourth floor premises with a precious fellow making ladies fashion dresses whom I threatened to toss down the lift shaft for a botched CMT job; of having to resort to using our silk fabric for ladies blouses, originally intended for ties, to sell to the boutique trade as a desperate cash flow measure; of the moment when I'd split my trousers and sat in my underpants conducting business when Ma Gerber -- the doyen of Johannesburg's fur trade - walked into the factory where I greeted this forbidding figure with a towel hastily strung around my middle; or of the nights we would work triple time and deliver the core of our workforce jammed into the hunting truck into the depths of Soweto in the late hours of the night.

After a mercurial beginning, facing bankruptcy on a score of occasions, Vinuchi finally arrived as a recognised player in the neckwear business. By the early 80s we had gathered together a formidable team of salesmen, designers, production workers and a skilled textile printing team. Our presence was beginning to be noticed. We were in demand. We had something new to offer. International awards began to come our way and such was the healthy state of the company that I could take time off chasing big game in faraway places whilst spreading the Vinuchi gospel in export markets. At this stage it is relevant to dwell on those pillars on which the Vinuchi company was built. Firstly, and most importantly, the technology that Vinuchi became renowned for, making it arguably the most sophisticated corporate tie maker in the world at that time. I am very serious on this claim. To give ourselves full credit, we had the ability of creating a corporate Hermes style product thrusting Vinuchi head and shoulders over the competition in the domestic and overseas markets which had traditionally relied on pedestrian club type designs made in woven fabric. And it must be remembered that in South Africa, the corporate, the military and the sporting sectors outweighed the fashion products sold through the retail trade in value terms.

This is when an extraordinary individual entered the fray. I had met John Kimber in my brief sojourn in the advertising world and I had taken our concept of a fashion orientated corporate tie to this controversial figure that was considered the country's finest and most innovative silkscreen printer. Either he was too successful at the time I approached him, or he was of the opinion that the scheme was a trifle harebrained, but he demonstrated scant interest until two years down the line when I received a call from the tempestuous fellow: "what the f... are you doing messing around with printing machines!" he bellowed down the line in his inimitable, irreverent style. "Get your backside down here tonight and we'll talk!" What had transpired in the two year span was that Vinuchi in its mercurial wisdom had laid out capital it could ill afford to import some serious printing machinery from France to facilitate the transfer of its avant – garde graphic designs on to cloth. Not one of the many silkscreen printers we approached had the ability, or the perseverance, to attempt to print our complex and detailed designs. There was only one man in South Africa, and probably overseas, who could attempt to meet the challenge and that was John Kimber. Yes, there were some sophisticated fabric printers in Italy and France who could achieve what we wanted but they demanded impossibly long runs which we could not hope to market.

Until Kimber's arrival, we had the vision and the designers, but not the printing expertise to propel us ahead of the pack that remained wedded to the well tried but pedestrian woven fabric route. It was evident that John Kimber had been observing the dizzy progress of the Vinuchi Company and he had timed his telephone call to perfection. Another three months of floundering around in the highly technical field of silk screen printing and Vinuchi could have sacrificed a brilliant idea. John Kimber had seen the angle. It took just two hours to forge a deal in Kimber's printing plant in downtown Johannesburg. Despite the cynics of Johannesburg's business community prophesying that the association between Callender and Kimber would erupt in a volcanic explosion within weeks, the partnership endured for some twenty years. Kimber, as with many artistic types, could be highly volatile and there were several occasions when the partnership threatened to split asunder but it stood the test of time.

Kimber was a genius in his field, the best in the silk-screening industry. The fellow had nightmarish people skills and his temper was legend. If he hadn't told half of South Africa's leading business houses to 'f... off', he would have become a billionaire with sufficient spare cash to buy Gucci. The man, formidable in build and resembling a hairy Goth of the fourth century, didn't particularly like his fellow brethren on the human planet. But he believed in himself to such an extent that if told there had been a misfire in his print, he would respond by threatening to march round to the client's office and hurl him out of the window. Despite rife speculation that the Vinuchi/Kimber combination would not work, it did and with the rich components of Vinuchi's marketing, production and design skills and Kimber's printing technique, we firmly attained our goal -- the Republic's finest corporate neckwear brand, an accolade it shared in the markets it exported to. *A success story.*

The second stanchion was Vinuchi's marketing strength. Vinuchi's growth in the decade the company thrived was partly due to its penetration of the corporations. In our heyday we covered 70% of the JSE top 100 companies. Our profile also slotted in admirably with the sporting and military sectors, not to forget the numerous associations and schools. Immense satisfaction was to be held in supplying the army and the air force defending the Republic's borders and it was a pleasure to travel around the various messes to meet the warriors in the different units ranging from the Para Brigade to the tank and artillery men, the infantry regiments and the aviators flying the Mirages and the Dakotas. Vinuchi manufactured a massive volume of product for the military and one took pride in being a cog in the Republic's fighting juggernaut. At the peak of the war on its borders, the fighting forces of South Africa were judged to be the best trained, motivated, and well equipped on the African continent. There was the occasion when we were called in by General Neil Webster at the South African Defence Force (SADF) HQ in Pretoria to design and make the Border Visit tie. The order was sizeable and prestigious for our company and it provided an enviable opportunity for me to partake in two tours to the military camps in Southern Africa. I describe one of these in chapter 11.

Life was never dull with the military. I took a telephone call one morning and the conversation went something like this: "Meneer Vinuchi, this is Captain X from General Malan's office. We need you to design a tie for the General. When is it convenient for you to come to his office?" The deep gravel voice had a heavy Afrikaans inflection. I believed this to be the work of a practical joker, a certain Steve Hodgson, who had caught me before with his pranks in posing as an inspector from the tax office that had me in a cold sweat; on another occasion as an official of the 'Iron Man' accusing me of cheating by catching a lift in the race and depriving me of a coveted silver medal which had me bellowing down the line in a red rage. I responded to the perceived humorist in my choicest Afrikaans telling the General's aide to *"voetsek!"* A pregnant pause followed and then a severe reprimand: *"I suggest you wash your mouth out. You understand who you are talking to? You want the business or not!"* I realised I'd made a terrible gaffe in suggesting an aide of the Chief of the SADF to jump in the lake with a very rude expletive. I apologised profusely and in due course took the brief to design the General's tie for his personal distribution. We were instructed to use a plain white lining in order that he could autograph his tie with a ball point pen!

Armscor, the giant armaments company of South Africa, provided us with a large chunk of business. The chairman, Commandant Piet Marais, dealt with me personally and under his wing we produced an impressive collection of product for the extensive list of companies supplying Armscor. It should be explained that in response to the world tightening its sanctions, the Republic reacted with resilience and punched well above its weight in the armaments industry. The skills of its scientists, engineers and technicians are best manifested by the South Africans making the atom bomb. Virtually every facet of the military and the arms industry was serviced by Vinuchi. It was hardly surprising as our profile was better suited to this channel of business than our competitors. As aforementioned, our face fitted and we had an empathy with the SADF and its myriad of associated companies.

The world of sport was another natural hunting ground. We were appointed as official suppliers to SA Rugby, SA Cricket, the National Olympic Committee of South Africa, and we covered a wide spectrum of sport. Perhaps being a participant in the major endurance events -- ultra marathons including the Comrades, the Two Oceans, the Duzi canoe marathon and the 'Iron man' - facilitated the significant business that we conducted for South Africa's sporting community. Vinuchi reciprocated the immense support it received from the various sporting bodies in sponsoring rugby, cricket, canoeing, inflation boat racing and contributions of university grants for boxing and gymnastics

The Johannesburg agent for Cravateur, our fiercest rival, believed he had the rugby business sewn up. This particular individual had played for the Transvaal which he used as a battering ram to bludgeon any competitor daring to encroach on his turf. I rang a friend, Lee Irvine, the legendary Springbok cricketer for advice on how to crack the lucrative rugby enclave and his solution was to arrange a lunch with Mickey Gerber, the supremo of Ellis Park. I had heard from my accountant, an irreverent Londoner called Derek Tucker, that Mickey Gerber disliked the English speaking fraternity. "He'll eat you for breakfast" was Derek's sage advice delivered in his distinctive cockney accent. "Waste of time and money giving him lunch, Michael, lad!" I thought this was somewhat a contradiction, reminding Derek that he was a regular attendant at the Wanderers club bar which Mickey Gerber patronized. It should be explained that Mickey

Gerber, who had played full back for the Springboks in his time, was a known supporter of Cravateur.

Lee Irvine was true to his word and lunch was arranged. Any misgiving I may have held on the destroyer of the English speaking community was disarmed by an engaging smile and an extended handshake. With him was a young man, Rian Oberholzer, marketing director of Ellis Park. The upshot of the lunch was that Vinuchi agreed to sponsor the Under 20's Transvaal side in return for benefits in the form of neckwear business and signage in the ground in a spectacularly prestigious position near the halfway mark. And, thanks to the advice from Willie John McBride, the sign was reproduced in black & white to catch the cameras. This meeting resulted in a successful sponsorship and until his death, Mickey Gerber and I remained good friends. Rian Oberholzer was to become the CEO of SARFU and his major achievement was masterminding the Super 14, the Southern Hemisphere version of the Heineken cup involving the strongest of the provincial sides of South Africa, Australia, and New Zealand, producing some of the most ferociously played rugby in the world. Rian's detractors will claim that his father- in- law, Louis Luyt, provided Rian with a silver spoon but those in the inner circle of SA Rugby would probably disagree. Rian with his legal degree and Stellenbosch University background contained the necessary corporate ability and street sense to reach the pinnacle of the jungle which SA rugby is.

As the sponsor of the Transvaal juniors, I had the privilege of a passing parade of past and present players of note that I would encounter in the 'Glasshouse', a cavernous room for the after match functions, at Ellis Park. I shared many a drink with such characters as Jomo King who sat on the Transvaal and SARFU boards and he was an entertaining speaker at the after match parties. I would frequently converse with Springboks including Kevin de Klerk, Richard Prentice, Jannie Breedt, Ray Mordt and many more. The 'Glasshouse' evokes many memories going back to the early eighties, well before the Vinuchi sponsorship commencing in 1988, when I used to accompany two colourful men of sport, Keith Gordon and Clive Noble who were linked to the rugby game. The former, a Macabbi

Games wrestler and noted sporting physiotherapist who treated many rugby players; and the latter, physician to the Transvaal Rugby Board and the SA Boxing Board of Control. These two would invite me to many matches viewed from the 'Glasshouse'. I met many fascinating characters as General Jannie Geldenhuys, the GOC of the SADF; rugby scribes such as Jan Retief; and the evergreens of Springbok rugby of the late 60's, men like Wilf Rosenberg, Des Sinclair, and Syd Nomis.It was in the 'Glasshouse' that I first met the legendary captain of the 1974 Lions Willy John McBride where a few years later our paths were to cross again.

Rugby apart, Vinuchi spread its tentacles wide amongst the sporting bodies. Cricket, boxing, gymnastics, rowing, canoeing featured heavily on its roll and we reciprocated by sponsoring teams and individuals in these sports. Vinuchi's respect for and commitment to sport was manifested by its staging *The Vinuchi Sporting Occasion.* This constituted an invitational lunch involving an auspicious collection of businessmen and sportsmen of national level; a guest speaker would be invited from overseas, in most cases a sporting legend, which was a valuable draw card as the country was in sporting isolation in those days. We managed to attract an illustrious collection of celebrities: Syd Millar, Tony O'Reilly, Willie John McBride representing rugby; Mark McCormack, founder of IMG; Sir Chay Blyth, the ocean solo yachtsman; and General Sir Anthony Farrar – Hockley, the renowned military figure. *The Vinuchi Sporting Occasion* proved to be a public relations triumph - it became a talking point in influential business circles but it also presented a healthy platform for industry to mingle with the sporting world.

The third pillar of Vinuchi's foundation was its financial structure. I will refrain from naming the bank that we initially used in respect for our big minded approach at Vinuchi. This institution was one of the major banks in South Africa. We made the cardinal error of placing our account at its head office, 100 Main Street – we'd met the manager through a friend - where I was given a particularly obnoxious sub manager to look after our account. He took a pernicious delight in trying to bully our emergent company. After one stormy meeting, stumbling angrily down the steps of the wretched bank in question, I had the good luck in colliding into my revered friend, Colonel Ian Mackenzie, the chairman of Standard Bank. "What are you doing here?" the venerable man demanded. "You may well ask, Colonel; I've had a shocking experience with this miserable lot". "You need help?" Since that bleak day in the late seventies, Vinuchi received excellent, unwavering service from Standard Bank. The chairman took the trouble to place the fledgling Vinuchi under the courteous care of Ginger Schmidt, the manager of the Marshall Street branch which serviced some notable giants of industry – Anglo American, De Beers, Boart International and a host of other monoliths. Five years later when Vinuchi had expanded, Ginger took early retirement and we invited him to handle our books. One of the wisest decisions made early on in the development of our company was the financial reporting systems we put in place, well beyond the expectancy of a concern of our size.

Not through marketing myopia in the Harvard Business School definition, the dream came to a shuddering halt in 1991. It took one short year for the tie market to implode in the Republic and this phenomenon included the retail trade. A combination of Nelson Mandela's release from jail in 1990 -- Mandela preferred 'Madiba' styled shirts to ties -- and a dramatic shift in international clothing trends leading to the 'open neck' attire, resulted in a catastrophic death blow to our product. The Western world experimented with the open neck dress code for a few years. However, the corporations in the G8 countries reverted to wearing ties including the sunny European countries -- Italy, Spain etc -- as they felt undressed without a tie around the neck. But South Africa and Australian businessmen felt that the tie was superfluous which says something, of course, for the level of taste down in the Southern Hemisphere! Vinuchi was forced to diversify into corporate clothing and up market corporate gifts, with neckwear taking a back seat. It took quite some time to adjust to this very different tack but it succeeded, largely due to our Managing Director's (Jonathan Evans) understanding of these products and the marketing strategies needed to keep Vinuchi's reputation and standing in the market place intact. Today, Vinuchi remains alive and thriving, with full credit due to Jonathan Evans and his team.

From very humble beginnings, it is with a modicum of pride that the Vinuchi enterprise threaded a path through South Africa's socio/economic maelstrom. Vinuchi had fought in a highly competitive, over traded channel of industry to become the brand leader of the corporate neckwear market. Through sheer stamina and gutzpah, the company is alive and well today, due in no small measure to the foresight and ability of Jonathan Evans. In its time Vinuchi became a world beater. It won the silver award for the 1985 Screen Print Association International competition in America; it exported to several markets, forming companies in Britain and Australia, and sales offices in Canada and America. It had made such diverse product as The New York Marathon tie, 'Britain means business' tie, a glittering Who's Who of varied business houses in the markets it operated in, and it achieved brand leadership in its domestic market.

Today, Vinuchi operates in a very different business climate. Gone are the halcyon days when captains of industry wrote letters to express appreciation of their corporate tie; when contracts were cemented on a handshake; when accounts were settled promptly. Over a recent lunch in Johannesburg with Jonathan Evans, we reminisced on Vinuchi's turbulent beginnings and the moments of close disaster and euphoric good fortune. The new leader and owner of Vinuchi turned to me with a serious expression. "Listen to this one – it sums up the precariousness of the business climate in this country. The other day, our ladies in the sales admin department came to me with a proposal –they wished to generate sales off their own initiative. I gave them full blessing on their enterprising spirit. These two ladies were doing a fine job of mopping up after the salesmen, ensuring their orders were accurate and correctly prepared for the computer, and following through with diligence checks on the customers. Despite their efficiency, the invoice for their first order was allowed to lapse to 90 days! They came to me scared to tell me of their dilemma– they had finally cornered the customer after numerous calls, only to be told: "I'm a criminal. I do fraud. Chase me once again for payment and I will come round and shoot you!" Michael, this may sound a hoot to you but doing business in this country is becoming hairy.

Bribing one day will become a norm of business. You've never bribed in Vinuchi and nor have I . But it's coming to this".

Postscript

I sent a copy of this chapter to Jonathan prior to publication for his approval as he's now the top honcho at Vinuchi. I received a prompt reply which reads:

A wonderful tribute to Vinuchi... I like the fact that you made significant reference to the unfortunate incident we suffered (ref last paragraph of the chapter). I think it very typically describes the bush war we are fighting these days in the SA market place!

I wish to add a postscript: "I joined Vinuchi in 1994 to work for an absolute maverick, Michael Callender. They say things happen for a reason; this move for me surely had reason. Michael taught me many things in my time with him, most of all he taught me honour, commitment, and a sense of adventure. He also made me realise that one should never give up on a dream and that sticking to something and making it work will surely bring success and happiness. He showed me how important it is to surround oneself with strong people, lead well and never let them know when one is feeling vulnerable. He also taught me the value of a brand and of marketing that brand which we are now doing again in a big way. The best part of my working life has been Vinuchi which still today remains a strong and well respected brand."

Fine words, Jonathan. I never knew that I was taking on a scribe in addition to your striking talents as an entrepreneur. If anything goes awry at Vinuchi, which I very much doubt it will, you have a job in my editorial department!

℘ ✦ ℘

CHAPTER THIRTEEN

Iron Man

Superb fitness and true grit are the qualities that make Iron Men and Women. But physical preparation and tenacity alone are insufficient; quite as important is a mental attitude that enables competitors to press on, and on, and on when body and spirit must be at the limits of their endurance. It is this spirit, this almost mystical challenge that people set themselves, which makes the Iron Man contest so special — and elevates all the contenders above the herd.

A T Myburgh – *Editor of the Sunday Times.*

THE IRON Man race was conceived in a bar by an officer in the US Navy stationed in Honolulu. Commodore John Collins, bored to tears with inaction, came up with the idea of the perfect athlete: a man capable of completing the Waikiki water swim, a cycle race around Oahu, and running the Honolulu marathon without stopping. In 1979 fifteen challengers, all male, inaugurated the Hawaiian Iron Man race of which a dozen completed the course. Four years later the race came to South Africa and in 1983, 303 men and 3 women set off at 5.00 am on the first leg of the 160km Iron Man. The race was given intense publicity many months before the start as the sponsor was the Rand Daily Mail and South Africa had never countenanced an event involving the diverse skills of canoeing, cycling and marathon running without a stop. The course was gruelling – 28 kms in the Hartebeespoort Dam which is a vast stretch of water that can be whipped into a choppy sea in minutes if the wind rises; 92kms of mind numbing hills for the cycle leg; and a cruel switchback of a road for the 42km marathon from Pretoria to Johannesburg. If the tortuous route was not sufficient to drain the strength and the stamina of the athlete, there was the added torment of the scorching heat of the Transvaal summer. South Africa at this period of time was in the midst of a seven year drought and the pundits were forecasting temperatures well into the late thirties centigrade for the day of the race.

I stood in the gathering dawn on the banks of the Hartebeespoort in a sheen of sweat and suffering from a bad attack of nerves. I could hardly canoe in those days, having started three months prior to the Iron Man and it was a race that favoured the canoeist, particularly the men of the Duzi who were conditioned to running hills with canoes on their backs. It was no great deal for these rugged men to learn to cycle. But the reverse applied to the marathon man or the specialist cyclist. They had to learn how to handle a sleek racing kayak for 28 kms over a choppy dam which took the paddler across long stretches of extremely deep water and woe betides him if he capsized. That could be his race over!

I had been cajoled into the contest by a close friend, Ian Green, who sadly was to lose his life six years later in the Duzi Canoe Marathon as mentioned in chapter 9. The ever-ebullient entrepreneur who had a great zest for life had phoned me in a state of excitement: "There's this amazing race we've got to do!" he yelled down the phone. "Drop tools and meet me for a beer right now". I needed no further encouragement. I was thirsty after a long day in the Johannesburg heat – exacerbated by the savage drought we were experiencing – and excitement was never far from my reach. Ian was waiting for me in a bar that we used to frequent and with a gleeful grin he thrust into my hand a newspaper cutting. "Read it, my man, we're in!" I scanned the article as I dipped into my beer and I nearly choked. "No man in his right senses would try this!" I spluttered. "160 kms nonstop – 13 hours of exposure in this heat. No, no, oh no!" I muttered. "Anyway, I'm approaching 44, but you can do it and I'll second you. You're ten years younger for a start and you can canoe. I've never sat in one of those boats and I'll drown. That Hartebeespoort Dam is big and it's deep. You've lost it, Ian. Forget it!" After two hours and many beers, my fate had been sealed. I was lured in by a triumphant Ian Green.

Then started the training routine: a rotation of a cycle leg of 60kms or a 15km run or a 10km canoe session at daybreak and a second session in the middle of the day. Triathlons were unheard of in those days. We were guinea pigs, not really knowing how to cross train effectively for such a race. We knew that the field would be tiny – 300 competitors drawn from the entire country was the estimate.

I remember calling John Feek, a Comrades silver medallist and a 'Duzi rat' of more than five Duzis, and a strong, competitive athlete. What was he doing about the cycle, I was keen to learn. His reply was that his backside had never been so sore after riding several kilometres on his wife's bicycle. In those early days of the race, we really didn't have a clue as to what equipment to use and how to train. Like John Feek, several competitors were of the belief that they could pedal near-on 100 kilometres on a bicycle with a shopping basket! It didn't take us long to learn that a racing cycle was requisite and so were strange shoes with cleats, and cycling vests to allow for circulation of air and such vital ingredients as peanut butter sandwiches and bananas to consume on the race. We secured the services of a Springbok cyclist, the tough-as-teak Alan Van Heerden who had recently completed the Italian equivalent of the Tour de France with a broken jaw. He taught us how to handle a racing cycle and he transformed us from slogging endlessly in low gears to the finesse of 'spinning'. Ian Green needed no canoeing lessons, nor did John Feek, nor such men as Mike Tindall and others who formed our impromptu training squad. I had to learn the hard way entering races without the help of a seat to secure my balance. I had a torrid time of falling out at the starts, tipping over in the rapids, and on more than one occasion I'd run the last 10 kilometres or so with a canoe on my shoulder to reach the finish point.

For four arduous months, including the Christmas holidays, we'd sweat up and down the hills surrounding Johannesburg. We'd learn to handle the grilling heat and the cross-disciplines of canoeing and cycling, cycling and running, running and canoeing and we began to assume highly honed physiques from the hours spent in a canoe, a discipline that I continued to battle with in those days. We learnt to eat on the cycle, and how to pass water standing on the pedals. We began to get accustomed to the leg numbing transition from cycle to run. Our diets began to assume strange patterns and out of the window went the desire to drink wine or spirits where beer was the flavour the body craved for in its need for carbo-hydrates. Meat gave way to mounds of pasta, bread and more beer, particularly stout. With the punishing regimen, mostly conducted under the blazing skies of the drought-stricken Transvaal, our bodies leaned down without an ounce of fat to show for the potatoes, the bread, the spaghetti, and the litres of glorious beer.

We stood there in the harsh glare of the television floodlights at 5.00 a.m. beside our canoes waiting for the gun in the dawn of February, 26th, 1983. The temperatures had already reached the mid 20's and the announcer's voice over the tannoy warned us of the impending heat, threatening to reach the late thirties centigrade. I took stock of the athletes around me. The expressions told the story. They stood looking grim, nervous, silent and alone in their thoughts. The 300 strong field were pioneers of a race that none had experience of. In anybody's language the 28 km of canoeing, 90 km of cycling and 42 km of running is a devastating challenge. Add to that the heat, the rare air of an altitude of close to 6000 feet, and then there is a race to strike a degree of dread into the hearts of the most stoical of the Duzi and Comrades veterans. There are not many tests of endurance which radiate that special kind of aura that I experienced on the dawn of that day. And then at last the gun went off and I can remember a tremendous cheer from the throng of onlookers as we entered the fray of jostling canoeists anxious to gain a good head start for the punishing journey that lay ahead.

That first Iron Man was to prove a punishing ordeal, more so that I had ever imagined. I fell out three times in the Hartebeespoort Dam, losing valuable time and precious energy. I lost my water bottle on the first capsizing and if a considerate fisherman hadn't come to my aid, I could have continued in a serious state of dehydration. I had also to thank a fellow competitor, a brawny rugby forward who gave me his water bottle as we crawled together across the depths of that massive stretch of water. In those early days of my canoeing career, I hadn't the confidence of swinging my body in the kayak and my shallow stroke reflected the nervousness of the novice. I lurched out of the water, third last in position and my wife and children and Peter Geikie-Cobb – a cousin from London – had given up hope, as indeed had Johnny Sack, my second, who proved to be a saviour later that day. Already I was dehydrating with 130 kms staring ahead of me and I knew that the spectre of acute heat exhaustion was to stalk me throughout that long, hard day.

My spirits began to revive as I passed competitor after competitor on the cycle leg. I saw men huddled in blankets staring sightlessly at the roadside, victims of exhaustion. These weren't soft men. They'd devoted 4 – 6 hours training a day for months on end with the ambition of finishing the race and winning a medal in the first Iron Man race staged in South Africa. And then disaster struck. 5 kms before the finish of the cycle leg, I took a wrong turning at a T-junction. I turned right instead of left and pedalled furiously – I had gained a precious second wind at this juncture – for some 20 kms before hurtling through a military roadblock. The startled officer in charge flagged me down to a screeching halt and demanded what I was playing at. "I'm in the Iron Man race", I gasped, "let me through. I'm late enough!" "Gott, meneer, no racer has been through these parts, you're very, very lost!" responded the well meaning officer. I swore to the heavens, turned my cycle round and pedalled furiously in the direction I'd come, only to see my old friend Tony Beith coming at me with full speed, signalling frantically for me to stop. "Hop in!" he yelled. "Hold onto your bike out of the window – you've done an extra 20 unscheduled kms. I'm dropping you off where you went wrong. You're not cheating – the marshals disappeared thinking no one's left in the race!"

At the start of the marathon leg, Johnny Sack was waiting to run with me for the last leg, assisted by Beith. I changed into my running clothes and it was adrenaline alone that kept me alive on that scorching day. I was barely conscious, my skin was beginning to pucker through dehydration, and I was literally on my last legs. The extra twenty kilometres on the cycle had taken its toll but Tony Beith knew me well and that I didn't give up easily. As I ran out of the military check point with a group of soldiers bidding me good luck, I muttered to Beith that I'd forgotten to put on underpants and I needed his for the marathon. The good man complied and we whipped off our running shorts simultaneously in front of a knot of incredulous and bemused spectators, including a representation of women, and I accepted my mate's scants with gratitude. That last leg was an experience of undiluted agony. I was facing the ignominy of defeat before setting off on the 42 km marathon under a tormenting sun. I had to complete the final leg in less than 4 hours. I had run a 3.08 marathon the previous year which is relatively swift for a 43 year old and I was now expected to complete 42 kms at a rate of 6 minutes a kilometre in a state of near dehydration and approaching exhaustion after virtually nine hours in the searing heat. The temperature had reached 38 degrees centigrade by 2.00 p.m. and I was asking the impossible from my wracked body. I ran in a daze and the mind had taken over from the body and will power alone kept me running those unforgiving hills of the old Pretoria-Johannesburg road. I then began to reach the back markers who were stumbling mindlessly along the harsh route and this gave me a fresh burst of adrenaline. I gave up mumbling good wishes to my fellow competitors as few were responding, they were that shot. I remember seeing men lying flat besides the tarmac out for the count. I recall my cursing aloud a 'bus' of runners and their seconds who were hogging the road as it took a supreme effort to run around the group. I collapsed at one stage with 15 kms before the cut off and that's when Johnny Sack gave me a vitamin injection in the buttocks. And then the final cruelty of being forced off the road for traffic safety by the police with barely two kilometres to complete. The bitterness of defeat then overwhelmed me after I'd recovered my senses. For a week I held my head in shame. I'd failed my mission of crossing the line in 13 hours. My fellow competitors were truly magnificent in their support but I needed more than consolation to retrieve my pride. The race had wreaked its toll and a friend of mine remarked on my appearance over a drink a week later. "You look withered", he said, "Do you feel alright". "In the body, yes." I responded. "My mind has to recover".

The following year I returned to the Iron Man with a vengeance. I'd learnt how to handle a canoe, which was the first step; I'd honed up on my cycling skills and purchased a sleek machine that made my first racer look like a donkey. Running had never proved a problem as borne out by my performance in the previous year where I'd run at a rate of just over six minutes a kilometre in my pitiful state. We were wiser, too, on how to train for this awesome race, remembering that 35 athletes had ended up on intravenous drips and three hospitalised after the inaugural event, and not forgetting my own traumatic experience. For four months we pursued a punishing routine of rising at 4.00 a.m. well before dawn to take to the roads. My running partners were the staunch Tony Beith and the talented Reginald Hunter-Blair (as referred to in the Comrades chapter) and we'd meet at the Fourways Crossing, north of Johannesburg and run that long hill past the Bryanston post office and down to the Bryanston shopping centre and back, covering 14 kms of hills. In the dawn we'd see a muscular, bull-dog of a man and we'd pass each other like ships at night. We'd grunt a greeting and we'd comment on this loner, a fellow we'd get to know well by the name of Dick Stent who'd recently left the Trucial Oman Scouts as a captain. I'd cycle with Ian Green, Mike Tindall, John Feek, Noel Stamper and in later weeks Dick Stent; an attractive personality in the form of Priscilla Carlisle of Comrades fame joined our illustrious group.

We'd think little of burning up 90 kms in the rising dawn on our racing cycles. We were perhaps strong on energy and short of finesse but we were conditioning ourselves to cycle the hilly 100km leg in between 3½ and 3¾ hours. Then the work on the water. The Dabulamanzi Canoe Club spawned several entrants for the race, the more colourful of which ranked 'Moggy' Lightfoot – the old man of the river; Andy Torr of Spitfire Fame; Frank Soll, a noted cyclist who raced in 11th place on the day; 'PG' Barry, an ex-Recce soldier; Mike Davies - one of the most gifted athletes and perhaps one of the idlest; and Geoff Mathews, a Duzi veteran and Comrades silver medallist. The race inspired an amazing camaraderie, perhaps on the realisation that only a few in South Africa had the capability and the focus to entertain a challenge of this enormity.

The race was still dominated by the canoeists who in addition to their skills in rivers and raging waters were capable of running marathons and this particularly applied to the Duzi men. The inaugural race in 1983 was won by Tim Cornish – the ex-British Olympic canoeist who won the Duzi doubles race with Graham Pope-Ellis. Both men were also competent runners achieving the coveted silver medal in the Comrades. Then there were men in the top ten such as Danny Biggs, a diminutive figure with an angelic choir boy's face, but this tough little competitor came in behind Cornish in second place. There was the big, muscular S A Defence Force soldier, Benny Reynders, who could power through the water and also soak up the marathon miles on his powerful legs. There were others such as Rory Pennefather and Mike Tocknell from Natal who reached the top ten. But the runners were beginning to talk of an extraordinary loner, Dr Eddie King, the farmer from Delmas.

I used to listen to the rumours with avid interest as I had actually met the reclusive figure under different circumstances. I'd been invited rough shooting by a friend of mine who worked in the coal business, a trained geologist and a fanatical lover of the outdoors known as Steven Finnemore. There were just the two of us with our dogs walking the grasslands of the farm to which Steven Finnemore had an introduction to shoot the guinea fowl and the francolin. I remember clearly that day under a brilliant, blue sky so typical of the Transvaal winter, and I pointed out to Steven a figure away in the distance depicted against the skyline and we couldn't quite understand what the lone runner was up to loping along the lands in the mid afternoon. He seemed out of place but I recognised the long, fluid stride of a true athlete. Strange, we thought, and then we turned our attention to the serious business of shooting birds over our gun dogs. We had picked up a reasonable bag as dusk was setting in and I decided to end off the day by taking a shot at a brace of yellow billed duck which were flighting in to a dam. The shot was true and down plummeted a duck and Tara, my springer spaniel, needed little coaxing to jump into the chilly water and retrieve the duck.

I nearly jumped out of my skin at the furious bellow from behind me. "What the hell do you think you're doing? You are trespassing!" I turned to confront a livid-faced fellow wearing running shorts, a singlet, and a cycling cap. I took in the lean frame and realised that this was the figure we'd spied earlier on. I explained my position as best I could and was relieved to see Steven Finnemore hurrying towards us with his letter of introduction in hand. However, it was obvious that there'd been a sorry misunderstanding as the angry farmer in his running garb had no forewarning of our presence on his land. The position was beginning to look somewhat bleak with threats of calling the police being bantered about, until I spoke up enquiring as to the reason for the land owner's unusual get-up. "I'm training for the Iron Man" was the fellow's reply. "Oh!" I said, "So am I". "You're doing the race?" asked the farmer. The mood had suddenly changed direction. "Carry on shooting and come and see me at the house when you've finished."

I spoke to Eddie King for two hours that evening with Tertia his wife and Steven Finnemore listening in, and so started a firm friendship. Much to the gratification of Steven Finnemore, our shooting grounds were secure for several years to come. Dr Eddie King – he was a practising GP in addition to his farming occupation – exploded onto the Iron Man scene in spectacular manner and came 4th in the 1985 race, breaking the strangle hold of the canoeists. He went on to win the 1986 and 1987 races before nearly writing himself off on a cycle accident, and shortly afterwards he departed for the United States. I came to know the famous Eddie King well and he was a most interesting eccentric. He and his pretty wife, Tertia, would come to the house for dinner. Eddie was a teetotaller, except for Guinness which he'd drink like an Irish farm labourer with both hands around the pint glass and noisily slurping back the black liquid. Eddie King was a very gifted athlete: a Springbok cross country trialist in addition to representing S A Universities and Western Province. He learnt to canoe on his dam on the farm, a minuscule stretch of water, and he trained the local postman, the only black entrant in the Iron Man, who was to put up a notable performance in the 1985 event before tragically drowning after capsizing his canoe in the Bronkhorstspruit Dam.

In that year of 1984, the second Iron Man race, I breasted the tape on ten hours thirty eight minutes with the leading lady, coming in 133rd position out of the 350 competitors. I had revenged my sad defeat of the previous year. A week before the start of the 1985 race, at a stage when the nerves were beginning to jangle, I decided to take John Feek's advice and follow what is known as the Soltan diet. This entails stripping the system of every shred of carbohydrate and pursuing a strict protein diet on the seventh to the third day prior to the race whilst continuing to train. On the third day, the reverse pattern is put into motion and a pleasurable carbohydrate programme is pursued in full vengeance. I'd remained somewhat sceptical about this Soltan diet revered by many an endurance athlete but I decided to experiment with this strange discipline. I decided to indulge myself on the seventh day before the Iron Man and I took my sales manager to Spaghi's restaurant in downtown Johannesburg and proceeded to consume a serious dosage of pasta washed down with enormous quantities of beer and red wine. The binge extended into the late afternoon and by 6.00 that evening I was truly intoxicated. I made a merry fool of myself that evening on my way home. I drove into a storm water culvert near the Johannesburg Country Club's golf course at Woodmead and leaving the vehicle marooned, I scared off several householders in my attempt to reach a telephone before an elderly lady of German origin ushered me in to her living room. She enquired what I would like to drink with a kindly smile. "Whisky, please" I promptly replied, to which she said that I could have water or lemonade as it was obvious that I'd had enough alcohol for that day. She was curious to find out what I did for a living to which I responded proudly that I was racing in the Iron Man. She looked at me quizzically for several moments and then peeled into laughter. "You'ze an Iron Man! Tonight I zink you'ze looking like ze jellyman!" I thought this extremely funny and I'm fond of recounting this anecdote over the years.

The next day I was weaning off my carbohydrate intake which had left with me a serious hangover. I'd met Moggy Lightfoot and Ian Green for a 90 km cycle along the Johannesburg – Pretoria road. My head was bursting and I was close to vomiting as we churned relentlessly back and forth along the marathon route that faced us in six days time. With us was a young fellow over from England, a first cousin of mine called Peter Geikie - Cobb, who was preparing himself for a career in the Irish Guards. We made him run in army boots whilst we pedalled along the hilly route in the warm sun of that early Saturday morning. I felt sorrier for myself than for the 21 year old being barked at by Moggy, who'd served as a subaltern in the Rhodesian African Rifles in his time. After three hours of furious riding, I besieged my Iron Man colleagues to call a halt and I told them of my experience with the Soltan diet. "Sounds like a load of bullshit" opined Ian Green and backed by Moggy Lightfoot. "There's only one way to get you right and that's half a dozen pints of beer in the Balalaika!" The motion was keenly supported by a heavily perspiring cousin and Moggy Lightfoot and that was the abrupt end of the Soltan diet experiment. But having said that, I was to try it in later races to great success and there's little doubt that the Soltan diet helps certain athletes and is not a programme to be scorned.

I finished that year well up the field, and in the top ten for the Masters age category (the oldest category for 40 years plus) and my strongest performance was the road marathon which I completed in 3 hours 54 minutes, rating 55th place for that particular leg, and 11th for my age group. But the most glorious experience that arduous day was the sight of Eddie King standing waiting for me at the finish line. He'd come fourth overall and in second place on the marathon leg.

The 1987 race was to be remembered for my fastest time for the event but in other ways a disappointing experience. An American from New York called Bunker Snyder had issued a challenge. He was considerably younger than me – some 15 years – and a capable cyclist but he was considerably less experienced in the canoeing and marathon running disciplines. I got wind of his braggadocio about beating the veteran Iron Man, Michael Callender, and I was quick to take up the gauntlet and show this cocky Yank a trick or two. We settled for a modest monetary sum as the bet but dinner was to be included and to be attended by wives and two seconds of our choice. This wager would add up to a significant cost and I thought the American a trifle ambitious. I'd meet Bunker at the canoe time trials at the Dabulamanzi and I'd leave him well behind on the 10 kilometre circuit. But what I didn't take into account was the bevy of seconds he'd coerced into training him for the road. Ian Green led the troupe – traitor! 'PG' Barry – another traitor – both acting as coaches for the marathon leg. They'd worked it out quite correctly that this was my strength and Bunker's singular weakness. Secretively, and with great stealth, he'd run parts of the course every afternoon in the last two months preceding the start. And accompanying him on these runs were Ian Green, 'PG' Barry, and a knot of experienced Comrades runners they'd hauled in for the week-end training sessions. On my part, I'd continue to train with the perennials: John Feek, Noel Stamper, Dick Stent, Mike Tindall, Priscilla Carlisle and Tony Beith.

Came the great day and I was probably the fittest I'd ever been in my life, including the army days in the deserts of Saudi Arabia. I was supremely confident of beating the American amidst the hype that had been created over the challenge. I entered the water with a focus rarely matched before and I paddled as if my life depended on it, knowing that I had to build up a 15 minute lead at least. Allowing for the American's cycling supremacy, my goal was to start the marathon leg at approximately the same time as the New Yorker. I had drawn in two seconds: the normally conscientious and dependable Tony Beith, and a Comrades veteran, Alec Browne. I'd briefed the two in minute detail well before the race so they knew what was expected of them. In contrast, Bunker Snyder had attracted a support team that would have been the envy of Eddie King and others of the top ten.

I charged out of the water (I was ten minutes ahead of schedule) with boat on shoulder and raced to the cycle pound but to find no sign of Tony Beith. Then followed a frantic ten minutes looking for the blond giant, but to no avail. I was forced to have him called on the tannoy system. I'd found my cycle but not my second and he was in possession of my helmet – now mandatory for the Iron Man – and bananas, water bottles and other critical paraphernalia for the cycle event. Up galloped Beith, gasping apologies, but my mood was very, very bleak. "You've lost me 15 minutes, Beith!" I growled as I set off muttering obscenities on the cycle leg, helmet askew, bananas hanging out of my cycling shirt. It should be mentioned at this stage that the change over in the triathlon game is critical. One learns to wear cycling pants in the boat and a few contestants even don their cycling cleats in the canoes. Long gone were the early days when taking a glorious cold shower at the end of the canoeing and cycling legs was a favoured practice. If you were racing for a silver medal, remembering that the cut off had been reduced by 30 minutes to 10 hours for the silver, you were expected to exit the boat smartly, heave it onto the shoulder in one smooth movement, race to the cycle pound and take to the road in under two minutes.

Past me surged the Springbok rugby hooker, Uli Schmidt, an Iron Man in every sense of the description. I remember his powerful legs pumping furiously as he swept past; and then cruising beside me, much to my extreme irritation - and I was already in a grim mood sensing that the fifteen minutes lost at the changeover could cost me the silver medal and the wager with the American - were the taunting faces of Ian Green, 'PG' Barry and a retinue of Bunker Snyder's supporters standing on the back of a pick-up truck festooned with pails, ice, sponges, towels, chocolates. These were professional seconds compared to the two that I had. The wretched men in the truck continued to drive slowly besides me as I sweated on those energy sapping hills. I had enough pressure on my plate, notwithstanding an extra dose from Bunker's army. Mercifully, they moved off just before a triumphant Bunker Snyder pedalled past me without a nod or murmur of acknowledgement. He looked ahead, pretending not to see the bedraggled cyclist with helmet skew and bananas falling out of his jersey. I swore again and I gritted my teeth as I ground my way through the gruelling course of the cycle leg.

Then a further insult awaited me at the change over for the running leg. You are now a seriously tired athlete. You've raced across the vast Hartebeespoort dam which requires full concentration or otherwise you risk a swim in the choppy waters and this could cost you a full twenty minutes, and you've punished your legs on the Magaliesburg hills on a course that is studded with steep ascents and descents. And now you face a full marathon in the heat of the midday. As you strip off your sweat-sodden clothes to don running shorts and singlet, modesty is cast to the winds and for a few seconds you are baring your body to the gawking audience. At the front of this throng stood Bunker Snyder's wife, a good looking lady called Suzie, and she was relishing the spectacle of a near-naked athlete who was being pounded into the ground by her spouse. To add salt to the wound she informed me smugly that Bunker had taken to the road a full thirty minutes ahead of me. And on top of this my seconds cheerfully told me that they weren't allowed to accompany the runner for the first ten kilometres of the course. Where they got this notion from one is not quite certain, as runner after runner which I managed to pass had their seconds with them, dousing their charges with ice-cold water and feeding them with sugar-filled sustenance.

I ran my heart out that day under the hot sun and my mood was resolute. I was determined to catch the American although my chances of victory were now exceedingly slim. However I noted with grim satisfaction the increasingly worried expressions of Bunker's seconds who had the habit of driving beside me at regular intervals with their walkie talkie sets. I sensed I was hauling in the American but inwardly I knew that the 30 minute handicap was just too severe to catch the younger man. As I crested the last hill before crossing the M1 motorway and with five kilometres to go, I caught up with the familiar figure of Dick Stent – a look alike of Marvin Hagler, the former middleweight champion of the world. Dick was grimacing with a severe attack of cramps and urged me to run on and to catch 'the sawn-off Yank' as he put it and it was obvious that Bunker Snyder was close to the finish line. And so it was to be. My adversary had come in on a commendable 9 hrs, 53 minutes, well inside the silver medal mark. The satisfaction for me on that day was that I'd reduced the American's lead of 30 minutes at the running changeover to 14 minutes and completed the course in my fastest time – 10 hours, 7 minutes. If the race had extended itself a few further kilometres, I would have reeled in the New Yorker, but that was of little consolation when walking away from the finish line. This was not the occasion to berate my seconds. They had had a thankless task and Tony Beith's distraction on the banks of the Hartebeespoort dam – probably a pert blonde and there were many out there on that day – was soon forgotten. I shook Bunker Snyder's hand and congratulated him on a magnificent race and he was, quite understandably, over the moon with his victory. I believe he still talks about his Iron Man race today in London where he lives and he'll remember for many years to come how he'd given his best over those pain-wracked hours in the hot Transvaal of South Africa.

I sensed that this would be my last Iron Man. I was approaching 50 years of age and I had set my sights on the Duzi as being my next major challenge. I therefore stayed on to the end of that day, filling my depleted body with countless beers and watching the competitors stream in, many limping but all wearing a triumphant smile to have finished this cruel course. I commented to John Feek – he'd put in his best performance to date, 9 hours 57 minutes – that the four months of training and sacrificing family and social life culminating in 22 kms of churning water, 100 kms of demonic hills on a cycle saddle, and the final mind-numbing 42 kms of a tortuous marathon, would be emblazoned on our memories to the end of our days. As darkness closed over the ground I saw the last competitor to finish before the 13 hour cut off point. He was in terrible pain and as he crossed the line, he collapsed in a motionless heap. The small boy that was presumably his son tugged helplessly at the inert figure when mercifully the fallen athlete stirred and two burly Iron men - both well-known rugby players -lifted him and carried the prostrate figure to the medical tent where doctors and nurses were treating dozens of athletes. I limped away from the ground, 4 kgs lighter and exhausted in body but strong in mind.

From those earlier days of 1983 I'd conquered the Iron Man and new challenges lay open. The race continues today. The event has become far slicker with athletes racing a course that is designed for swimmers as well as canoeists. Shorter in length and assuming more the configuration of an international standard ultra triathlon, the race has lost some of its rugged appeal. It was with a degree of nostalgia those seventeen years after the 1983 inaugural Iron Man when I seconded my son, Sean, in the race, and I was to proudly watch his coming in on 20th position in the canoe leg. As I ran the last 15 kilometres of the running leg with him my mind reverted to those pioneering days when the Rand Daily Mail devoted pages to the majestic event that the paper sponsored. The memories remain vividly etched. I can still see the extraordinary sights of powerfully built men writhing on the ground from the scourges of stomach cramps, of blanket wrapped athletes staring into space as they were lifted onto stretchers by the tireless St John's Ambulance men, of the leaner middleweights – suitably built for a race of this type – running with a natural cadence along the marathon route, of the inspiring sight of the crowds lining the route with their words of encouragement barely recognised by the dazed athletes.

CHAPTER FOURTEEN

Rambling with a shot gun

The natives especially regard a bird shooter as mad.
They cannot understand why a man spends time
and energy blasting away at birds when there are
2000 pounds of eland over every hill and sleepy topi
standing under every bush.

Robert Ruark 'The Horn of the Hunter'

I HAVE enjoyed forty years of shooting game birds in Africa taking me from crocodile infested rivers to grassy savannah lands where lions lurk to bush strewn hills hiding the Cape cobra. It is inevitable that comparisons are drawn between the traditional driven shoots in Britain or Europe to the rougher equivalent on this continent. Both have their merits, albeit strikingly different. I could be contentious when I say that the essential difference between a driven grouse or pheasant shoot in Britain and a rough shoot in this neck of the woods is that the former is a time hallowed tradition, a predictable set of events, and the other is an adventure where the unforeseen can happen.

Bird shooting has drawn me to several African countries and varied terrains - Malawi, Zimbabwe, Botswana and South Africa itself. I've discharged thousands of cartridges at geese, ducks, guinea fowl, francolin, partridges, pigeons, doves, sand grouse and even hand-reared English pheasant. And indeed I've let loose when the larder was empty in certain hunting camps with a variety of weapons – from a .375 down to a .22 - at birds in the trees or on the ground. This will set the purists muttering! I've shot in mixed company of eminent bird shooters and game hunters – the latter remain a touch sceptical of a shot gun.

When I first came to South Africa, I was imbued with the idea of purchasing a rifle and taking to the bush in pursuit of game. Bird shooting was not high on my agenda until Mejor Cullinan, referred to earlier in the book, gave me a serious dissertation on the joys of wing shooting. I listened to this gifted shot and it was he more than most that persuaded me to look to this sport. In 1969, the cost of big game hunting was a pittance to what it is now. An elephant licence in Botswana could be obtained for a mere R100! Today we're looking at many thousands! But in those days I was making my way in a country where I knew hardly anyone, in a new environment, and the father of two young children earning a modest salary. Both the time and cash required then for big game hunting, sadly, was beyond my means. Bird shooting, however, cost little – a bottle of brandy for the farmer in most cases - and practical in terms of availability.

* * * * *

In the winter season of those early days in South Africa, I would spend virtually every weekend chasing guinea fowl through the meilie fields or firing at ducks and geese in those few wetlands that were accessible from Johannesburg. The shooting was rough and ready but fun. Frankfort in the Free State is a good case in question. We'd discovered a headwater that contained a prolific population of duck and teal. On one memorable occasion half a dozen of us had spent a lucrative three hours collecting a serious bag of yellow-billed duck. We'd been up since four in the morning and the weather gauge showed freezing well after daybreak and we were looking for something to do to while away the hours until the evening flighting. We decided to investigate a pan which we hadn't shot and to our amazement the water was seething with a mass of wild fowl. We couldn't believe our eyes. However, there was certain opinion amongst those present that the pan formed part of a conservancy and out of bounds for shooting. Then up roars Mejor Cullinan in his red bakkie. He'd driven down from Olifantsfontein for the evening flight and he joined us on the banks of this particular pan. "Are we permitted to shoot here. Are we legal?" Mejor Cullinan asks. "I guess so" I reply, aided and abetted by David Vanrenen, an ebullient character who now lives in France, and a Cornishman, Philip Cadman, then busy marketing an inflatable boat that never seemed to work. "Take my rubber duck" offers Cadman. Ever resourceful, Mejor takes to the water in the inflatable boat with his African horse groom perched on the prow to pick the birds off the water. He entertains us for an hour, with a masterful display of shotgun expertise and down cascade dozens of ducks and geese. We were all quite envious that we were not partaking in this magnificent sport when over the hill roars a troop of bakkies bristling with guns. The Flora and Fauna men have arrived! A local farmer, no doubt, had tipped off Nature Conservation that a protected conservancy was under siege. Mejor was oblivious to the intrusion but we on the bank were becoming very nervous. We'd placed Mejor in this predicament and the possibility of having to bail him out of jail assumed a strong reality, added to which Mejor's legendary short fuse posed a further problem of note.

Mejor continued to blaze away with contentment until the African groom sensed something was awry. We were too far away to warn the sportsman. Philip Cadman's rubber duck at this stage was brimming with birds and the craft was dangerously close to sinking which wouldn't be anything unusual for Cadman's inflatables! We watched Mejor gesticulating, pleading, imploring with the men in uniform. "I'm getting the hell out of here", muttered David Vanrenen, "there's going to be hell to pay! Deal with it, Mike, he's your mate". "Great", I replied, "so you're running off and leaving me to face the music!" "No, seriously I've got to go. I'm in enough trouble at home" replies Vanrenen. To my extreme disappointment with the baseness of the human race, all present on the bank took the cue to leave me alone to face Cullinan's wrath. I climbed wearily into my vehicle and slowly made my way to the far shore. Fortunately, I had a bird shooting licence, my ID book and my gun licence for the stern looking men to scrutinise. That was something in my favour as was with Mejor who also had his paper work in place, unlike the disorganised Vanrenen and others no doubt in the party that had evaporated into the thin Transvaal air. Did I know that this pan was a conservancy, I was asked. Another wished to know if I was an Englishman. I was facing a collection of aggressive Afrikaners. The first question I replied to in the negative and the second I responded to being of Scots/Irish descent which alleviated the mood a trifle.

Two hours later Mejor and I were ensconced in a kroeg (men's bar) in Frankfort. He was mellowing a little but still smarting from a near-arrest. "Look what you idiots got me into. I should kill the lot of you. Where are the rest of your mates anyway? They ran off leaving you to face the music, didn't they?" "Not really", I replied, "they had to get back. But they did apologise for putting you into the dam. How did you manage to talk your way out of it by the way?" "I told them that I had shot in the Springbok trials, I was a responsible man and I was joint MD of Cullinan Refractories and I was a Springbok deep sea fisherman and that there'd been a terrible misunderstanding". I had to grin at this reasoning and bought Mejor another drink. "Tell you what we'll do, Mejor, we'll phone Vanrenen and say that you've been locked up and that he must drive down tonight with R1000.00 for bail money!" I called David there and then with Mejor gleefully listening in. David answered the phone and there was a long pause before he replied: "I've just got back and we've got in-laws for dinner and I'm in enough trouble for reneging on a party last night. Anyway Frankfort is a two hour's drive from here and I can't make it". "We'll have to bail Mejor out" I said. "He's as much as your pal as mine. You can't let him down". Vanrenen was in a state of panic. "I cannot raise the bail as I've no cash on me and they won't accept cheques". Revenge was sweet. I could hear an angry wife, Heath, buzzing in the background leaving a fraught David Vanrenen racking his brains how to raise R1000.00 in cash – a sizeable sum in those days – late on a Saturday evening. Mejor Cullinan was all for David driving to Frankfort but I came clean and let him off the hook.

* * * * *

In an earlier chapter I made mention of a wild character, Faan Fourie –
'Die Leeu van die Oos'. I was to achieve the unusual privilege of being
the first 'rooinek' that I knew of for receiving an invitation from a leader
of the AWB (the notorious right wing movement) to shoot on his farm
near Lydenburg, some 350 kilometres north east of Johannesburg. This
was unprecedented as the AWB was virulently anti the English speaking
community.   However, not all men of the AWB could be discarded
as Nazi style bullies. You have in Faan Fourie a charismatic giant of a
figure, fluent in English, with a strong sense of culture as manifested by
his knowledge of Shakespeare, added to which his empathy with diverse
creeds of men provided they remained clear of politics. Faan Fourie was
an essential part of the mosaic that constitutes the rich variety of the
peoples of South Africa. This larger-than-life character remains a legend
in the Lydenburg district. He had to flee the country with a loaded truck,
as he would have been a prime target for the African National Congress.
I asked him recently what he was up to in Zambia. He was running a
wildlife photographic venture and a farming scheme, he told me, and that
he was in partnership with a local tribal chief. Faan had me puzzled as the
big Dutchman wasn't known for his sympathies with the black brethren.
"I'll explain, my rooinek friend. This chief is an excellent African. You
see, he has a legitimate claim to the land going back centuries – unlike
our brethren in South Africa. He is a good man. I can teach him about
farming and wildlife conservation and he can teach me the local ways.
He is confused, mind you, because my neighbour is a New Zealander and
when the chief comes to my house for dinner he can't understand why I
call my mate an 'All Black'. But he's pure white says the chief and when I
say grace in Afrikaans, the chief asks if the Lord above understands my
funny language!"

The day I went to shoot on Faan's farm he was absent. He'd left a note
to say that sadly he couldn't be present as he was on 'military duty' in
Welkom. I had selected the men for the shoot - Tony North, Michael and
Barry Victor, and my son, Sean - all capable of speaking Afrikaans in case
it was needed for the occasion. The sport that morning was a desultory
affair and we had bagged just one guinea fowl before lunch. The lands had

been cropped and the birds had flown but we were enjoying ourselves. Towards dusk we found ourselves in an apple orchard but not before Barry Victor had come across a kleinhuisie (a privy). Mike, his brother, was standing by and I was initially a little shaken to see them pelting the outhouse with number seven shot. "A francolin has just scuttled in there", cried an exuberant Barry Victor, an Eastern Transvaal farmer. "We must get it". However, the francolin had flown out of the kleinhuisie from sheer fright into a fruit orchard measuring some fifty hectares and perhaps as well — Faan might have taken exception to having his kleinhuisie riddled with bird shot! We followed the francolin and we then had the most amazing sport. Several coveys of francolin whirred up and the four of us had excellent shooting. Between us we collected a sizeable bag and to celebrate this we gravitated to the Lydenburg Motel. We were a motley looking collection in our dusty khakis but the service was prompt as the food was ordered in Afrikaans, and no doubt the staff assumed us to be an AWB vigilante group.

* * * * *

Bird shooting in Africa is very different to the highly controlled, well regulated sport as understood in Britain and Europe. Indeed, there are the hardy wildfowlers and the rough shooters who endure the blisteringly cold winds and sleeting rains of the Northern climes but in general the syndicated English pheasant shoots or driven grouse in the Scottish Highlands are predictable affairs. I have experienced a line of guns startled out of their wits on a driven francolin shoot in Botswana's Okavango Delta by a leopard streaking out of the undergrowth; I've waited for the flighting of sand grouse at dusk not far from a pride of lions lying nearby; I've experienced the thrill of shooting white-faced whistling ducks in the Shire Swamps of Malawi when the sudden swirls in the water signals the presence of crocodile swallowing a fallen bird. There have been confrontations with lions while chasing francolin through elephant grass in Zimbabwe and even in the more predictable terrains of the Transvaal Highveld, the sight of a coiled puff adder is not a rare occasion.

Over recent years a group of us have enjoyed a spectacular shoot in the 'Splash Camp' hunting concession situated in the northern reaches of the Moremi Reserve in Botswana. This is an enviable event for a host of reasons: brilliant setting, quality and variety of birds, a proliferation of wildlife and the company of kindred spirits. This entailed flying to Maun, clearing immigration and customs, refuelling, and then on to a tented hunting camp, our base for four nights. This was a highlight on the shooting calendar for us lucky souls who were privileged to shoot in this pristine corner of Africa. We'd start the day waiting at a pan, one of many in the Okavango Delta, for the early morning flighting of sand grouse. This is a desert-dwelling bird and the description 'grouse' is a misnomer as a sand grouse resembles more closely a brightly coloured pigeon. They usually occur in flocks of up to 20, but they congregate in hundreds near water holes in the early morning and dusk. The namaqua and double-banded are the species shot in the Moremi. It is a thrilling bird to shoot: swift – it can reach 50 knots – and devious in flight. This strikingly coloured bird with pointed wings that differentiate it from the pigeon can quickly confuse a shooter with its sudden swoops and swirls. When shooting sand grouse, the shooter is tempted to fire into the flock, not a sporting practice when the sky can blacken with the flying birds. The secret is to crouch behind an anthill and search the sky for the tell-tale signs of a flock in the distance and let the birds come in close before selecting a target to shoot. At dusk the shooting is fast and furious and usually over in 20 minutes. But in this short space of time the pace is that frenetic that the gun barrels become unbearable to the touch. Sand grouse are great game. The shoot manager, usually a professional hunter as this concession is big game territory, will allocate the rest for the day for geese or guinea fowl or driven francolin. The hunting camp staff will be given the task of beating the thickets known as 'islands'. These beaters – trackers, skinners, and cooks – are taken out of their normal milieu and they form a stark contrast to the English country-folk on pheasant drives. The Africans create an unholy racket, sufficient to frighten the odd lion out of the thickets. I exaggerate not. On one famous occasion a lioness burst out of the undergrowth much to the consternation of the point gun. Luckily no harm came to the startled guns as the lioness kept her line and raced on into the horizon. The fearsome cacophony created by the beaters is effective. Francolin explode out of the trees in all directions, making the shooting unpredictable and testing for the sportsmen encircling the islands.

I recall a certain evening where the birds were flying in their droves and we created a competition among ourselves and recovering the birds was essential to our personal tallies. I was standing next to Barry Victor, the Eastern Transvaal farmer. We were positioned at the far extremity of a large pan on the edge of the water and in front, some 50 metres away, was the tree-line. We had eager young locals, keen as mustard, to gather our birds. Off they would race whooping and hollering in the direction of the trees to pick up the downed sand grouse. When darkness fell, the other guns including Michael Deacon, Michael Victor, and Paul Hatfield joined us at the spot where Barry and I had been firing like demons. In the lights of the truck we saw a pride of six lionesses get to their feet and slink off, a mere 60 yards in front of where Barry and I had been shooting! Our retrievers had been racing to and fro from where we'd been firing, directly at the lionesses in wait, and it had been a miracle that they hadn't suffered a grisly fate. That's Africa!

Those shoots in the Moremi left indelible impressions. Here one is shooting game birds in an active big game hunting concession. Whilst waiting for the birds to flight in, I would wonder at the breathtaking panorama of the crystal clear waterways of the Okavango swamps, fringed by yellow grasses and papyrus reeds and the ubiquitous acacia trees. Then the game. Only those who've been privileged to hunt animals or shoot birds in this beautiful corner of Botswana can bear testimony to the abundant wildlife: roan antelope, blue wildebeest, sable, waterbuck, lechwe, and elephant – all there to be seen. The Moremi is lion country, adding another dimension to the shoot, and there would be certain thickets to avoid because of the cats in the vicinity.

* * * * *

It was a congenial and interesting group of men that Piers Taylor had assembled for an Easter bird shoot at his Matetsi concession near Victoria

Falls, Zimbabwe. The proliferation of button quail was phenomenal that particular Easter weekend and none of us could quite explain the migratory pattern of this diminutive game bird that provided us such excellent sport. Quail of this multitude tend to be uncommon in Southern Africa. But over that weekend, hundreds of these sporting birds sprang up all over the savannah. Piers made an impressive shoot manager – all six foot, seven inches of him directing the line. He was firmly in control, except for his pointer dogs that ran riot over the African veldt. They were drawn more to the scent of game, and the sight of Piers' hounds wailing off into the horizon scattering sable, roan and other forms of wildlife, would cause a furore in field trials.

There was an interesting diversion to this shoot. Early one morning, Sean, my son, then 14 years old, Jonathan Taylor (an apprentice professional hunter but no relation to Piers) and I had the unnerving experience of a confrontation with five lionesses in elephant grass. Piers had dropped us off in a stretch of savannah and had chugged slowly off into the distance to brew coffee and wait for us. We began to walk through the high grass when a strong acrid smell hit me. I put this down to buffalo. Piers had been fairly nonchalant as to the likelihood of lion that were rampant in the area. In fact, it came to me as I waded through the thick grassland that Piers had bumped into a lioness the previous year while walking up guinea fowl. As legend had it, he'd thrown his cap at the growling cat bellowing 'voetsek' (an expressive Afrikaans expletive) and the lioness had slunk off.

Jonathan then brought us to an abrupt halt muttering "lions – watch out!" We formed a triangle and full marks to Sean who kept his nerve and was a brave chap that morning as we inched forward. Jonathan whispered that there were five cats surrounding us, and all we had were guns loaded with number five shot – mere confetti against a lioness! It took 30 nerve-racking minutes to cover 500 metres when we spotted the lionesses creep out of the savannah and climb onto a small ridge. I looked at Jonathan, he looked at me, and Sean looked at us both. Our sunburned faces had been transformed into pale shades of grey. Jonathan began to laugh nervously at first, and then great guffaws. We were all howling when we reached Piers. "Only you, Piers, only you could get us into this scrape",

I gasped. The lanky professional of the bush remained imperturbable. He turned to Vivienne who was with us that morning. "We didn't see lion? What are they on about?" Sean's mother wasn't quite so nonchalant and she remonstrated with Piers as to how irresponsible he'd been. Piers is used to all sorts of invective, particularly from hunters' womenfolk. He just shrugged and grinned. "They chose to clamber through the grass, and I warned them that this is lion country", the piratical-looking figure grunted, staring at us with a gold-toothed smirk, daring us to contradict him.

* * * * *

Malawi is the land of Livingstone and Lake Malawi was used for two centuries for the transportation of thousand of slaves to be sold in the slave markets on the East African coast. This small country is not much larger than Germany's Bavaria with a population of 10 million spread over only 36,000 square miles, a quarter of which is the lake itself. Not many sportsmen trek to this picturesque corner of Central Africa as permits to hunt are virtually non-existent owing to the relative scarcity of game and an inheritance of Dr. Hastings Banda's strict gun laws. Lake Chilwa, lying parallel to the Zomba plateau, and the Shire swamps in the Chiromo vicinity below the escarpment were a paradise for the wildfowl enthusiast.

I had heard of Malawi's legendary flight lines from several adventurers and felt compelled to venture forth to this relatively unspoilt part of Africa. The opportunity came in 1981 when Daniel and Val Oxberry suggested that I and a mutual friend, Tony North, try our hand at bird shooting on the lake. Daniel involved Ed Hammond and Daryl Botha, local business dignitaries, who were instrumental in arranging some excellent sport. Both men saw to it that each shoot was an adventure worthy of recording.

This was bird shooting in true colonial style. We found ourselves blazing away at white-faced whistlers and spurwing geese without another gun present in the entire country. We had Malawi to ourselves as Dr Hastings Banda, Malawi's long serving dictator, regarded guns and cartridges as a threat to his personal safety. It was rumoured that Banda personally signed each permit, such was his distrust of guns coming into the country. Rifle licences were taboo. If it was not for the standing of Daniel Oxberry and Ed Hammond, there would have been no shooting permits. We also learned that there was a strict limitation on ammunition in Malawi. The allowance for a Malawian resident was a paltry 250 shotgun shells per annum, an afternoon's ration on pigeon in the Transvaal, and we were fortunate in being able to bring in over a thousand rounds each.

Our first shoot in Malawi took us to the Shire swamps below the escarpment, due south of Blantyre. There were three of us that day who experienced an explosively exciting sport. Daryl Botha fished for tiger from the middle of the boat he'd brought for the occasion whilst Tony North and I fired at the continuous flocks of white-faced whistlers from opposite ends of the craft. This bird shooting was very different, and I relished every moment of that hot, steamy morning in the swamps. Everything was right. The water was teeming with crocodile, hippos were grunting on the banks, and the scenery was stunning, set against the backdrop of a string of islands inhabited by a water tribe. The sport was unbeatable. Flight after flight came in low over our heads, and after half an hour of constant firing, we began to ignore low flying birds and concentrated on more testing shots. We were piling up quite a bag but avoided the temptation of slaughter. Meanwhile Daryl Botha was casting furiously for tiger fish. He knew what he was about and was hooking these razor-toothed fighters continuously. Landing them was another story. We carried on throughout the morning, oblivious to the swamp flies and the heavy humidity, having a field day. We called a halt after our host had landed four sizeable tiger fish and the shooters thirty or so ducks. It cannot get better than that. On the return journey we stopped at a bar off the beaten track in the middle of a large dried out swamp. This hostelry was called 'The Elephant Marsh Inn'. The establishment itself was fairly dilapidated, to say the least, but the Carlsberg was ice cold. The menu was something else. Fried gecko for the starter followed by hippo steak, rounded off with toasted mealie cobs with sugar! If you were brave enough to sample the fare, you could distribute further largesse in the inn and offer a coca cola to the women and your entertainment for the night was sealed! It wasn't exactly difficult to avoid such temptations! 'The

Elephant Marsh Inn' became a favourite watering hole on subsequent visits – for the cold lager and not the food nor the local sirens!

Tony North and I returned in 1983 to revisit the Oxberrys and to pursue more wildfowl shooting. This time Ed Hammond arranged for us to stay with the men from the Sugar Corporation (SUCOMA) in Chiromo. Daryl Botha, the manager of the African brewery, had sadly departed and we missed the 'white bull' as Val Oxberry was fond of calling him. He knew the Shire swamps and was fun on a hunt. The shooting was patchy on this occasion, and the birds weren't flying as they had previously. I remember standing close to the water with my back turned, and one of the guns, Don Pye, the Chairman of the Tobacco Export Corporation, suddenly bellowed a warning for me to move further inland if I did not want to be taken by a crocodile. Far shades from standing in a West Country field in England!

The third foray into Malawi (1986) was also eventful. I had arranged the Malawi visit with the help of Ed Hammond as the Oxberry's had moved to the U.K. The very day after I had been flattened by a buffalo in the Charara Reserve, Zimbabwe, we travelled to Limbe via Kariba and Harare. Ed Hammond directed our party - Piers Taylor, Tony North, Ted Siebenman from Chicago and me - to the rice plantations bordering Lake Chilwa. We waited and waited for the flight lines. Eventually Piers seized the initiative and questioned a group of passing African fishermen in fanagalo – a distillation of African tongues used in the gold mines. Off we set in an easterly direction and an hour later we were in the thick of the action. The white-faced whistlers flew wondrously and the four of us proceeded to knock the ducks out of the sky. We had a band of young Africans in tow and these little fellows made excellent retrievers. We enjoyed excellent sport that sunny morning in the shallows of Lake Chilwa, firing continuously at the swarms of ducks. What seemed incredible was that the wildfowl were impervious to our presence and to the commotion that the locals created with their wild splashing and loud screeches of excitement while picking up our ducks. We remained oblivious to the leeches clinging to our legs, and I forgot the pain from my recent buffalo accident, the action was that fast and furious.

The next day we moved down the escarpment to Chiromo and the Shire swamps. As with the previous day, we found ourselves in the flight lines, and that afternoon the spurwing flew over in droves. The problem, however, was that we were loaded for ducks, not geese. Everyone was aware of this. Although we were bringing down several spurwing we ran the risk of wounding a number of them. Piers' ethical instinct brought us to our senses and we listened to his advice of not shooting unless we were confident of head shots. We took heed and packed away the shotguns shortly after that. Members of the Sugar Corporation were waiting at the SUCOMA club, and they entertained us regally. These were good men, and we were happy to leave them with our shotgun ammunition which pleased them greatly.

I spent an uncomfortable night as the groin was playing up, but Piers and Ted suffered to a greater degree. The mosquito screens and the air conditioning in their room were ineffective and both men received a mauling from both rampant insects and the oppressive heat. The next morning Piers was in a sorry state. We all believed malaria had afflicted him, but the SUCOMA men immediately had him checked out in their hospital. Fortunately, malaria hadn't struck Piers, but we agreed to forego further shooting and head for the escarpment away from the stultifying humidity that was getting to all of us.

I tried to return to Malawi. However, in 1990 I received a letter from the authorities stating that all permits for guns had been withdrawn for an indefinite period. Dr Hastings Banda had died, both the Oxberrys and Ed Hammond had moved from Malawi and our allies from SUCOMA had departed. The Shire swamps and Lake Chilwa hold special memories. Those who have hunted wildfowl in these picturesque lands will not forget the joys of swinging a gun in this charming corner of Africa. And, of course, there's 'The Elephant Marsh Inn!

* * * * *

The Eastern Cape deserves special mention. Here is an area of South Africa renowned for its plains game hunting and greywing partridge, arguably South Africa's most prestigious game bird. This genuine partridge is found in the mountainous regions spreading from Molteno through to Graaff-Reinet. I have wandered around the Eastern Cape for many years with both rifle and shotgun on the estates of such prominent farmer/hunters as Robin Halse, John Broster and Louis Marais. One shoot in particular epitomises the lure of greywing shooting. Miles and Jill Browne, a charming Eastern Cape couple, were the hosts to Sean, our son, Mike Viljoen, Bill Bedford and Bob Warren-Codrington, both from Zimbabwe. The first morning we walked, and we walked, down, up and across the mountains looking for greywing. Ranging in front were Miles' pointers, good dogs, but the day was uncharacteristically hot for July - mid-winter in South Africa. Scent was scarce and, as experienced as we were, we began to wonder whether there were any birds in the region, but we remained positive that there would be greywing. My son, however, lost his focus and started looking for snakes to while away the time. There are plenty of cobras lurking under the rocks in the Eastern Cape hills. To break the tedium, he would upturn the odd rock to see if his luck was in. Sure enough Sean discovered a Cape cobra and called me over to inspect his find. I don't like snakes and usually give them a wide berth. However, I had to show face in front of the youngster, by then barely out of his teens, and I walked over to inspect his wretched prize. The Cape cobra wasn't the largest of its kind. In fact it was on the young side, but it looked unpleasant enough. Sean was prodding the serpent and, predictably, the venomous snake became angry. It slithered straight at me and cursing volubly at the cobra and Sean who was responsible for this attack, I backed off hurriedly only to trip and land flat on my back. The snake graciously retreated but I was not on my feet in time to avoid the attention of Bill Bedford and Bob Warren-Codrington, both beside themselves with mirth at my misfortune.

Talking of these reptiles, I came out of the jungles of the Congo on one of my big game hunts and never encountered a snake whilst wading through the swamps. Then on a bird shoot, shortly after my return,

I nearly tripped over an evil looking puff adder with enough venom in it to down a horse. Such is the unpredictability of bird shooting in this part of the world.

We sat down to a cold lunch in the veldt. We had not shot one greywing and were feeling somewhat despondent. Then that afternoon, we encountered covey after covey and began to amass a sizeable bag. The pointers were on to the partridges like forest bees to a honey tree. The sight of an English pointer with another pointer backing up, standing nose in the grass with tail rigid, is poetry and the pulse starts to race when you walk up waiting for a sudden explosion of birds to burst in every direction. The gun has to be quick on the draw as greywing can move like bullets, particularly in the strong winds prevalent in the mountains of the Eastern Cape.

The following morning we tramped over another range of hills and had only moderate success until we encountered one huge covey made up of various coveys that had converged. This is a rare phenomenon and we were amidst the largest grouping of greywing that Miles Browne and we guns had ever experienced. We estimated 30 - 40 birds and we were in the thick of them. I was shooting on the flank and downed four birds in a row. Sean to my right was having a field day and so were the others. Bob was lethal with his 20 bore that afternoon. Finally Miles Browne called a halt. We had taken a third of the covey and this was enough. We had never seen anything like it in our days on greywing shooting. Then the rains came – or rather the hail stones. We had three kilometres or so to reach the truck and there was nowhere to shelter on the bleak hills. Following the previous day's heat we were clad in shirts and little else. The hail was savage and we took a beating that afternoon and a severe soaking. I reckoned we were close to hypothermia after eventually reaching the truck. Greywing shooting – mountains, cobras, heat and hail but worth every minute of it. In my opinion the king of the game birds in this region is the greywing.

* * * * *

Close to Johannesburg are many farms producing sunflower crops and cattle feed lots, attracting swarms of speckled pigeons known locally as 'Rockies'. Pigeon shooting tends to be regarded by the non initiated as an inferior sport. Any such notion should be dismissed as this species of game bird is a truly testing challenge to the wing shot.

I have had magnificent sport on rock pigeons and red eyed doves and it's rare not to return after a day in the sunflower fields with a sackful of birds. They make excellent eating at very little cost, remembering that the farming community actively encourage licensed sportsmen to deal with these rapacious birds that threaten to decimate their crops. A typical pigeon shoot can be described following a telephone call from a Rob Bailey. "We're shooting at Randfontein (An hour's drive from Johannesburg). Usual thing. Bring some meat for the braaivleis and your drink. The farmer tells me the birds are flying in their droves so have plenty of ammo. I'm getting there by 7 am to catch the early morning flight. See you on Saturday."

The best flight times are usually predictable – the early mornings an hour after day break when the Rockies come in from the mining shafts and the towns to feed and the return flight back to their roosts just before dusk. As with most field sport, the midday period is quiet. There are several tricks to the trade in successful pigeon shooting. These birds have phenomenal eyesight. Camouflage clothing is essential and the aficionado will use camouflage cream on the face. Portable hides are necessary such as specially designed netting which is light to carry. Decoys are useful and certain experienced pigeon men will use either artificial decoys, or defrozen birds from the previous shoot and attach these to the stalks of the sunflowers within shooting range. Certain sportsmen are indolent and avoid the effort to walk into the centre of a field, remembering that farms in the Transvaal or the Free State are large in comparison with those in Europe or the UK. Flight lines change during the day, requiring some energy to position oneself effectively. Light shot is recommended – sevens & eights – and plenty of ammunition is needed as a good day's sport can account for two hundred cartridges or so depending on the accuracy of the wing shooter. Pigeons move at the rate of knots;

this bird jinks, swoops, dives – they never fly in a straight line. The experienced hand will tell you that if you can shoot pigeons, you can shoot any bird. This explains the tendency of over leading guinea fowl at the start of a season.

I arrive at 7 am. sharp to find Rob Bailey, David McGillivray, and Bruce Brothers, the early risers. Andrew Allen and Christo Mackeurtan of the Molopo shoot fame – as described later in the chapter – will be present if available. These capable shots are keen exponents of pigeon shooting. The indolent men - Derek Noyes - Smith, Neville Glasser and Geoff Cox will arrive later. It pays to reach the shooting grounds early as a sunflower field can attract an army of guns from various shooting clubs and it's advisable to claim a good position.

I drink Rob Bailey's coffee hurriedly and wade through the tightly sewn sunflowers lugging my paraphernalia of weapon, ammo, netting, shooting stick which all add up to a fair weight. I settle into position where I remember the birds flighting in from the previous foray and I wait. I scour the sky in all directions for the tell tale specks on the horizon and my prediction that morning is correct. The first flight swarms in with a characteristic swoosh of beating wings. I miss with both barrels, committing the cardinal error of not focussing on one bird but shooting into the flock. For three hours the action is fast and furious and I've collected three dozen Rockies despite countless misses and a crack shot would have downed many more. But I'm happy and I'm looking for a cold beer. I pick up the empty cartridges – a mandatory practice for ethical sportsmen – gather my equipment, and struggle back to join the team. Watching Rob Bailey is an experience. He shoots perched on a camp stool with his pipe clamped in his teeth and he rarely misses. He's a fine shot and he doesn't believe in unnecessary effort. He has trained his gardener to mark the birds where they fall and collect them during a lull in the flightings. Derek Noyes – Smith and Neville Glasser have opted as they are wily men for a flight line over a clump of wattle trees. They are ensconced in the shade on this very hot summer's morning, leaving 'mad dogs and Englishmen' to travail under a blazing sky! To be seen nearby is Paul Hatfield, a seasoned shot and observing him swing a gun is poetry in motion. I used to shoot ducks with Paul and his henchman, Tony Scuil, in the early days at Koster in the West Transvaal and these shoots were adventures not to be forgotten. We'd drive back to Johannesburg with a boot brimful of yellow bill ducks and some Egyptian geese and these were the halcyon days when radar police traps and breathalysers were virtually unknown. The conversation would get riper whilst the cold beers were being sunk in tribute to a great day's sport.

The pigeon shoot is not complete without the traditional braaivleis. Rob Bailey has this down to a fine art. He's trained his faithful gardener not only to collect his birds but to braai the steaks and the boerewors to a perfection. By midday, the action has quietened down and the guns assemble for the lunch break. The conversation borders on barrack room humour with David McGillivray leading the pace and we ask him to take us through his experience with the thief who broke into his house. McGillivray was woken early one winter's morning to discover a robber in the hallway. He gave chase stark naked in the cold where he was to be seen sprinting after his unwelcome guest in the midst of Dunkeld, a smart suburb in Johannesburg, when the commuter traffic is at its peak. The early morning drivers were entertained at the sight of McGillivray rugby tackling the felon in all his naked glory. To this day, an indignant McGillivray rails against the drivers in the traffic jam which he had caused for not assisting him with his wriggling captive in giving him a lift to the nearest police station! "I was freezing my bollocks off gripping the thief who was not exactly a puny fellow and no – one came to my aid!"

* * * * *

I'd heard the old timers speak of *"the Natal surround"*. I'd given scant attention to this technique of bird shooting until I attended the Wales International shoot near Petrus Steyn in the Free State. I had received glowing reports of this particular tourney hosted by Peter Wales and supported by a varied collection of enthusiasts drawn mainly from the Transvaal and Natal provinces. In the five shoots I've attended the assembled guns were generally speaking experienced game shooters and there was a strong camaraderie amongst the farmers, the surgeons, the lawyers and entrepreneurs who congregated each year to partake in some first class sport. Peter Wales had a long nurtured ambition to commemorate his father's tradition of hosting an annual shoot for his friends, most of whom were farmers who used to buy his fertiliser and seed. To grant Peter his full due, he perpetuated this fine tradition in an exemplary manner. He was able to fulfil his aim with the cooperation of the local landowners who remembered Wales senior with respect and with the assistance of a shoot captain called Braam Cronje, a charismatic Natal farmer who ran the shoot in a commendable manner. Braam was a major asset in the splendid way he controlled the thirty guns with a firm handedness but with a natural leadership which he'd obviously inherited from an illustrious forebear, General Piet Cronje – the Boer war hero who inflicted significant defeats on the British at the turn of the century.

I'll describe a typical Wales shoot: the sportsmen would arrive late on a Thursday afternoon and congregate at the bar of the shooting lodge which Peter had built on his father's estate. Here'd be thirty odd characters, as aforementioned, most of whom were acquainted through previous shoots, and all shared a sport in common. Dinner would be served on three long refectory tables with the fare consisting of venison or game birds during which Braam Cronje would brief the guns on the plan for the following day's shoot. Then some serious carousing would follow and the die hards would lurch to bed in the small hours of the morning. The sleeping quarters are reminiscent of a boarding school: two dormitories, one up, one down, in an adjoining annexe to the lodge. As in the private school tradition, two showers and four toilets to service thirty men! There were a few who whinged about the privation of queuing in line for a shower, usually cold for the latecomers, or the noisy toilets. This was all part of the charm of the shoot.

We'd then awake at 5 am, get dressed, grab a coffee, and prepare for the first beat on a very cold Free State dawn. The guns would be divided into four groups with each group leader assigned a radio. The objective is to place a company of guns in a wide circle where the guinea fowl would be surrounded from all sides and where they would be slowly entrapped until they'd finally attempt to escape in small bunches. The guns are now in position- no mean feat as this exercise of marshalling this multitude of guns is undertaken in the dark – and the section leaders wait for Braam Cronje's signal to move forward. Usually the first shoot of the day is centred on a copse as this is where the prey roosts before dispersing to feed in the surrounding mealie fields. The birds bolt out of the trees in spectacular fashion, and the sport is on. Over a two days shoot comprising of an average of six beats per day, the bag will reach at between seven and eight hundred birds, mostly guinea fowl and a few francolin. It should be explained that wild guinea fowl – not the domestic bird found in Europe - are the hardiest game bird in Africa. Wily, cunning, this bird understands how to survive in the harsh environment they habitat. And they are tough to bring down unless with a head shot. Experienced sportsmen will tell you how a wounded guinea fowl with a heavy load of no 4 shot in its chest can continue to fly for two kilometres or more until they land. The African guinea fowl is excellent to eat, provided the cook knows how to marinate the fat free bird. Many an overseas shot has been humbled by this game bird that they'd dismiss as "shooting apples in a barrel". Perhaps slower than the English pheasant, the guinea fowl is a testing target, especially in full flight behind a wind. Prick a pheasant or partridge in Europe, and the bird comes down. But not the wild guinea fowl, unless accurately shot.

The technique of *'the Natal surround'* is worth focussing on: reconnaissance of the shooting terrain is essential to determine where the flocks are, the size of the flocks, and where they roost. The Wales shoot is conducted over several farms in the Petrus Steyn area which obviates overshooting the flocks. The guns are briefed prior to each beat with each gun assigned to one of the four sections. The section leader keeps in touch with the shoot captain. He will be responsible for shepherding his team to the assigned destination and to keep them in line when the signal is given by the shoot captain to start closing in. If properly executed, *'the Natal Surround'* can be devastingly effective, remembering that the radius of the circle can extend to four kilometres or more. Each section leader knows how essential it is to close gaps in the circle for guinea fowl are born survivors and will fly through a hole in the line if given the chance. The guns are instructed not to shoot at birds flying in the direction of the centre for both safety and sporting purposes. The effect of the manoeuvre is to disperse the flocks into small groups that will attempt to escape the tightening noose by flying out in singles or pairs.

Most of the beats as described were conducted in the manner planned. However, certain were not without some incident. There was the case when one section, poorly selected in this instance as most were the least fit in the party that year, went on strike and refused to obey their section leader, a young Natal farmer. As they lagged further and further behind, placing this particular beat in jeopardy, the farmer stormed up to Braam Cronje bellowing" these palookas are not fit to be on the shoot – I'm resigning – find another leader!" Then there was the infamous incident in which our host acted out his party trick in roaring around a corner force spinning his vehicle towards the assembled trucks in spectacular fashion. But on this occasion he misjudged the space between the four wheel drives and swiped a brand new Mercedes Benz amidships. The expression on the owner's face told the story. Luckily for Wales, the fellow was of a placid disposition but he never returned to the shoot.

A section leader's task can be unenviable. I know this as I was selected to replace the aforementioned Natal farmer. In the pursuit of one's task, one cannot fully enjoy the shooting. However, on a particular beat where the birds came over our position in a constant stream, the temptation was too severe and I dropped the radio in the veldt to shoot the birds and so intent was one on this marvellous sport that the radio was forgotten. Only in the truck returning to the lodge that one remembered the missing radio, and these are valuable and Peter can be highly excitable in nature. I confided with Braam and luckily there was a spare and the host was kept in blissful ignorance! Braam and I quietly went off to search for the radio, my bribing Braam with a dozen Guinness's in the local kroeg, and we found the radio in the thick grass – a needle in a haystack!

* * * * *

There is unpredictability in bird shooting in this part of the world. I came out of the jungles of the Congo on one of my big game hunts and never encountered a snake whilst wading through the swamps. And then on a shoot last year in the Settlers area, near Warmbaths north of Pretoria, organised by the Dodds brothers, there were snakes! And how! An Egyptian cobra, highly venomous, was caught by the farmer on his homestead stoep on whose ground we were shooting that very morning. I had noticed that several of the guns were wearing heavy canvas trousers and knee high gaiters. "For the snakes – plenty of them around!" they cheerfully told me. And Rob and Ian Dodds were hardly reassuring: "You'll see snakes and this morning's hot. Just keep an eye out!" They weren't exaggerating. There was the aforementioned three metre long cobra in all its glory. Then we had Rob give us the riveting news that he'd picked up on his shortwave radio that a black mamba had bitten a shooter on a neighbouring farm necessitating a casevac by helicopter. We didn't know whether to believe him or not. And little did he know that his black humour hovered close to reality. One of our party had a black mamba slither across his track an hour later! This certainly sobered us up and I spent an inordinate amount of time searching the grass for mambas, cobras, and puff adders. Despite this diversion, we managed to collect a respectable bag of francolin.

* * * * *

Shooting birds in South Africa itself has its own special attractions. Overseas sportsmen have come to experience our greywing partridge, guinea fowl, francolin, sand grouse and speckled pigeon. More driven bird shoots are being developed and special train shoots are promoted wherein enthusiasts are transported to various interesting shooting grounds in Southern Africa. I have a prediction that more hunters will venture here for a combination of big game and bird shooting in the belief that South Africa offers these field sports at their optimum.

Perhaps the one shoot which I would rank as best reflecting the aforementioned sentiment is an event known as the Molopo conducted by

Andrew Allen and Christo Mackeurtan. I have been one of the charmed to have been invited on this superb private shoot. When I'm overseas in the field, I take every opportunity to expound on this truly magnificent sporting event which has few peers in my extensive shooting career. Andrew Allen and Christo Mackeurtan have run the Molopo shoot for many years and they make a formidable team. They are crack shots, they understand how to provide the guns with magnificent sporting birds over a vast terrain of sandveldt, they are splendid exemplars of shooting ethics, and highly companionable and generous minded people to be with. I've had the pleasure of knowing these two characters for many years. Andrew comes from a Suffolk farming family and he started to pot ducks and geese still wearing his nappies! Andrew is built for ribaldry and the British boarding school humour is well in evidence when he's around. And then Christo. This fellow embodies the description 'nature's gentleman' through his background and his demeanour. His manner in the field is less vociferous than the stentorian Andrew Allen who would have made an ideal RSM in a British regiment and his skill with a gun is magnificent to witness.

The pair knows instinctively the habits of the guinea fowl, how they will react to the wind, the direction in which they will fly when walked up, the size of the flocks, where they are likely to be feeding dependant on the time of day. They accordingly make their action plan in consultation together for the drives which can differ in accordance with the various cattle camps we will be shooting over. A favoured tactic on the Molopo is the 'L' shape configuration where certain of the guns walk behind each other, well spaced out, at right angles along a boundary fence, with the beaters and the remaining guns following slowly behind in line coaxing the guinea fowl over the guns moving ahead along the fence. Andrew and Christo have perfected the technique of 'the bounce back' encouraging the guinea fowl to fly over the guns rather than risking open ground. As with the 'Natal surround', this is a highly effective method of guinea fowl shooting. On other drives all the guns will walk up with the beaters interspersed to pick up the birds. Prior to each drive, the guns will receive a brief from the shoot captains so that they will be left in no doubt as to what is expected of them. Most who attend the Molopo are experienced shots; they know the terrain and are unlikely to get lost, using their shadow from the sun as a bearing; they are conversant with the safety drills and the need to warn the line on a lost bird; and most importantly they respect the sporting ethics of bird shooting.

The lively notes of an Irish jig cascaded over the moonlit sandveldt against a hum of cheerful laughter and animated chatter. There was a merry shindig in progress at 2 a.m. in a farmhouse on the Molopo River. That evening will have me grinning to the grave! This particular Molopo shoot had come to a conclusion on a Sunday when the main party had returned to Johannesburg leaving the shoot hosts, Andrew and Christo, and Andrew Glencross and the author to break camp on the following day. That afternoon, Andrew Allen and Christo departed to discuss a forthcoming commercial shoot with Kevin Keeley and Verona at their nearby farm. On their return, they announced that we had been invited to dinner but they suggested that we stoke up on snacks & whisky before presenting ourselves as it was likely that there wouldn't be much to consume being the end of the week. We duly arrived at 7 p.m. to be greeted by an extraordinary sight of a dining table laden with such delicacies as oysters, prawns & other special titbits. This was just the start of a bacchanalian feast. Fine wines, malt whisky, French brandy were on offer plus a huge tantalising fillet of steak which would have put Simpsons in London to shame! We'd wagered on an early night, little knowing that the revelry would last into the small hours of the morning. It was probably the wine that had Christo and Andrew Glencross warbling like canaries after a sumptuous meal on their war exploits in Angola. The stories grew more outlandish as the hours ticked by. Andrew Allen was out of it has he'd fallen firmly asleep as is his custom but our hosts were reduced to helpless mirth as was I at the improbable spectacle of Christo taking the flags of surrender from the enemy wherever his tank took him in Angola and Andrew Glencross blowing up half Southern Africa with his mortar team. They were on an unstoppable roll and our laughter, punctuated by Andrew Allen's snores, only exacerbated their verbosity. And the greater the merriment, the more brandy and whisky was consumed.

Keeley's Irish jigs played at full blast on his music system resounding over the silent sandveldt certainly contributed to the delightful bizarreness of the occasion.

Over the many years of running the Molopo shoot, Andrew and Christo have assimilated a group of carefully selected individuals drawn from a variety of backgrounds and pursuits. They share one common interest – appreciation of the quality of the Molopo shoot which all know too well is rare to come by. There is no discordance within the party; there is no show of naked competitiveness or poaching of birds so often displayed on commercial shoots; there is no jockeying for pole position – the guns are placed by the organisers and they do what they are told to do without discontent. The spirit of the camaraderie is vibrant; the humour is abundant. Without a sense of humour you are not invited. Co-operation in assisting on the preparation of the meals is expected as with the housekeeping in the cottage at the start and finish of the weekend. The shirkers are quickly recognised and run the risk of not being invited again. Friendships are struck at the Molopo shoot and likely to stand the test of time. Then there are some farmers from the district who operate their own shoots, characters like Rob Schulze and Neil Hobson, who are regulars at the Molopo. They are true assets to have as they are conversant with the tactics, they are good shots, they provide extra beaters which are always useful, and add in no mean way to the bonhomie. I have been lucky to have attended several of Rob Schulze's guinea fowl forays on his Nonen farms which are again run in a most professional manner and I had the very good fortune of being involved in a family reunion organised by Neil Hobson for his extensive tribe from all over South Africa. To celebrate this occasion, Neil held a splendid shoot on his farm in the Setlagole district. I recall vividly one of his coveys numbering some 500 guinea fowl – one covey!

The Molopo River serves as the border between South Africa and Botswana for most of its length. It runs dry in the winter months where the borderline is marked by a wire fence. The farms in this corner of South Africa are large and well spread out, stretching from Bray to Setlagole over a distance of some 150 kilometres. The shooting takes place on farms in the Bray district which are best suited to cattle ranching and game as the sand veldt is harsh for crops. However, the farmer is efficient in his estate management and his irrigation system facilitates the planting of maize and groundnuts which attract the guinea fowl from several kilometres afar, explaining the rich abundance of game birds.

The cottage which serves as the shooting lodge on one of the farms has a charm which will appeal to the true sportsman; there are no artificial trappings which would ill suit the gold tap brigade and the facilities are perfectly adequate where there is plenty of hot water and an excellent outdoor shower. A major feature is the camp fireplace where most of the food preparation takes place and each gun is designated a meal. This reminds me of the brunch which I was designated to produce some years back. It was uncharacteristically warm at midday and I was not relishing the thought of cooking over an open fire for the ten assembled guns. It took almost an hour for the heavily perspiring chef – the intake of whisky the night before hadn't helped - to scramble some two dozen eggs. Rob Schulze was good enough to alleviate the tedium – he can be an entertaining character and he acted as the sous chef with the more menial chores of preparing the bacon, tomatoes, onions, peppers, potatoes, liver, kidneys under my supervision, of course – and he'd told me whilst all this was going on that there was a certain amount of cynicism prevalent in the camp that I could cook! This only encouraged me to add a few exotic ingredients not usually included in the cookery manuals – in went a handful of chillies, tobasco by the mugful, and other eastern delights. The party was suitably awed at the sight of the feast when brunch was finally announced but not one gun wanted to eat the eggs! Andrew started the rot: "No eggs for me, I don't eat them"; Tom Bramwell- Jones, usually a prodigious trencherman, apologised: "Eggs have cholesterol – I'll do without"; Philippe Anderson's healthy appetite had lapsed with an apologetic "I only eat boiled eggs"; and then, Rob, my own sous chef, had the effrontery to complain "after what you've put in the eggs, I'll pass". My fuse was already at a dangerous low and with this last insult, I stormed off to the cottage with the frying pan bellowing the worst insults I could muster at the snickering ensemble, and proceeded to gobble the eggs in haste. Denis da Silva – usually a dependable ally – had originated the jape and a contrite assembly of bird shooters arrived with their plates asking politely for eggs! I think it was Christo who informed me that the last laugh was on me – for some reason or other, most of the party suffered a serious bout of the runs the following week! Since that day, I have been pardoned from cooking breakfast – any other meal but breakfast.

The Molopo shoot is a difficult act to beat. The game birds are abundant and the birds are magnificently presented -- high shots, long shots, sometimes in droves or small coveys. There's game – kudu, warthog, duiker, jackal. The terrain is striking – not a power line in sight, just open sandveldt. Then at night, the awesome silence descends under a brilliant canopy of stars in the high sky and the sound of a jackal in the distance. This is a special corner of Africa, unspoilt, unsullied, and esoteric. I'm a lucky man to have had the rare pleasure of experiencing the Molopo.

* * * * *

During a span of 35 years carrying a shotgun in Southern Africa, there is rarely a dull moment in the platteland, mountains or bushveldt. I've often reflected on what separates a big game hunter from the wing shooter. How is it that the world of bird shooting is considered an acceptable sport, more 'politically correct' than its big game hunting counterpart? After all, both forms of sport involve the act of killing, whether it is bird or beast. Bird shooting is essentially a pastime where etiquette plays a dominant role and where the demands on the sportsman are different. Trophy hunting is an intensely serious game. Days can pass on a safari where a hunter will not pull the trigger. Either the quarry has escaped the hunter, such as my experiences on elephant and lion, or the trophy is not up to expectation. On one occasion after seven days of lion hunting in Botswana, I did not pull the trigger once, and on another it was only on the sixth day of a three-week safari in Central African Republic that I fired a shot. Two weeks in the Congo on another hunt accounted for only three spent rifle cartridges. The average bird shooter would think it a poor day's sport if 50 shells had not been fired at least. And triple that on a pigeon shoot. A miss at an easy bird encourages a barrage of friendly banter from down the line. A miss at a trophy animal can create a deathly pall in a hunting camp. I missed a Marco Polo sheep in the Pamir Mountains in Tajikistan and my Russian guide wouldn't speak to me for five hours. Walking up guinea fowl is a relatively relaxed pastime. Conversing with a fellow gun is acceptable in the field. After all, controlling one's dog involves noise. Stalking an animal is very different. As the column of trackers, gun bearers, hunter and back up gun (if there is one) close on a herd of buffalo, or a pride of lion, or an exotic antelope, the tension can be cut with a knife. There is no small talk, no bonhomie, just concentration on the prey and an adrenaline rush that courses through the system, burning every nerve end.

The participants are different too. The wing shooter is generally gregarious and sociable. He is generous with words and praises a good shot. He likes his comforts, whether it be a good lunch, or taking a noggin in a jeep in a downpour between drives. The dedicated big game hunter knows little of this and has to be immune to freezing cold, sodden clothes, searing heat, little sleep and a cursory congratulatory nod on achieving a trophy. However, there is usually empathy between the wing shooter and the hunter. They are both familiar with weaponry and hold a common love for the pursuit of sporting game. There is a saying that a capable rifle shot makes a pedestrian wing shooter and vice versa. I don't necessarily concur. I have witnessed some very adept riflemen who are capable with shotguns; perhaps this is not generally the case in the reverse. Most of the men I shoot birds with show little inkling to hunt. Not that they are adverse to it. Indeed, they can be most generous spirited in their outlook on big game sport. And there are those who are proficient with both rifle and shotgun. A good example is Michael de Pelet who shoots pheasant and hunts roe deer on his Dorset estate. He roams Britain and Europe banging away at birds and hunting deer, wild boar and other species. He's hunted in Africa on several occasions and has a variety of big game trophies to his credit. He's a first class shot on both bird and game. I've had the pleasure of shooting some very testing birds on his estate and I recall one Christmas when Sean and I, together with six other guests, were given a briefing by Michael. I was half listening, trying to keep warm on that cold frosty morning, when my host counselled the guests: "Avoid, please, the low flying birds….not sporting….and a danger to the beaters…..and this particularly applies to my colonial friend from South Africa who'll shoot anything that moves!" Later that morning, Sean, who was sharing my stand, couldn't understand my passing up the low birds. "You'd shoot them in South Africa, wouldn't you, Dad. Why not here?" Sean had a point, remembering that our own rough shooting doesn't boast quite the same finesse as driven bird shooting in Britain. I explained this was a different kettle of fish as firstly our host wouldn't take it kindly if a beater was peppered and secondly it was "not quite sporting" to blast away at a low flying bird.

One December, I was helping out on a shoot that Michael de Pelet was hosting for a party of fee-paying Americans. I felt a little conspicuous as the visitors arrived impeccably kitted out. Their tweeds were new, probably purchased in Holland & Holland, and here I was fresh from hunting Marco Polo sheep in Tajikistan bordering Afghanistan and I had arrived over for the Shikar Club's annual dinner in London. My host cast me a disparaging glance as I stood with the group in front of the de Pelet manor house as he ran through the form for the bird shoot. I was wearing a Polish fur hat, thick canvas trousers tucked into mountain boots, and a Gortex arctic jacket pulled in by a wide leather belt. It mattered not. The leader of the American party was an urbane, well dispositioned merchant banker whose son was being given the shoot as a 21st birthday present. The group came from the East Coast of America. The banker learned that I was from Johannesburg and said that his son and friends were visiting South Africa. What could I tell him about the country? The net result was that a few weeks later we hosted the banker's son and his friends in Johannesburg. In response, the banker generously invited us to Wisconsin to hunt white-tailed deer on his ranch. So much for my Russian hunting gear – it had obviously made an impression!

CHAPTER FIFTEEN

Invictus

Then we realised that the whole country is behind us,
and for this man to wear a Springbok jersey was a sign,
not just for us, but for the whole of South Africa, that
we have to unite, and we have to unite today.

Joost van der Westhuizen,
Springbok scrum half - 1995 World Cup

FOR MANY South Africans, there are four milestones in the country's recent history: The first democratic elections held in 1994, the Rugby World Cup victories in 1995 and 2007, and the successful staging of the FIFA world Cup in 2010.

The Vinuchi sponsorship of the Transvaal Under Twenties – we had some future Springboks who played in the 1995 World Cup in the form of James Dalton, hooker, and Japie Mulder, centre – gave me access to the Luyt family box located beneath the 'Glasshouse'. It was from here that I enjoyed the special privilege of watching the World Cup final of 1995. This was a dramatic day which will remain indelibly in my memory and surely in the minds of the 70,000 spectators that crammed into Ellis Park to witness Francois Pienaar and his men take the cup. The film 'Invictus', directed by Clint Eastwood, immortalised the Springbok triumph. How can one forget the raw excitement that permeated the streets of Johannesburg the day prior to the final. There was a remarkable surge of support for the Springboks from all sectors of the population. The cry 'Amabokoboko' (the Xhosa word for Springbok) rang around the city. This was the first major event to be staged in what Bishop Tutu dubbed "the Rainbow Nation". I arrived early in the Luyt box and with me was Sean and I introduced him to Louis Luyt and Rian Oberholzer. Already the famous ground was simmering with excitement and the tension was electric. One should remember that the Springboks were seeded ninth owing to the years of isolation when they were only readmitted to the international arena in 1992. But the men in the green and gold defeated Australia, Romania, Canada, Western Samoa, and France to play their traditional rivals, New Zealand, in the final.

The Luyt box was a marvellous venue to be on this historic day. I recall having a chat with 'Zulu' Coetzee, the rugged chief of security for Ellis Park. I had got to know this charismatic character over the three years of the sponsorship when I used to meet him with Rian Oberholzer for a few beers after work at Ellis Park – the ground was close to our factory. Perhaps the most thrilling action prior to the kick-off was the incredible sight of the SA Airways Boeing 747 with a message emblazoned on its undercarriage 'Go Springboks' skimming over the stadium. This stupendously daring act had the crowd on their feet and, no doubt, 'Zulu' Coetzee's security team in jitters. It was a remarkable derring - do on the pilot's part – he had taken his own initiative to stage this stunt - and not once but twice did he thunder over the packed ground.

The All Blacks captain, Sean Fitzpatrick, perhaps best summed up the raw emotion that permeated Ellis Park that memorable afternoon in June 1995: "To see him (Mandela) walking into the stadium with Francois' jersey on, and to hear 72,000 people start chanting Mandela, Mandela ...... then there's 15 of us there looking, thinking 'God, how are we ever going to beat these buggers!" And Jonah Lomu, the giant winger for the All Blacks who had single handed demolished England in the semi finals, had an uneasy feeling on the day. In his words he felt intimidated shaking Mandela's hand before the game and he could sense that Mandela had united the country after years of conflict "and on that one day they all came together".

The epic was a close run thing with the South Africans pipping the all Blacks in the play-off after a 12/12 tie with a dropped goal by the Springbok fly half Joel Stransky in extra time. The massive crowd witnessing this milestone in South Africa's sporting history was incredulous at the sight of Nelson Mandela walking across the pitch towards the podium wearing a number six Springbok shirt, matching the vest of the captain, Francois Pienaar, an Afrikaner who had inspired his side that afternoon to bring glory to the Republic. Mandela's gesture was characteristically magnanimous and a stepping stone in crossing a divide between black and white South Africans. Nelson Mandela later wrote: "It was under Francois Pienaar's inspiring leadership that rugby became the pride of the entire country". Driving through Johannesburg later that evening was a fairy tale where massed crowds of cheering South Africans of all creeds were dancing and shouting 'Amabokoboko – Amabokoboko'. The nation was truly one that night.

The ecstasy that the 1995 World Cup triumph created in the hearts of South African rugby aficionados was eclipsed in the dark years that followed this euphoric victory. Racism, political infighting, panic within the coaching ranks, despondency in the players, crowned by the infamous Kamp Staaldraad led to an inevitable failed performance at the 2003 World Cup. The very ethos of the Springbok was under threat. But from the ashes rose the Phoenix in the form of a rejuvenated spirit extended by the coach Jake White, another inspirational figure in the mould of a Kitch Christie, who became the architect of South Africa's meteoric rise to the ascendancy of the world rugby game. But it was not a clear run through to the pinnacle in the 2007 World Cup. The Boks a year previous had lost seven of their eight tests. Jake White prophesied that the team that would win would be the side that knew how to defend its line. To substantiate his belief, he would refer to history when in four consecutive World Cups between 1987/ 1999, the winners did not concede one try in the final. The traditional strength of the great Springbok sides has been in the domination up front; Springbok rugby has rarely received accolades for brilliant ball playing flair. The hard, ruthless physicality and the relentless intensity of Springbok play and the conservative low risk approach is a proven World Cup winning formula for the men in the green & gold.

The team that went to France in 2007 was ranked as second favourites to the All Blacks. But it was a team that struck fear in the opponents. Bakkies Botha and Victor Matfield were rated as the best lock combination in the world; Juan Smith, Schalk Burger, and Danie Rossouw as the most deadly back row in the tournament; John Smit as a captain of inspirational leadership on the level of Francois Pienaar and Sean Fitzpatrick; Bryan Habana as a winger of genius; and Fourie du Preez and Butch James as the best half- back combination in international rugby to dictate the direction and flow of a game. Then added to this awesome collection of rugby gladiators were the likes of Percy Montgomery, destined to win more caps than any other Springbok, and the highly respected front row forward, Os Du Randt, the sole remnant of the victorious 1995 side. This was the squad of battle hardened stars, the core of which had grown from boys into men from the ill fated 2003 side, that won over the hearts and minds of the French in Paris and other towns where the players strolled without armed escort with a quiet confidence and dignity with the knowledge of being a world class side.

As most predicted, the Australians and the New Zealanders were the only sides capable of beating the Boks, a tribute to the accepted supremacy of the Southern Hemisphere in world rugby, largely due to the titanic Tri – Nations competition and the Super 14 tournament. The 36 – 0 pulverising of the English by the Springboks in the preliminary rounds sent out the message in clear terms. The often posed question at the World Cup 2007 was how Australia and New Zealand allowed themselves to be beaten by France and England respectively. Both nations were playing well below their best capability. The semi – final between these sides was accorded as a game of mediocrity and described by the Independent Newspapers Group as: "England, we know, can't play. And France, in Paris, we saw for a second time in the tournament, were too scared to play!" The other semi – final produced quality rugby. The Springboks scored four tries to one, a win by the second highest margin recorded in a World Cup semi – final, 37 – 13. The ruggedness of the Boks defence was awesome and the line-out performance was flawless with the Boks stealing eight of the Argentinean 19 throw ins whilst conceding one only out of 19 of their own. "We were facing the best line – out in the world" stated the Pumas no 8, Gonzalo Elia.

I watched the final on TV in Durban where the game ended late at night and I had four hours only before the start of the Amabokoboko cycle race along the route of the Comrades marathon, Pietermaritzburg to Durban. I pedalled the tortuous route with a well deserved hangover and with a pride from witnessing the controlled decimation of the English XV. The Springboks commenced their World Cup campaign with an indestructible defence and they ended it with a ferocious display of hammer blow hits. As Jake White has always decreed: defence wins World Cups. The Springboks were indomitable in the collisions, converting ruthless defence into turnovers and subsequent deadly attacks. I was witness that evening to an awesome display of confrontational physicality meted out with an iron discipline that marked this side as the exceptional team of the tournament. The colossal performance in the line-outs by the incomparable trio, Juan Smith, Bakkies Botha, and Victor Matfield was majestic; even the mercurial scrum – usually a perennial strength of Springbok sides but an inherent weakness in the 2007 World Cup, came together in the final; The half-back combination of the world class Fourie du Preez and the experienced Butch James clinically controlled the pulse of the game in one of the finest Springbok half - back performances for many a year that had the English reeling backwards for most of the play. But it was the total commitment of the players, exemplified by Os Du Randt in his relentless forward surges and Percy Montgomery who played the last 30 minutes with torn ligaments in his left knee, that won the day for the South Africans. As I pedalled the long, hot road, with a throbbing head and a parched tongue, I had one thought only – to raise a glass to Jake White, his inspirational coaching team, and the magnificent Boks that have provided the Republic with a new rugby story to talk about.

The four years leading up to the FIFA 2010 World Cup hosted by South Africa were studded by uncertainty fuelling the doomsayer's predictions of unfinished stadiums, chaotic transport infrastructure, and the ever present threat of crime. FIFA must have had many nervous moments with the political machinations of the Mbeki/Zuma power struggle, the rash of xenophobic outbursts in the townships, and the electricity blackouts threatening to cripple the country's industry. Rumours abounded that FIFA had an alternative plan in place if South Africa appeared incapable of staging the mega sporting event.

The Republic confounded the critics when it delivered in flawless fashion the world's largest sporting event to hundreds of millions overseas and a near record three million spectators, which included 500,000 overseas visitors, attended the 64 matches – the third highest attendance in the history of the World Cup. In excess of 30 billion Rand had been invested in the preparation for the games, an investment that has been rationalised by the ANC government as forming part of a long term development plan for the country. Possibly the most important return on investment in the 2010 World Cup was the massive boost of confidence that the country gained in successfully hosting a tournament of this gigantic size and the uplifting of its standing in the international community in delivering a world class infrastructure and organisational capacity.

In the months preceding the games, an extraordinary catharsis was kindled where a social cohesion came about in a country with its lingering legacy of racial disharmony. South Africans of all creeds and colours were to be seen wearing Bafana Bafana shirts, flying flags from their vehicles, with wing mirrors and bumpers adorned by covers sporting the national flag. With days to go before the kick – off, World Cup fever was reminiscent of the 1995 World Cup but on a far grander scale. There were office blocks, private balconies, walls of mansions draped with the national flag. Blacks and whites amassed in the streets, arms entwined, blowing vuvuzelas. It was a massive display of national unity and spirit in South Africa's support of not only the home team but the many other national sides that had come to compete in Africa's first World Cup. John Smit, the Springbok rugby captain stated: "We have seen some unique scenes in our country before ... we will be following closely the progress of the Bafana Bafana and we wish Aaron Mokoena (captain) and the boys all the best of luck". This quote is significant in that white South Africa is wedded to rugby, regarding soccer as a predominantly black sport. The FIFA World Cup, however, encouraged many whites to share ownership of the national team and will it to victory despite its low international ranking. One must remember that this one factor separated the two World Cups in that the Springboks were in with a good chance to win whereas the Bafana Bafana were virtual no hopers. On the day of the opening ceremony held in Johannesburg's awesome soccer city stadium – 'One of the most beautiful in the world' as described by Sepp Blatter, FIFA's president – the entire country came to a grinding halt. The streets of the cities were transformed into seas of yellow and gold, with a mass of people dancing, singing, and blowing the vuvuzela. FIFA accorded South Africa a near perfect nine out of ten for its hosting of the 2010 World Cup. The vastly improved perception of South Africa internationally could have an enormously beneficial impact on its economy and on the continent as a whole.

CHAPTER SIXTEEN

Africa - A hunter's grail

Glancing down into the valley again, I saw bundles, heads and
heaving torsos along the waving sea of yellowing grass. Like a
slowly slivering python, I thought, that weaving zigzagged line of
porters with their bobbing burdens, stretching away down the path
and into the valley, until lost from view, at the tail end by a bend
in the trail by bamboos and riverine growth bordering the
last stream through which we had waded.

Harry Manners – Professional ivory hunter

THERE ARE many that ask me why I chose to live in South Africa. My answer would be manifold – a hankering for space, a yearning for adventure, and a born wanderlust. There's little doubt in my mind that Kenya, the birth place of the modern day safari, enticed me back to Africa. South Africa was the natural choice as one of the many adventurers in our family, a favourite uncle, Peter de Pentheny O'Kelly, had blazed the trail into this extraordinary land at the tip of the continent. I arrived at a time when an elephant licence cost the equivalent of a mere one hundred rand in Botswana, when a full scale three week safari would amount to a fraction of the staggering cost today, and when most of the African countries on the continent beckoned hunters. I often say that I should have been born in an earlier generation as when I reached these shores in 1969 with my wife and a one year old daughter, I had little means to afford big game hunting. I was making my way in a new environment where I hardly knew anyone and both time and cash required for big game hunting were beyond my means. Bird shooting cost little –

a bottle of brandy for the farmer in most cases – and practical in terms of availability. However big game hunting lay deep in my psyche. It was just a question of time before my dreams would be realised.

It was fortuitous that early on in my career I was to meet a stocky, cannon-ball headed Afrikaner sporting a jutting jaw and clear blue eyes that could twinkle mischievously or bore through one pitilessly. He was Vladimir Steyn, South Africa's Secretary of Defence in the mid-1960's, and by repute he was an excellent man for the job but ill-equipped for bureaucracy. He was too outspoken, too forthright, and too honest and he could be vindictive if he smelt duplicity amongst fellow bureaucrats. I observed him once reduce a senior executive of the S A Tourist Board to a quivering wreck. He'd deduced that the man had committed a mistruth. I had the honour of meeting Vladimir shortly after arriving in South Africa when he had, to use his own words, been demoted to Secretary of Tourism for berating a cabinet minister as an incompetent and a fool. It was my good luck that this formidable man took a liking to me, particularly when he learnt that I was a keen disciple of hunting. Over frequent dinners at his home, I listened avidly to his stories of hunting lion, red forest buffalo and elephant. Vladimir Steyn was a hunter in the old tradition, having faced many close encounters with dangerous game and he enthralled me one night with a vivid account of following up a wounded lion in thick riverine whilst carrying only a shot gun with ball load. Vladimir Steyn could quote from Shakespeare and could appreciate a fine wine. He was a man in the true sense of the word and a valuable mentor.

It is not every day that a modern hunter is given the privilege of meeting one of the last of the old time hunters that shot big game for a livelihood. Harry Manners accounted for 1100 elephant in his 35 years as an ivory hunter. Mozambique was his domain and his adventures are part of African hunting folklore. I am privileged to have known Harry and in my study hangs an initialled photograph showing him with the second largest tusks ever collected in the annals of big game: 187 pounds on one side and 185 on the other! Harry hunted that elephant in the Milange District in Mozambique, near the Malawi border. Contained inside his wonderful book, 'Kambaku', are five letters that he wrote to me. I read them frequently. Just before he died in 1995 he wrote to me: "I figure that a few lines to you, even at this late stage, will not go amiss and show that I have not forgotten you as a good friend. I have had you frequently in mind and have wondered whether you have been away on one more game hunt.........." I wrote back: "Last year was a good hunting season for me where I shot several species of game, including a bull hippo, two buffalo, two kudu, one duiker and several impala. I had nine days in the Zambezi Valley at Camp E; three days in South West Africa; four days in the Matetsi region, near Victoria Falls, Zimbabwe; and three days in Eastern Transvaal. This year I return for fourteen days to the Zambezi valley, taking a camp closer to the Mozambique border, sited on the Zambezi River. Harry, I cannot wait". Harry Manners was considered by many as one of the greatest elephant hunters in Africa, a man in the league of William Finaughty, Frederick C Selous, Jim Sutherland, 'Karamojo' Bell and others.

I feel lucky to have met, if only briefly, another legend – Harry Selby. This is the Kenyan that Robert Ruark immortalised in his book, 'Horn of the Hunter'. Harry Selby was his guide on a safari in East Africa in the 1950's and the model for the hero of Ruark's best seller 'Something of Value'. He was born and raised in Kenya, fought the Mau-Mau, and learned to hunt from an early age. Before hunting was banned in Kenya – and by this time Harry was a partner in the thriving safari company, Kerr Downey and Selby – he made his way to Botswana and continued to guide hunters. I first met him in Kasane when tiger fishing in the Chobe River in the late 1970's. I met him again more recently at his home in Maun, Botswana. David Lincoln, a local professional hunter, kindly arranged this meeting knowing that I held a .318 Evans rifle in my collection and that I would enjoy comparing notes on the gun with this doyen of the hunting world. We had an interesting hour chatting about this calibre on which hangs a tale. Robert Ruark had a .318 rifle custom built for his safari with Harry Selby but it didn't suit him and he gave it to Harry who learnt to use it with deadly precision. This .318 came to be Selby's favourite weapon.

Peter Hamilton Flack is arguably the most prolific hunter of game on the African continent alive today. I had heard many an account of this versatile and talented character before we met in Johannesburg to discuss hunting in the Central African Republic which he'd had extensive experience of. His reputation as a prominent business man – at the time we met he was heading Randgold & Exploration Company – was impressive but I was more concerned about his vast experience of chasing game in some of the remotest pockets of Africa and to him I turned for advice on hunting Bongo and the Lord Derby Giant Eland. I took an immediate liking to this tall, solid fellow who offered me some excellent information on the game, terrain, and hunting techniques that I would experience in the vast hunting concession on the Bouye River. For this I have to thank both Andre Roux, whom I mention later in the chapter and Rodney Kretszchmar, my taxidermist who spoke highly of Peter. I had been warned that Peter Flack had ice in his veins but I discounted this uncomplimentary summation and others which were invariably from the lips of business adversaries. From our initial encounter in the mid eighties in Johannesburg, I have always appreciated his company and I have found him to be a most interesting and sincere individual.

Peter has written several books on hunting with 'African Hunter 2' being, possibly, his most intensive work which he co-produced with Craig Bonnington as a sequel to J Mellon's highly respected book of the same title. My particular favourite is Peter Flack's 'Heart of an African Hunter' and in reading his accounts of the big five and the often overlooked 'the tiny ten' as he refers to the smallest species, his genuine appreciation and respect for the game he has tracked is readily apparent. Apart from his exploits throughout the African continent where he has collected more trophies than possibly any other recorded hunter, the man is an ardent conservationist and a proven exponent of hunting ethics. His contribution to conservation in creating the Agtersneeuberg Nature Reserve in the Karoo is testimony to his passion for wildlife. I have had the pleasure of hunting on this magnificent game reserve which measures close on eighty thousand acres of pristine wilderness in the Eastern Cape where over twenty different species of antelope roam the mountains and plains.

Before I sign off on this charismatic member of the hunting fraternity, I am fond of recounting the several times I have been mistaken for this formidable businessman/ sportsman. I was standing alone in the car park of The Johannesburg Country Club, Auckland Park, when I was approached by a fellow whom I knew by sight only who proceeded to interrogate me on the gold market. I listened politely to this intensive questioning with some perplexity and then the coin dropped. "Cocoa is what you should be looking at", I finally replied, and the bemused expression on the businessman's face was a picture. "You are Peter Flack?" to which I replied "I wish I was!"

Another remarkable character that I had made mention of in chapter 8 is Colonel Ian Mackenzie. This highly decorated soldier, businessman and hunter stands tall amongst men. I met the Mackenzie's through Jane, one of their daughters, when I first arrived in South Africa. Ian Mackenzie lived life to the full. He travelled the world in his sporting pursuits and he was a rare captain of industry who led a balanced life and allocated time to follow his widely varied interests. One of the colonel's greatest trophies is a huge lion that lies on his stoep at his game farm. There is an interesting story to this lion. Early one morning in the 1960's, the colonel was woken by one of his staff at his game farm in the Sabi Sand reserve. "Lions, boss Ian, come quickly. They're eating the wildebeest!" The colonel had recently invested in a herd of blue wildebeest to complement his plains game. Ian Mackenzie jumped out of bed with a curse as the story goes and marched out of the gates in his pyjamas with a .375 in hand. He strode fearlessly into the snarling pack of lions and shot a male that was hanging onto the hind quarters of a wildebeest. The pride backed off in earshot of the colonel's shouted obscenities. Several years later Ian had his substantial trophy collection measured by Steve Smith, a fellow hunter and publisher of the 'Rowland Ward Records of Big Game', who was able to inform the colonel that his lion ranked first in the book.

At a recent Shikar club dinner in London, I had the pleasure of conversing with Tony Sanchez-Arino, a Spaniard who has spent more than four decades hunting and can be included in the role of honour of the great hunters of old. In his capacity as a veteran ivory hunter in his earlier days, he accounted for 1250 tuskers in addition to 2000 buffalo, 320 lion, 150 leopard and 130 rhino. He can rank with his own heroes who he writes of in his books – George Rushby, Harry Manners, John Hunter, and Phil Percival. Tony Sanchez-Arino knew Harry Manners well and in his words described him 'my old friend, the great elephant hunter'. Such men humble us modern era sportsmen who've never truly experienced the hardships of hunting for four months at a stretch with 40 or 50 African porters in tow to carry the ivory, the rations of porridge, tea and salt, and the barest necessities for hunting in remote regions. The gun was the means for their livelihood and many didn't survive to tell the tale.

I inherited the love of the great outdoors and the ways of the gun from my two grandfathers who gave me the wanderlust, a symptom which is characteristic of many Celts and Anglo-Saxons. Visiting new country has always been a magnet and hunting is a wonderful reason to explore distant lands. Cities hold little fascination for me, except a certain few in Asia or the Far East, and beaches in the populated Cote d' Azure and Costa del Sol and others are of little allure. But, where there's exciting country with unusual animals to hunt, the challenge is on. Challenge is the emotive word. To reach the Rain Forests, the Arctic wastes or the Pamir mountains requires steady nerves, the patience of Job, and a stoical attitude as regards adversity. Run-down airports, unreliable airlines and endless waiting for clear weather or delayed flights, and mountains of documentation can test one's endurance. Added to this, depending on where one is, are the scourges of freezing or scorching temperatures, altitude sickness, tsetse fly bites, malaria and hunger and thirst. All can strain the body's system. The drawbacks are nothing, however, when one experiences the supreme achievement of collecting rare trophies in remote lands, creating an inner jubilation which sends the spirit soaring to the highest peak. I have been fortunate in visiting the more remote parts of Africa before these territories finally succumbed to the ravages of horrific poaching, unbridled corruption, and bloody civil wars leaving the wild regions denuded of wild animals.

* * * * *

In 1994 I found myself hunting in a sparsely populated and remote region, the Mboki-Mbomou triangle in the Central African Republic. This hunting concession was vast, an 8500 square kilometre tract of virgin country made up of savannah woodland, and patches of rain forest. The grass is so high in most parts of this unspoilt terrain that it's necessary to set light to it to find the quarry. I was one of the last to hunt game in this wild, remote corner of Africa before the Sudanese poaching gangs, armed with AK 47's and donkey caravans, made the region totally unstable and posed a threat to human life. As a result, Andre Roux had to close his concession the very year after my hunt with him.

We hunted relentlessly for three weeks in the manner of the old time hunters, on foot from dawn to sundown, requiring the hunter to be extremely fit and endurance trained. This particular safari was a beacon in my sporting career. I took eight Rowland Ward records including the exotic Lord Derby giant eland, giant forest hog, north western buffalo, sing-sing waterbuck, lelwel hartebeest, oribi, western kob and red duiker. The CAR is one of the few African countries that hold the Lord Derby giant eland and the bongo, these two species rating amongst the most coveted trophies in Africa. The giant eland is Africa's largest antelope measuring up to 5ft to 6ft in height at the shoulder and weighing between 1500 – 1600lbs.

For nine days and for fourteen hours a day Andre Roux and I, and his trackers Martin, Pierre and Francois, trekked after this 'ghost of the savannah' so aptly described by the old timers owing to its fleetness of foot and silence of movement as it flits through the woodlands and savannah. Hunting this animal can be a gruelling affair. Each morning, we'd wake up to an early call at 3.00 am followed by a six to twelve hour march on the tracks, returning to camp at 10.00 at night, then a hurried meal without alcohol, and tumbling into bed dead to the world. The moods would vacillate during those hot exhausting days. The tedium of marching for days on end can lead to a momentary lapse of concentration and a ruined opportunity. Such was one morning when it was midday and the sun was broiling and we were tired and not a little dispirited and we were whispering about the options of moving camp to another corner of this vast concession when a female eland suddenly appeared on the trail we were following. We'd dropped our guard, and we cursed our ill fortune as the female eland stared at us for a full ten minutes and then it turned alerting the herd which cantered off in a cloud of dust, and all I could glimpse was the tantalising sight of a pair of huge horns within the herd.

As tough as it was on us, the nine days of the relentless slog was also hard on the women in the camp, Vivienne and Nicky Kretchzmar. There was little to eat and the conversation was desultory over the dinner table. We were that exhausted. There was one enjoyable diversion during those testing days. We took Vivienne with us to a large saline (salt pan) to look for some light game to shoot for the pot. We needed meat badly as we were surviving on guinea fowl. The game bird was beginning to pall on the palate. For six days we had concentrated on the eland and I hadn't fired a shot. I was chatting quietly to Andre from our vantage point overlooking the saline. Dusk was beginning to settle when in the far distance emerged a curious looking animal – dark in colour and huge in size. I hadn't seen anything quite like this before. Andre gripped my arm in a fever of excitement and whispered: "giant forest hog. We have to get it. You don't see this animal very often. We've got to get it. It's rare, very rare!" We crawled on our bellies towards this gigantic wild pig with scarcely any cover to hide us. I had heard about the giant forest hog from those few who'd seen this nocturnal forest animal. Up we crept as silently as possible, taking our time but the light was fading fast. When we were approximately 100 metres from the target, Andre motioned to Martin for the shooting sticks. This is a crude but effective bipod made out of saplings, bound together at the tip with strips of rubber. When opened the sticks form a 'V' – a useful support when shooting over long distances with no rest at hand. As a point of interest, the famous elephant hunter, 'Karamoja' Bell, used such a device a hundred years ago. He was a meticulous hunter and he used to have his porters carry ladders so that he could shoot over the elephant grass.

We crawled on, halting every few paces, to avoid detection. But time was precious as the hog could have caught our scent and take off and a running shot in poor light would be precarious. About 50 metres from the prey, I took careful aim which was difficult owing to the thudding of my heart, I was that excited, and released a .375 cartridge at the left rear flank trusting that the bullet would rake through the vital organs. The 300 grain nosler bullet did its job brilliantly and the beast collapsed on the spot and died instantly. We stood in silence in the gathering dusk as we gazed down at this awesome trophy. There was food at last for the team, all 500 pounds of it, and I had gained a coveted and extremely rare trophy. The head was massive; the grey-black body was massive; the black bristles were massive. If one was to confront this animal in the dead of night in the heart of the forest, it would be a scary apparition. Imagine a long head with a knot of bristle around the nostrils, a swollen growth of gristle in front of menacing looking eyes, and pointed ears fringed with long bristles. The body is approximately six feet long, supported by short, stout legs. The tusks are not particularly impressive, perhaps smaller than those of the average warthog, somewhat out of kilter with the enormous frame. At the appropriate moment, Andre turned to me: "this is Rowland Ward. Nicely done". He was correct. Since the first records were accepted in 1908 for this species, there are only 90 entries in the book. This bears testimony to the rarity of this shy creature which was only discovered in 1904 owing to its nocturnal habits.

For a further three days we sweated after the giant eland. We persevered in the heat, taking turns in marching swiftly or jog-trotting at intervals, drinking out of the streams and eating wild bananas for sustenance; and I had to heap praise on Andre Roux and his chief tracker, Martin for their ability to concentrate for hours on end and to keep cheerful even in the deepest lows on the hunt. He drove me, this ex-paratrooper, and he expected results from his client. He and his trackers reasoned that if the hunter was physically and mentally in tune, the chase could be continued until the prize was in his grasp.

The following days passed with no result. We came onto various spoor and we'd spend up to three hours of merciless jog-trotting after the herds which had a habit of catching our scent and barrelling off into the scrub. Little sleep, sparse meals and endless marches in the heat were beginning to take their toll. Andre Roux used to speak to me at length on the long drives back to camp. "Up here in the CAR many hunters have returned home without trophies. They gave up, simple as that. They were not physically up to it; or if they were, the days and days of returning without the giant eland would get to them. They would insist on changing course and they'd opt for looking for bongo on the pretext that they could return to the giant eland. But it doesn't work like that". It was the ninth day and the early morning drill was becoming a well-worn routine. Up at 3 am, a cup of black coffee and a slice of toast smeared with Bovril. Then a quick check of equipment and on to the truck with a perfunctory nod at the trackers. I was beginning to feel the strain of equatorial Africa. I'd been bitten several times by the angry forest bees – this is no place for anyone allergic to these insects – my legs were ripped by thorns, my eyes were bloodshot through continuous exposure to the sun, and my frame was beginning to look spare. My mind was beginning to wander that morning in the cab. I began to question if I would obtain any trophies in the Mbomou triangle!

Then the familiar banging on the roof. Sight of fresh spoor. I lifted myself wearily out of the truck, summoning as much enthusiasm as possible, and involved myself in the routine inspection of the tracks left from the night before. This morning promised to be different, I gritted, the born optimist. We disembarked and just after two hours caught up with the tail end of a herd. The 'Judas wind' hadn't yet arisen. This is the dreaded breeze that eddies in all directions and warns the prey of danger. A female eland was lingering at the rear and she was looking at us and we had to freeze in our tracks. We'd been caught off guard and despite our diligence we were about to be held to ransom again by a single female eland that could, in one swift movement, spook the herd. For ten minutes the five of us stood stock still, not daring to look at the inquisitive antelope. It didn't move; it didn't stop staring at us; we didn't even dare to blink. Then the herd rose to its feet and walked off, apparently unaware of our presence, and the female turned and followed. Relief swept over us!

Another hour of swift marching ensued. I suddenly caught a glint of an eland horn and I tugged at Andre's sleeve and all of us sank on our haunches to observe the herd. We estimated that there were 40 – 50 grouped together in fairly dense brush. Andre whispered that there had to be at least two or three good bulls amongst them. Another thirty minutes and the herd drifted on and we with it. As we moved slowly forward, Andre cautioned me to be ready. "Don't waste time with your binoculars. I'll warn you if you should shoot. You'll only have a split second to fire. This could be our chance!"

It was now 2.30 p.m. and the heat was oppressive. The herd was taking us into deep thickets and the toll of the morning's effort was beginning to make itself felt. It's times like these when the hunter begins to question his ability to hold the rifle steady, to shoot accurately, and to react as he should. Tension fills the air. He'll glance at his guide and the trackers and notice the grim concentration illustrated by knitted brows, pursed lips and squinting eyes. The hunter knows that he dare not disappoint. The team has worked hard for him. The time for pay-back has come. His heart is thudding, the sweat streams down his face and back, and his mouth is bone dry. Francois was in the lead. He suddenly whipped round, whispering furiously, "Le Grand Male – Le Grand Male!"

Between us and the herd was a small outcrop of rock. Andre whispered tensely, "Get ready to shoot – a magnificent bull – he's just around the corner!" Seconds passed by. Andre whispered, "Take him. He's looking at us – face on – fifty metres in front of us!" This was the moment of truth after nine gruelling days. I dare not miss – I dare not miss! My eyes swivelled around the rock face and there it stood, in all its glory – the ghost of the savannah! This vision and that of the leopard I'd taken in the Zambezi Valley are beacons in my hunting career in as far as the sheer impressiveness of an animal is concerned. There was only a split second to react; otherwise the precious quarry would vanish. Eyes bored into my back, particularly those of the hard man, Martin. Okay, I'll show you my friend, I gritted, and I aimed my faithful .375 at the eland's chest and squeezed the trigger without hesitation. I felt Andre's hand on my shoulder. "You've got him, you've hit him well!" I was drained. I had seen the eland buckle, but over the years I have learnt never to count my eggs until they hatch. The trackers ran to the spot where the giant eland had been standing and sure enough there was the blood spoor. Pierre was tearing through the bush in the front. We then heard him shout with excitement, "Il est tombe, Il est mort!" It was the finest sound I had heard for a very long while. We chased up to find Pierre pointing to the fallen eland. It was a very emotional moment and highly charged and I quietly thanked St. Hubert. Everyone in the group was thrilled, including the tough Martin who allowed me a wide smile and a "bien fait". We shook hands and stood gazing down at the fallen monarch. Words were superfluous in the silence of the forest. Andre broke in, "nice shot – through the heart. You've got a Rowland Ward. You've deserved it. Nine long days which you won't forget!"

We got down to skinning the animal. The truck was at least three hours' march away and Pierre was dispatched to fetch it. Then the forest bees swarmed in. They'd smelt blood. Andre and I raced for our lives through the forest for a full twenty minutes and we were lucky to get away with a few stings on the arms and face as bees in this multitude have been known to kill. We returned eventually to the eland which was covered like a carpet with the bees. I watched with apprehension as Martin and Francois skinned the animal with apparent oblivion to these ferocious insects. Andre and I then loaded all the gear we could manage to meet up with Pierre and the truck.

We arrived at the camp just after midnight. The taking of a bongo, giant eland or lion has a special tradition in the C.A.R. hunting camps. The truck was decorated with branches and foliage and the trackers sang a legend about the 'ghost of the savannah'. The camp staff could hear the singing from two kilometres away and they all turned out en masse to welcome the hunting party. At the head of the ululating throng stood Vivienne and Nicky Kretzchmar and then the party started. Beer, wine and brandy flowed into the small hours of the morning and it was a pure joy to know that there was no longer a need to clamber out of bed at 3.00 a.m.

That twenty one day safari will reign supreme in my memory. I'd taken one of the most highly prized trophies in Africa in a manner that the old timers would have approved of. There was no expediency, no short cut in the process of bagging this magnificent prize. Just hard work, perseverance, and a belief that the long hours of preparation – the rifle range and the road work for endurance training – would ultimately pay off. The remaining ten days were spent in chasing buffalo, fishing the Ouarra River for bream, and collecting a marvellous bag of varied trophies. We searched for bongo from a forest camp near Ouagou, south east of the Oubangi base camp, when the mornings would find us creeping through the thickets, glades and rivulets after this elusive and prized antelope. We were working in oppressive heat, a build up to the rainy season which was forcing the bongo deeper into the forests. During those last four days of the hunt we covered miles on foot in our search for this shy, spiral horned antelope - another rare species indigenous to this part of Africa stretching from the Ivory Coast to Kenya. The promise of the 'double' was fast waning and I was not destined for the ranks of the envied few who had scored the giant eland and the bongo in the same hunt. After three strenuous weeks, I had shed 4 kilograms and I'm a lean man. The shaving mirror reflected a gaunt face but why to worry? Those hunting days in the C.A.R had ranked amongst the finest in my career. Despite aching feet, bee stings, tick bites, periods of searing thirst, I had had the time of my life.

＊　＊　＊　＊　＊

Seven hundred kilometres north of Brazzaville lies a remote hunting concession bordering the Parc Nationale d'Odzala close to the Gabon border. We were in the French Congo in 1993 and I was searching for forest sitatunga, red dwarf buffalo, a variety of duiker, and harnessed bushbuck. After two weeks of hunting I had collected a red dwarf buffalo and a harnessed bushbuck – a sparse bag by many a hunter's standard. But I was happy. I was fortunate to experience the rain forests of the Congo. For sheer impressiveness this part of Africa is difficult to beat. For hunters accustomed to savannah and mopani woodlands that constitute the bushveldt in the main, rain forests are foreign. Hunters from the South have no conception of the big rivers, the massive trees, the luxuriant undergrowth, the primary and secondary forests and the swamps and streams that make up equatorial Africa.

To reach the Congo's rain forests, the hunter is routed through Brazzaville – not a comfortable place. This is, in fact, a veritable hellhole. Johannesburg by comparison is Paris. The airport! How does one convey what this dank cesspool is all about? The fetid smell in the immigration hall is offensive. The visitor is shoved and elbowed by 'les grandes marchandes,' the heavy-buttocked, melon-breasted amazons who jostle and barge their way for pole position, balancing huge cardboard boxes on their heads. Within minutes of arriving in the immigration hall or shed would be more accurate, one's clothes are soaked with perspiration. The temperature is swirling around the 100 Fahrenheit mark and the air conditioning system has remained in disuse for years. To reach immigration control is a nightmarish ordeal. One wrestles with gun cases, luggage and travel documents, all to be stolen in a trice if the traveller's attention wanders. Immigration forms had run out long before I and Vivienne reached the immigration desk guarded by two harassed officials. French is the only language spoken and Vivienne being fluent was a valuable asset. God help the hunter who doesn't speak it. I watched an American tourist being elbowed unceremoniously out of the queue by one of the 'grandes marchandes.' The disbelief and anger on the fellow's face was a sight to behold as his bellowed summons for the chief of immigration fell on deaf ears in the tumultuous din.

It took a full hour to reach immigration and this is where I resorted to bribery for the first time in my life. When we were told to return to the end of the queue for lack of an immigration form – there were now 100 passengers behind me (the result of a jumbo jet recently landed) – I discreetly proffered a dirty 1,000 CFS note, equivalent in value to US$3.00. This did the trick. We were waved through to the baggage collection point. This was even in a worse state than the immigration hall. There were pools of stagnant water where the equatorial rains had leaked through the roof. Neon lighting, or what was left of it, cast an eerie glow over the hall. The customs checkpoint was a seething shambles of shouting, gesticulating Africans overwhelming a hopelessly understaffed team of four officials.

Then, fortunately, the agent employed by our professional guide, Eric Stockenstroom, finally arrived to negotiate the clearance of guns. The heated dialogue between the agitated agent and a group of impatient customs officials indicated that there was something terribly wrong. "You cannot bring guns into the Congo", explained the agent finally. "There's an arms embargo that's new to us – apparently it's only just been introduced". I was now facing the bitter truth that the two most coveted guns in my collection were to fester for two weeks in this appalling airport at a likely risk of these being stolen.

That night I was close to cancelling the hunt and returning to Johannesburg. I ran through all the options with Vivienne at the hotel in Brazzaville – a mockery of the 5 star status that it boasted. As I drank the tepid beer from the broken down fridge, pacing up and down the bedroom, I even considered calling up my hunting friends in Zimbabwe. Perhaps they had a vacancy that would provide me with an alternative. The recurring nightmare was the guns. My trusted .375 Browning and highly valuable .475 Jeffrey double were to lie rotting at that hideous airport. I had the necessary receipts but these could be worthless in this forgotten hell-hole of Africa. I recovered my spirits the next day when the charter aircraft landed at Etoumbi airstrip after a three-hour flight from Brazzaville. I immediately questioned Stockenstroom on the gun issue and he gave me to believe that the Minister hadn't signed the permits in time. I learned later after returning to South Africa that a total embargo on any form of weaponry had been in place for many years in the Congo. It was a case of who was bluffing who!

The first leg of the journey to the hunting camp included crossing a vast river in a hand-operated ferry. This took one hour. Then followed a further three hours of jolting over a rough track – the highway in this remote part of the world – through primary and secondary forest until we reached Mbomo. Stopping in this village consisting of a handful of huts and sparse population was quite eventful. Eric Stockenstroom, the sole professional hunter in the region, was asked to attend to an African woman who had haemorrhaged severely after a self-induced abortion. Stockenstroom then informed us that he and another white man, Ian Manning, whom we were to meet later, were the only Europeans in an area of 80,000 square kilometres, the size of Wales. In these remote parts, the white man as Stockenstroom explained, was looked on by the locals as a mixture of doctor, counsellor and keeper of the peace.

The first three days were spent hunting red dwarf buffalo. This smallest of the buffalo family is an unpredictable creature whose habitat stretches across the central band of Africa. It is primarily found in the rain forests of Cameroon, Congo and the Democratic Republic of the Congo (formerly the Belgian Congo). Although half the size of its cape counterpart, the red dwarf is more aggressive and is known to charge without provocation. As its name suggests, the animal is red in colour with horns more akin to the Asian water buffalo which curl backwards – very different to the other African species – to give this forest animal greater freedom of movement in dense vegetation. The red dwarf buffalo may appear far less intimidating than its cape cousin but they account for the deaths of several unwary Africans each year in the jungle. In fact, in remote regions such as where we were in, this is the one species that has escaped the ravages of untrammelled poaching. The Africans leave them alone, such is their reputation for ferocity.

It was a revelation as I marched through the tall elephant grass, the glades, the streams, rain forests and swamps. I had never encountered such country as this but had read about it in the works of the well known French hunter and explorer of the last century, Paul du Chaillu. The grass was so high in places that searching the skies for the tiny tick bird became an essential part of the hunting. This 'tell-tale' little bird swoops out of the sky onto the buffalo and the other creatures that roam this jungle; the 'tell-tale' bird was a gem of a guide to the herds hidden in the high grasses. And as for the water! We were in the central reaches of the Congo, consisting of a series of forest belts broken up by rivers which were tributaries of the mighty Congo River. This region claims the world's second highest water flow, and the Congo is mostly waterlogged with the central and northern parts made up of rivers and rain forests. This is the dark Africa of Tarzan-style jungle – a natural habitat for Pygmies and exotic animals such as bongo, forest sitatunga and gorillas. Each day the skies opened and drenched us to the skin. One hunted in a perpetually soaked state from the torrential rain and humidity. Because of the climate, there was a paucity of roads, tracks, or footpaths. There was just one main road, the 'highway' linking Etoumbi airstrip and the north. This was the forest track that we had driven to reach our camp and this would be rendered totally impassable in the rainy season.

The tick bird did not let us down. In the far distance, two kilometres or so, that minuscule black speck hurtled from the heavens, and we marched swiftly to the point we had carefully marked. In 20 minutes we encountered the herd. It was my first sighting of these forest buffalo. My immediate impression was how gentle these animals looked compared to their menacing cape counterparts, but Stockenstroom warned me never to underestimate this species. We positioned ourselves on a small rise to view the herd. It contained two bulls and six cows. We studied them through the binoculars for 10 minutes before the breeze must have eddied. Without warning the beasts cantered off in the direction of the forest. Stockenstroom shook his head, "Leave them. Once they're in the forest they are devils. You can't see them in the undergrowth and often it's too late when they are on top of you. There'll be more".

Our luck was in that morning. We had with us the trackers, Anbia, Soula, and Opounda and we headed back to camp taking a different route through the forests. Approximately four kilometres from camp, Anbia stopped abruptly in his tracks as we were emerging from the trees in single file. We slipped onto our haunches and 100 metres ahead in a small glade were two bulls grazing. We had not been seen. Stockenstroom whispered that we should crawl to a fallen tree separating us from the buffalo that had their backs to us. Nonetheless we had to take our time over the open ground with little cover other than the tree. We had almost reached it when the nearest bull turned. It had heard our approach. I took a running shot at the buffalo, aiming for its shoulder. It cantered on but I was confident that it had been hit reasonably well which was the case as proved by a pool of blood. "Careful", warned Stockenstroom, "he could be lying up waiting for us". We walked slowly through the grass in a line, 15 metres apart, and that familiar surge of adrenaline was coursing through me. A downed buffalo is always dangerous, whatever its size. From what I had read and the stories I had heard of this forest species, I certainly wasn't about to relax until we found it.

It was Anbia who came across the bull which was lying prostrate in a dense clump of grass and reed. I would never have seen it because it was so deeply buried in the vegetation. I remained behind with the buffalo while the trackers went to retrieve the vehicle from camp. Fortunately the ground in the vicinity was reasonably firm and near a track. Had we taken a bull from the herd seen previously, we would have had to cape the trophy in the swampy terrain, leave the meat until later, and carry out the horns. Hunting in the Congo is on foot and beware the unfit hunter!

We were looking for duiker when I encountered my first gorilla and it was an electrifying experience. Eric Stockenstroom and Anbia were in front of me. The foliage was particularly dense in this part of the forest and we were moving silently over the matted forest floor. All of us froze to a standstill at the sudden crashing, followed by a bloodcurdling barking and shrieking of a gorilla troop. Anbia was seriously agitated and he was signalling furiously at me to make ready with my gun. He was on his knees peering into the thick vegetation. Gorillas can be highly mercurial in temperament and lone males in particular have been known to attack. The primates could have not have been more than 20 metres away. Stockenstroom appeared relaxed in contrast to Anbia. However, I wasn't experienced with these jungle creatures and I kept my rifle at the ready and I had to admit to being nervous. The troop leader was creating a fearful racket and we could clearly hear the thumping of fists on his chest. I was by now extremely tense as the foliage around us was literally shaking and the noise was deafening for about fifteen minutes before the troop disappeared into the jungle. This was the making of my day, however, as few hunters experience getting so close to a gorilla and it is an unforgettable occurrence.

The western sitatunga known more generally as the forest sitatunga is distributed throughout Equatorial Africa stretching from Gambia and Sierra Leone through Liberia, Cameroon, Congo, the Central African Republic, the DRC and Northern Angola. This antelope can best be described as an aquatic bushbuck with distinctive spiral horns and peculiar shape of hooves which are pointed and more elongated than in other antelopes. At the rear of the foot is a distinctive pad, allowing the hoof to splay out thereby giving support in water. It lives in marshes, papyrus swamps and reed beds and is extremely shy, seldom leaving its lair except to feed at night. When threatened, a sitatunga submerges into water leaving only its nose exposed above the surface. This is a big antelope measuring 45 inches on average at the shoulder, weighing up to 250 pounds, and is a prized trophy on account of the testing challenge it presents to the hunter. Our game plan was to set off down the Mambili River. I was a fortunate man because according to Stockenstroom only a handful of Europeans had ever ventured down this waterway. His experience of the Mambili was limited and the river was swollen after the recent rains so we were apprehensive of what lay ahead of us.

At the crack of dawn, Stockenstroom, I and four Mboko tribesmen set off down the river which looked ominous and menacing in the gloom of the rain forest. These were foreboding waters, conjuring up images of sinister reptiles. Eric Stockenstroom said that few white men had penetrated this area. In previous centuries Arab slave traders had passed through but few white hunters worked this region as it was country difficult to traverse and it was inhospitable with disease rife and where the game could easily disperse into the forests. The first section of the river was tricky with tree blocks and floating flotsam from the recent rains and our small fibre glass boat with its 25 hp engine made slow progress. It took us three hours to complete 30 kilometres. If we'd chosen the pirogue – the traditional African transport made out of a hollowed-out tree trunk - we could have been in dire trouble. My canoeing experience dictated that with a river such as the Mambili, an upturned boat could mean weapons and provisions lost and potential drowning. A pirogue in an uncharted river in the depths of the Congo would have been a grave risk.

We reached a confluence after the 40 kilometre mark. Here the river widened substantially and the going became considerably easier. After four hours in the boat, we stopped to stretch our legs at an abandoned poacher camp and consumed a light lunch of bread and tinned sardines. Poacher camps were numerous along the river as this is the only means of transporting game in this jungle. The swarms of tsetse flies were proliferating in the torpid heat and their savage bites were a torment. Anbia was in the prow of the boat and he suddenly hit the deck without any warning, leaving Stockenstroom to work his bolt furiously. I followed suit as I heard him mutter "poachers – load up!" We jumped on to the bank ready to open fire and we found that the poachers' cooking coals were still burning and it was evident that they'd fled only minutes before into the undergrowth. They could have shot at us with ease from the protection of the forest and we were lucky not to have been involved in a fire-fight. As I scanned the forest for sign of the poachers, Stockenstroom and his trackers stripped the camp and appropriated a diary and documents. We then fired bullets into the poachers' pirogue to sink it.

With only two hours remaining before dark, Anbia led us to a saline that he remembered from his poaching days. There came an awesome sound high in the sky like a powerful squadron of jet airliners. The eerie rumbling crept closer. There was no sign of sitatunga spoor at the saline but plenty of red buffalo tracks and evidence of forest elephant. Then the skies opened and the rain sheeted down in torrents. We waited sodden in the undergrowth in case a sitatunga glided into the clearing. We made our way soaked to the skin to the base camp that Stockenstroom's trackers had prepared for us earlier that afternoon. The torrential downpour had created havoc in camp and the stoves, chairs, tents, and food stuffs were all under water. But I was not to grumble. We were in the thick of the rain forests where few hunters had ever ventured.

We ate sparingly that evening – cold spaghetti washed down by whisky. Conversation was limited as Stockenstroom can be taciturn, as I can also be, in a situation of this sort. We were in bed early that night and the rains crashed down making sleep difficult as the tents leaked and the water poured in. However, a serious hunter learns to endure harsh conditions and to accept acute discomfort when chasing a prized trophy. Early the next morning we set off downstream heading for a sitatunga habitat that Anbia remembered. It was a large flooded glade and looked a perfect setting for the western sitatunga. There was water, trees, and swamp grasses – all perfect cover for the shy animal. Stockenstroom warned me to be on the alert for the slightest movement in the swamp. But the sitatunga never came. For the whole of that day we chugged down a number of tributaries in search of this elusive antelope. The terrain fascinated me. There was water everywhere and it was similar, I imagined, to parts of the Amazon, judging from the reports that I had read on jaguars. The humidity at midday was serious and my body was covered in tsetse bites but I was beyond caring about discomfort as the experience was unforgettable: soaring trees, tributaries - sometimes too narrow to navigate - salt licks and silence and poachers to boot! We tried everything that day to find the sitatunga but it was not to be. We sighted a female early on which renewed our hopes and we startled a small herd of buffalo on the banks of a salt lick.

We returned to camp just after dark in time for the sky to unleash yet another devastating torrent. For the entire night the rain thundered down. The tents couldn't withstand the deluge and the water poured in making sleep impossible. In the early hours of the morning, we decided to break camp and at 6 a.m. the rain abated. Stockenstroom was concerned about the state of the river as this was now in full spate. We held a brief discussion on the merits of continuing the hunt but two problems were evident. We needed to take to the river without delay as the debris from the storm could build up endangering our return; secondly, our chances of sighting sitatunga were seriously diminishing. The game would vanish further into the forest as there was so much water. The picture was a little bleak so we decided to cut our losses and return to base camp but it wasn't to be that simple. After a breakfast of sardines and biscuits, the rains returned and we huddled under a tarpaulin makeshift, staring into space. For three long hours we remained huddled in this remote part of the Congo, remaining as cheerful as possible under the circumstances.

Then the rain ceased and we packed the boat in haste knowing that the skies could open again.

One must give full credit to Stockenstroom for his skill in navigating the river. The first part of the journey was fairly uneventful and we reached the confluence quickly as the river was running swiftly after the heavy rains. However, shortly afterwards we began to encounter fallen trees and this part of the river was narrower and at one stage it looked as if we would have to portage around a tree block, a serious problem as the boat was heavy. We were six in number but it would have taken us hours to haul the bulky craft around the debris. The remainder of the trip was slow going as the narrow river was beginning to collect serious flotsam. On two occasions we nearly overturned which would have been a nightmare with the guns and the cargo aboard. Capsizing in this deep river with the force of the current could pose a serious threat of drowning. We finally reached camp at dusk with one thought in mind - hot water and a dry bed.

The last two days of the safari were devoted to finding a sitatunga. On one of the mornings, I picked up a handsome harnessed bush buck, an excellent trophy and not to be found in South Africa. On the last day we decided to hunt the area that Stockenstroom had reserved for game viewing. This was a salt lick where a hide had been built for viewing forest elephant and sitatunga that were known to inhabit this particular stretch of swamp. To reach it we needed to trek silently through the rain forest in case sitatunga were present. We reached the hide after two hours on foot but, alas, no sign of sitatunga. A herd of buffalo was feeding on the far side but there was no other species in sight.

We then waded through the swamp adjoining the saline and this proved a highly unpleasant experience as at times the mud reached our knees. It was tough going as we squelched through the ooze encountering numerous thorn thickets and it was difficult to move silently owing to the sucking noise of the mud when lifting the feet. If our prey was in the vicinity, then we surely would have scared them off. We did manage to sneak close to one sitatunga which turned out to be a female. I was also intent on looking out for snakes whilst wading through this thick, glutinous swamp. I asked Stockenstroom about this later that morning and he cheerfully replied that there were plenty of poisonous species around! We just hadn't sighted them. As regards snakes, I've seen more in the dry South than when hunting in the jungles of the Congo and the CAR. In fact, a week after returning from the swamps of the Parc d' Odzala, I was shooting guinea fowl when I nearly tripped over a huge puff adder coiled close to an ant hole.

Some hunters have frequently asked whether I had any regrets about spending the money and time on that trip to the Congo. My spontaneous reply was that hunting in the rain forests of the Congo was a unique experience, so totally different in terrain and game to which we have in Southern Africa. I would further expound that sport hunting should not be judged solely on trophy acquisition. The challenges of hunting in Equatorial Africa was worth every cent in the proud knowledge that only a few hunters have braved these inhospitable regions. The constant irritation of tsetse flies, swamp mosquitoes, drenchings from the torrential rains, and the sparse food are overridden with the indelible reminders of the rain forests of the French Congo. The red dwarf buffalo and harnessed bush buck trophies serve as appropriate tokens of a great and unusual adventure in darkest Africa.

CHAPTER SEVENTEEN

White water and
a tragic death

The fear of death follows from the fear of life.
A man who lives fully is prepared to die
at any time.

Mark Twain

CRADOCK IS a picturesque, somewhat sleepy dorp in the heart of
the Karoo in the Eastern Cape. Once a year a thousand odd canoeists
descend on the town to compete in the two day Fish river marathon. The
citizens turn out en masse as do the farmers and they extend boundless
hospitality to the men, and a few women who hurtle down the fast flowing
waters of the Great Fish River. The natives of Cradock are well prepared
for this raucous festival that rocks the town to its core. Canoeists are a
rumbustious breed – they have to be to handle the hurly-burly, 'every-
man-for-himself' nature of river racing. And they understand a party
with a no-holds barred approach. After one such fish marathon I had to
depart for Johannesburg in a hurry, a seven hours drive, without having
the pleasure of taking part in the post-race bash in the Masonic Hotel.
I happened to stop to reach into the cold box for a beer. My thirst was
fairly acute after several hours of paddling beneath a blazing sun and I
could hear the noise three kilometres distant. I could visualise the scene
- several hundred shirtless canoeists jammed into the kroeg served by

half a dozen sweating barmen tossing six packs into outstretched hands, followed by the 'races' down the main street in canoes battered from the Fish River.

Cradock comes to life in the first week of October when the Fish River is run. This event is arguably the most popular on the racing calendar for a variety of reasons. The Karoo has its own fascination – the vistas are breathtaking, unmarred by telephone wires or pylons, stark in comparison with the softer, Mediterranean ambience of the Western Cape, perhaps, but the ranges of hills that undulate to the horizon catch the breath. There's a silence and a stillness and a sense of space that is peculiar to the Karoo. And then the roads. These stretch like ribbons into the horizon, straight as an arrow and without a vehicle to be seen. It's unwise to drive too fast, not on account of the speed traps which barely exist but the splendid sight of the springbok grazing on the ubiquitous game farms will be forsaken.

Sportsmen from all over the Republic converge on Cradock where they are made to feel at home by the friendly locals who manifest their unstinting generosity by the meals and the liquor they lay on for the two day race. This is staged over eighty kilometres starting at the Grasmere Dam and finishing at Cradock. The water flows swiftly facilitated by the opening of the sluice gates of Grasmere allowing 22 cubic metres per second which is a vast volume of water. The Fish is clear and cold and can shock the canoeist if he takes a spill if the weather is inclement, which it can be at this time of year. It's a testing river, characterised by low lying trees over the first part of the river which the canoeists hold great respect for. Then there are the weirs to shoot, low lying bridges to hurtle under and some testing rapids. The Fish River has every form of challenge for the river racer, let alone the distance. The start itself can be gruelling and the wind tends to whip the Grasmere Dam into a veritable sea at the end of which is a steep wall over which the boats have to be man-handled, presenting the sizeable crowd of onlookers with an entertaining sight of scores of cursing canoeists jostling, barging, and shoving to put their boats into the river. There are no prisoners taken in river racing!

Tony Beith and I took a very nasty swim one year just after the put-in behind the wall. Here the river is deep and the banks are sheer and covered in reeds, making it extremely hazardous to empty the boat, get back into it, and fix the splash covers which is easier said than done owing to the fast flow of the water. And then a few kilometres down river is the first major obstacle known as 'Keith's flyover'. A mere fifty odd intrepid boats out of an average field of seven hundred attempt this boat- breaker of big rapids ending with a sharp dog leg and only the very skilled or the very reckless attempt 'Keith's'. The race can be over if the canoeist gets his line wrong, remembering that 'Keith's flyover' lies eight kilometres from the start and there's forty to go to the first day's finish post. Smashed boats and broken bones can be the canoeists' lot and Keith's flyover claims a 30% failure rate each year. Without shame, I can state that I've never chanced this awesome rapid. The river is then relatively straight forward, except for the tree blocks. One year, Tony Beith and I crashed through the low lying branches of a willow tree using sheer force – we were hacking at the branches with our paddles – only to take a cow broadside on. The beast bellowed with fright and took off up the bank and on we sailed. Then our steering cable snapped so we struck for the side and I hopped out to stabilise the canoe to find myself totally submerged and out of sight. It felt like a mine shaft that I'd dropped into and a life time before I spluttered to the surface. A similar situation, tragically, didn't have quite the same happy ending when Tony Beith had a comparable experience in the Klip River some years later, never to emerge. He lost his life and I pay tribute later in the chapter to this great friend and constant companion in river races.

The Swaelkrans weir is the next challenge and a number of contestants portage around it. However it's feasible with the help of three steel poles that the farmers have thoughtfully placed in position. The strategy is to get the line right and then valuable minutes are saved, but approach the chute at an angle and into the chilly waters the canoeist will tumble. Then follow two of the trickier hazards of the Fish- the low level Murray Bridge threatening a nasty crack to the head as punishment if the canoeist misjudges the line, immediately followed by a challenging set of rapids which can throw the unwary racer into the swirling white water. This is Swartkrans and on one occasion Tony Beith and I drove down the centre without mishap although we nearly beheaded two fellows who were floundering helplessly in our path. In another race, I was pairing with Tony Lightfoot – the year we had one of our finest races ever. Lightfoot had discovered a 'sneak' channel and we popped up much to the amusement of the hordes of spectators present amidst a clump of bushes bypassing the main stream of the notorious Swartkrans boat breaker.

The second day is considerably more straightforward with the major obstacles in the form of Gauging weir and Cradock weir. I will never forget Gauging weir as one year Lightfoot and I managed to shoot it successfully but found ourselves sailing down the river backwards before crashing into the reeds to discover another Masters pair, Benham and Egan, extricating themselves after a tumble over the weir. The final obstacle in the race is the Cradock weir and attempting to shoot this can waste precious time as the canoeists are banked up to wait their turn to challenge this impressive wall of water. The portage takes a mere two minutes and we've never waited in line to shoot the Cradock weir although the sensation is awesome by all accounts.

The four times that I have raced the river with either Tony Beith or Tony Lightfoot, the Fish River has been an adventure. There's never a dull moment. We've always done relatively well in the race in coming half way up the field, and in one notable year – 1990 - Lightfoot and I were seventh in the Masters category and 221 out of 670 boats, taking 6 hours and 57 minutes for the two days.

* * * * *

The Breede River in the Western Cape is worthy of mention. This is a two day race in the scenic winelands from Robertson to Swellendam. The Breede is not as dramatic as the Umkomaas, the Fish, the Berg or the Duzi but is testing for its low lying trees and weirs which can overturn the unwary canoeist in a trice. A strong attraction of the Breede is that the Fraser-Jones family is to be found in Swellendam. Billy, the youngest son then running one of the two family farms, was a canoeist himself and he not only kindly volunteered to have Lightfoot and myself to stay in his magnificent home - a National Monument in the Cape Dutch architecture - but he served as a very capable second. In addition to this, Billy out of great generosity allowed a number of the Dabulamanzi Canoe Club to party at his home at the end of the race. Billy Fraser-Jones and a neighbouring farmer in the area, Hasie Lourens, were well renowned in the four day Berg river canoe marathon. The Breede was their training ground and Hasie gained his river craft as a youngster, gambolling down the Breede on a tyre tube.

In the late eighties Hasie and Billy were racing the major rivers of South Africa in an inflatable boat sponsored by Vinuchi, notching up a commendable number of victories, gaining valuable publicity for our company. The Vinuchi boat was pictured in the press in the 1990 Breede River. The drama of a near drowning was illustrated in a series of vivid close-ups of a young husband and wife team capsizing at the base of the Secunda weir and being sucked in to the 'washing machine', the dread of every canoeist. A 'washing machine' is the descriptive given to the turbulent water that boils at the base of a weir or a crop of rocks and often the cause of a death in the river. There were close-ups of the inflatable in full Vinuchi livery with marshals aboard hauling the pair aboard.

Billy Fraser-Jones, his brother Andrew who farms the second family property near Swellendam, and Hasie Lourens in earlier days turned out for the Swellendam rugby XV with Billy resembling the archetypal rugby hooker in build and temperament with the sinewy Hasie – as tough as you'll find them – as a flanker. In his day Hasie Lourens created a reputation for himself as one of the foremost veterans in the Western Cape canoeing ranks and his reputation, wildness included, spread far and wide.

Tony Lightfoot and I set off from Johannesburg for the Breede on a clear Transvaal winter day, August 1989. We were in high spirits as we had a canoeing race ahead of us in new waters and the welcoming company of the Frazer-Jones tribe abetted by the aforementioned Hasie Lourens. Ian and Jeanette Frazer Jones as the clan chiefs gave us their full blessing from Johannesburg. The wheels began to come off on the Bloemfontein – Colesberg stretch of the highway linking Johannesburg to Cape Town. The eccentric Moggy insisted on playing Mantovani which I was forced to listen to as he tapped his feet out of time whilst we sank two packs of long-tom beers between us. We were carefree as we were away from the freneticism of Johannesburg and in the midst of the wonderful Karoo. We hit Colesberg and booked into a motel to meet up with two Dabulamanzi characters – Dick Stent and an Irishman, Cavin Rothwell. Dick had served time in the Rhodesian Light Infantry as an officer and had spent a short period in the SAS before the country was handed over to Mugabe. He'd moved on to become a captain in the Trucial Oman Scouts in Muscat. Cavin Rothwell was a foil to the mercurial Stent – affable in manner and possessed of Irish charm. We had dinner and a deluge of alcohol before calling it a day in the small hours of the morning.

We set off for Robertson the next day, arriving in the mid-afternoon and feeling slightly worse for wear. Moggy and I made our way to the Goudmyn weir, one of the trickier spots in the river. The Breede was swollen from the melted snows of the Ceres Mountains and was so full that most of the obstacles were flooded over, including Drew Bridge, the finish of the first day. We found a knot of Dabulamanzi canoeists that had converged on the weir to reconnoitre a huge and menacing 'stopper' wave at the base of the weir. Dick Stent and Cavin Rothwell were there, looking a little green, possibly from the alcohol from the night before and at the sight of the stopper. There was a vigorous debate underway led by the Dabulamanzi 'hot shots': Brian Longley, Garth Watters, Niels Verkerk and Graham Cross. In his inimitable style, Moggy Lightfoot took it on his shoulders to drag his reluctant partner - I was feeling very jaded that afternoon – to challenge the stopper. The Dabulamanzi newsletter described the story: "The belated arrival of 'Lightning Lightfoot' and 'the Great White Hunter' restarted the whole discussion of where to shoot the weir. After carefully checking the line, they paddled upstream, turned and came down at a frightening pace and went through the weir without even a break in the stroke rate. A truly professional effort and a beautiful sight to behold!"

Then came the race day. The start was a sheer shambles as the river was running at a ferocious rate and the more experienced river men termed the start as the worst they'd experienced. The flooded river and the typical lack of discipline of the canoeists - the dictum 'every man for himself' applied here in full form –led to the gung-ho contestants ignoring the starter and barging their way into any spot they could find. The river was probably running at 20 knots and all of us had to grab on to reeds, trees, anything that would prevent one sailing down the river before the gun.

It was a dark day and bitterly cold. The snows on the Western Cape Mountains were threatening to fall on our heads and we were freezing as we were wearing only singlets as is the custom upcountry. We'd picked a good spot for the start amongst the seeded hot shots. We kept quiet and looked nonchalantly away as one of the officials barked at us for proof of our seeding. But this is river-racing – 'every man for himself' runs the dictum. I saw a number of men I knew, mostly in a state of disorder, and Joe Torlage and John Rhynes his partner were trying to slide under their splash covers to prevent the organisers spotting them as they'd opted for sixth place in the seedings illegally. The novices were having a grim time and several boats had capsized and others were holding onto each other – a risky thing to do in a fast flowing river. Certain seeded paddlers couldn't even get their boats into the river, the melee was that severe, and after three unsuccessful attempts to start the race, the organisers decided to let the first twenty boats go before the pack. This was the cue for the more experienced river men to follow suit, to hell with the starter, and the gun went off five seconds after the front runners had started sprinting, including the Lightfoot/Callender team!

After the pandemonium of the start we enjoyed an uneventful forty minutes through some pleasant waves and then came Goudwyn weir. Our previous day's glorious effort hadn't gone unnoticed and ten boats were lined up behind us, including our friends Stent and Rothwell. Lightfoot, however, had one of his customary rushes of blood to the head and was paddling like a maniac to the right of the river and not down the centre as we had so successfully done the day before. Needless to say we capsized and so did the ten boats behind us in quick succession amidst a stream of curses. The water was icy, a legacy of the melted snows of the Ceres Mountains, and the tumble into the fast flowing river was not a joyous experience. The race was fairly uneventful after the pantomime at Goudwyn weir but then the organisers had decided to emulate the Tour de France and incorporate a time trial fourteen kilometres from the finish. This involved the canoeists climbing out of their boats and standing on the bank shivering on this cold, grey day whilst they waited for the first thirty boats to leave at two minute intervals before the pack was allowed to set off in batches. It was a crazy move on the organisers' part. Our spirits were lifted by the sudden appearance of Billy Fraser-Jones who'd witnessed the fiasco at the start and the chaos at Goudwyn weir and like many seasoned river men, he couldn't believe the unwarranted time trial interrupting the flow of the race. It took quite a while to thaw out once we set off for the finish and woe betide any canoeist who fell into the Breede at this stage. There were the unfortunate paddlers who collided into trees or misjudged the whirlpools, including a wild man −'Bull' Turnbull, a Scotsman and a fellow Dabulamanzi mate. He'd misjudged an overhanging tree and had taken a big swim.

The start of the second day was to prove as chaotic as the first. A number of experienced canoeists had illicitly joined the ranks of the seeds, including 'Bull' Turnbull who was determined to pick up positions after his swim on the previous day. The organisers were yet again having a nightmarish time trying to control the throng of hyped canoeists who were venting their wrath for the ill-considered time trial and they decided to employ a helicopter to video the defaulters. This ruse backfired as the din of the low-flying helicopter was deafening, drowning the starter's instructions. Again 'the every man for himself' syndrome! Boats crashed into each other, boats capsized, and canoeists were rammed amidst a howl of threats and curses. The helicopter's fearsome racket resulted in the starter giving up and the boats were off with the 'Bull' (lying 101st from the first day) neatly packed in with the top seeds! The Torlage/Rhynes team were well up there with the seeds, having hidden again beneath their splash covers to conceal their race number from 'the eyes in the sky'. A cunning duet, this Torlage team. Needless to say 'Bull' Turnbull was creating chaos in the front 'diamond' (a term in canoe racing where an arrow shaped pack is formed creating a slip stream, similar to the peloton in cycling) until he hit a tree for the second time and went 'crayfishing' much to the satisfaction of the leading hotshots. There were many upsets that day for a number of crews. The river was still pumping and the Breede's notorious channels wreaked their toll and several boats were spun out by the whirlpools into the low lying trees. The Lightfoot/Callender team scored well on that second day and took fourth position in the Masters Category and 168th overall. Turnbull, whooping and hollering raucously down the river in his inimitable style, picked up 23 positions and scored 78th and the Torlage duet made 27th position.

That night Billy Fraser-Jones gave the men from the Transvaal a roaring send off. He hauled in Hasie Lourens who was known to a number of the Dabulamanzi veterans, and his brother Andrew and his charming wife, Anneke. I cannot remember much about the details of the hoolie, apart from finding 'Bull' Turnbull fast asleep at daybreak in the straw of the pigsty. I don't believe he went to bed and Moggy and I departed for Cape Town and Turnbull and his rumbustious crew for Johannesburg, canoes skew on the vehicle roof-tops and looking very worse for wear. The men from the Dabulamanzi still talk about Billy-Fraser Jones and he in turn tenderly asks after the fortunes of the 'Dabulamanzi cultural section'. It's an amazing thing he said that those men who knew how to party the night through left not one thing broken in the house.

* * * * *

The over-organised, highly litigious western world would be incredulous at the goings-on in the 'Wild South' of South Africa. They'd despair at the antics where canoeists take the most perilous of challenges in their stride in addition to handling the grade 5 rapids in the big rivers. Nico Viljoen, a Springbok paddler and winner of several races overseas including the Scandinavian Arctic canoe marathon, was struck on the head by stone-throwing youths in the Umkomaas marathon. Take the Duzi where kids amuse themselves by dropping boulders off low-level bridges and panga wielding Zulus attack the back markers. Graham Monteith, a leading light in his day in S A canoeing, received a rubber bullet in the head racing down the Jukskei river near Johannesburg from an enraged landowner who held a pathological hatred towards canoeists. He believed he owned the river, mistakenly as it was demonstrated in court, where he was charged for attempted manslaughter. The races that I've just referred to would be burdened with a bible of regulations if these were staged in Europe and other parts of the world. I've heard from South Africans living in Australia that even that country – a haven of outdoor sport – regulates the canoeist in an alarming manner. As one sportsman put it to me the other day: "Imagine the Duzi being organised by the Europeans or the Australians or the Californians. There'd be a life saver every kilometre down the river and we'd look like Christmas trees with helmets, flashing lights, whistles, life jackets and we'd have a problem fitting into our boats. There'd be marshalls along each bridge and set of rapids preventing the spectators from getting too close to the river in case they might fall in and sue the organisers". On this very point, two Dabulamanzi members who emigrated to Australia, Glen Armstrong and Gert Visser, regularly participated in the Hawkesbury Classic, the biggest canoeing event in NSW. They'd race in their 'comet', a veteran boat of several Duzi, Fish, Breede and Umkomaas marathons, dented and scarred by many a rock in the African rivers. The boat, a typical racing canoe in the South African tradition, was the object of intense interest from the Australians, a highly conservative bunch compared with South African canoeists. Furious debate would rage at the start of Australian races that the 'comet' could survive a dam, let alone a river. Then Armstrong and Visser noticed how safety conscious Australia was, largely due to public liability where the race organisers did not wish to be held responsible for a drowning or a broken limb. All boats, therefore, were closely scrutinised before being allowed onto the water and the Hawkesbury classic is a flat water race, 110 kilometres in length, rather similar to the Vaal Marathon near Johannesburg. Each paddler had to wear luminous clothing, carry a torch (ostensibly to shine at speed boats that could run the canoeists down at night!), a compass, a map of the course and a whistle. Glen Armstrong and Gert Visser were caught dumping this paraphernalia, including the luminous clothing, at the start – the ill-disciplined South African canoeists at play – and were forced to reload the discarded baggage. Further, the rules stipulated that each boat has to have a land crew. The race rules state 'Land crews must also provide their paddlers with sustenance, support and encouragement. They must have a good sense of humour and be constantly tolerant of the paddler's often forgivable bouts of irascible behaviour"! The average seconding team in the Duzi would snort with derision. Certain Duzi competitors race without the help of seconds. I've personally witnessed many seconding teams in the Duzi lambasting their charges for being slow on the river and not for all the tea in China would they wait at the next stop! The two aforementioned stalwarts of the Dabulamanzi canoe club concluded that Australian crews might win gold and silver medals at the World championships and the Olympics. But if a Dabulamanzi team came over for the Hawkesbury race it would probably take eight of the top ten places.

* * * * *

I recall a conversation with a colourful character called 'Cockroach' Simpkins who has represented South Africa in the sport. He describes the 'Sella' descent, Spain's major canoe event. "Rapids?" he snorts derisively, "What rapids? They can't understand how we race in these narrow boats of ours. They think we're mad". Frankly, I don't blame anyone thinking 'Cockroach' is unhinged. Every time I have had the misfortune of being ahead of 'Cockroach' and his cronies in a race – and that's only on those rare occasions when the batches are reversed on the second day of a marathon to even out the finish – I hear this appalling shriek in imitation of a British accent: "There's the man who shoots polar bears! What a spiffing time we're having, what do you say, old boy!" And on he surges, cackling dementedly, his paddles whirring like a windmill. The canoeing sport epitomises the South African philosophy to life: "Give it a full blast

– whatever the consequences!" Indeed, the race organisers of the major events have now become acutely aware of the hazardous nature of the sport, sometimes sadly culminating in a death, and qualifying points have to be earned before a competitor can take part in a major race. If the rivers are in full spate in the rainy season, the rules will stipulate crash helmets and life jackets, but after that the canoeists are on their own. If they capsize and smash up which regularly happens, the responsibility is theirs to make their way back to civilisation often through rugged and snake infested terrain as with the Umkomaas, the Crocodile and the Duzi events.

* * * * *

There's a race on the Crocodile River in the Eastern Transvaal that took the competitors down hippo infested water in the final reaches until they altered the course. The race once assumed a sort of survival test as the canoeist warily weaved his way through these angry behemoths. I came last in this particular race when I lost a paddle in a rapid and I found myself propelling the boat with bare hands. There wasn't a fellow canoeist in sight and it was a hot day reaching 40 centigrade and I was faced with ten kilometres to reach the finish. I nearly trod on an evil looking snake that afternoon and received a fright from a startled bushbuck that was lying low in the undergrowth. I was hot and seriously sunburnt when I reached the finish at 6.00 in the evening. There was only the indefatigable Moggy Lightfoot and Andrew Gutchi left to welcome me with a six pack of ice cold beers. Imagine the scenario in Europe! Firstly, there'd be no hippos in the water, or poisonous snakes lurking in the undergrowth, but there would be a flotilla of search parties scanning the countryside for a lost paddler!

* * * * *

Canoeists take their lives into their hands and it is a dangerous sport and every year rivers claim victims. The recent loss of a close friend, Tony Beith, will never be erased from my mind. We were pairing a K2 in a race in the Klip River near Johannesburg –a hazardous, narrow waterway studded with tree blocks, testing weirs, low lying bridges, and rapids along its seventy kilometre course. The Klip River is an 'A' graded river, meaning that it's a top qualifier for the major races on the S A Canoe calendar. The Klip is notorious for its tree blocks and the tree block is an obstacle that needs the highest respect from all paddlers. What is visible in the water is not what necessarily lurks below the surface. The chance of a canoeist falling out of his craft and being sucked into the tentacles of a tree and related debris beneath the water are slim. But to reach the afflicted canoeist in such circumstances is tenuous. I can write about this with firsthand experience as I was with Tony Beith that dreadful day he died in the Klip, October, 2002. A friend of thirty-two years standing, I had shared many a revelry and adventure which could fill fifty pages of condensed type. I had paired with him in three Duzi marathons, four Fish river marathons, two Vaal river marathons, and a multitude of other river races, including the Duzi fifty miler. I had trained with him for months on end in the cold wintry dawns for the Comrades marathon. He competed in two and in the first of which he achieved a commendable 9 ½ hours, despite his considerable size and powerful physique. We were part of a squad that prepared for the Iron Man as described in full in a previous chapter. We hunted together. We used the same gyms. I was his best man at his wedding to Philippa, his wonderful wife, and I had the fortune of knowing his parents, John and Jean, and his offspring since they were tiny. Such was our closeness that he would confide in me, knowing well that I respected discretion. So it was a great shock when he jumped into the water to haul the boat to the bank and never surfaced. The evidence at hand indicated a massive heart seizure and we all trust it was. Perhaps it was appropriate that Tony Beith died in the manner befitting the man. Not from a bullet from a mindless hijacker, or an accident in the skies - he was a capable pilot - or on the roads, or from an incurable disease, but with a paddle in hand amongst canoeists, a breed that he always revered.

CHAPTER EIGHTEEN

Johannesburg - no mean city

We do face a problem living in a town like Johannesburg,
where the pace is furious, where life is lived close to the
edge, but when each day promises a fresh adventure,
sometimes unpalatably raw, sometimes invigoratingly
vibrant, which charges us with an attitude that ill prepares
one for living in tamer climes.

The Author

SOUTH AFRICA is a huge land with vast tracts of emptiness and
endowed with a rich mixture of terrain that earns itself the rightful claim
of being 'a World in One', the size of France and Britain combined, and yet
its principal cities can be counted on one hand. Pretoria and Cape Town
share parliaments – a contentious issue to the tax payer where the rule of
the land is alternated between the two cities at a huge duplication of cost.
Durban is host to Africa's largest port and claims to be the cradle of the
finest English spoken in the country. Bloemfontein stands as the judicial
capital of South Africa and is positioned geographically in the centre of
the Republic. This leaves Johannesburg, still today a city rooted in its
wild pioneering history -a bustling mining town in spirit. Before setting
foot in South Africa, Johannesburg was described to me as the New York
of the African continent. This is a true description. Driving from the
airport - the largest and most modernised in Africa - the first impression
of the city is a cluster of skyscrapers set in a bowl of surrounding hills.
There's a pervasive sinister feeling, a Sodom and Gomorrah aura in a

fashion, when Johannesburg is viewed from a distance. It's somewhat a sad thing that the mine dumps have been recycled and grassed over, all within the last thirty years. These yellow mounds were reminiscent of the raucous, brawling gold rush just over a century ago.

Johannesburg was a bustling metropolis in the 60's and 70's. The Central Business District housed the hub of South Africa's industry and commerce: the Stock Exchange, the mining houses, the Rand Club - the latter with an enviable reputation around the globe and commanding a waiting list of seven years. The restaurants were packed and the night clubs throbbed to live bands. Crime in the city was negligible, the lights worked, and the streets were clean and shopping malls were almost unheard of. It was a great city to do business in, to shop in and to celebrate in. Johannesburg buzzed.

Things have dramatically changed in a short forty year span. Most service industries and light industry have moved away from the city centre and the CBD is unrecognizable to what it was. The once-proud city is on its way to becoming a Calcutta, or a Lagos, or a Harlem. The Johannesburg skyline still presents one of the most impressive sights modern architecture has to offer but enter the city and foreboding will set in. Many of the skyscrapers are lying empty, festooned with "to let" or "for sale" signs. The pavements are congested with hawkers, a sure symptom of a third world country. Certain landmarks, once proud relics of Johannesburg's history, are lying derelict where vandals have smashed windows and stolen priceless clocks and weather vanes. What were solidly built apartment blocks with handsome facades are today squalid squatter dwellings. On the streets, both pedestrians and motorists pay scant attention to the law. It is probably the only metropolis in the world that actually encourages the driver to roll gently across a red light at night - the danger of hijacking is that rife - and despite the town earning a reputation as a criminal's paradise, a policeman is rarely in sight.

My entire working life in South Africa, save for the recent years when after our financial controller had a gun stuck into his ribs by a dope-crazed thug and I relocated our company to the north of the city, has been spent in the bowels of Johannesburg. I have watched the degeneration of

Hillbrow, Johannesburg's Chelsea of London, which I and most other Johannesburgers held nostalgia for. The very first hotel that I booked into when reconnoitring South Africa was the Casa Mia, then a respected hostelry set in Hillbrow. This was Transvaal's clubbing capital, a district with exciting bars and cosmopolitan restaurants where intellectuals, yuppies, and out of town revellers rubbed shoulders. Hillbrow has deteriorated into a Harlem, a hub for Nigerian fraudsters and the sub-continent's drug and prostitution centre where buildings are rotting and alley ways seeping with rats and garbage of every form of inconceivable filth. Hillbrow is ungovernable - a cesspit of murder, extortion and vice.

Then to be mentioned are the artisan precincts of Yeoville and the area known as the Market Theatre. The urban decay is spreading its grimy fingers into these once-proud centres where the youth congregated in the coffee shops and pubs. Johannesburg has been allowed to fall into decay and disrepute through nothing other than bad management. The 'New South Africa' had the chance of developing Johannesburg into the greatest multi-racial city on the continent. The new city masters inherited an enviable infrastructure: an impressive skyline, a harbour for the nation's industry, a collection of famous landmarks, and a cosmopolitan population. Despite the well worn platitude of 'Apartheid is to blame', the current city council was handed a capital that could be developed into a great metropolis to the envy of Africa. It is evident that the Johannesburg Municipality attracted a second rate legion of bureaucrats. Any capable black politician was either scrabbling for power in the national legislature or heading for the lucrative world of big business. Tokyo Sexwale was regarded as the man big enough and powerful enough to stop the rot when he was appointed to the top job in Johannesburg's administration. Shortly after he took office, this charismatic black leader, one of Mandela's inner circle on Robben Island, opted for the business world where he amassed a fortune in mining and other enterprises.

Johannesburg has moved its pivot to the suburbs surrounding the CBD, in the same manner as many American cities – Atlanta, Philadelphia, Dallas, St Louis to mention a few. But for all this the Johannesburger remains proud and there are many reasons. As with the New Yorker, Johannesburgers are conscious of their ability to survive the crime, to wear the scars of hijacking and violence, and look to the benefits that are unsurpassed anywhere in the Republic. The climate is brilliant, and the city's bright sunny skies and its proximity to the African bush vie with the fast tempo of the life in the city. I remember from my several visits to New York the constant threat of danger - the muggings in Central Park and the sinister over-spill of Harlem into the upper reaches of Manhattan. New York has been cleaned up since its 'zero tolerance' policy and perhaps there is ultimate hope for this southern hemisphere metropolis of five million people standing at 5500 feet high. Johannesburg is a little madder than most big cities in South Africa. Michael Deacon, a good friend of mine and a bird-shooting companion, now residing in Cape Town, described it as such: "Johannesburg is a lunatic asylum. Up here, they drink too much, they drive too fast, they eat on the hoof, and they work and play like people facing their last day on earth!" Johannesburg could be reminiscent perhaps of London in the war years or Salisbury when the Rhodesians were fighting Mugabe and his freedom fighters. The Johannesburger might be harder than his counterpart in Durban and Cape Town, Bloemfontein and East London but he's generous in heart. He's more receptive to change. In fact he'll try anything - he's big spirited.

I've been fortunate to have travelled to many places in the world and I'm pressed to find a livelier, bigger minded and more red blooded breed as the Johannesburger. They are very special. Sir Chay Blyth, the British sailor, often ribbed me about South Africa as "diddy land". I corrected him saying he's referring to Cape Town - the city that vies with Johannesburg for supremacy. In my business experience I've tried every ruse known to man to persuade this cliquish, self satisfied breed to buy our product. It's been sold in London, Sydney, New York, Toronto, but Cape Town, no. I've tried various strategies: the veneer of a true-blue Brit, an Afrikaans speaker, an English speaking South African. I've worn London style pin striped suits, tan suits, chino trousers and blue shirts. I've attempted all sorts of dialects, expressions, mannerisms but the Capetonian wouldn't budge. I was a menace, a threat. I'd come from the north of the Hex River mountains. Cape Town is a secluded enclave, a protectorate of its peoples that see themselves as a privileged sect, not to be contaminated by the dreaded uitlander. They are charming and civilised but parochial to a severe degree.

Johannesburg people can laugh at themselves. They have a highly developed sense of the ridiculous. They adapt to crisis more easily than the denizens of the other cities because, perhaps, they live constantly on the edge. Soweto, the sprawling Black township of over two million, is on the door step. Alexandria, a squalid slum settlement, sits in close proximity to one of Johannesburg's most affluent suburbs, Sandton. This is a mean city where robbers have learnt to dope Dobermans and rat-poison Rottweiler's, and they have worked out how to dig under electrified fences and pose as security guards to hoodwink the unwary householder. A businessman told me how he would drive to dinner parties in khaki bush gear and running shoes so that he could either give chase to or flee from the hijackers, depending upon his situation. He's that eccentric that I believed him. There is a fearless woman we know who abjectly refused to be intimidated by a hijacker. She brushed aside the gun waving in her face and admonished the astonished young thug to grow up, to stop being so utterly absurd, and could he step aside so she could proceed on her way!

The Vinuchi delivery van used to carry large and realistic decals of snakes and scorpions with the message in big letters: "dangerous reptiles in transit" and for several years there was not one theft from the vehicle. The receptionist was well tuned to handling callers wanting to know if Vinuchi could arrange to have their plague of rats dealt with by a leased python, or if it would oblige in adopting a pet cobra who'd poisoned their cat!

Johannesburgers have become street wise in not only outsmarting hijackers but the drink and drive traps that are sprung each Christmas around the busier thoroughfares. There was a time that the practice became rife of munching half a dozen or two spring onions on the drive back from the office or from a favourite drinking hole. My own ruse was to change into running gear with a canoe strapped onto the roof of the car. Many a time this worked with one sailing unchallenged through police blocks until I returned home one particular evening and was asked what on earth I thought I looked like. The sweat stained singlet was well in place but I'd overlooked the lower section which beggared belief with immaculately pressed pin striped trousers and Jermyn Street's finest footwear firmly in play! I knew a character who had the nerve of the devil and his method would be to move over to the passenger seat at a police bloc and sit there leaving the infuriated police banging on the windows only to be told that the driver had fled in panic into the bundu.

In Johannesburg one experiences extraordinary sights that would turn heads in normal capital cities. Here the Johannesburger exhibits a déjà vu at the apparition of a scantily clad Naomi Campbell-like figure soliciting a stream of BMW and Mercedes Benz drivers at a busy intersection in the heat of the day; or a melon breasted, ample buttocked Amazon vision balancing three suitcases on her head weaving through a throng in a shopping centre; or the spectacle of a road labourer pumping his arms and legs furiously in time to a rap tune blaring from a radio. Such sights that would have Parisians or Berliners rubber necking are common place to the Johannesburger. He's seen most things in his time.

Baragwanath Hospital is reputedly the biggest in the world with 3200 beds. Situated at the edge of Soweto - the huge sprawling township verging on the west side of Johannesburg - 'Bara' is a notoriously rough place to work, even by standards of the violence hardened Johannesburger. Medical students from all over the world apply to work in 'The Bara', a veritable bedlam where interns and registrars mill around, tending to anything up to thirty-five patients a night and triple that over weekends. The main surgical focus point is the notorious 'pit'- Baragwanath's casualty ward where every conceivable variety of wound is on gory display - and it's not unusual to see victims staggering in with axes embedded in their skulls, or knives protruding from their shoulder blades. Compassion is a rare commodity. The nursing staff, mostly black, are intolerant of whingers. They are hard people. Any sympathy is lost: "Baba, we have to cut you from here to here, otherwise you die!" And the regulatory consent from the patient is usually confined to an inky thumb print on a piece of rough paper, the patients are that spaced out. A friend's son spent a year as an intern at Baragwanath and his story is riveting. In his words, 'Bara' is so overcrowded that patients languish on trolleys for hours unattended to. The more badly injured have a red sticker slapped across their foreheads. The wariness and the cynicism of the Johannesburg native are never more evident than in the expression of the 'Bara' veteran. He's seen it all before. The young man speaking to me on his 'Bara' experience was in his early 20's. I could only admire him for his matter of factness and his calm disposition as he went on to describe a typical Saturday night. "It took me three months to acclimatise to those hapless creatures with stab wounds, with smashed up faces and shattered limbs, and the hours we spent with splints, matching blood, draining chests, arranging brain scans. The pace is so frenetic that we assist in a three hour operation without passing a pleasantry to our fellow staff. The foreign interns at first cannot believe what they are seeing but they go back to Britain or Europe or Latin America with a life time experience condensed into one year".

Living in Johannesburg makes one aware, very aware of danger. When one treks abroad the question is self-asked: "Are we seriously out of kilter with the world, or they with us?" I clearly recall one visit to Sydney in the mid 80's. The Australian press was flooded with lurid pictures of South Africa of white policemen bludgeoning blacks with truncheons, of buildings ablaze, of total mayhem in general. Amidst these stark headlines of carnage ran the main story of the day in a Sydney newspaper of the price of butter rising by 8%! Then there was this quaint, peaceful setting in a country inn in Dorset, England, on a Saturday morning and I overheard one local in his thick West Country burr talking about the badger he'd seen in the road and I thought back to the week before when a friend of ours had been bludgeoned to death by a fence pole wielded by a revengeful labourer who'd been retrenched for abusive behaviour.

That's Johannesburg – no mean city.

CHAPTER NINETEEN

The next generation carries the torch of adventure

Those who choose to search for adventure

make their own decisions about

living and dying.

The Author

THERE'S A company in the adventure business called Kayak Africa and we are proud of that company as one of the two founders was MaryAnne Callender, our daughter. Her brother, Sean, is a charter pilot who covers some of the remotest and darkest destinations of the African continent. Both offspring have succeeded in perpetuating our family's adventurous spirit.

We were recently reminiscing with Pierre 'Bushy' Bester. He was the co-founder of Kayak Africa when the two drove a second hand land rover up to Cape Maclear in 1995 to set up camp to build Malawi's foremost adventure company. Kayak Africa is an enterprise offering sea-kayaking, spear fishing, scuba diving, mountain biking and custom made adventure trips for the more intrepid. One glance at the makeup of the team driving the enterprise will tell you where Kayak Africa comes from. The Bester brothers were born with the outdoors in their blood and from an early age they took to mountaineering and the corporate life was not for them.

Shortly after completing his military service as an officer, Clive Bester joined his brother and MaryAnne and with his natural marketing flair began to build the brand name. A large measure of the success of Kayak Africa is Clive's talent in harnessing the media and it wasn't long after the creation of the company that the television screens were filled with images of this exciting company and the adventure magazines began to carry articles on the enterprise.

And then entered Jurie Schoeman, an ex officer of the Marines, a highly specialist unit in the SADF. Jurie Schoeman's sense of adventure took him to Bosnia as a mercenary and from there he gravitated into the French Foreign Legion where he put his deep sea diving experience to good use. He was appointed an instructor to a garrison of legionnaires based in Djibouti. He's a useful man in a fight endorsed by a tale that Jurie is reticent to recount. When completing his five year service in the Foreign Legion, Jurie met an attractive Danish girl called Eban who was a part time employee in a bar in Castelnaudary in France. His attentions to the beautiful girl inspired a jealous inn-keeper to call in a collection of local thugs to fix the legionnaire. As the story has it, Jurie Schoeman single handed laid out six Frenchmen and proceeded to chase the terrified inn-keeper down the street kicking his backside along the way. Jurie Schoeman is firmly of the 'strong silent' mould but, as with my ancestor Ronald Brodie also of the Foreign Legion, not a man to be crossed.

The expression "a cat has nine lives" aptly applied to Pierre Bester and MaryAnne. The horrific ordeal they endured at the hands of two hijackers in Johannesburg has been described in detail in chapter 3 and it would have been tragic if these two adventurers had had their lives shortened by a shot to their heads. The hippo incident which was a near run thing has been narrated in chapter 7. But as Pierre Bester said to me that night whilst reminiscing on the stoep of our home, there were several other dices with death that remained untold. Apart from such lesser incidents such as MaryAnne rolling a truck which threw her into a ditch and where the truck landed on top of her with the depth of the ditch saving her, there was the happening when a single engine Cessna in which they were flying force-landed in Lake Malawi and sank in fifteen metres of water where the six occupants nearly drowned. On this occasion, a close friend of the pair, Matt Slaven from Johannesburg, was flying his plane under the watch of his flight instructor when the engine cut out leaving the instructor to hedge-hop over the lake towards the shore. The propeller hit the water capsizing the aircraft and the weight of the engine dragged it down to the bed of the lake, mercifully shallow at this point. Matt Slaven, the co-pilot, and another in the party managed to crawl through the splintered wind screen and swim to safety, whilst MaryAnne and another girl were treading water to keep their heads afloat at the rear of the Cessna. Pierre Bester was under water, trying to wrench a side door open in spite of the massive pressure of the water, and he was rapidly running out of breath. This he managed to succeed owing to his prodigious strength and his deep sea diving experience, thereby saving two lives from a certain drowning.

Shortly after this incident, danger was to rear its head again when Pierre and MaryAnne were returning from Blantyre with a truck laden with goods and camp equipment. They'd followed a short cut through the bush when to their astonishment they saw a white fellow running towards them, naked except for his underpants. This was now in the dead of night and he was screaming for help and Pierre, being an experienced man in moments of danger, slowed the truck in pace with the frantic character who was now hugging the dashboard and screaming "They're waiting to ambush you - turn round!" The couple hauled him aboard and gunned the vehicle down the way they'd come from, leaving pots and pans and other paraphernalia flying into the bush. Back at camp MaryAnne nursed the fellow's bloodied feet whilst Pierre took note of his story. He was a visitor from South Africa. He'd been assaulted by a gang of thieves who'd taken his shoes and marched him to their village, stripped him of his clothes, and told him to walk along the road ahead of them. They were using him as bait to rob the first vehicle that came their way. The ruse had nearly worked as the sight of a near naked apparition racing down a deserted track in the middle of the bush would be sufficient for an unwary victim to stop. Despite his life being saved, he never returned the R700.00 or the clothes and the shoes which the trusting pair had lent him. The money was a small fortune to Kayak Africa in those days.

And then Pierre reminded me of a hair-raising ordeal which he and MaryAnne experienced in Mozambique. The two had decided to chart an adventure trail along the coast in a klepper sea kayak and they needed a driver to second them. The driver they took on in Cape Maclear was an Irishman who seemed capable for the job until they realised they had a dangerous paranoiac on their hands. During the drive through the bush to reach the Mozambique coast, the Irishman became obnoxious and it was evident to the two that they had a drug addict and an alcoholic for company. MaryAnne was able to prevent Pierre taking the knuckles to this deranged Irishman as they needed him to collect them down the coast to return to Malawi. But then the true drama started. The pair commenced their canoe trip at the mouth of the Rovuma River on the Tanzanian border to reach their goal, Porto Amelia, a distance of 300 kilometres along the coast. On one of their stops they had to haul the canoe across mudflats and Pierre, shoeless on this occasion, had his feet covered with the needles of sea-urchins. He was allergic to the poison and that night he incurred a heavy fever with his face swelling alarmingly and where he couldn't breathe. He instructed MaryAnne to cut an incision in his throat with his Swiss army knife and he showed her how to do it and the poor girl refused believing that if she erred on the incision, that would be Pierre's life. She then trekked through the snake infested bush and it was a miracle that she eventually found a bush doctor. It took two days for Pierre to recover before they could resume their sea trip and then to find their paranoiac team mate drinking himself into a stupor. Again MaryAnne had to intervene as Pierre Bester was in the mood to end the wretch's life. Once back at Cape Maclear, the Irishman decided in his wisdom to vanish into thin air.

Kayak Africa runs river adventure trips and the Bester brothers decided to explore the Rovuma River which serves as the border between Tanzania and Mozambique. They attracted two volunteers, David Evans – a mountaineer and outdoorsman well known to Pierre Bester - and Gary Harper, an avid supporter of Kayak Africa and friend of the partners. The source of the Rovuma lies inland from the eastern shore of Lake Malawi and for two days the party of four, aided by porters, portaged their canoes and their supplies through the bush to the Messinge River which flows into the Rovuma. This river has never been navigated by white men with the exception of David Livingstone, the 19th century missionary/explorer, who correctly believed that the source of the Rovuma in the Indian Ocean would lead into Lake Malawi. Livingstone had to abandon his attempt in 1862 when his party encountered a set of massive rapids 160 kilometres upstream, making further progress impossible. For most of its 1000 kilometre length, the Rovuma runs wild, without any bridges, or roads leading into it, endorsing the belief that the men of Kayak Africa were the first to attempt to navigate this stretch of untamed Africa.

For twenty-three days the canoeists paddled an average of 50 kilometres a day. In the Messinge tributary leading into the Rovuma, David Evans experienced a near drowning when his kayak threatened to wrap around a rock which would have entrapped his legs. Fortunately, Clive Bester was behind him and was able to go to Evan's aid and leverage the boat to safety. It took some days before the paddlers met up with the Rovuma itself which has its source in the mountains on the eastern shore of Lake Malawi. The Messinge was a stream compared to the fast flowing Rovuma. Then came the hippos and the crocodiles in great numbers which were to accompany the party for the rest of their journey up to the last ten kilometres before the river mouth. As Pierre Bester was to say later, these were the biggest crocodiles he'd ever encountered in his bush experiences. The hippos and the crocodiles aside, the Rovuma presented several daunting challenges. The river would separate into narrow channels, leaving the canoeists to guess which channel was navigable. The vines of huge trees would intertwine from one islet in the river to another, creating tunnels which David Evans would describe as 'winding through a magic jungle'. At one stage elephants crossed the river immediately in front of the canoeists, forcing them to follow an alternate channel only to find a pod of hippos wallowing in the water. This necessitated yet another turn to where two hippos boiled up in front of the kayaks threatening to capsize them, leaving the paddlers to make for an island to let the mayhem settle down. Pierre Bester was first to step ashore when a crocodile bolted out of the reeds, passing him with feet to spare! On one occasion the four crawled through a dense jungle thicket to reconnoitre the river ahead of them. This took them to the lip of a 60 ft high, rainbow shrouded waterfall. With nerves stretched to breaking point, they had to ferry-glide across the current above the falls after which they portaged slowly down the cliff. Many of the rapids encountered along the river were reported to be grades 3, 4 and 5 which dictate an advanced state of proficiency from the canoeist.

The area was extremely wild and remote and the Kayak Africa team found Africans living in caves and making fires by rubbing sticks together and they'd flee at the sight of the canoeists. Having studied Livingstone's diaries, they believed that the descriptions 'regular pirates inhabiting the sandbanks 60 miles from the mouth' would be well out of date. But to the contrary! Exactly in the same place, 135 years later, the explorers came across a group of wild-eyed, turban-headed, shaggy bearded men shouting at them, chasing them in dug-outs shrieking "passport-passport" as a ploy to get them to stop. There were bands of these men in groups of 100 strong loping along the banks waving pangas and the canoeists had to paddle furiously and their speed, and no doubt the crocodiles as a deterrent, saved their lives. But, two hours further down river when they thought they were safe, they were again confronted by more pirates, standing thigh deep in the water with their arms behind their backs, concealing the pangas with which they had intended to use on the explorers. The four had their flares ready to fire off to scare the pirates away and they paddled furiously past the bandits who were attempting to reach the canoes despite the crocodiles. A few days after their dice with the river pirates, the Bester brothers, Gary Harper and David Evans reached the mouth of the Rovuma, having paddled 1087 kilometres and portaged 41 kilometres in the space of 25 days. Kayak Africa decided that the risks were just too great to offer this as a river trip to their clients.

Jurie Schoeman and Pierre Bester are highly experienced divers. They'd think little of spear fishing in the shark-infested raging waters off Krommetjie near Cape Town, and to be accorded the honour of training the Foreign Legionnaires in diving is a mark of Jurie Schoeman's prodigious skill. A ferry boat some years back sank in Lake Malawi and the pair decided to salvage the engines after the owners of the ship had declared all lost. This was an immense feat, requiring skill, strength and stamina to operate in 500 ft of water. Defying all odds, permission having been granted by the sceptical authorities, the pair achieved the seemingly impossible and salvaged the valuable engine and repaired it with their own hands. They then purchased a vessel, installed the renovated engine following which Pierre Bester and a diving instructor employed by Kayak Africa called Morne, and sailed the boat over to Madagascar from the shores of Mozambique to set up a new camp at the Masoala Peninsular on the eastern tip of the island.

Sean, our son, is his own man – a self dependent character that dislikes any form of self-aggrandisement as is the trait of many individualists. It's not extraordinary why brother and sister both beckoned to the call of the wild, scorning the shackles of corporate life. Their affinity with the wilderness is in their heritage. A few years ago Sean was tiring of his studying for a B-Comm Accounting degree. We could sense his heart wasn't in it although he is a bright young man and when he told us in London where he was earning pocket money pulling beer handles that he wanted to be a pilot, we gave him our full support. It was, therefore, a natural progression that he found himself initially flying in and out of the swamps of the Okavango Delta, notching up useful hours flying amongst the islands. His experience of landing and taking off from remote air strips stood him in good stead in his later assignments flying in diverse African countries such as Ruanda, Madagascar, the DRC, Angola, and Sudan. He's earned his captaincy status and is qualified to fly the latest Lear jets. It's likely that in the near future he will operate his own commercial charter business. His plans to set up a sea plane service based in Dar es Salaam are nearing fruition.

Sean has many a tale to tell but to coerce them out of the young man is like drawing hens' teeth. One story which he's hesitant to elaborate on is his tackling the notorious rapids 5 – 18 of the Zambezi River in a white water canoe. He brushes the experience aside with a terse comment "it's no great deal" but when I talk to the more experienced white water men in canoeing circles, it certainly is. There are not many canoeists who have the experience and the daring to challenge these extremely dangerous waters. According to Sean, he turned up one day with boat on shoulder and obtained the services of a guide, a young Black. "That's the hero – not me" said Sean and if I'm to believe him, then this makes two very daring men as this section of the Zambezi we are talking about is a fearsome stretch of grade 4 and 5 rapids, some of the largest to be found anywhere in the world. Vivienne and I shot these same rapids as part of a team in an inflatable in the early eighties before running the Zambezi in a rubber duck became the popular adventure challenge it is today. I describe this as an awesome experience, and the sound alone of those huge rapids is enough to have the sturdiest tremble. Each year the inevitable accidents occur and these are hushed up as the river-running companies would be out of business - but they happen. So here's Sean who in his casual, unassuming manner rocks up with his slalom boat at the base of the Victoria Falls and braves these massive waters of the Zambezi (this stretch is not be confused with the downstream Zambezi where game-viewing trips are staged). Sean passed the regulatory proficiency test handsomely, having learnt how to 'Eskimo roll' in the Colorado River which is a mandatory technique for serious white water canoeists. Even Sean had to admit that he had 'a close shave' when he had difficulty surfacing after a tumble in one of the massive 'washing machines' at the foot of a 5 grade rapid. Like his sister, Sean falls in the adventurer mould and we are proud to see the family flame for adventure firmly alight.

∽ ✦ ∾

CHAPTER TWENTY

Finale

It is bientot and not adieu, Africa.

The Author

I STARTED the story in a freezing Europe and I finish in a sweltering Africa. I believed my task was done before setting off for Johannesburg and that my manuscript was in the safe hands of the publisher. My complacency was short lived as I walked through O R Tambo airport that had been refurbished for the recent FIFA world cup. I wondered if Johannesburg had received the same treatment, if it had enjoyed a face lift and become a saner place. Any illusion on this was shortly shattered in the underground car park as a frantic looking local hurtled straight at one's hired vehicle – he was obviously late for his flight – and with a manic twist of the wheel I avoided a nasty collision. Reaching the bright sunshine of a typical Highveld day, we were coasting along smoothly until we hit a massive traffic jam. It was only 7 am but I'd forgotten this city arises early and we were in the thick of the commuter traffic. But it was an upturned truck that was the cause of the delay. We were reduced to a crawl but not for all. The freneticism of the city came to its fore and the black taxis were hurtling down the safety lane and in their slipstream lurched a hunting truck driven by a White dressed in khaki with sandwich clenched in mouth, mobile jammed in ear, and elbows steering the wheel. We were truly back in good old Joeys!

That evening I was in the robust company of the shotgun brigade and I regaled the unruly lot with some vivid excerpts from my book – I wanted to gauge their reaction. And then started the fun! "You've forgotten this, you've forgotten that" and unfolded a series of incidents which had escaped my memory. For example the night when a mate and I stopped off at the Balalaika after a day's guinea fowl shooting in Standerton and we bought a round for the crowded pub, only to discover we had no cash on us. We decided to pay by other means and dumped a sack of guinea fowl on the bar to be told by Dougie, the barman "we don't accept cheques or guinea fowl". This novel practice increased the tempo in the smoky bar and the air was filled with guinea fowl hurtling in all directions with feathers everywhere and in walked the owner, a Michael Firth whom we all knew, and to give him his due he saw the comical side of things. He had little choice with 50 odd South Africans in full flight!

Then one of the guns told me the hilarious happening when a lion tamer - a Vicky Brooker whom I know well - had her zebra kick down the fence and escape from her property in Chartwell. Apart from the animal decimating the hydrangeas and hoofing rotweillers to the skies, there was the problem of the gaping hole in the fence that could cause a problem to Vicky's security. So could she return immediately from her dinner, cried the worried servant who'd phoned her in a panic. She duly drove home, only to find a curious phenomenon of her driveway strewn with a trail of cigarettes. And then it dawned on her that some thieves had seen an opportunity to help themselves to the contents of her house only to find themselves staring straight in to the yellow, baleful eyes of a fully grown lion tethered to a tree! They, of course, gapped it the way they entered but scattering an open pack of fags in the process! Another day in Africa!

I was reminded of the tale when Rick Currie, an old friend and a colourful character, had suggested that we conduct a guinea fowl shoot in the centre of the Monte Casino entertainment complex in Fourways.

Some background to this unlikely yarn is needed before the anecdote is discarded as Irish blarney. Rick had engineered a successful coup for the Currie family when he brokered a sale of the ancestral home consisting of 80 acres of prime real estate bordering on what is today the large Fourways intersection, north west of Johannesburg. I used to shoot pigeons on this farm with Rick's younger brother, Hamish, who is mentioned in chapter 5. As Rick declared at the time "Fourways had lost its rural charm – and so why hold on to our home amidst an urban sprawl". Some years later, Rick called me with this idea of holding an informal guinea fowl shoot on the open ground facing the Monte Casino hotel. The scheme became more enticing as Rick expounded on his plan and the next evening we held a site inspection and worked out where to build a hide. I had the necessary weaponry – a .22 rifle with a silencer. We even got to the stage of planning the exit with our sacks of guinea fowl to avoid attention from the security guards and the operation looked feasible. Rick went one stage further and laid on some seed to attract the birds and we calculated that we should bag about 200 guinea fowl to boost our deep freezers. However, the scheme was preposterous – an analogy can be drawn to staging a pheasant shoot in St James Park in central London – there would be little chance of *not* being arrested, having one's gun collection confiscated, and our faces splashed across the front pages of the Johannesburg tabloids - a threat too ghastly to contemplate! We reluctantly dropped the scheme.

Another tale that evening: a Somali pirate attack was directed at a cruise ship some few months back. What the pirates had not taken into account was that a bunch of South Africans were aboard. Whilst the rest of the ship's complement were cowering under cover, the South Africans were hurling deck chairs, decanters, and any other missiles they could find at the raiders swarming up the side of the ship, yelling "Voetsek, you focken rag heads, voetsek!" which did the trick and the pirates fled! South Africans again to the fore!

The next day I was crossing the hectic Fourways intersection in the slipstream of a huge pantechnicon when I was brought to a screeching halt by a lady traffic officer who'd executed a weird sort of star jump. I was somewhat impatient as she stuck her head into the window. I was late for a meeting with my good friend Charlie Gough but I was damned if I was to be coerced into a bribe, particularly as I believed I was innocent of any crime. I sat there poker faced, shrugging my arms as I replied in French to her voluble threats "that I was in very, very deep trouble for shooting a red light!" I could sense her eyes fasten on to a euro note as I fished my French drivers licence out of my wallet. But she was a wily one, this traffic officer, as she cried out in triumph: "Michael Peter Callender – you'll have to follow me to the police station and you'll have to pay a R1000 fine!" However, I have survived the Johannesburg system for many years and I remained implacable, continuing to respond in French. If she'd understood what I was saying, I would definitely be behind bars and calling for Andrew Cullinan to bail me out once again! The charade took ten minutes but I was finally waved on by a very frustrated lady of the law.

We flew to Malawi that weekend to regain breath after the frantic pace of the brawling mining town. This country is a backwater but there is a charm to the gentleness of the people and the soothing panorama of the rolling green countryside with the mountains in the distance as one drives the five hour trip from Lilongwe to Cape Maclear. We were greeted by two excited grand children and Jurie Schoeman, our son in law, and we were truly ensconced in our second home. The aura of MaryAnne is omnipresent when the old timers of the Kayak Africa staff such as Ash, William, and Lainess line up to give you a warm greeting. In the welcoming throng was Renee Watson, Jurie's new lady. We'd heard a lot about her from Jurie so were naturally curious to set eyes on her and she met the descriptions well. With her vibrant looks and personality she will no doubt be an asset to Jurie. Renee is an interesting person; she travels extensively overseas to train teachers in the Pilates discipline, having started a successful enterprise in Cape Town. She recently returned to South Africa with her family from Canada where she had spent many years and she met Jurie in Cape Town last year.

We enjoyed a glorious week, mostly on Mumbo Island with Renee, Jurie, and the children, spending our time swimming, kayaking, and walking over the island. This is a gem of a retreat and a stark contrast to the gritty metropolis of Johannesburg or the sanitised climes of Europe. Undoubtedly, there will always remain an overhang of MaryAnne's sad end in the Lake, but the melancholia is quickly dispersed with the cheerful company of our family up here and the welcome addition of Renee. My favourite time of day on Mumbo is the sunset when one surveys the Lake deep in contemplation with only the strident cries of the fish eagles disturbing the silence. Memories of MaryAnne come flooding back as indeed of others who've been claimed by the powers above by meeting a sad , premature end – Ian Green & Tony Beith in rivers; Johan Bellingan & Alastair Travers on the horns of a buffalo; Andrew Crutchley, Charlie Vanrenen, and Michael Tindall through other tragic circumstances. And then one's reflections meander in a different direction – the destiny of Africa and can it cast aside the shackles of the graft, corruption, and tyranny inflicted by the 'Big Men' of the continent and can it follow the footsteps of such successful emerging markets as Brazil, India, and China or will it submerge in a morass of civil wars and internecine savagery.

Back to the pulsing metropolis. This time I meet the hunting men from the Tembo chapter of the S A Hunters Association - Andrew Kayser and his band of carpet - baggers. They entertain me with exciting tales of the bush and the animals they have tracked in my absence. I list these diverse characters in the Miscellany but it's worthwhile to digress on how the Tembo chapter evolved in the first instance. The SA Hunters Association has a current membership of some fifty thousand registered hunters which are catered for by a collection of different chapters dispersed throughout the Republic. This led to a need for an English speaking body and it was left to a charismatic Afrikaner, Wilhelm Greef, to form such a body and it was termed Tembo for whatever reason known to Wilhelm or his henchmen sitting on the SA Hunters committee. Despite my collecting the 'Hunter of the Year' award in 1988 with my trophy collection harnessed in the Central African Republic, I had to go back to school as with all registered hunters to qualify for recognition by the Dept of Police who had instigated an ill conceived five year plan to re-register all fire arm licence holders in the Republic. This was a cumbersome concept which more sophisticated nations had found impractical and had discontinued, Canada for example. Wilhelm Greef ran courses for the competency test, where he suggested I join Tembo which he had created to meet the aspirations of the English speaking hunting community which was vastly outmatched in the S A Hunters Association by the Afrikaners. This involved a monthly gathering held at the Morningside country club which was patronised not only by the English speaking but by a growing band of Afrikaners who'd heard that Tembo was a very entertaining and lively chapter to belong to. It was at one of these raucous gatherings, mostly conducted in a rich mangle of English and Afrikaans under the chairmanship of Andrew Kayser, that the *Callender Giant Forest Frog* floating trophy came into existence. How this came about was through a lively debate on pig shooting where I stood up and delivered a treatise on how to hunt a Giant Forest Hog in the CAR. There was some misinterpretation by the Afrikaners present who thought I was warbling on about a giant forest *frog*! This led to some ribbing at the Rooinek's expense naturally, but Bertie Lombard, a stalwart of Tembo, saw an opportunity to recognise the hunter of the Tembo chapter with the finest trophy for the year and donate a cup which he generously did. This happened to fall in the hands of the author the very first year the award was introduced on account of his CAR collection. However, I did pass this on to allow a youngster to steal the honours!

Another few days in the Johannesburg bedlam led us to look for some welcoming company in Natal – this being my favourite province for a variety of reasons: its collection of warriors (Gerrard, Crutchley, Robinson, Brett to name a few); farmers (Cronje, Mitchell – Innes, Henderson, Ralfe, Eustace, Benson amongst others) and excellent veldt for hunting. Braam Cronje & his attractive wife, Yvette, were waiting for us with a case of champagne which was consumed by all except the temperate author who satisfied himself with a bottle of fine chardonnay. Dinner was hilarious as the celebration of our arrival was exuberant and the duck roasting in the oven was forgotten about. When it was finally served up close to midnight, the bird seemed to be upside down with its fearsome claws extending into the heavens. Braam managed to carve this strange looking fowl with his fingers and I swear he had cooked a crow as a prank to play on his guests the following night.

At 4.30 am the next morning Braam and I had a bosberaad in the kitchen. He was in dire pain from a pinched nerve in the back, but I think it was a hang- over. His plan was to take me to a cattle auction later in the morning but not before he'd conducted some cash crop business in the mealie fields. At 7 am we found ourselves hurtling along a dirt road with some six labourers holding on for dear life in the back of his bakkie. I was gripping the dashboard with whitened knuckles. "We're late, we're late" Braam kept on muttering. "I'm third on the list and I don't want to lose my place in the line-up as otherwise we'll be there all day and there'll be nothing for you to do except to get drunk in the Dundee and District club". We were barrelling along at a furious rate and Braam was ignoring my pleas to slow down. "Stop panicking, man, there's no traffic on this road!". As he said this, we turned a corner and there was an African lady sitting on a stool twirling a makeshift sign saying 'stop/ go'! There was a queue of trucks waiting their turn at what appeared to be a road works. We skidded to a halt with Braam muttering obscenities whilst the visibly nervous lady was shielding herself under her sign. We reached Helpmekaar miraculously in one piece to refuel when Braam cursed aloud – the front right tyre had exploded. Imagine the scene if this had occurred at the road works! We then proceeded to a farm to load up the cattle for the auction and we had some time to spare and I read aloud to Braam a poem on the battle of Magersfontein whilst he was taking a breather lying in the grass. Pertinent, I thought, with his distant forebear wreaking such damage on the 51st Highland Division. He enjoyed this peroration as he did the prologue to my book which I delivered in suitably sonorous tones.

The cattle auction was well worth experiencing as it was not my first as auctions go, but this was a trite more robust than the more genteel affairs I've attended in Bond Street! I was particularly intrigued with the arrival of a 750 kg ox in the sawdust ring and I asked Braam if there were any accidents at these auctions. "Plenty", he replied, "particularly when the bulls panic. The cattle attendant in the ring either plays the bull as he would at a bullfight or he scampers behind the barrier". I remain uncertain if Braam is having me on or if there are serious accidents; I will have to return to Dundee to find out. Braam managed to achieve his target and off we sallied to the Dundee and District club to seek a cold beer for the morning's work. The establishment was a true relic of colonial times with its game trophies adorning the walls and its billiard tables, now sadly gathering dust. The arrival of a stock theft detective named Dorf Kruger boosted the proceedings and if it wasn't for my host having to pay wages being the week end, the party doubtless would have carried on for longer. The return trip was less hectic than the outgoing version but equally as entertaining with Braam's stories on the incorrigible Dorf Kruger and his anti stock theft antics. "Would they allow this sort of thing in Dorset?" I was asked. "For example, what would your friend Michael de Pelet do with a poacher?" I reply: "He and his game keeper dig fox hound pits as fox hunting disturb the pheasants and there's a cemetery in the vegetable garden with a row of crosses; poachers, I guess!" The Dundee farmer was most impressed with this piece of information on the West Country. Braam then proceeded to tell me about a recent incident which nearly had me out of the truck with mirth. "I have a neighbour who out of the kindness of his heart lent his labourers a tractor and a trailer to drive to Dundee to purchase their Xmas presents. All went well until the inevitable – they got drunk in town and overturned the trailer on their way back. There were bodies everywhere and a farmer happened to drive by and stopped to walk amongst the sprawl of bodies enquiring "anybody hurt?" and one faint reply reached his ears. "Not *yet*. Our baas hasn't arrived!" Typical South African farm humour that will possibly be lost on certain readers, except Michael de Pelet and his game keeper.

We celebrated Braam's successful cattle sale that evening with Derek Ralfe, his wife 'Tutu', George Mitchell-Innes and Gerta, his Austrian wife, and ourselves. We were in cheerful company as I'd met the Ralfes on several occasions in the Cronje household. Derek is a Duzi veteran and one of the distinguished few who have competed in the One Day Duzi – a gruelling test of endurance, strength, and river craft. George is also an interesting man: farmer, military historian owning a museum, and hunter operating his game ranch near Ladysmith. A kudu hunt was planned for the following morning on one of Braam's farms near Helpmekaar. However, on the way Braam had to attend to a tractor that had broken down and by the time this was sorted out, it was late on in the morning but we decided to check out the kudus that had been sighted the day before by one of the farm workers. This proved unrewarding and we tracked Rob Gerrard down in Dundee and we had a glorious reunion which I've made mention of in chapter 8. So another fine day in the rolling grasslands of Natal.

The following morning we set off for Nottingham Road to have lunch with Monty Brett.The Colonel of the paratroops is standing by to greet us with his customary cheerful disposition. It only takes a few minutes before Monty embarks on a favourite topic – crime prevention. He tells us there have been some unsavoury incidents in the region and he's in his finest mettle when Vivienne enquires on how to deal with an armed intruder. She's forgotten the days of Chartwell since residing in rural France. "Come, I'll show you, Viv. Michael's seen it all before but let me show you my drill" and with this he proceeds to his armoury and takes Vivienne through his well rehearsed procedure. I cannot digress further as this would let Monty's anti crime secrets out of the bag and he would have my nuts on an electric fence for this so we will fast forward to his 'immediate action' where he shows us how to shoot a robber and keep within the law. I'm tempted to pass this on to a Brigadier – Chef of police I've come to know who operates a riot squad in Avignon!

There's more excitement yet ahead of us. We are staying with Jack Crutchley and his wife, Rosalie. They live in Kloof in fine style in one of those gracious Natal homes. It was an entertaining evening and full of lively conversation with two other couples invited for the occasion. The preamble to dinner was marked by typical Jack Crutchley humour. "I assume you like this sauvignon blanc I'm about to pour you?" "I do indeed" says I. "That's good, I've been trying to off load this donkey's piss for years!" and proceeds to leave me with the bottle in easy reach on the mantelpiece. The next morning I suggested we take a walk, thinking this would be a gentle stroll along the leafy Arbrie road before a breakfast of eggs & bacon which I had longed for since putting my foot into Africa. Jack had other ideas. I was attired in shorts and beach shoes which I thought was suitable for the ramble around picturesque Kloof. I therefore watched with some surprise Jack strapping on a service pistol and jamming a wicked looking serrated knife into his waistband. He thrusts a heavy knobkerrie into my hand and off we set for a nature reserve known as 'Long Shadow' which Jack briefed me on whilst careering down the tranquil Kloof lanes in his jeep. "We're heading for a special spot – the nerds avoid the place like the plague for the black mambas and the odd thug. But you are with me – in safe hands", chuckles Jack dementedly. We set off on foot down an overgrown narrow track and I hear a river some 800 foot below. "I'm taking you to a waterfall if you're game" he says, looking at my beach shoes with an evil smirk. "You look like a true poofter dressed like that", Jack chortles. "You lead" I say, "You know where the mambas are". He turns to me. "I'm very serious, watch out; they are here – masses of them". I believe him as the flora is typical of that found on the northern coast of Natal, bright green & venomous looking. "By the way", my cheerful guide continues, "mambas have a habit of pecking the second in line & you're a dead ringer in those shorts of yours!" Two hours later we'd slid down a rock face where scorpions apparently lurked and home to some fearful spiders, crossed a narrow river skipping over slippery rocks, and reached the promised waterfall which, in all truth, was an impressive sight in this patch of jungle separating Kloof from Hillcrest. Jack had obviously enjoyed his morning stroll – it had taken him back to his SAS training days in the Matopos – and the adventure had increased my appetite for those eggs & bacon promised to me earlier by Rosalie. On the way back, Jack was busy explaining how he carries an oversized pencil on to an aircraft in the event of a hi-jacking. "Here, take a look at this" and he hauls out of the glove compartment a thick twig which he's fashioned into what at first glance is indeed a pencil. "This fools them at the security gate" and with this he jabs my thigh with his weapon. This is Mad Jack in full flight!

The remainder of the trip was relatively tame. We spent quality time with our son, Sean, who was commuting between Luanda and Johannesburg whilst we were in Africa; with my old friend, Grahame Wilson, where we had some property business to attend to; a riotous luncheon at the Noyes Smith household; a meeting with a General Neil Vaux who'd led the Royal Marines in the Falklands war in the home of another ex Royal Marine, John Stroud; and the day before flying out, a most pleasant lunch with Gary Ralfe under the oaks at the Johannesburg Country Club who amongst many interesting topics outlined his plans to drive a vehicle with his brother from Sussex to Saxonwold in Johannesburg, a ten week safari through dark Africa. Gary is one of those rare captains of industry similar to Colonel Ian Mackenzie – he retired recently from running De Beers – who hankers after adventure, like his nephew, the aforementioned Derek Ralfe. This was a most befitting end to an action packed month in 'The Wild South'

Epilogue

AFTER LEAVING school, I wanted to become a journalist. Writing had been inculcated in me from an early age. I was grateful to those teachers recognising my academic strengths in steering me to study English literature and History at Advanced level. To construct history essays it is essential to be competent with the pen. It was in the latter stages of my forty year span in South Africa, shared with Vivienne and our children, that it struck me what a vibrant and fascinating land I had chosen to live out the best years of my life. I felt compelled to write about it. History is about not forgetting. To comprehend who we are and why we act is to understand our forebears. So when putting this collection of stories together, I began to research my family using diaries, letters, and such references as Burke's Landed Gentry of Ireland. It then became patently clear that I descended from an abundance of adventurers who lived dangerously to get the best out of life. In turn this encouraged me to research certain aspects of Africa. Fortunately, I collect antiquarian books on Africana, most of which are written by eminent explorers and hunters of the nineteenth century. I delved into David Livingstone, Henry Morton Stanley, Sir Samuel Baker, Sir Richard Burton and then it dawned on me that my own sojourns had taken me into some very remote and primitive corners of Africa.

Until composing this book, I had taken for granted my roaming into the Congo (DRC), the French Congo, the Central African Republic, the Luangwa valley in Zambia. I'd ventured into regions where few white men had stepped. Only a handful of Europeans had navigated the Mambili River in the Parc d'Odzwala. This is a wild tributary of the Congo where Eric Stockenstroom and myself cleared a poachers' camp and shot up their pirogues (refer chapter 16). We encountered gorillas emitting blood curdling shrieks behind screens of matted vegetation in the rain forests. The safari with Andre Roux in the Mboki – Mbomou triangle in the Central African Republic covered a vast terrain of 8500 square kilometres. I was one of the last to hunt in this unspoilt stretch of Africa before the Sudanese poaching gangs rendered the region totally unstable. MaryAnne, our daughter, and her partner, Pierre Bester, had chosen to base their adventure company in Cape Maclear on Lake Malawi near to where a distant forebear, David Livingstone, had lived out his last years. And then the Rovuma river saga involving Pierre Bester, his brother, Clive, and two fellow adventurers which is covered in chapter 19. This intrepid crew were amongst the first adventurers to follow Livingstone along this remote river of 1000 kilometres in length housing huge crocodiles and 'wild eyed and shaggy headed river pirates' which Livingstone referred to in his diary.

Then follows a further coincidence. Peter Flack, referred to in chapter 16, introduced me to an old African hand, Brian Marsh, one of the last old time hunters, at a game fair in Johannesburg. He told me that he'd hunted crocodile on Lake Malawi in the nineteen sixties. His book 'A pioneering hunter' describes Cape Maclear in 1960 as "an uninhabited sandy beach, where the empty shell of the once luxurious Cape Maclear hotel still stood". The hotel was built for tourists flying in to Cape Maclear using the Catalina Flying Boat Service but then abandoned when the air service was discontinued. In the period after WW1 and the nineteen sixties, sea planes were widely used throughout Africa. Now we have Sean, our son, pioneering a sea plane business operating out of Dar es Salaam which promises to come on stream next year! Brian Marsh's book describes how he boated into Mumbo Island, some 10 kms from the shoreline of Cape Maclear. Mumbo is leased by Kayak Africa & is a major attraction for their clients. Marsh's trackers were terrified of 'The Spirit of Mumbo' and Jeremiah, the chief tracker, did his best to deter him from hunting crocodile on the island believing it to be bewitched, stating "nobody goes there because it is well known that evil will befall anyone who does". The hunter persisted in his quest and discovered a 'line of monster crocodiles sunning themselves on the narrow beach'. I have stayed on Mumbo Island several times with Vivienne and have kayaked into the caves that Brian Marsh referred to. Since his days, the crocodile species still exist in the Lake but in reduced numbers.

Shelby Tucker's 'The Last Banana' will tell you that slavery existed in Africa long before the Europeans engaged in this grisly business. I bore this in mind when roaming with a rifle in the central parts of Africa which were on the slave routes whilst contemplating on Livingstone's crusade to abolish the trade. Between 1450 and 1880, ten million slaves were sold to Arab slavers by African chiefs for cloth, guns, cattle, beads etc. Mungo Park's 'Travels in the interior districts of Africa', published in 1799, describes how the slave trade was thriving well before the Europeans became involved in the early 19th century to supply labour for the Caribbean and American colonies. A prominent forebear, George Burke O'Kelly, owned sugar estates in St Croix, West Indies. I am descended from a slave owner, it would appear!

I followed some of my forebears to South Africa as an antidote to the drabness of a hum drum life in Britain. Peter de Pentheny O'Kelly couldn't settle down after five years fighting in the frontline of WW2. He sailed to the shores of South Africa in an impossibly small craft with two fellow warriors of 'Shimi' Lovat's 4 Commando. His cousin, Renfric 'Rex' Arundell de Pentheny O'Kelly, was despatched as a remittance man by despairing parents to Australia to shear sheep to mend his wild ways. To their surprise, the open spaces of the Southern Hemisphere were to his liking and he chose to settle in Tasmania, becoming one of the largest sheep ranch owners and a prominent racehorse owner. As 'birds of a feather', Rex visited Peter who'd made good in South Africa, establishing a thriving farm on which stands today the Swazi Spa. Rex, having no children, wanted Peter to inherit his vast estate in Tasmania which Peter elected to turn down, he was that proud of what he'd achieved in Africa. There's Raymond Arundell de Pentheny O'Kelly, my great uncle, fighting the Boers and I have a letter from his Commanding Officer describing how he and fellow horsemen of Lock's Horse, plus a contingent of Irish Mounted Infantry, were led into a trap and were chased across the Free State veldt by General Christiaan De Wet's men. He ultimately died of his wounds and was buried in Wolvehoek. Two other brothers fought in the Boer War: Henry Arundell de Pentheny O'Kelly who survived the deadly marksmanship of the Dutch farmers only to be killed at Ypres in 1915, and Edmund de Pentheny O'Kelly.

I am proud of our offspring, Sean and MaryAnne, both of whom returned from spending a lengthy sojourn in Europe to live out their lives in Africa. They found Britain too tame. MaryAnne's intrepid exploits are covered in chapter 19. She had a leaning for fellow adventurers such as the Bester brothers and Jurie Schoeman, the father of our grandchildren. Jurie's grandfather made his way to America by merchant ship and became the Golden Gloves lightweight boxing champion of the US. Jurie followed in the footsteps of his adventurous grandfather by fighting as a mercenary in the Bosnian war before signing up with the French Foreign Legion. Thus the Callender line became intertwined with Conan Doyle's 'hard bitten farmers', a fitting sequel to the path followed by myself and Vivienne to South Africa. The story would be incomplete if mention was not made of Sean's exploits as a bush pilot traversing a fair slice of the African Continent. He has flown mining missions into Angola, Sudan, the Democratic Republic of the Congo; he has completed survey work in Madagascar; he has been based in Kigali in Rwanda; Luanda in Angola; and Maun in Botswana. He's about to settle in Dar es Salaam in Tanzania.

The flame of adventure continues to burn.

80 ✦ 03

Acknowledgements

To the Republic of South Africa. This vibrant, pulsating country is the raison d'etre for the book. In my extensive travels, I have yet to encounter a land of such varying beauty and immense vistas and it does not stop there. I have had the honour of meeting more adventurers, mavericks, warriors, sportsmen emanating from one land which, for a reason of its own, breeds such wild spirited people.

To Michael & Dominique Whitehead for suggesting the route I have taken on having the book published.

To Mindy Gibbins-Klein at Ecademy Press, the Publishers, and her team - Emma Herbert, Michael Inns, and Karen Gladwell - for their valued assistance in the design and layout of the book. Their skill and professionalism has been of inspiration to the the Author.

To Maxime van Hanswijc de Jonge, a fellow author and hunter, for his invaluable assistance on the images and for teaching me how to use photo filtre.

To the South African press namely 'The Star', 'The Sunday Times', 'The Sunday Independent', for the various excerpts extracted and modified for the chapters *'Life on a razor wire'* and *'Death and close encounters in the wild'.*

To Sir Arthur Conan Doyle and Thomas Packenham for their histories on the Boer War and their tributes to the 'White tribe of Africa' and the band of 'the hard bitten farmers' who withstood the might of the British army.

To President Theodore Roosevelt, Ernest Hemingway, and Jacques Vettier for their pithy quotations on hunting and other matters. Refer to Miscellany 'favourite quotations'

To the following authors for use of their material: Rudyard Kipling *If*; John Simpson *A mad world, my master*; Robert Ruark *The Horn of the Hunter*; Hugh Dormer *Hugh Dormer's diaries*; Shelby Tucker *The Last Banana*; Lord 'Shimi' Lovat *March Past*; Edwin Way Teale for his quote refer chapter *'The Duzi Rats'*; Harry Manners *Professional Ivory Hunter*; Mike Hoare *Congo Mercenary*; Mark Twain for his quote refer chapter *'White water & a tragic death'*; *The Daily Telegraph Book on Obituaries 2* for the material on 'Dodo' Lees; Mark Keohane *Champions of the world*; Brian Marsh *A Pioneering Hunter* .

To the explorers of the nineteenth century for their inspiration: David Livingstone; Henry Stanley; Sir Richard Burton; Sir Samuel Baker.

To the sportsmen for their descriptives: Wilf Rosenburg & Peter Pollock on the Comrades race; Joost van der Westhuizen on the 1995 World Cup Springbok victory; Grahame Pope – Ellis on the Duzi with his reference to Tim Cornish & 'Burma Road'; Dr Tim Noakes on the Comrades race.

To Philippe and Beryl Andersson for their magnanimous friendship and for the generous loan of their charming home where this book was completed.

Miscellany

Andrew Fraser – Adventurer & big game hunter. Youngest son of Lord Lovat of 4 Commando fame.Refer chapter 7.

Anthony Cable - Resides in Santiago , Chile. Lived in Johannesburg late sixties, early seventies.Noted character.

Anthony Fitzgerald - Distant cousin of author's on Irish side.Educ Ampleforth, of same generation as Rob Gerrard (See Rob Gerrard). Married MaryAnne Fitzgerald(see Ladies of Good Repute) daughter of Gordon & Mary Richdale by whom 2 daughters.Remarried to Roseanne. Lived in Nairobi & Johannesburg prior to current home in Berkshire.

Alastair Vere Nicoll - Arctic adventurer. Author of ' Riding the ice wind' narrating his Antarctica crossing by kite & sledge. Colin Payne, Alastair's grandfather , represented Vinuchi in Cape Town.

Alastair Travers - Co – founder of Ingwe Safaris. Killed by the same buffalo as Johan Bellingan. Refer chapter 7

Adam Fleming – Educ Eton; Scots Guards; Chairman Wits Gold; scion of Fleming Banking family.

Bill Bedford - Co – founder of Ingwe Safaris with Alastair Travers aforementioned. Served in the Rhodesian SAS in the Rhodesian war, 1969 – 1980. Hunted on numerous occasions with author in Zambezi Valley.Refer chapter 7.

Bob Warren – Codrington - (major   Rhodesian SAS ret'd).Represented Rhodesia at Olympic Games for Trap shooting & Equestrian events. Experienced big – game hunter.Hunted with author in Chirisa & Dande, Zhimbabwe. Refer chapter 7.

Braam Cronje – Natal farmer.m Yvette by whom 3 children. Great, great grandfather fought at the battle of Blood River and distant forebear General P Cronje of the battle of Magersfontein fame where the 51st Highland Division were soundly beaten.Keen field sportsman.Northern Natal rugby.Eleven Comrades marathon medals & five Duzi canoe marathon medals.

Bridget Martin - Gossip columnist in late eighties/early nineties for Star. She wrote "An unprecedented 1500 strong crowd at the International Exhibition of Wildlife and Natural History held at the Everard Read Gallery.....not everybody is into the deification of the rhino or interested in paying R 25000 for a painting of a cheetah (by David Shepherd); they want the real thing...dead, stuffed and mounted – Michael Callender for instance.He is well known here in *les circles sportif* and is off to the North Pole to shoot a polar bear, laden down with guns, chill proof bullets, a battery of cameras to record this epic moment and a posse of Eskimos to eat the carcass...". An enraged Johan Bellingan phoned author whilst on his return from Arctic suggesting he sued the Star!

Brigadier General Zvi Kantor (ret'd), Israeli Defence Force - Military attaché to S Africa. Fought in 6th Day War 1967; War of Attrition 1967/70; Yom Kippur War 1973. Founder of the Museum of the Jewish Soldier in World War 11 in Latrun, Israel. Refer chapter 8.

Brian Wright – Endurance athlete (Iron man/ Comrades/ Duzi). Field Sportsman & member of Cornwallis & Molopo shoots.Entrepreneur & aspirant novelist.

Blades of Johannesburg - Peter Allen; Robin Susman; Rob Muller; Mark Edey; Tony Niemeyer; Peter Gallo; Robin Stubbs; Tony Worthington; Tony North;Simon Docherty; Dale Purcocks;Steve Finnemore;Adrian Hickey; Johny Bothner; Tony Philips; Hal Rosholt; Doug Band; Rob Hewitt; Nick Style; Steve Hodgson; Christopher Greig; Rick Currie; John Daniels; Conrad Penney; Michael Gristwood; Alfie von Merveldt.Charlie Proudfoot; Greg Marthinusen. Mike Campbell – Young; Denny Hayden.Mike Hyslop.

Charlie Gough – British Parachute regt; British Army soccer capt(1962);Captained Highlands Park soccer(1967 -72).Son, Richard, played for Scotland 61 occasions. Captained Rangers.

Chay Blyth(Sir) – Noted adventurer. First came to fame through rowing the Atlantic in 1966 with John Ridgeway as fellow paratroopers of the British Parachute Regt. Served under Farrar – Hockley(refer chapter 8). First to sail solo around the world against the prevailing winds & tides.

Chartwellians - Sally&DavidBaikie;NicLeontsins;Rick&JaneMcArthy;JohnyKn esovitch;MikeThompson;MikeWilson;Mike&IngridKearney;Ian&ViFindlay;Gr ahame&CarrieWilson;PaulSmith;LSaad.Rob&MandyDodds;VickyBrooker;Rob Beneke;Laurence Saad.

Cameronians - Unique part of Scottish history. Regiment named after Richard Cameron,'The Lion of the Covenant'. The Cameronians legendary fighting spirit was carried in campaigns all over the world for 300 years. 1750 the Cameronians were identified as 26th Regiment of Foot, The Cameronians. In WW1 supplied 27 battalions in which 7000 soldiers lost their lives. In WW2 the 1st Battalion spent the entire war in the Far East and formed part of the famous Chindits led by Brigadier Orde

Wingate who defeated the Japanese in Burma (refer chapter X1).Since WW2, the 1ˢᵗ Battalion fought with distinction in Malaya, served in Germany, then in the Arabian Peninsular, Kenya, and Jordan as experienced by the author.The Earl of Angus , the 14ᵗʰ Duke of Hamilton, took the salute on the sad occasion of the disbandment of the regiment at Douglas , May 14ᵗʰ, 1968.

Colonel A C A Mackinnon MBE - CO of the 1ˢᵗ Battalion Cameronians in Bahrain, Trucial Oman, Kenya and Jordan whilst author served in Bn .On first interview with Colonel Mackinnon, author was reminded of his forebear, Major Ronald Brodie, under whom Colonel Mackinnon served as a subaltern and that he had a reputation to live up to. Ronald Brodie remembered for many things, including training the Bn in bayonet fighting in mid winter in shirt sleeves.

Colonel Hugh Mackay OBE - Adjutant of the 1ˢᵗ Battalion The Cameronians in Bahrain when author joined the regiment. Hugh once referred to author 'as one of the worst behaved officers he had the displeasure of knowing'(refer chapter X1). This fine commander of men, however, softened his stance when commanding D company in Jordan, where author was platoon commander, suggesting he sign on for a further term. Ultimately rose to full Colonel and appointed Regimental Trustee.

Lt Colonel J. Orr OBE - Ist Battalion Cameronians. Second in command of D Company where author served as platoon commander (refer chapter X1). Transferred to Parachute Regiment where he served under Colonel A Farrar – Hockley in 3 Parachute Battalion. Lt heavyweight boxing champion of Sandhurst. Lives in Kirkudbrightshire, Scotland.

Officers ,NCO's, and men well remembered in 1st Bn Cameronians (in addition to aforementioned). Majors T V Gilfillan, H Worthington - Wilmer, R Parkes, AR Kettles, A Galloway, WC Weir, AM George, R Robertson, JMH Scott, CGI Harper. **Captains** D Cameron, D Sinclair, KM Cooper, JND Lucas, WAL Rodger, A Campbell, WNF Carter. **Lieutenants** BAS Leishman,R Gibson, DR Craig, J Spiers, W Bullard, A Lindsay, IK McBain, J Burrell. **2ⁿᵈ Lieutenants** J Irvine, NSI Daglish, DGP Heathcote, JD Muir, ADI Nisbet, G Stevens. B Powell – Harper. **WO's, Sergeants & Riflemen** J Murray(RSM), A Henderson (WO11), H Anderson(WO11), J Mathieson(Pipe Major), Allan (Bugle Major), Priestly(Sergeant), Docherty(Corporal), Mcluskey, Grant, Duffin, Boyle, Sharp, Cassidy, Smith, Macfadzean.

Captains of industry – Sir H Oppenheimer, J Oppenheimer, G Relly (Anglo American); G Ralfe (De Beers); A Rupert, J Rupert (Rembrandt); M Rosholt, J B Maree, A Philips(Barlows/Barloworld); B Davidson(Anglo Plats);C Adcock(Toyota); C Ball(Barclays/FNB); D Hough(Total Oil); Ian Mackenzie(Standard Bank); GT Ferreira(First Rand); P Flack(RandGold); Ian Haggie(Haggie Rand); Meyer Kahn (SAB/Miller); Paul Harris(RMB Holdings); Laurie Dippenaar(RMB Holdings). J Crutchley(Romatex; CG Smith); Steve Mulholland(Sunday Times); Doug Band (Gallo, Premier)

Carel Carol – Molopo farmer of Irish descent.Carel's grandmother married a cousin of Jurie Schoeman's grandfather.

'Cockroach' Colin Simpkins Chairman Dabulamanzi canoe club; Springbok canoeist;Winner of Liffey descent, Dublin.

Conrad Penny – Property surveyor & evaluator.Geneologist; m Theresa by whom 4 children.

Cullinans of Olifantsfontein – Author introduced to the legendary Irish clan based in Olifantsfontein by his maternal grandmother.Sir Thomas Cullinan (of Cullinan diamond fame) father to Dougie (friend of author's grandmother); Mejor (son of Dougie); Reginald & Margaret Cullinan,parents to Andrew;Andrew Cullinan(see below);Tim Cullinan;David Cullinan;'Uncle Billy' Cullinan. Refer chapter 2.

Andrew Cullinan – Educ Michaelhouse; Edinborough University.Olifantsfontein farmer.m Janis.Sons: Conrad, Rhys, Damon; Tyron. Richard and Sally by first marriage.

Charles Huguet (Colonel) – Special Forces Belgian Army in Congo. Member of the Inanda Club.

De Villiers & Schonfeld – refer chapter 12

David Vanrenen - Residence: Monte Carlo & Provence.Known to locals as 'Mayor of Oppede'. Entrepreneur. Bon vivant. Married to Heath with children – Jamie, Daniel(author's godson); daughter 'Tiggs';Charlie (deceased). Refer chapter 14

Donough McGillycuddy - Clan chief of The McGillycuddy of the Reeks, Eire. Married to Wendy. Ex Eton & Irish Guards. Resides in Himeville, Natal. Accompanied author on hunts in Underburg & Himeville. Bestower of attribute to author – 'One Shot'.

David McArthy-Irishman living in Johannesburg . Author met Jean,David's mother,at Howth Castle. Eminent shot. Author taught him to fly fish. Married to Laurie. Two children & one poodle.

Dennis de Pentheny O'Kelly – Son of Peter de Pentheny O'Kelly.Refer Geneology. Entrepreneur based in Geneva..Keen shot.

Eaton Hall OCS contemporaries – The Hon J Byng; J Lodge; N Stobbs; 'Thunderflash' Emery; J Ormonde; B Eley; 'Pug' Davison; J Gould; 'Spare parts' Wallace; 'Jock' Fee;'Taffy' Philips.Refer chapter 8.

Derek Watts – TV celebrity and producer of 'Carte Blanche'.

Edward A Hoare – Educ Eton m.Susan; Family C. Hoare & Co Bankers; Adventurer – nearly losing life four times. Keen shot.

Field & Stream

Bird shooting

Molopo River - Andrew Allen; Christo Mackeurtan; Peter Johnson, Miles Johnson, Ant Johnson; Rod Schulze; Neil Hobson; Tom Bramwell- Jones; Derek Noyes – Smith; Dennis da Silva; Jarl Christierson; Philippe Andersson; Brian Wright; Martin Joubert; Andrew Glencross.

Moremi, Botswana - Michael Deacon, Paul Hatfield; Michael Victor; Barry Victor.

Lions' Den, Zhimbabwe - Steve Seward; Giles Raynor; Bob Warren – Codrington; Bill Bedford; Michael Deacon; Andrew Halstead.

Peter Wales International, OFS - Peter Wales; Braam Cronje(shoot capt); Neville Glasser;Tony Petter – Bowyer; Chris Laas; Paul Hatfield; Bruce Brothers; Michael Deacon; Lew Gerber; Doug Cole; Brian Slater; Rob Bailey; Geoff Cox; Victor Brothers; Grahame Naylor; Andrew Crookes.

Lake Chilwa & Shire swamps, Malawi – Dan Oxberry; Ed Hammond; Piers Taylor; Ted Siebenman(USA);Tony North. Daryl Botha.

Eastern Cape - Michael Browne; John Broster; Luke Bell; Louis Marais; Peter Murray; Robin Halse.

Koster, W Tvl Tony Scuil; Paul Hatfield

Settlers, Gauteng – Rob Dodds; Ian Dodds; Derek Noyes – Smith; Neville Glasser.

Gauteng Pigeon shoots - Rob Bailey; Derek Noyes – Smith; Bruce Brothers; Neville Glasser; Andrew Allen; Christo MacKeurtan; David McGillivray;Paul Hatfield; Geoff Cox.

Purse Caundle (UK) – Michael de Pelet; Colonel Tim Earls; Patrick de Pelet; Colonel Michael Goldschmidt; Edward Hoare. Anthony Geans. Gamekeeper: Anthony Sprake.

The Hunting Brigade

South Africa_- Peter Flack; Mike Viljoen; Peter Becker; Johan Bellingan; Louis Serrurier; Diana Serrurier; Ian Fraser – Jones; Jeanette Fraser – Jones; Eban Esbach; Col 'Pottie' Potgieter; Louis Marais; Robin Halse; Bertha Halse; Michael Murray; Meyer Steyn.

Africa - Atholl Vrylink, Ian Manning (Zambia); Eric Stockenstroom (Congo); Andre Roux(CAR); Bob Warren – Codrington, Bill Bedford, Piers Taylor, Jonathan Taylor (Zhimbabwe); Dave Lincoln (Botswana)

UK - Michael de Pelet, Peter Geikie – Cobb, Simon Albertini, Andrew Prendergast.

Tembo Chapter – Wilhelm Greef, Andrew Kayser, Wim Lamprecht, Leon Winterboer, Trevor Starke, Rod Duggan, Ed Knieps, Bertie Lombard, Ben Rheede, Avril Pagel.

Old Timers: Harry Manners(Mozambique); Baron Werner von Alvensleben (Mozambique);Ian Henderson (Doddieburn Ranch, Zhimbabwe); Vladimir Steyn; Colonel Ian Mackenzie; Tony Sanchez – Arino; Brian Marsh;Harry Selby.

Trackers - Bandit, Contella, Flex, Adom (Zhimbabwe); Martin, Pierre, Francois (CAR); Anbia, Soula, Opounda (Congo); Kent (E Cape).

Gunsmiths & Taxidermists: Lucas Potgieter (Powder Keg); Tony Rogers (Rogers Sporting Arms); Alex Holmes,Louis,Eugene (Roy Swaydin); Bill Ritchie & Vincent (WJC Ritchie);James Dunlop, Geoff Smith (African Rifles);DC Joubert; Jurie Mejoor; David Winks (Holland & Holland); Peter Chismon (Holland & Holland); Jeremy Clowes ((Holland & Holland); Hugh McKelvie (Holland & Holland); John Ormiston (H&H, Churchill); Robin Hawes (W Evans); Rodney Kretzchmer (Trans African Taxidermists); Dieter Oschenbein

Fishermen - Doug Starling;VincentTaylor;Barry Kraut; Tony Niemeyer; Christo Mackeurtan; Tony Scuil; Hamish Currie; Royce Rosettenstein; Ian Ritchie; Peter Allen; Mark Edey; Rob Muller; John Feek; Jan van Huysteen; Simon Malone; Neville Glasser; Philippe Andersson; Lew Gerber. B Davidson.

Favourite quotations

"Or walk with Kings – nor lose the common touch" - Rudyard Kipling's *'If.'*

"Roaming with a rifle has won you your spurs. It demonstrates clearly that you have mastered the change in discipline required in switching from fiction to fact without losing the ability to hold the reader's interest" - General Farrar Hockley:

"The encouragement of a proper hunting spirit, a proper love of sport, instead of being incompatible with a love of nature and wild things, offers the best guarantee of their preservation" – President Theodore Rooseveld

"An elegant dinner, eminently Parisian. Sitting beside a pretty woman, cafe – jet society and titled a 'demi – mondaine'. Knowing my passion for the hunt, she attacks me through the main course and the dessert, forgetting herself when she deplores the fact that her chef can no longer find venison at the better grocery stores." – Jacques Vettier 'Big game hunting in Asia, Africa and elsewhere'

"The climate in Paradise is fine, but the fellows below are more interesting" - Ernest Hemingway

"Take a community of Dutchman of the type of those who defended themselves for 50 years against all the power of Spain and at a time when Spain was the greatest power in the world. Intermix with them a strain of those inflexible French Huguenots who gave up home and fortune and left their country for ever at the time of the revocation of the Edict of Nantes. The product must obviously be one of the most rugged, virile, unconquerable races ever seen upon earth. Take this formidable people and train them for seven generations in constant warfare against savage men and ferocious beasts, in circumstances under which no weakling could survive, place them so that they acquire exceptional skill with weapons and in horsemanship, give them a country which is eminently suited to the tactics of the huntsman, the marksman, and the rider. Then, finally, put a finer temper upon their military qualities by a dour fatalistic Old Testament religion and an ardent and consuming patriotism. Combine all these qualities and all these impulses in one individual, and you have the modern Boer -- the most formidable antagonist who ever crossed the path of Imperial Britain. Our military history has largely consisted in our conflicts with France, but Napoleon and all his veterans have never treated us so roughly as these hard -- bitten farmers with their ancient theology and their inconveniently modern rifles" – The Great Boer War by Arthur Conan Doyle.

"Men & liquor improve with age" – Rosalie Crutchley

Farmers in S A - Apart from the trials of drought & flood, they face a running battle with poachers of stock and wild game. Hosts of some fine game & bird shoots. Braam Cronje (Dundee,Natal);Derek Ralfe (Dundee) George Mitchell – Innes(Lad ysmith);Robin&BerthaHalse(EasternCape);Neil Hobson(Setlagole,Stellaland); Rod Schultze(Setlagole,Stellaland); MikeBenson(Karkloof,Natal.CarelCarol(MolopoRiver);LeeSouthey(Colesburg,NCape);DavidSouthey(Middelburg,NCape);AndrewCullinan(Olifantsfontein,Gauteng);EdKing(Springs);PatEustace((Underburg,Natal);FaanFourie(Lydenburg,ETransvaal); Andrew Fraser – Jones(Swellendam, W Cape); Billie Fraser – Jones(Swellendam, W Cape).

Father Harry Wilkinson - Presides over Rosebank Catholic Diocese. Well loved by parishioners. Conducted memorial service for MaryAnne (daughter).

Geneology

These forebears instilled in me the drive for adventure and a free spirit which led me to the Republic of South Africa. This in turn motivated me to write the book. What may appear to be a pretentious and irrelevant recital of a family lineage, the pantheon of lords, squires,military men, and adventurers are there for a reason. Most had either fought in battle – the extreme adventure of killing foes - or were explorers and adventurers of one form or another. Hence there is direct relevance in the listing of such men as the de Pentheny O'Kellys' – George, Henry, Raymond, Edgar John, Renfric, Peter.These were warriors and émigrés to new territories where the homeland was too tame. Add the characters of the ilk of Sir Richard Burton and Hamilton O'Malley – Keyes and it is readily evident that a wild spirit permeated the maternal side of the author's ancestry. It should be noted that the linkage of the de Pentheny O'Kelly family and those of Talbot of Malahide and Arundell of Wardour reflect the intertwinement of the prominent Catholic families in Britain in those times and it was only recently that the taboo of mixed marriages – Catholics with Protestants – fell away. To illustrate this point, my grandmother's conversion to Catholicism was met by disapproval from the Presbyterian side of the family which led to a schism and relatively little is known of the Callenders & Callender- Brodies in Scotland. However, sufficient evidence is there to indicate a lineage of adventurers and sportsmen – David Livingstone, the New England lot, Ronald Brodie and Leonard Callender,my grandfather.

Paternal side

The Callenders of Scotland - The Scots spelling of the name (Callendar, Callander, Callender). Callenders are linked to the town of Callander situated 16 kms north of Glasgow. Callender history dates back to the ancient castle in Callender county, Scotland, residence of the Earl of Callender.The Callender family and the Livingstone family originate from the Earl of Callender from which are descended David Livingstone (African explorer), John Callender of Craigforth (antiquarian of great renown), and the Callenders migrating to New England producing a governor, a mayor, and a certain John Callender, reputed to be one of the roughest and rudest politicians of his time in the mid 18th century.

Idvies House, Angus, Scotland - Owned by Anne Catherine Brodie who married John Sharp Callender (great uncle to Author); member of the Royal Company of Archers (King's Bodyguard in Scotland). John altered name to Callender – Brodie. Their daughter, Phoebe, and author's father, a regular visitor to Idvies,were first cousins and close friends

Ronald Brodie - Member of the Brodie clan who joined the French Foreign Legion in Sidi bel Abbes 1912.Served five years, fighting in 5 campaigns in Algeria. Military career covered special mission in Albania 1918/1919; Attached to Iraq army 1925/1928; Major in the Cameronians 1931 and remembered by author's Commanding Officer, Colonel ACA Mackinnon. Married countess from Hungary.

Leonard Callender - Author's grandfather. Younger brother to aforementioned John Sharp Callender-Brodie. Born in Manor Place, Edinborough. Keen field sportsman representing Scotland at equestrian (eventing) and teaching youngsters to stalk deer at Idvies & other estates in Scotland. His son, **Leonard Callender** (author's father) born Manor Place, Edinborough. Educ Downside. Senior partner at Arnold , Fooks, & Chadwick, leading catholic legal firm in London. Awarded Knighthood of the Order of St Gregory the Great by Pope Paul V1. Cardinal Basil Hume (Archbishop of Westminster 1976 – 1999) wrote on his retirement: "We were very sorry indeed to hear that you will be retiring on 30th of April, 1971. This is an avowedly selfish attitude on our part, but it is the measure of our confidence in you and gratitude for all that you have done for us...."

Mildred 'Rudy' Callender - Author's grandmother. On death of her husband, Leonard Callender, converted to Catholicism and elected to leave Scotland and reside in Palace Place Mansions, Kensington Court, London. She raised author & Mary, sister, in the early stages of WW2. One of the first women to cross the Sahara on camel.

Dody Wellesley – Colley - Sister to Rudy. Married into branch of The Duke of Wellington's lineage. Mother of Anthony Wellesley – Colley (see below)

Lieutenant Philip Anthony Wellesley – Colley - Born 1919. First cousin to author's father. Educ Downside. Served in Lord Lovat's No 4 Commando, one of the first units to land on the Normandy beaches on D Day. Struck by a machine gun bullet as he left the landing craft but led his troop across the beach and collapsed in the wire defences. Lord Lovat wrote in his autobiography 'March Past'... "Anthony Wellesley – Colley, a Downside boy with a cheerful smile,lay against the pack of a sergeant who had pulled him into shelter. He was shot through the heart. Tears were running down the NCO's face. "Mr Colley's dead, Sir. He's dead. Don't you understand? A bloody fine officer..." 1994, the 50th anniversary of D Day, a memorial service given for P A Wellesley – Colley in St Mary's Church, Louth, and a memorial bench dedicated to him as the first allied casualty on D Day.

Michael Callender - 1917 – 2001. Uncle & Godfather to author. Educ: Downside; Commissioned into the Irish Guards in WW2 and saw action with the Guards Armoured Division.Hand blown off in Normandy. Keen shot & fisherman. Holland & Holland taught him to shoot without a right hand. Married Elizabeth Grant mentioned below by whom five girls; Sally, Petronella, Charmian, Lucy, and Anne.

Rear Admiral John Grant CB DSO - Brother to Elizabeth Callender (aunt of author as aforementioned). Admiral Grant was one of the Royal Navy's foremost experts in anti submarine warfare and a major architect of victory in the Atlantic in WW2. His fiery temperament matched his red hair and he had a first lieutenant relieved from one of the ships he commanded because" he was not only ignorant but *wet* to the point of being dangerous".

Mary de Laszlo - Sister to author. Married Philip de Laszlo, grandson of the famous portrait painter , Philip de Laszlo.Two daughters: Laura, Tanya(god daughter). Co – Founder of SOS Poland 1982 under the auspices of the Polish Knights of Malta Association. Patron: Count Rafal Smorczewski. Primary aim to assist persecuted Solidarity supporters and to send out medicines, food, clothing to Poland. Awarded the Officers Cross of the Order of Merit with the citation:"It does take a lot of inner steel to help the poor against overwhelming odds – and succeed. Years ago you cheerfully set up the organisation SOS Poland to minister to the desperately needy, reduced to stark poverty, by either blind fate or political oppression,or both.You have since then delivered aid to countless destitute Polish households in areas of South Eastern Poland which were too remote or too rugged for other charities. Under martial law, some of them were thought just ideal for internment camps. I cannot read other people's minds, but I am inclined to believe that this thought precisely shot through the mind of President Lech Walensa, himself a former internee, when he was conferring upon you this prestigious decoration". Mary de Laszlo's other decorations include Medaille d'argent de l'ordre ' pro merito melitensi' and the Croix de l'ordre " pro merito melitensi".

The Callender girls – Sally m. Richard Worthington with 3 children, Camilla, Simon, Selina. Live in Hants, England; Petronella m. P Donaldson(deceased) with 4 children, Lorna, Patrick, Emma, Rebecca. Lives in Ayrshire, Scotland; Charmian m. Ian Tulloch with 2 children, Leesa, Gillem.Lives in Ayrshire, Scotland. Lucy m J Bolton; Anne m. R. Henderson with 4 children, Robert, Horatia, Christian, William.

Maternal side

George Bourke O'Kelly of St Croix, West Indies - Grandson of Edmund O'Kelly of the Ard Coll or Mount Kelly line. 1799 married Mary Pentheny descended from an old Anglo – Norman family settled in Counties Louth & Meath of Ireland (ref Burke's Landed Gentry of Ireland).

Edmund de Pentheny O'Kelly of Barretstown Co Kildare - Grandfather to Edgar John (below).1822 married Blanche, 2nd daughter of Hon Thomas Arundell, brother of 9th Baron Arundell of Wardour **.**

Lt Colonel Edgar John de Pentheny O'Kelly DSO - Author's grandfather. Served on North West Frontier 1908; Gallipoli 1915 mentioned in despatches for gallantry; France 1916/1918.Highly decorated and mentioned in despatches several times whilst commanding the Royal Welch Fusiliers in the trenches of the Somme. The Divisional Commander wrote to the GOC 113 Infantry Bde...."unbridled admiration at the bravery & determination of the troops...I especially wish to congratulate the 16th Bn Royal Welch Fusiliers on a magnificent performance of dogged endurance and courage" (Edgar John was commanding this Bn). In one of his letters to his wife, he wrote" Tell her (referring to his mother) not to worry about me. *I am absolutely in my element".* Educ: Beaumont. Married Nora Agnes (see below) by whom six children:Peter (see separate);Noelle (Mother to author); Thomas(see separate);Eleanor Mary 'Sadie'(see separate); Moira; Julia Ann(see separate).

Nora Mary Agnes Bland - Grandmother to author. Daughter of Frederick Millbanke Bland who married Julia Isabel, daughter of JRF Talbot of Malahide.Co - heiress of Kippax Park (see below).

Kathleen Mary Eleanor Bland– Great Aunt & Godmother to author. Co – heiress to Kippax Park. m. Captain J Weld of Weld of Chideoaks line.

Kippax Park - Purchased by Sir Thomas Bland in 1595 from the Earl of Essex. Enlarged by Sir John Bland (notorious gambler) in 1750. Wagered a bet with Lord Rockingham that Kippax was longer than Wentworth Woodhouse. Despite the staggering length of its 600 feet, John Bland lost. Wentworth Woodhouse is the longest house in England with 49 bays. Kippax subsequently requisitioned by National Coal Board.

Raymund Arundell de Pentheny O'Kelly - Brother of grandfather. Served in Lord Loch's Horse in Boer war. Captured by General de Wet's rear guard near Wolverhoek, Tvl and died of wounds in Kroonstad hospital, Tvl, S Africa. Letters from his brother officers in Lock's Horse detail the account of his capture and the gallant fight they put up as described by one of Boer captors: "I must say, I admire you fellows for making a good stand."

Henry Arundell de Pentheny O'Kelly - Great uncle to author. Served in Boer War. Killed in action at Ypres, France 1915.

Noelle Alicia de Pentheny O'Kelly–Mother to author. Married Leonard Callender of Manor Place, Edinborough, Scotland.

John Richard Arundell, Lord Talbot of Malahide - 2nd cousin to Noelle Alicia Callender as aforementioned. Educ Stonyhurst & Sandhurst.

Renfric 'Rex' Arundell de Pentheny O'Kelly -1st cousin to Noelle Alicia Callender. Educ; Downside. Emigrated to Australia and then to Tasmania. Leading sheep farmer & race horse owner.

Peter de Pentheny O'Kelly - Uncle to author. Educ: Ampleforth, Sandhurst, Trinity College, Dublin. Commissioned Irish Guards. Transferred to Lord Lovat's No 4 Commando and saw continuous action in WW2. Emigrated to South Africa. Employed in mines; Stipend Steward, Johannesburg Turf Club; owned Rathcoel farm, Ezulwini,Swaziland. Married Jeanne O'Sullivan O'Moloney in Johannesburg & had 4 sons: Seamus, Dennis, Hugh, Peter – Rory.

Thomas de Pentheny O'Kelly - Uncle to author. Educ Downside. Racing correspondent for 'Irish Field' Dublin. Race horse owner & farmer. Married Anne Weld –Blundell of Ince Blundell hall. Four children: Louise, Carmel, Marie Claire, Edmund.

Julia Ann de Pentheny O'Kelly. Aunt to author. Married A Geikie – Cobb. Two sons: Peter & Ivo. Author raised in WW2 at Pyt House by Edgar & Nora (grandparents), with Julia & Sadie (see below).

'Sadie' Eleanor de Pentheny O'Kelly - Aunt to author. Married Major Hamilton O'Malley -Keyes (refer Chapter 1 & Howth Castle below). Downside & Irish Guards. Ross House , Westport, Co Mayo.His first marriage to Lady Iris Mountbatten dissolved.

Sir Richard Burton - Explorer, writer, soldier. Married Isobel Arundell of Wardour (refer Edmund de Pentheny O'Kelly).

Dolores 'Dodo' Lees – Distant relation on the maternal side through the Welds of Chideock.Twice awarded the Croix de Guerre. Captain Michael Lees,Dodo's brother, was parachuted as SOE into Yugoslavia to assist General Mihailovich's resistance fighters. Dodo served in General de Gaulle's Free French force and in 1944/45 crossed the Germans' lines continuously dressed as a civilian to assist resistance fighters in the Vosges mountains. A chapter on Dodo's war exploits is included in the Daily Telegraph ' Heroes and Adventurers obituaries.'Pictures of Dodo & brother, Michael, hang in Special Forces Club, Hans Place, Knightsbbridge, London.

Howth Castle, Howth, Dublin - Author's grandmother 1st cousin to Christopher Gaisford St Lawrence's mother. Since 1180 the St Lawrence family have been the Lords of Howth. Christopher Gaisford St Lawrence m Penny Drew deceased,direct descendant of the Howth family,is the current incumbent of the castle.Place laid at table each day for the pirate Grainne O'Malley – direct forebear of Hamilton O'Malley as aforementioned.According to the legend,'The Pirate Queen'abducted the grandson of the 8th Baron Howth for having the gates of the castle closed on her whilst paying the Baron a courtesy visit in 1576.She released the grandson on a promise from the family to have the gates opened to unexpected visitors and to have an extra place laid for each meal. The agreement is honoured to this day.

Gum Cutters - These men had me constantly under the scalpel sorting out my gums and teeth. I got to know them as friends who managed to have me writhing in the chair at their constant ribald repartee: Robin Meyeroff; Sandy Goldbaum; Stan'Butcher' Butz; Sheldon Jones.John Dresner.

General Constand Viljoen – Formerly GOC of SADF. Leader of The Freedom Front Party. According to Mandela's aides, General Viljoen was deeply trusted by Nelson Mandela. As a military leader, General Viljoen had experience of war and realised that military action against the ANC would lead to an ultimate bloodbath. "I know the price of war. It would have led to great suffering of my people & other people in South Africa. It would have meant a disaster to the economy and it would probably have led to international interference".General Constand Viljoen has since retired from politics and farms near Lydenburg in the eastern Transvaal.

Gerhardt Batha - Renowned modern artist in Johannesburg.

Grahame Callie - Vikings Rowing Club. Coached author & Rob Gerrard in sculls & pairs.

Gary Wilson deceased – Mercenary in Major Mike Hoare's 5 Commando fighting in the Congo early sixties.Ex Sandhurst. Highly respected by Hoare. Led a company attack into Lisala, killing 160 Simbas with no loss of life to his own troops. Married to Joanna. Farmed in Tvl, SA.

GT Ferreira – Prominent Johannesburg banker.Big game hunter.Nearly lost life to robbers. Refer chapter 2.

Gary Magnussen – Capt 1st Parachute Bn. Trained A Tucker & author in parachute jumps, Wonderboom.

Germiston Lake Rowing Club – Bob Tucker, Keith Mayberry, Jopie Van Hooten.

Gordon Richdale (deceased) – President Engelhard Industries.Chairman Hill Samuel SA.mMary by whom Jeremy. MaryAnne.

Hamish Currie – Noted wild life vet. Founded the ' Return to Africa' project (reintroducing game from overseas zoos to Africa). Deep sea fisherman. Married to Alison (refer Findlay,chapter5). Lives in Cape Town.

Hilton Hamman - Author' Days of the Generals'; Sunday Times military correspondent; weapons expert.

Hunting licence fees Rhodesia 1968 - General game licence GBP 10.00 for a resident of Rhodesia & GBP 25.00 for non resident.This allowed for Bushbuck(1); Duiker(4); Impala(4); Warthog (2); Wildebeest(2); Zebra(2); Kudu(1); Grysbok(1); Steenbuck(1). Big Game – Buffalo(GBP 10.00); Elephant(GBP 30.00); Lion (GBP 30.00); Leopard(GBP 30.00).

Hugh (The Hon) & Mary Morrison - well known horse trainer & field sportsman. Estate owner in Islay.m Mary – wife & mother to Rory Sweet (see Rory Sweet & Ladies of Good Repute).

Hugh de Pentheny O'Kelly – Son of Peter de Pentheny O'Kelly refer Geneology. Lives in California. Past president of the Gunmakers Guild (USA).

Horst Kollrep - Keen field sportsman. Shoots & fishes in many parts of the world. Resides between Provence, London, & Johannesburg. Married to Maureen.

Ian Ritchie – Educ St Andrews College, Grahamstown. Commanding Officer 2Para battalion.Youngest Commandant in SADF Civilian Force.Handed Bn over to Monty Brett on retirement.Pilot,hunter,fisherman,entrepreneur.

In Memoriam – MaryAnne Callender; Charlie Vanrenen; Ian Green; Ian Ritchie; Mike Tindall;Tony Beith;S Copelowitz; Johan Bellingan; Alastair Travers; Geoff Mathews; Tony Rowney; Patricia Hall; Harry Hall;Ian Fraser – Jones. Derek Tucker; Mickey Gerber; Andrew Crutchley;John Hatfield ; Steve Smith; Geoff Smith; Kent; John Mackenzie; Guy Fletcher; Colonel Ian Mackenzie.Gordon & Mary Richdale.

Iain Grahame Major ret'd – Served with Kings African Rifles in Uganda when Idi Amin was a sergeant in the regt. Leading UK antiquarian book dealer specialising in Africana. Lives in Suffolk,England.

Ian Ovenstone - father–in –law to Alastair Vere Nicoll as aforementioned.Resides in CapeTown. Accomplished business man & raconteur.m Lindy

Ian MacKenzie Colonel ret'd DSO. Deceased. Distinguished WW2 soldier. Hon Colonel Transvaal Scottish; Chairman Standard Bank; African Finance Consolidated & director of other public companies.Chancellor of Rhodes University; big game hunter,keen field sportsman. Collector of Africana books & paintings.Resided in Stonehouse, Parktown, Jhb. m.Anne with whom John, William, MaryAnne, Jane,. Refer chapter 8.

Ivor Sander - Noted Johannesburg historian & leading light of Rand Club. Author of several works on prominent business houses .Grandfather was FRN Findlay, noted big game hunter in late nineteenth century. Married to Heather.

Jake Francis – Jones - Downside 1949 – 1953. Dartmouth Naval College. Executive secretary of St Gregory society (inaugural role) & responsible for rejuvenating the OG family worldwide. Captain Royal Navy. Flag Lieutenant to Vice Admiral Sir Fitzroy Talbot (see separate). Delivered eulogy at Admiral Talbot's funeral.

Jason Gard – Commissioned Green Jackets Regt; Entrepreneur; Cresta Run; Son in law of Sir M Jackson GOC British Forces(retd). Resides in UK & France.

Jeremy Richdale – prominent business figure in Hong Kong & Far East. M brett by whom luke, kate, kelly.

Johny Sach – Prominent GP Johannesburg. Seconded author in Iron Man & Comrades. Accomplished athlete. Lives in US

Jonathan Evans - CEO of Vinuchi. Innovator of the corporate uniform & gifts divisions. Previous experience with Cadbury Schweppes, Promardis, prior to establishing a fresh foods business.

Johan Bellingan - Founder of Prima Bank. Served on the Board of Trustees,University of the Free State & Chairman of the University Foundation.Killed by a buffalo whilst hunting in the Dande area of the Zambezi Valley, July 1992.Close friend of the author. Married to Denise with son & daughter.

John Yetman - (Colonel ret'd).Resided in Dorset. Shot with grandfather.Owner of largest private deer herd in England. Proposed author for Shikar club.

John Flemming – Mercenary, adventurer, big game hunter, bird shot, fisherman. Specialist on hand surgery. Introduced to author by Brian Wright. Major Mike Hoare, mercenary leader of 5 Commando in Congo, described him in his book 'Congo Mercenary': "Young, tough, adventurous, and efficient.... at times I felt he was wasted as a doctor, he would have made a magnificent infantry officer....he had tremendous dash & courage. His ambulance is the only one I have ever seen leading a column into battle!"

John Stroud - Holland & Holland representative in Johannesburg. Ex Royal Marine, British army.m Ayla (Mackenzie).

John Robbie – Irish rugby int, Tvl rugby, radio celebrity702

Johannesburg Sportsmens' Club - formed to host dedicated sportsmen of Johannesburg. Current chairman – Hugh Bladen. Proposed to club by Bill Emmett.

Keith Gordon – Leading sports physiotherapist in Johannesburg. Represented S Africa in Maccabi Games at wrestling. Author frequented K Gordon's gym in Rosebank. Seconded author in Iron man.Lives in US with wife,Marlene.Refer chapter 6.

Kayak Africa – Pioneered by MaryAnne & Pierre 'Bushy' Bester (refer chapters7 &19). Leading adventure company. Recently publicised by Conde Naste as a top tourist destination in Southern Africa. Directors: MaryAnne (deceased); Clive Bester; Jurie Schoeman.

Kingston, Jamaica – A rumbustious three years with Suzanne & Carol Issa; Raymond Miles;Bernard Weil; Gordon Hewatt; Nick Galtress & Jane; Gavin Gordon; Neville Ten;Arnold Sherman; Donovan Hailstone and a host of other wild spirited men & women.

Legal men – The men who strived to keep author on straight & narrow. Micky Schneider; Frankie Nino ; Derek Brugman; Rob 'The Loony Lawyer'Thompson; Louis Serrurier; Les Civin.

Ladies of Good Repute - MaryAnne Callender (Founder of Kayak Africa);MaryAnne Fitzgerald (author of 'Nomad', adventurer, jailed in Kenya for criticising President Moi's corruption);Major (ret,d) Jeanette Fraser – Jones(hunter, SADF pilot);Tina Fraser – Jones(Iron Man SA Veteran champion);'Crazy Rain Forest' (hunter & horsewoman);Patricia Carlisle (Comrades gold medallist);Jane Halse (Proprieter of Rowland Ward records of Big game; hunter);Diana Serrurier (Hunter & field sportswoman);Patricia Glyn(adventurer & author);Vicky Brooker (Lion tamer & game expert);Kim Batha (Vinuchi Tie designer & wife to Gerhard Batha);Mary Morrison(equestrian & field sportswomen; married to The Hon Hugh Morrison; mother to Rory Sweet);Liz Mulder (1st lady Iron Man).

Loftur Johannesson - Godfather to MaryAnne(daughter).Renowned pilot & mercenary flying supplies for Red Cross in Biafran war & Vietnam for US military. Armaments adviser to Pentagon.Resides in Washington,Bahamas,France & London.

Michael Westmacott - Ex Eton & Guards. Army ski champion. Veteran Cresta Runner. Resided in Johannesburg early seventies.Resides in Edinborough.m Louise.2 children.

Michael Johnson deceased - Fine bird shot. Ex Eton & Guards.

Michael de Pelet – Educ Downdside.m.to Charlotte by whom 2 daughters.Estate owner in Dorset. Member Shikar Club. Big game hunter (Europe, Africa, Central Asia). Keen shot & fisherman.

Maxime van Hanswijck de Jonge – Ambassador for the Netherlands to several countries.Hunted big game in Europe, Sumatra, Mongolia, Alaska, Namibia.,New Zealand,and Venezuela. Author of three books.m.Laetitia with 3 children.Lives near Aix – en Provence.

Michael Whitehead–educ Michaelhouse. Investment adviser. Resides in Provence, France. m Dominique by whom 2 children.

Neil Callie - Brother to aforementioned Grahame Callie. Leading head hunter in Johannesburg. Placed J Evans with Vinuchi. Now resides in Australia.

Paul Edey - Celebrated headmaster. Previous posts: Marist Bros; KES; current: St Andrews College, Grahamstown.

Philip Cadman – His rubberducks sank without fail.Johannesburg entrepreneur.m Suzie du Toit.

Paul Mills - Leading antiquarian book dealer specialising in Africana. Originally with Clark's Bookshop, Cape Town. Now works independently.

Philippe Andersson– Educ St Aidans Grahamstown. Owner of Dolobran,(national monument),Parktown, Johannesburg.Co – founder of Ferminore. M Beryl by whom 3 sons.Great grandfather C J Andersson acclaimed mid 19th century hunter, explorer,author.

Peter Geikie – Cobb – First cousin. Educ Eton.m. MaryAnne with 3 children. Keen shot. Hunted buffalo with author in Zhimbabwe. Lives in Dorset,, England.

Peter-Rory de Pentheny O'Kelly – Son of Peter de Pentheny O'Kelly. m Paola with 4 children. Lives in Tuscany. Noted wine maker 'La Casa di Bricciano'.

Peter Hamilton Flack –Prominent big game hunter residing in Cape Town. Film producer 'The South African Conservation Success Story'. Top businessman chairing various companies in mining.Now ret'd. Author of several books. m Jane with one son and daughter.

Rand Club – Founded in 1887 by Cecil John Rhodes and Dr Hans Sauer. Strong historical links with the mining magnates of the late nineteenth century and synonymous with the development of Johannesburg's mining history. The site where the Jamison raid was planned.Author launched book 'Roaming with a rifle' at a lunch held in the club.

Rand Athletic club – leading running club in SA. Renowned organisers: Dick & Vreni Welch.

Sir Ranulf Fiennes OBE – Educ Eton. SAS. Acclaimed adventurer.Polar explorer awarded the Polar medal with two clasps.Led over thirty expeditions inc first polar circumnavigation of universe.Successful author inc 'Mad dogs & Englishmen', 'Living dangerously' & several other titles.

Roger Crawford – Rugby referee,sportsman, businessman, President US Chamber of Commerce Jhb.

Rory Sweet - Antarctic adventurer, hunter, computer tycoon. Game farm owner in Northern Transvaal

Rembrandt – Multi global tobacco giant founded by Anton Rupert in S Africa. Noted philanthropist & patron of arts. Present chairman Johan Rupert- supporter & sponsor of sport, notably rugby (Saracens, UK); golf (Ernie Els); adventure (Mike Horn). Also chairman of boards inc Richemont, Geneva.

Richard Durlacher deceased - Best man at author's wedding.Son of 'King'Esmond Durlacher of Durlacher,City of London. Keen sportsman. Member of 'Benedicts', renowned London dining club. Enjoyed company of adventurers. Married to Wendy(see separate) by whom Noel (son), Natasha and Samantha. Died 2005.

Rob Gerrard - Educ Ampleforth; Captain Gordon Highlanders (regt commanded by father Lt Col BJD Gerrard DSO);Seconded to Sarawaka Rangers, Borneo. Renowned Zulu War historian & author. Member of Royal Geographic Society. Rowed for Vikings RC with author in pairs. Author best man at his wedding at Drummond, Natal. Gerrard wrote " many,many thanks for being my best man... the concept of a formal wedding certainly fell away pretty quickly as one drama occurred after the other, so called ushers arriving after the bride, organist pissed in a pub, priest improperly dressed, no food and finally kids running amok flattening guests' tyres.... who wanted a formal wedding anyway!"

St Gregory Society - In memory of Downside School: Dom Wilfred Passmore; Dom Aelred Watkin: Dom Martin Salmon; Dom 'Wappie' Wulston; Dom Brendan Lavery; Dom Ceolfrid O'Hara; Dom J Crouzet;Dom Raphael Appleby; Hugh Watts; C Brasher; Jake Francis – Jones(see separate); The Hon Jamie Drummond (Captain of boxing); Michael Brufal, Marquis of Lendinez (Cambridge blue boxing & 1st XV for three years); Archer Hardy (contender with author and Robin Watson for the most whipped boys of their generation);Teddy Maynard (gifted rugby player/ cricketer);

Tim Melhuish (RNC Dartmouth 1ˢᵗ XV);TremayneRodd (RNC Dartmouth Royal Navy boxing champion;Scotland rugby int);Jose D'Aguirre(1ˢᵗXVrugby);Peter Doyle (1ˢᵗ XV flanker); Jammie Clinch (1ˢᵗ XV rugby hooker – father & grandfather played for Ireland); Byeyard McHugh (1ˢᵗ XV winger); John Coward (Admiral, Royal Navy); Michel Morris(Lord Morris); Peter Raven(Oil magnate);Tom Chetwynd (author). Fergus Blackie (Supreme Court Judge in Harare, Zhimbabwe); Michael Gogarty (Former golf champion of Kenya); and others of prominence inc Edward Pryce; Auberon Waugh; Silvio Canepa; Tony Lesser; Simon Bingham (Lord Clanmorris); Nicolas Franco (President of CIC); Nicholas Bellord.

Simon Murray CBE - Born 1940.Educ Bedford. French Foreign legion 1960;5 years fighting FLN in Algerian war with 2eme REP (Legion's Parachute Regt).Wrote 'Legionnaire' selling over one million copies.Auspicious business career based in Far East spanning Jardine Matheson, Hutchison Whampoa (10 yrs as Group MD), Deutsche Bank(Exec Chairman); currently operates own private equity investment fund. Chairman Glencore and sits on 129 boards including Vodaphone, Richemont. Adventurer completing the arduous Marathon des Sables – 240 km across the Moroccan desert- and oldest man(64) to trek to South Pole unaided and accompanied by famous explorer Pen Hadow.Member of Royal Geographic Society. Married to Jennifer (1ˢᵗ woman to fly solo around the world) and three children.

Shikar Club – Formed in late nineteenth century by British army officers serving in Asia to commemorate big game hunting. Membership based on invitation only. Author proposed by Colonel John Yetman(deceased) then the oldest member at 90 yrs of age and seconded by Michael de Pelet. The Shikar Club convenes annually at a dinner held at the Cavalry & Guards club, 137 Piccadilly, London. Chairman: The Lord Charles Cecil; Secretary: Chisolm Wallace, Scots Guards ret'd.

Sculptors - Roy Sarkin & Donald Greig.

Sporting world

Cricketers: Clive Rice, Grahame Pollock, Dr Aly Bacher, Lee Irvine, Vince van der Byl; Jimmy Cooke;

Rugby: Richard Prentis; Syd Nomis; Wilf Rosenburg; Des Sinclair; Kevin de Klerk; Uli Schmidt; Jaap Mulder; James Dalton; Tommy Gentles; Ray Mordt; Johny Buchler; Jannie Breedt; Morne Du Plessis; Micky Gerber; Chick Henderson; Burger Geldenhuys; Willie – John McBride, (Lions Captain 1974; Vinuchi Sporting Occasion); Syd Millar(Irish International & former president of IRFU; Vinuchi Sporting occasion). Sir Anthony O'Reilly (Irish International; Vinuchi Sporting Occasion). **Rugby Administrators**: Louis Luyt (President SARFU); Rian Oberholzer (Mktg Director of Ellis Park & CEO SARFU); Gary Grant(mktg manager SARFU)

Boxing: Willie Toweel; Kallie Knoetse; Stan Christodoulo; Brett Taylor.

Cycling: Alan van Heerden. Frank |Soll.

Athletics: Paul Nash; Gert Potgieter; March Fiasconara;

Karate: Stan Schmidt; Norman Robinson; Malcolm Dorfman; Peter Bunckle. Jimmy White.

Tennis – Gordon Forbes; Abe Segal; Owen Williams.

The Johannesburg Sportsmens Club-Hugh Bladen(president);Peter Bunckle; Neil Smith;Tom van Vollenhoven. Bill Emmett.John Imrie.

The Sports Institute - Clive Noble (Member of Boxing Board of Control; Transvaal Rugby Board).

Iron Man/ Duzi/ Comrades - Grahame Pope – Ellis; Danny Biggs;Tim Cornish; Ian Green;Michael Tindall; John Feek; Tony Beith; 'Moggy' Lightfoot; Patricia Carlisle; Geoff Mathews; Dick Stent; Cavan Rothwell; Brian Wright; Lionel Gaddin; Andy Balme; Dave Hodgkiss; Steve Britten;Jomo King;Geoff Mills;Bill Turnbull;Gary Boast;Brian Jordan.Eugene Jordan.Jomo King.Author.

Duzi/Comrades- Bruce Fordyce; Adrian Hickey.Stan Copelowitz; Braam Cronje;

Ironman/Comrades- Noel Stamper. Rob Rutter.

Iron Man/Duzi- Eddie King; Colin Balderson; Maurice Stacey;Uli Schmidt.

Duzi - Neil Evans; Mark Perrow;Garth Watters; Colin Simpkins;Brian Slater;Meyer Steyn; Nigel Briggs;Ant King;Vaughan Richardson.Grahame Cruikshank.Dave Drummond.Andrew Gutchie. Paul Cooke.Derek Ralfe.

Comrades- Jackie Meckler; Alan Robb; Lew Gerber; John Sawers; Chris Griffiths; Hamish Gilfillan; ; Reg Hunter- Blair; Bob Tucker; Alan Tucker.Mike Gahagan; Olav Andersson; Caspar Greef; Clive Lucas – Bull; Dick Welch.

Iron Man-John Stroebel; PG Barry; Bunker Snyder; Joe Skono;Andy Torr;Richard Prentiss;Keith Gordon;Eugene Jordan.

Dabulamanzi Canoe Club (The Plymouth Brethren) - 'Cockroach' Colin Simpkins; Lionel Gaddin; Neils Verkerk; John Rhynes; Mark Perrow; 'Moggy' Lightfoot; Brian 'Scatter' Slater; 'Jomo' King; Joe Torlage; Andrew Gutschie; Alan Witherden; Andy' Spitfire' Torr; 'Bull' Bill Turnbull; Meyer Steyn; Grahame Cruickshank; Dave Ferguson; 'Big' Brian Longley; 'Headbanger' Vaughan Richardson; Tony Beith; Brian Wright; Geoff Mills; Ant King; John Skuse; Garth Watters; Grahame Cross; Gareth Peddie; Mark Cluttey; Gary Boast; Geoff Mathews; Tony Rowley; Stan Copelowitz; Dave Drummond; Andy Balme; Dave Hodgkiss; Brian Jordan; Eugene Jordan.

Vice Admiral Sir Fitzroy Talbot KBE, CB, DSO(With bar). 44 year naval career covering two sinkings,a near fatal air crash and shrapnel wounds to win a DSO & bar and to attain flag rank. Appointed C in C South Atlantic based at Simonstown, Western Cape, South Africa in early sixties. Author privileged to stay with him and his wife on several occasions at their home in Dorset. Lady Elizabeth Durlacher second wife (Richard Durlacher's step – mother). On reading his autobiography 'Old Rope',author saw Jake Francis – Jones mentioned (see J Francis – Jones) as the Admiral's Flag Lieutenant.

Van Zyl & Robinson –Refer introduction & chapter 12

Vinuchi Pty ltd – Refer chapter 12

Vinuchi Sporting Occasion – Syd Millar; Sir Anthony O'Reilly; Mark McCormach; Sir Chay Blyth; WJ McBride; Gen Sir A Farrar – Hockley. Refer chapter 12

Vikings Rowing Club – Jhb. Dan Robinson, Ernest Geering, Peter Thompson, Grahame Callie, R Lonman – Davis, Henry Watermeyer, Peter Mitchell, Martin Mayne, Dave Baker, Rob Jeffrey, RJanisch & many other splendid men who teached Rob Gerrard, Adrian Hickey & author to row.

Warriors – General Constand Viljoen; General Jannie Geldenhuys; Lt General Dennis Earp (Chief of South African Airforce);General Sir A Farrar – Hockley; General Svi Kantor (IDF); Witkop Badenhorst; Jan Breytenbach; Ian Mackenzie; Grahame Wilson; Jack Crutchley; Simon Mann; Peter Barry;Sej Dunning;David Christie; Dave Barr; Monty Brett; Charlie Gough; Sir Chay Blyth;Rob Gerrard; Lew Gerber. Refer chapters 8 & 11.

Willie John McBride MBE – Legendary captain of the British Lions.The might of the Springboks was humbled on the famous tour of 1974 where the Lions beat the S Africans 3 – 0 with one draw. Willie John instigated the notorious '99' war cry in retaliation against any brutal play from the Springboks.m Penny.2 children. Resides in Ballymena, N Ireland.

Wits Rifles - Affiliated to Cameronians. Officers remembered: Col John Job; Majors O'Halloran, Carton – Barber, Kevin Townsend.

Wendy Durlacher – Widow of Richard. Close friend of author and Vivienne. Resides in London, Guildford, and Beaulieu, France. Adventurers would find Wendy simpatico with her huge humour, ability never to get phased, and striking looks!

Magersfontein

Battle of Magersfontein. - 11 December, 1899   Poem by an Unknown Soldier

Tell you the tale of the battle ?
Well, there ain't so much to tell,
Nine hundred marched to the slaughter,
And nigh four hundred fell.
Wire and the Mauser rifle :
Thirst, and a burning sun,
Brought us down by the hundred
Ere' that black day was done.
You didn't read all in the papers,
You folks that read them at home :
You don't read the truth of the battle,
So please leave our actions alone.
Tell you just how the thing happened ;
Tell you the way it was done ?
Well, listen ! I tell the story
Of how a hard fight wasn't won.

Cold was the night, wet and dreary,
Chilled were the men to the bone :
Bivouacked there in the open,
Thinking, maybe, of their homes.
Midnight they came round to wake us,
Forming us up in the dark ;
Officers whispered their orders,
Never a light or a spark.
Onward we went till the dawning
Showed in the east, grey and drear,
While in the front os us looming
The kopjes' bold skyline showed clear.
Away on the left of the kopjes
We noticed a light burning bright,
And just as the column had halted
It suddenly vanished from sight.

Then ere we knew what had happened,
Two shots on our left ringing out.
To the Boers in their trenches gave warning,
And rifle balls answered our shout.
Some one yelled "Charge," and we started,
Rose and rushed out on their fire,
Meaning to give them the bayonet,
But checked and stopped by the wire.
Bullets nor shells ne'er appalled us,
Trenches nor boulder-strewn hill,
But just in a few strands of wire fencing
Brought us nonplussed, standing still.

Over the wire, men, or through it,
Drive the charge home to the hilt ;
Vain were the struggles in climbing,
Deep stuck the barbs in the kilt.
Strong grew the light of the morning,
Hotter the lead on us rained ;
Still we remained there before them,
Holding the ground we had gained.
"Down on the face and seek cover ;
Nothing could live in that fire ;
Off to the right, men, and flank them !"
"Forward !"   "Lie down, men !"   "Retire !"

Then we looked back and cursed them ;
Took home the truth with a groan -
The rest of the Brigade are retiring ;
Now, we must stick it alone.
"Form a line here, men ; we'll hold them !"
MacFarlane spoke, standing erect.
Volley on volley we gave them,
Till their fierce fire we checked.
Then round the Audjutant rallied
Remnants of different corps,
Some of the Black Watch and Argyles,
Some gallant Seaforths of yore.

All day long in position,
Watching the lyddite shell burst,
Lying with dead men and dying.
Lips, swollen blue black with thirst.
Not thirty yards from the trenches,
Brave General Wauchope lay dead ;
The Colonel, too, lay beside him,
Their lives by the Boer bullets sped.
Then, with the dust came retirement,
Weary and thirsty and sore,
Gathered together in regiment,
All that was left by the Boer.

Such was the day for our regiment ;
Dread the revenge we will take ;
Dearly we paid for the blunder -
Some one has made a mistake ;
Not a man knew when we started,
What we were going to do,
Take up or rush a position,
Were the Boers many or few.
Had they retired ? Were they coming ?
Had they slunk off in the night ?
Should we attack in the morning ?
Shall we attack them to-night ?

Why weren't we told of the trenches ?
Why weren't we told of the wire ?
Why were we marched up in column ?
May Tommy Atkins inquire.
Why were no scouts sent forward ?
Why were no scouts on our flanks ?
Why did they not send us water,
Although it was putrid and stank ?
Mourning that day of black sorrow
In Scotland are women and men -
The sound of the piper's Lochaber
Re-echoes in city and glen.

Over eight hundred our loss is -
Englishmen, Irish, and Scotch ;
Half of it fell on one regiment -
God help the noble Black Watch.
Still, we must take the position,
And vengeance will take for the slain,
And every Boer's check shall grown paler,
When he speaks of black Magersfontein.
Such is the tale of the battle -
Easy for tongue to tell ;
Nine hundred men in a death-trap,
And nigh four hundred fell.

Suggested reading

Badcock Peter *Images of war*

Barlow Eeben *Executive Outcomes*

Baynes John *The Cameronians*

Bell 'Karamoja' W *Bell of Africa*

Blyth Sir Chay *A fighting chance*

Boyes John *The company of adventurers*

Bredin Neville *Blood on the Tracks*

Breytenbach Colonel Jan **Eagle Strike.** *The Buffalo Soldiers*

Bull Bartle *Safari*

Butcher Tim *The River of Blood*

Callender Michael *Roaming with a rifle – big game adventures in Africa and other far away places*

Cole Barbara *The Elite – Rhodesian Special Air Service*

Crutchley Jack *Live longer – Live stronger*

Daily Telegraph *Military Obituaries Book 2*

Doyle Arthur Conan *The Great Boer War*

Du Preez Max *Of warriors, lovers, prophets - unusual stories from South Africa's past*

Edgerton Robert B *Like Lions They fought- The last Zulu War*

Fiennes Sir Ranulf *Living dangerously*

Godwin Peter *The fear The last days of Robert Mugabe; Mukiwa; When a crocodile eats the sun*

Hamman Hilton *Days of the generals*

Hoare Major Mike *Congo mercenary*

Hochschild Adam *King Leopold's ghost*

Keohane Mark *Champions of the world*

Klatzow David *Steeped in blood*

Knight Ian *Go to your god like a soldier*

Livingston David *Livingston's last journals; Expedition to the Zambezi*

Manners Harry *Kambaku*

Marsh Brian *A pioneering hunter*

Morris Donald *The washing of the spears*

Munnion Chris *Banana Sunday*

Murray Simon *Legionnaire*

Packenham Thomas *The Boer War*

Reitz Denys *Commando- a Boer journal of the Boer War*

Ritter E A *The rise of the Zulu empire*

Stanley Henry Morton *In darkest Africa*

Selous F C *A hunter's wanderings in Africa*

Tributes

*I was enthralled with this adventure which is reminiscent of
'Jock of the Bushveldt' and Michael Callender certainly stirs
the blood in his fast paced book.*

Simon Murray CBE

*Reading this narrative and having experienced South Africa for myself,
this is true excitement and a pulsating, red blooded account of a life
that is refreshing in its stark contrast to the dreary, over cosseted
world of today. We who aspire to adventure are fortunate people
to comprehend what the real meaning of living is about.*

Sir Chay Blyth CBE, BEM

*I first encountered Michael Callender in 1974 when leading the British
Lions against the Springboks – I doubt South Africa has forgiven this
team of mine! Understanding both the vibrant spirit of this special
land and that of the multi faceted author, this is a glorious portrayal
of a big hearted country. He writes it well and vividly.*

Willie John McBride MBE

*The soldiers, frontiersmen, explorers, hunters, and traders that abounded
in South Africa in its formative years and who forged the foundations of
this country of ours are given true recognition in this fascinating story.
A 'must' read for those who possess an adventurous spirit.*

Colonel Jannie Breytenbach DVR, SD, SM

About the author

MICHAEL CALLENDER currently spends his time between his home in Provence and Africa. He is married to Vivienne and has a son and daughter (deceased). His first book "Roaming with a rifle" was published in America.

Synopsis

This is the story of an adventurer, Michael Callender, who is of Scots/ Irish descent and who lived for 40 years in the Republic of South Africa. His title is an apt description of an extraordinary land that is made up of a brilliant scenery, charismatic peoples, and an inheritance of savagery. The *leopard* is a creation of beauty, *razor wire* a symbol of harshness. In the author's belief, this summarises South Africa — a country of raw contradiction. Michael Callender presents a collection of rousing stories as a British immigrant who witnessed a wildly oscillating pendulum from the peak of Apartheid in the late 1960s to the 'New South Africa' as termed today. His portrayal of the 'Wild South', as he describes this domain, is presented in a manner that is in harmony with the author's independent spirit that found deep inspiration in a challenging and exciting land. The descriptions of the warriors, the adventurers, sportsmen, and the mavericks that he encountered, set against the kaleidoscopic panorama of a country that remains a frontiersland, is an essential read for those that are either linked to the country or have aspirations to learn more about this controversial and emotive land.

Lightning Source UK Ltd.
Milton Keynes UK
UKOW031604251111

182702UK00001B/1/P